Navigating Innovative Technologies and Intelligent Systems in Modern Education

Madhulika Bhatia
Amity University, India

Muhammad Tahir Mushtaq
Cardiff Metropolitan Univesity, UK

A volume in the Advances in Educational Technologies and Instructional Design (AETID) Book Series

IGI Global
PUBLISHER of TIMELY KNOWLEDGE

Published in the United States of America by
IGI Global
Information Science Reference (an imprint of IGI Global)
701 E. Chocolate Avenue
Hershey PA, USA 17033
Tel: 717-533-8845
Fax: 717-533-8661
E-mail: cust@igi-global.com
Web site: http://www.igi-global.com

Library of Congress Cataloging-in-Publication Data

CIP PENDING

Navigating Innovative Technologies and Intelligent Systems in Modern Education
Madhulika Bhatia, Muhammad Tahir Mushtaq
2024 Information Science Reference

9798369353707 (h/c)
9798369353714 (s/c)
9798369353721 (elec)

This book is published in the IGI Global book series Advances in Educational Technologies and Instructional Design (AETID) (ISSN: 2326-8905; eISSN: 2326-8913)

British Cataloguing in Publication Data
A Cataloguing in Publication record for this book is available from the British Library.

All work contributed to this book is new, previously-unpublished material.
The views expressed in this book are those of the authors, but not necessarily of the publisher.

For electronic access to this publication, please contact: eresources@igi-global.com.

Advances in Educational Technologies and Instructional Design (AETID) Book Series

ISSN:2326-8905
EISSN:2326-8913

Editor-in-Chief: Lawrence A. Tomei, Robert Morris University, USA

MISSION

Education has undergone, and continues to undergo, immense changes in the way it is enacted and distributed to both child and adult learners. In modern education, the traditional classroom learning experience has evolved to include technological resources and to provide online classroom opportunities to students of all ages regardless of their geographical locations. From distance education, Massive-Open-Online-Courses (MOOCs), and electronic tablets in the classroom, technology is now an integral part of learning and is also affecting the way educators communicate information to students.

The **Advances in Educational Technologies & Instructional Design (AETID) Book Series** explores new research and theories for facilitating learning and improving educational performance utilizing technological processes and resources. The series examines technologies that can be integrated into K-12 classrooms to improve skills and learning abilities in all subjects including STEM education and language learning. Additionally, it studies the emergence of fully online classrooms for young and adult learners alike, and the communication and accountability challenges that can arise. Trending topics that are covered include adaptive learning, game-based learning, virtual school environments, and social media effects. School administrators, educators, academicians, researchers, and students will find this series to be an excellent resource for the effective design and implementation of learning technologies in their classes.

COVERAGE

- Bring-Your-Own-Device
- Educational Telecommunications
- Web 2.0 and Education
- Game-Based Learning
- Social Media Effects on Education
- Collaboration Tools
- Curriculum Development
- Instructional Design Models
- Adaptive Learning
- Hybrid Learning

The Advances in Educational Technologies and Instructional Design (AETID) Book Series (ISSN 2326-8905) is published by IGI Global, 701 E. Chocolate Avenue, Hershey, PA 17033-1240, USA, www.igi-global.com. This series is composed of titles available for purchase individually; each title is edited to be contextually exclusive from any other title within the series. For pricing and ordering information please visit http://www.igi-global.com/book-series/advances-educational-technologies-instructional-design/73678. Postmaster: Send all address changes to above address.

Titles in this Series

For a list of additional titles in this series, please visit:
http://www.igi-global.com/book-series/advances-educational-technologies-instructional-design/73678

Transforming Education for Personalized Learning
Afzal Sayed Munna (University of Sunderland in London, UK) Husam Alharahsheh (University of Wales Trinity Saint David, UK) Alessandro Ferrazza (University of Sunderland in London, UK) and Abraham Pius (York St. John University, UK & Arden University, UK)
Information Science Reference • copyright 2024 • 312pp • H/C (ISBN: 9798369308684) • US $225.00 (our price)

Teacher and Student Perspectives on Bilingual and Multilingual Education
Hung Phu Bui (University of Economics, Ho Chi Minh City, Vietnam) Truong Cong Bang (University of Economics and Law, Ho Chi Minh City, Vietnam & Vietnam National University, Ho Chi Minh City, Vietnam) and Cuong Huy Nguyen (International University, USA)
Information Science Reference • copyright 2024 • 296pp • H/C (ISBN: 9798369353653) • US $245.00 (our price)

Enhancing Education With Intelligent Systems and Data-Driven Instruction
Madhulika Bhatia (Amity University, India) and Muhammad Tahir Mushtaq (Cardiff Metropolitan Univesity, UK)
Information Science Reference • copyright 2024 • 337pp • H/C (ISBN: 9798369321690) • US $245.00 (our price)

Supporting Activist Practices in Education
Natasha N. Ramsay-Jordan (University of West Georgia, USA) and Andrea N. Crenshaw (University of West Georgia, USA)
Information Science Reference • copyright 2024 • 362pp • H/C (ISBN: 9798369305379) • US $230.00 (our price)

Practices and Implementation of Gamification in Higher Education
Veronica Membrive (University of Almeria, Spain)

For an entire list of titles in this series, please visit:
http://www.igi-global.com/book-series/advances-educational-technologies-instructional-design/73678

IGI Global
PUBLISHER of TIMELY KNOWLEDGE

701 East Chocolate Avenue, Hershey, PA 17033, USA
Tel: 717-533-8845 x100 • Fax: 717-533-8661
E-Mail: cust@igi-global.com • www.igi-global.com

Table of Contents

Detailed Table of Contents

This study arises from an innovation in initial teacher education aimed at designing immersive gamified ecosystems (IGEs), instructional resources where gamification converges with the use of augmented reality and artificial intelligence. The objectives are: a) to analyse university students' opinions on the generated motivation, ease of elaboration, group work, educational value, and future intention of application; b) to identify the level of acceptance of the methodology; and c) to analyse the mediation effect between the different variables. The research is empirical, non-experimental, descriptive, and inferential. A questionnaire adapted from the TAM model was used. The results demonstrate that the level of acceptance of the methodology is very high and is related to high motivation, ease of elaboration, contributions of group work, the educational value assigned to IGE, and the intention to apply it. Finally, this methodology proves suitable for teacher training by confirming its formative potential and increasing the intention to implement IGEs in their classrooms.

The health monitoring system has become increasingly popular in recent years due to its unique features and wide range of medical applications. The OneLife IoT-based self-monitoring healthcare system is a smart health monitoring system to detect and predict diseases by monitoring various health-related data such as body temperature, pulse rate, heartbeat, blood pressure, oxygen levels, and sugar levels. It helps track a patient's specific metrics every day and provides analysis for a week, month, and year to predict the patient's condition. It is implemented and tested on two groups of five patients each and achieves accuracy by measuring the general parameters in a controlled environment. It provides the users with the measured results, on LCD including heart rate, blood sugar level, temperature, etc. By incorporating internet of things-based self-monitoring healthcare systems into educational systems, the health of the students can be easily monitored.

Online learning platforms have accelerated tremendous growth since the inception of the Covid pandemic. Learning platforms such as Khan academy and BYJU's had shown significant rise in the enrolment figures of candidates willing to pursue online education. The Covid-19 pandemic, at one time, depicted a picture that online education is the only future as schools and colleges were forced to shut down. However, accessing online education was not easy for every student due to several hindrances. The right to access online education can be hindered by data packs, electricity etc. The state has to look into the fact that economic, cultural, or social barriers are not restrictions for a child to access online education. Online education has been emphasized in different educational policies; several judicial pronouncements but lack effective mechanism to put it in the right place. The most ignorant part is the collection, storage, and dissemination of students' personal data, as the shift from physical to online mode of education involves data transfer of students either directly or indirectly.

Like many sectors affected by the Coronavirus (Covid - 19) pandemic, the higher education sector was disrupted globally and needed immediate re-adjustments to provide distance learning solutions. Educational management contingency plans were initiated in many parts of the world to reach out to students isolated due to the pandemic; however, it quickly became clear that one size (or plan) did not fit all, especially with regards to students with online learning constraints. This qualitative research explores the online learning experiences of students during the pandemic in the Kingdom of Bahrain. The study employed an online survey to investigate Bahraini students' perceptions of online learning as a new initiative during the pandemic. The findings of this survey suggest that the digital divide, digital inequities, and differences in e-learning opportunities have been experienced by students through the implementation of online learning. The study also revealed different perceptions of the educational technologies available to students.

Structural violence has a profound psychological impact on Venezuelan college students, leading to increased levels of stress, anxiety, depression, and hopelessness. This study investigated the psychological impact of structural violence on individuals and served as the basis for the collaborative action on transmedia human rights (CATHR) program design as a peaceful disruptive methodology to counteract violence. The CATHR program is an interdisciplinary educational strategy based on a challenge-based learning framework that fosters civic commitment, democratic values, the defense of human rights, and socio-environmental awareness. The study found that the CATHR program was effective in reducing stress, anxiety, depression, and hopelessness in college students. The study also found that the CATHR program empowered learners to resist and overcome the challenges they face. This chapter highlights the importance of addressing structural violence and its psychological consequences to promote the well-being of individuals and communities worldwide.

The chapter commences by examining the evolving role of social media in the digital age and its pervasive influence on communication, collaboration, and information dissemination. It navigates through a diverse array of social media platforms, exploring their unique features and potential applications within educational contexts. A critical focus of the chapter lies in the pedagogical implications of incorporating social media into teaching strategies. It discusses how educators can leverage these platforms to foster interactive and collaborative learning environments, empowering students to actively participate in knowledge creation and dissemination. The exploration extends to the cultivation of digital literacy skills, emphasizing the importance of guiding students in navigating the complexities of online information.

Preface

Navigating Innovative Technologies and Intelligent Systems in Modern Education, co-edited by Madhulika Bhatia and Muhammad Tahir Mushtaq, stands as a beacon for educators seeking to revolutionize their teaching methods in the ever-evolving landscape of modern education.

This groundbreaking book goes beyond traditional educational paradigms, presenting cutting-edge strategies and techniques to inspire and equip teachers with innovative tools. The aim is clear: to transform classrooms into dynamic spaces that foster enhanced student learning outcomes.

In assembling this comprehensive guide, we, the editors, drew upon the expertise of seasoned educators, ensuring a rich tapestry of practical insights, real-life examples, and step-by-step guidelines. From the effective integration of technology to the creation of collaborative learning environments, this book covers a spectrum of topics, providing educators with the necessary resources to remain at the forefront of modern education.

Impact and Audience

Central to our vision is the empowerment of teachers as catalysts for change in the classroom. This book serves as a guide to engage students, ignite curiosity, and promote critical thinking skills. With a focus on a student-centered approach, educators are armed with the tools to create inclusive and interactive learning environments that nurture each student's unique talents and abilities.

The exploration of digital tools and resources within this book underscores the importance of leveraging technology to enhance teaching and learning experiences. From interactive multimedia presentations to online collaboration platforms, educators will discover innovative ways to integrate technology effectively into instruction, assessment, and feedback.

Revolutionizing Education

Ultimately, this book seeks to revolutionize education by encouraging educators to reimagine their teaching practices, adapt to evolving student needs, and instill a lifelong love of learning. By embracing these revolutionary methods, teachers can create classrooms that inspire, motivate, and empower students to reach their full potential in the 21st century.

The book explores a diverse range of topics, each contributing to the overarching goal of transforming education. From flipped learning to gamification, personalized learning to project-based learning, augmented reality to blended learning, culturally responsive teaching to inquiry-based learning, integrating social media to mindfulness, and beyond, these topics offer a holistic perspective on modern educational methodologies.

This reference book is designed for faculty, school teachers, and experienced educators seeking to enhance their teaching practices. It is our sincere hope that this book serves as a guiding light, inspiring educators to embrace innovative strategies, adapt to changing educational landscapes, and create impactful learning experiences for their students.

ORGANIZATION OF THE BOOK

Chapter 1: Enhancing Digital Technology Planning, Leadership, and Management to Transform Education

Authored by Kathirvel Ayyaswamy, this chapter delves into the transformative potential of virtual reality (VR) in education. It explores how VR can provide teachers with safe, realistic learning experiences, challenging or impossible to reproduce in a traditional classroom setting. The focus is on enhancing digital technology planning, leadership, and management to harness the power of immersive and engaging learning experiences.

Chapter 2: Coding and Computational Thinking Empowering Students for the Digital Age

Authored by Rahul Dwivedi, Siddhant Bisen, Mayank Yadav, and Amit Yadav from GNIOT, India, this chapter explores the intricate relationship between coding skills, computational thinking, and student empowerment. Through an in-depth analysis, it provides insights into the transformative potential of coding education, emphasizing problem-solving skills, logical reasoning, and creativity among students.

Chapter 3: Design of Immersive Gamified Ecosystems: Acceptance of the Methodology and Predictors of Future Implementation from the Perspective of Future

Authored by Nerea López-Bouzas, Jonathan Castañeda Fernández, and M. Esther Del Moral Pérez from the University of Oviedo, Spain, this chapter explores the design and acceptance of Immersive Gamified Ecosystems (IGEs). The methodology combines gamification, augmented reality, and Artificial Intelligence to enhance motivation, ease of elaboration, group work, and educational value, proving suitable for teacher training.

Chapter 4: OneLife IoT-Based Self-Monitoring Healthcare System

Authored by Ritu Punhani, Shalini Puri, Vivek Jangra, and Ishika Punhani, this chapter introduces the OneLife IoT-based self-monitoring healthcare system. Focusing on predictive disease detection through health metrics monitoring, it emphasizes the potential application of Internet of Things-based self-monitoring healthcare systems in educational settings for monitoring students' health.

Chapter 5: Right to Online Education Vis a Vis Privacy: A Global Transition of a Basic Human Right Since Covid 19 Pandemic

Authored by Mili Gupta and Gagneet Singh from Presidency University, Bengaluru, India, this chapter critically examines the right to online education and its global transition since the COVID-19 pandemic. It addresses challenges hindering access to online education, emphasizing the importance of considering economic, cultural, and social barriers.

Chapter 6: Perceptions Remote Teaching by Diverse Student Cohorts in the Kingdom of Bahrain: Emergency Remote Teaching

Authored by Fatema Wali, George Toworfe, and Henk Huijser, this chapter explores the experiences of diverse student cohorts during emergency remote teaching in the Kingdom of Bahrain. The findings highlight the digital divide, inequities, and differences in e-learning opportunities experienced by students, revealing varied perceptions of available educational technologies.

Chapter 7: An Investigation into Primary School Teachers' Perceptions about the Delivery of Physical Education (PE) Lessons through Distance Learning, in the Republic of Ireland, During the COVID-19 Pandemic

Authored by Conn O'Hanlon and Xiuping Li, this chapter presents a study investigating primary school teachers' perceptions of delivering PE lessons through distance learning using Google Classroom during the COVID-19 pandemic. It addresses challenges, strategies, and the significance of PE teacher training for supporting students' physical health and mental well-being.

Chapter 8: The Combination of Flipped Classroom and ICTs Towards Effective Instruction in an EFL Environment

Authored by Antonio Juan Rubio from the Universidad de Granada, Spain, this chapter explores the combination of flipped classroom and ICTs for effective instruction in an English as a Foreign Language (EFL) environment. It emphasizes how flipping the class using ICTs can cater to diverse student needs and promote learner-centered teaching.

Chapter 9: Collaborative Action on Transmedia Human Rights Program: A Digital Strategy to Improve the Well-being of Students Facing Structural Violence

Authored by José Luis Jiménez from FAU, Venezuela, this chapter introduces the Collaborative Action on Transmedia Human Rights (CATHR) program. It explores how this program, based on Challenge-Based Learning, counteracts the psychological impact of structural violence on college students, promoting civic commitment, democratic values, and socio-environmental awareness.

Chapter 10: Socially Connected Learning Harnessing Digital Platforms for Educational Engagement

Authored by Dhiraj Gupta, Arbaaz Ali Khan, Abhishek Kumar, Manoj Singh Baghel, and Ayush Tiwar from GNIOT, India, this chapter examines the role of social media in the digital age. It navigates through various social media platforms, exploring their potential applications within educational contexts and emphasizing the pedagogical implications of incorporating social media for interactive and collaborative learning environments.

Chapter 11: Embedding Social Media in Education Cultivating Engagement and Collaboration in the Digital Learning Environment

Authored by Arti Kumari, Mohd Sahil, and Mohd Jarjis Raza from GNIOT, India, this chapter delves into effective strategies for incorporating social media tools in education. It explores transformative roles, practical examples, and case studies, addressing challenges, opportunities, and the impact of social media on fostering a sense of community and collaboration among students. The chapter aims to provide educators with insights, methodologies, and best practices for successfully integrating social media into teaching strategies in the rapidly evolving landscape of digital education.

IN CONCLUSION

In the culmination of "Navigating Innovative Technologies and Intelligent Systems in Modern Education," we witness the convergence of diverse perspectives, insights, and transformative methodologies that collectively redefine the landscape of education in the 21st century. Through the dedicated efforts of esteemed contributors, this reference book serves as a compass for educators navigating the dynamic waters of educational innovation.

From the immersive realms of virtual reality (VR) to the empowering domain of coding and computational thinking, each chapter unearths the potential of technology to revolutionize teaching and learning. The exploration of gamified ecosystems, self-monitoring healthcare systems, and the right to online education sheds light on the multifaceted challenges and opportunities presented by the digital era.

As we journey through the chapters, the integration of flipped classrooms, ICTs, and social media emerges as a powerful force for change, fostering collaboration, engagement, and learner-centric approaches. The insights into the impact of emergency remote teaching and the collaborative action on transmedia human rights underscore the adaptability and resilience of educational systems in the face of global challenges.

We conclude with the conviction that this book is not merely a collection of chapters but a manifesto for educators, policymakers, and researchers to embrace innovation, inclusivity, and student-centered pedagogies. The commitment to reimagining education is palpable, and the potential for positive transformation is boundless.

As editors, Madhulika Bhatia and Muhammad Tahir Mushtaq, we extend our gratitude to the visionary contributors who have enriched this volume with their expertise and dedication. It is our sincere hope that the insights and strategies shared within these pages will empower educators worldwide to navigate the complex intersection of technology and education, creating classrooms that inspire, motivate, and prepare students for the challenges and opportunities of the digital age. Together, let us embark on a journey toward a future where education knows no bounds and every student can thrive.

Madhulika Bhatia
Amity University, India

Muhammad Tahir Mushtaq
Cardiff Metropolitan Univesity, UK

Chapter 1
Enhancing Digital Technology Planning, Leadership, and Management to Transform Education

Kathirvel Ayyaswamy
https://orcid.org/0000-0002-5347-9110
Panimalar Engineering College, Chennai, India

ABSTRACT

A computer-generated simulation known as virtual reality (VR) submerges viewers in a three-dimensional setting. Users using VR headsets can interact realistically with items and situations while giving the impression that they are in a different location. VR has the potential to transform education by enhancing learning through immersive, engaging experiences. The use of VR in teacher education has drawn more attention in recent years. This is due to the fact that VR may be used to give teachers safe, realistic learning experiences that are challenging or impossible to reproduce in a conventional classroom setting.

INTRODUCTION

VR has the potential to transform education by enhancing learning through immersive, engaging experiences. The use of VR in teacher education has drawn more attention in recent years. This is due to the fact that VR may be used to give teachers safe, realistic learning experiences that are challenging or impossible to reproduce in a conventional classroom setting.

DOI: 10.4018/979-8-3693-5370-7.ch001

The Potential of Virtual Reality for Teacher Education

By enhancing its effectiveness, immersion, and engagement, virtual reality has the potential to completely transform teacher education. In a conventional teacher education program, lessons, readings, and fieldwork are used to teach students about ideas and methods of instruction. However, the extent to which these approaches can adequately prepare students for the actual difficulties of teaching may be constrained.

VR can be used, for instance, to develop interactive simulations that let students test out various pedagogical approaches and techniques.

Field trips: Students can travel virtually to locations they would not otherwise be able to visit using VR. Students could use virtual reality to tour well-known museums, historical sites, or other educational facilities, for instance.

Hands-on learning: Virtual reality (VR) can be utilized to give students hands-on learning opportunities. Students could, for instance, utilize virtual reality to construct a model of the solar system, carry out a science experiment virtually, or practice instructing a certain skill.

Assessment: VR can be used to evaluate students' advancement in teacher preparation. Students could, for instance, utilize VR to complete a series of assignments that evaluate their understanding of instructional strategies or their capacity to control a classroom.

We can anticipate many more creative and successful uses of VR in teacher education as the technology progresses.

Innovations in Virtual Reality for Teacher Education

Virtual reality (VR) is a quickly evolving technology that could completely alter how we learn. In the subject of teacher education, virtual reality (VR) can be utilized to deliver immersive and interactive learning experiences to pre-service and in-service teachers that can aid in the development of the knowledge and skills they need to be successful in the classroom.

Virtual Field Trips

Virtual field trips are one of the most creative applications of VR in teacher education. Students can experience real-world locales through virtual reality field trips without ever leaving the classroom. Students who reside in rural locations or who cannot afford to travel may particularly benefit from this (Bowman & McMahan, 2007).

SIMULATIONS

Virtual reality (VR) can also be used to build simulations that let students practice their teaching techniques in a secure setting. Pre-service teachers can use this to hone their classroom management abilities, discover how to provide education, and practice providing feedback to students (Kemp & Issroff, 2016).

There are numerous VR simulations available that cover a variety of themes. Virtual reality simulations can be used to give students performance feedback and to assist them pinpoint areas where they need more practice (Lai & Bower, 2018).

Environmental Immersion

VR can be utilized to construct immersive settings that let students experience various cultures, historical eras, or even fictitious worlds, in addition to virtual field excursions and simulations (Plass et al., 2015). This can be a beneficial way for kids to grow in their comprehension of various viewpoints and to build a greater app around them.

Obstacles to VR Use in Teacher Education

The use of VR in teacher education is not without its difficulties. These difficulties include the high cost of VR devices and software, as well as the scarcity of VR content (Sadiq & Nosrati, 2019).

APPLICATION OF VIRTUAL REALITY IN TEACHERS EDUCATION.

Teachers Content Knowledge: Virtual reality can be a useful tool for teachers to improve their comprehension of subject-matter expertise. Teachers can investigate complicated ideas, historical events, scientific occurrences, and more through realistic simulations and virtual worlds.

Developing Pedagogical Skills: Practicing and honing educational abilities in a safe and controlled environment is possible with virtual reality for educators. The Stanford University simulation known as the "Virtual Classroom" serves as one illustration (Johnson, 2016).

Preparing for Diverse Learners: Virtual reality can play a crucial role in preparing teachers to meet the needs of diverse learners. In order to establish an inclusive and encouraging learning environment for all children, educators need to have the empathy, cultural awareness, and effective communication skills that come with these simulations.

Challenges and Opportunities of Virtual Reality in Teacher Education

Technical Challenges: Limitations of Hardware and Software: VR experiences require top-notch gear, including head-mounted displays (HMDs), motion sensors, and potent computers. Additionally, user-friendly, reliable, and frequently updated software is needed to create and transmit VR content (Bower et al., 2015).

Connectivity and Bandwidth: Since VR experiences frequently demand high data transmission rates, poor internet connectivity and bandwidth limitations may make them difficult to use.

Compatibility and System Integration: Integrating VR technology into current educational systems might be challenging. Technical know-how is necessary to allow seamless integration in the event that compatibility problems between VR systems and Learning Management Systems (LMS) develop (de la Fuente et al., 2020).

Cost Considerations:

Costs associated with gear and infrastructure: The initial outlay for VR hardware, such as HMDs, sensors, and processors, can be significant. Costs associated with ongoing maintenance, such as software upgrades and equipment repairs, should also be taken into account (Ke & Im, 2013).

Creation and Licensing of Content: The creation of high-quality VR content necessitates the expertise of designers, programmers, and subject matter experts. For teacher education programs with tight budgets, the costs of content generation, such as licensing fees for external VR experiences or simulations, might be a major hurdle.

PEDAGOGICAL CHALLENGES

Curriculum Integration: Careful planning and alignment with learning objectives are essential for successfully integrating VR into teacher education curriculum. VR activities must be made sure to fit with the overall educational strategy and curriculum layout (Kreijns et al., 2003).

Faculty Support and Training: In order to design and facilitate immersive learning experiences, teacher educators must receive training in the use of VR technologies. They should have technical knowledge of VR and be skilled at instructing pupils.

Ethical Considerations: VR experiences have the potential to be emotionally impactful and may give rise to ethical questions, especially when imitating difficult classroom scenarios or delicate subjects 13].

PLANNING TOOLS AND STRATEGIES INTO PRACTICE

The community should start creating an implementation strategy as soon as they have decided on the best planning instruments and approaches to reduce risks. Regardless of the particular tool, the following are typical implementation steps:

Decide who to speak with initially.

Think about whether or not to put together a team.

The community should start creating an implementation

Give instances from different communities.

Determine the financial sources.

Create a completion schedule.

Establishing a projected schedule for completion, along with designated responsibilities for important activities, deliverables, and milestones, can assist support momentum management.

Implementation of Planning Strategy

Enhancing planning results can be achieved by addressing a task or topic through the use of current networks and the development of new professional and community contacts. Strengthening community capacity, improving communication, developing resources, and better informing and coordinating specific actions through relevant expertise are all made possible by networks, which facilitate linkages between persons and groups.

Acquiring this knowledge will facilitate the process of determining the kind of extra knowledge, political backing, and community involvement that your community's work requires. In particular:

1. Determine the experts on the issue.
2. Look for instances from different groups.
3. Determine additional resources and best practices.

LEADERSHIP IN DIGITAL TEACHING

Acquiring this knowledge will facilitate the process of determining the kind of extra knowledge, political backing, and community involvement that your community's work requires. In particular:

Leaders need to know how members of their team relate to and use that platform or technology (Rohit, 2022). Effective leaders in this situation should design appropriate training programs for their team members. This is how wise decision-makers make a wise adjustment for their company. With the right leadership, the issues may be resolved and a powerful social message can be developed as shown in the Figure 1.

MANAGEMENT OF EDUCATION SYSTEMS IN DIGITAL TEACHING

Learning management systems (LMS) come in a variety of forms because to the use of digital technology in education. The use of virtual classrooms, where a teacher can communicate with students in real time, exchange resources, give a lecture, evaluate their learning, get feedback, and address their questions, has been encouraged by these LSMs. These platforms, often known as EMS or

Figure 1. Digital leadership for teachers

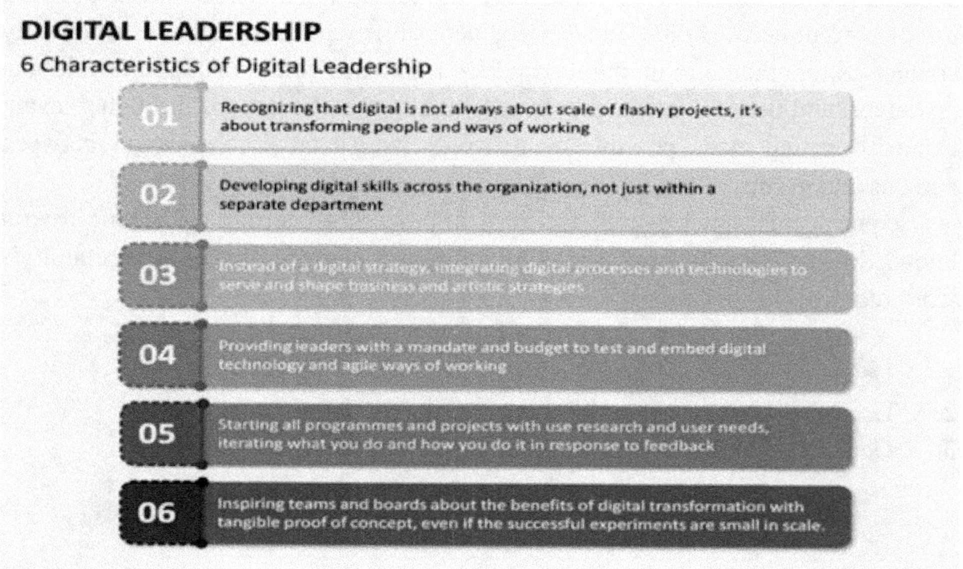

AMS (Academic Management System), handle data in educational institutions like schools.

Management software supports administration, academic management, teachers, and students by assisting in addressing the day-to-day difficulties of this intricate industry.

1. It enhances the ability to make decisions.
2. It boosts the output of groups.
3. It enhances users' normal organization
4. Dropout rates are decreased.
5. It encourages sectorial integration
6. It streamlines procedures
7. It makes an organization's finances better.

This holds true for vendors, staff members, and pupils. In order to reduce mistakes and delays, management systems can create invoices, remind users of deadlines, and manage the complete supplier portfolio.

CONCLUSION

In conclusion, the future of teacher education could be completely transformed by virtual reality (VR). As a result of its immersive and interactive features, virtual reality (VR) can offer aspiring instructors one-of-a-kind educational opportunities that connect theory and practice. VR gives teachers the opportunity to practice critical abilities, broaden their pedagogical expertise, and handle challenging classroom dynamics by mimicking real-world circumstances. The future of VR in teacher education must be shaped through collaboration between educators, researchers, and technology developers to ensure its successful inclusion into current programs. Virtual reality has the potential to completely reimagine how we educate and prepare teachers for the challenges of the future with sustained research, innovation, and investment.

REFERENCES

Akhtar, R., Zulkhairi, M. H., Raza, A., & Khairi, K. M. (2019). Cultural Competence Training Simulator: Virtual Reality Application for Inclusive Education. In *IEEE International Symposium on Mixed and Augmented Reality (ISMAR)* (pp. 346-349). IEEE.

Bower, M., & Sturman, D. (2015). VR Education: A Historical Perspective. In M. Bower & D. Sturman (Eds.), *Virtual Reality for Teaching and Learning* (pp. 1–16). Springer.

Bowman, D. A., & McMahan, R. (2007). Virtual reality: How much immersion is enough? *IEEE Computer Graphics and Applications*, *27*(6), 16–22.

Columbia University. (2017). *The Body VR*. Columbia University. https://www.columbiaradiology.org/research/3d-virtual-reality-vr-human-body

de la Fuente, M. J., Ortega-Múnez, J., & Amado-Salvatierra, H. R. (2020). Virtual Reality in Teacher Education: A Systematic Review. *International Journal of Educational Technology in Higher Education*, *17*(1), 1–28.

Johnson, C. (2016). *Virtual Classroom: A Platform for Teacher Training*. Stanford Press. https://online.stanford.edu/programs/virtual-classroom-platform-teacher-training

Ke, F., & Im, T. (2013). Virtual-Reality-Based Social Interaction Training for Children with High-Functioning Autism. *The Journal of Educational Research*, *106*(6), 441–461. doi:10.1080/00220671.2013.832999

Kemp, J., & Issroff, K. (2016). The potential of virtual reality for teacher education. *Journal of Computer Assisted Learning*, *32*(4), 311–320.

Kreijns, K., Kirschner, P. A., & Jochems, W. (2003). Identifying the Pitfalls for Social Interaction in Computer-Supported Collaborative Learning Environments: A Review of the Research. *Computers in Human Behavior*, *19*(3), 335–353. doi:10.1016/S0747-5632(02)00057-2

Lai, C., & Bower, M. (2018). Virtual reality in education: A review of the literature. *Computers & Education*, *122*, 109–122.

Minocha, S., & Roberts, D. (2018). An Evaluation of VR for Learning Maths and Spatial Awareness in Primary School. In S. Minocha & D. Roberts (Eds.), *Interaction Design and Virtual Reality* (pp. 39–66). Springer.

Plass, J. L., Homer, B. D., & Kinzer, C. K. (2015). The effects of virtual reality on learning: A meta-analysis. *Journal of Educational Psychology*, *107*(3), 525–546.

Rohit, K. (2022). Digital leadership in 21st century education. *International Journal for Research Trends and Innovation, 7*(7).

Sadiq, S., & Nosrati, A. (2019). The role of virtual reality in teacher education: A systematic review of the literature. *Computers & Education*, *132*, 132–145.

Chapter 2
Coding and Computational Thinking:
Empowering Students for the Digital Age

Rahul Kumar Dwivedi
https://orcid.org/0009-0003-1347-1434
Greater Noida Institute of Technology, India

Siddhant Bisen
Greater Noida Institute of Technology, India

Mayank Yadav
Greater Noida Institute of Technology, India

Amit Yadav
Greater Noida Institute of Technology, India

ABSTRACT

In an era characterized by swift technological advancements, the integration of coding and computational thinking into education is essential for preparing students to excel in the digital age. This book chapter explores the intricate relationship between coding skills, computational thinking, and student empowerment. Through an in-depth analysis of pedagogical approaches, curriculum design, and real-world applications, the chapter aims to provide educators, researchers, and policymakers with insights into the transformative potential of coding education. The chapter initiates by delving into the core concepts of coding and computational thinking, elucidating their significance in fostering problem-solving skills, logical reasoning, and creativity among students. It navigates through the dynamic landscape of educational technologies, emphasizing the role of coding in cultivating a profound understanding of computational principles.

DOI: 10.4018/979-8-3693-5370-7.ch002

INTRODUCTION

The introduction sets the stage by emphasizing the dynamic nature of our globalized society, where digital literacy is no longer a luxury but a fundamental skill. We delve into the foundational concepts of coding and computational thinking, unveiling their significance in nurturing critical skills such as problem-solving, logical reasoning, and creativity among students. In the face of the imperative to equip the next generation with the tools necessary for success, exploring effective pedagogical approaches and curriculum design becomes paramount for educators, researchers, and policymakers alike.

The chapter further unfolds by surveying the dynamic landscape of educational technologies, illustrating how coding serves as a gateway to understanding the core principles of computation. Real-world case studies and success stories from diverse educational settings provide tangible evidence of the positive impact coding can have on student engagement, motivation, and academic achievement (Resnick, 2017).

Addressing the challenges and opportunities associated with integrating coding into the curriculum, the introduction navigates through considerations of accessibility, equity, and the crucial role of teacher professional development. It highlights innovative teaching methodologies, hands-on projects, and collaborative learning environments that enhance the effectiveness of coding education across different grade levels.

As we journey through the pages of this chapter, we will explore the symbiosis between coding skills and various academic disciplines, shedding light on how coding acts as a powerful catalyst for interdisciplinary learning. The narrative extends beyond the confines of the classroom to examine the broader societal implications, discussing how coding education can contribute to nurturing a generation of digitally literate citizens poised to address and solve global challenges.

In conclusion, the introduction foreshadows the synthesis of key findings and practical recommendations that will follow in subsequent sections, ultimately advocating for a paradigm shift in educational practices. By understanding and harnessing the transformative potential of coding education, we aim to empower students to not only thrive but also shape the unfolding narrative of the ever-evolving digital landscape (Wing, 2006).

- Global Perspectives on Coding Education:

Explore international initiatives and best practices in coding education. Compare and contrast how various countries are incorporating coding into their educational systems and analyze the resulting impact on student outcomes.

- Inclusive Practices in Coding Education:

Investigate strategies for making coding education inclusive and accessible to all students, irrespective of gender, socioeconomic background, or learning abilities. Highlight successful models that prioritize diversity in coding classrooms (Grover & Pea, 2013).

- The Role of Industry Partnerships:

Examine collaborations between educational institutions and industry partners that aim to bridge the gap between classroom learning and real-world applications. Showcase examples of successful partnerships that enhance students' readiness for the workforce.

- Assessment and Evaluation in Coding Education:

Discuss effective methods for assessing and evaluating students' progress in coding. Explore alternative assessment approaches beyond traditional exams, such as project-based assessments, portfolios, and peer evaluations.

- Coding Across the Curriculum:

Showcase examples of how coding can be integrated into various subject areas, fostering interdisciplinary learning. Illustrate how coding projects can enhance understanding in subjects like mathematics, science, language arts, and social studies.

- Teacher Professional Development Programs:

Explore successful professional development programs for educators, ensuring they are equipped with the knowledge and skills to effectively teach coding. Emphasize the importance of continuous learning for teachers in the rapidly evolving field of technology.

- Coding in Extracurricular Activities:

Investigate the role of coding in extracurricular programs, such as coding clubs, hackathons, and coding competitions. Discuss how these activities contribute to students' passion for coding and foster creativity (Kafai & Burke, 2014).

- Coding for Social Impact:

Explore initiatives where coding is used to address societal challenges. Discuss projects where students leverage their coding skills to create solutions for issues like environmental sustainability, healthcare, or social justice.

- Ethical Considerations in Coding Education:

Discuss the ethical implications of teaching coding, covering topics such as data privacy, cybersecurity, and responsible AI development. Highlight the importance of instilling ethical considerations in students from an early stage.

- Parent and Community Engagement:

Investigate the role of parents and the broader community in supporting coding education. Discuss strategies for engaging parents in their children's coding learning journey and building community support for coding initiatives.

BACKGROUND

The background study of "Coding and Computational Thinking: Empowering Students for the Digital Age" revolves around the dynamic shift in education prompted by rapid technological advancements. This era of the digital age has brought about a transformative paradigm where computational skills and coding literacy are increasingly recognized as indispensable components of a comprehensive education. This context is essential for comprehending the escalating significance of integrating coding and computational thinking into educational frameworks.

In recent times, there has been a fundamental change in the skills deemed crucial for success in the contemporary world. As technology permeates various aspects of life, the ability to comprehend and apply computational concepts becomes paramount for individuals navigating an interconnected and technologically-driven society. In response to this shift, educators, policymakers, and researchers have redirected their focus towards incorporating coding and computational thinking as fundamental pillars of education (Papert, 1980).

The background also acknowledges the broader societal and economic implications of this shift. The digital economy necessitates a workforce armed with skills extending beyond traditional subject areas, emphasizing qualities such as problem-solving, critical thinking, and creativity – all intrinsic to coding and computational thinking. Within this framework, educational institutions are reassessing their curricula to ensure students are not merely consumers of technology but active contributors and innovators.

Additionally, the background takes a global perspective, recognizing that the demand for coding skills is not confined to specific regions or industries. Internationally, countries are acknowledging the need to prepare their citizens for a digitally-driven future, resulting in diverse initiatives and approaches to integrating coding into educational systems.

The background also considers the challenges and opportunities associated with this educational transition. It underscores the necessity for inclusive practices, addressing issues of accessibility and equity to ensure coding education is available to all students, regardless of their background. Concurrently, it acknowledges the potential of coding education to bridge gaps and cultivate diversity within the tech industry.

As the background unfolds, it lays the groundwork for a thorough exploration of pedagogical approaches, curriculum design, real-world applications, and the broader societal impact of coding and computational thinking. It establishes the foundation for understanding the transformative potential of coding education in empowering students to excel in the digital age.

Coding and Computational Thinking in Digital Age

The integration of coding and computational thinking has become increasingly pivotal in the digital age, reshaping education to meet the demands of an evolving technological landscape. This symbiotic relationship between education and technology is not merely a response to the digital age but a proactive strategy to equip students with essential skills for navigating and contributing to the contemporary world (International Society for Technology in Education, 2016).

- Coding as a Fundamental Literacy:

In the digital age, coding is emerging as a fundamental literacy, akin to reading and writing. It empowers individuals to communicate with technology, understand its language, and shape its functionalities. As technology permeates every facet of our lives, the ability to code becomes a valuable skill, providing agency and fluency in an increasingly digitalized society.

- Computational Thinking as a Problem-Solving Framework:

Computational thinking, characterized by a systematic approach to problem-solving, is at the core of the digital age skill set. It involves breaking down complex problems into manageable parts, recognizing patterns, and designing algorithms to devise solutions. This mindset not only underpins coding but also cultivates a broader analytical and problem-solving capacity crucial in various fields.

- Preparation for Future Careers:

The digital age is marked by an unprecedented pace of technological innovation. Coding and computational thinking are not just academic pursuits; they are essential skills for future careers. Proficiency in coding opens doors to a plethora of opportunities in technology-driven industries, from software development and data science to artificial intelligence and robotics.

- Interdisciplinary Applications:

Coding and computational thinking transcend disciplinary boundaries. They serve as interdisciplinary tools applicable across subjects. Whether in mathematics, science, humanities, or the arts, the application of coding enhances understanding, fosters creativity, and encourages students to explore connections between seemingly disparate fields.

- Technological Innovation and Creativity:

The digital age thrives on innovation, and coding is a conduit for creative expression and problem-solving. Teaching coding empowers students to become creators of technology, fostering innovation rather than mere consumption. This creative aspect is crucial for cultivating a generation of thinkers and innovators capable of addressing complex global challenges (National Research Council, 2010).

- Adaptability and Lifelong Learning:

Coding and computational thinking instill adaptability and a mindset of lifelong learning. In a rapidly changing technological landscape, individuals need to embrace continuous learning. These skills go beyond specific programming languages; they encompass the ability to learn new languages and technologies, adapting to the evolving demands of the digital age.

- Global Connectivity and Collaboration:

The digital age has ushered in an era of global connectivity. Coding facilitates collaboration on a global scale, as individuals can contribute to open-source projects, participate in online communities, and collaborate across borders. This interconnectedness not only enriches learning experiences but also prepares students for a globally connected workforce.

Coding and computational thinking in the digital age are not merely educational trends but essential components of preparing students for a future where technology plays a central role. They empower students with the skills and mindset needed to thrive, innovate, and contribute meaningfully in an increasingly digital and interconnected world.

Block Diagram of Coding and Computational Thinking

Problem Definition

- Identify and understand the problem to be solved.
- Clearly define the desired outcome or goal.

Decomposition

- Break down the problem into smaller, more manageable steps.
- Analyze each step to determine its role in solving the problem.

Analysis (Planning)

- Evaluate each step for potential challenges or complexities.
- Develop a plan for tackling each step effectively.

Design (Problem Solving)

- Create algorithms and data structures to solve each step.
- Design user interfaces for interaction and data input/output.

Coding (Implementation)

- Translate the design into code using a programming language.
- Ensure code is well-structured, documented, and maintainable.

Testing (Verification)

- Conduct unit tests to verify the correctness of individual components.
- Perform integration tests to ensure seamless interaction between components.

- Conduct user acceptance tests to validate functionality and usability.

Evaluation (Assessment)

- Measure the performance, efficiency, and scalability of the solution.
- Assess the solution's usability, accessibility, and adherence to design principles.
- Evaluate the solution's security, data protection, and error handling mechanisms.

Computational Thinking

- Abstraction: Identify essential features and ignore irrelevant details.
- Pattern Recognition: Recognize patterns and regularities in problems and solutions.
- Algorithmic Thinking: Develop step-by-step procedures to solve problems.
- Evaluation: Assess solutions based on criteria and identify areas for improvement.

Coding

- Syntax: Understand and apply the grammatical rules of the programming language.
- Semantics: Understand the meaning and purpose of each language construct.
- Error Handling: Anticipate and handle errors gracefully during program execution.
- Debugging: Identify and fix errors in code to ensure proper functionality.

This block diagram illustrates the relationship between coding and computational thinking. Coding is the process of writing instructions for a computer to follow. Computational thinking is a way of thinking that involves breaking down problems into smaller, more manageable steps, and then using algorithms to solve them. Coding and computational thinking are closely related, as coding is a way of implementing computational thinking solutions (Partovi, 2017).

Merger of Digital Age With Coding and Computational Thinking in Student Perspective

In the ever-evolving digital age, the convergence of coding and computational thinking emerges as a transformative force in the educational journey of students. From the

Figure 1. Block diagram of between coding and computational thinking

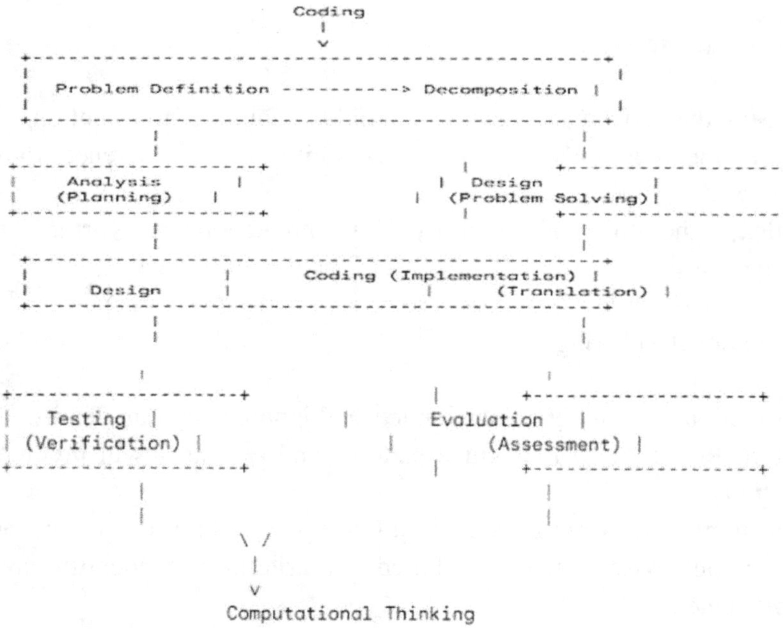

perspective of learners navigating this era, the integration of these skills becomes not only a pathway to technological proficiency but a gateway to unlocking creativity, problem-solving capabilities, and a deeper understanding of the interconnected world.

- Digital Literacy as a Cornerstone:

For students, coding becomes a fundamental literacy in the digital age, similar to mastering a language. It empowers them to communicate with technology, enabling them to navigate, understand, and manipulate the digital tools that permeate every aspect of their lives.

- Problem-Solving Mindset in Action:

Computational thinking, viewed through the lens of students, becomes a practical problem-solving mindset. It encourages breaking down complex issues into manageable parts, recognizing patterns, and devising algorithms to craft solutions. This mindset extends beyond the confines of coding projects, offering students a holistic approach to addressing challenges in various subjects and real-world scenarios (Wing, 2011).

- Career Readiness and Technological Fluency:

From a student's perspective, acquiring coding and computational thinking skills translates into readiness for future careers. It opens doors to diverse opportunities in technology-driven fields, instilling confidence in their ability to navigate an ever-evolving job market where digital fluency is not just an advantage but a necessity.

- Interdisciplinary Exploration:

Students experience the interdisciplinary nature of coding as they apply it across subjects. It becomes a tool for exploration in mathematics, science, humanities, and the arts, fostering a holistic understanding of how these disciplines interconnect. This approach not only enhances academic performance but also nurtures a well-rounded perspective.

- Innovation as Personal Expression:

In the eyes of students, coding transforms into a medium for personal expression and innovation. They become creators rather than mere consumers of technology, using code as a canvas for imaginative solutions to real-world problems. This creative aspect of coding empowers students to envision and shape the future.

- Adaptive Learning and Continuous Growth:

Students recognize coding and computational thinking as catalysts for adaptive learning and continuous growth. In a world where technology evolves rapidly, the skills acquired go beyond mastering specific programming languages. Instead, students develop a mindset of lifelong learning, embracing new languages and technologies as part of their educational journey.

- Global Collaboration and Connectivity:

From a student's perspective, coding facilitates global collaboration and connectivity. They become part of a global community where they can contribute to open-source projects, participate in online forums, and collaborate with peers from diverse backgrounds. This interconnectedness broadens their worldview and prepares them for a globalized workforce.

In essence, the amalgamation of coding and computational thinking in the digital age, seen through the eyes of students, becomes a transformative experience. It equips them not just with technical skills but with a mindset that fosters innovation, adaptability, and a profound connection to the interconnected world they are poised to shape.

In the digital age, students are invariably immersed in technology, utilizing it for communication, learning, and recreation. The acquisition of coding and computational thinking skills has become indispensable for students to thrive in this digital landscape. Coding involves the formulation of instructions for computers, while computational thinking encompasses the adeptness to deconstruct problems into more manageable components.

As students engage in coding, they cultivate a cognitive approach akin to that of computers. They learn to dissect problems into smaller elements and apply logical reasoning to devise solutions. This cognitive skill set proves invaluable across various domains, including computer science, engineering, and mathematics, laying a foundation for success in these fields.

Moreover, computational thinking contributes significantly to the development of students' problem-solving abilities. Those versed in computational thinking demonstrate proficiency in problem identification, analysis, and solution generation. These competencies extend beyond academic realms and are fundamental for success in diverse aspects of life.

Furthermore, coding and computational thinking serve as catalysts for fostering creativity in students. The process of coding necessitates creative thinking to formulate innovative solutions to problems. This form of creativity is transferable to other domains, such as art, music, and writing, enriching students' overall creative capacities.

In summary, the integration of the digital age with coding and computational thinking is imperative for student success. Through acquiring these skills, students not only become adept learners and problem solvers but also cultivate creative thinking abilities, positioning themselves as empowered individuals poised for leadership roles in the future.

Methodology

- **Engaging Pedagogy:**

Employ student-centric and engaging pedagogical approaches utilizing the digital age. Utilize interactive online platforms, coding games, and collaborative projects to ensure that learning coding and computational thinking is enjoyable and relevant for students.

- **Project-Based Learning:**

Figure 2. Functional diagram of the merger of the digital age with coding and computational thinking in the student perspective

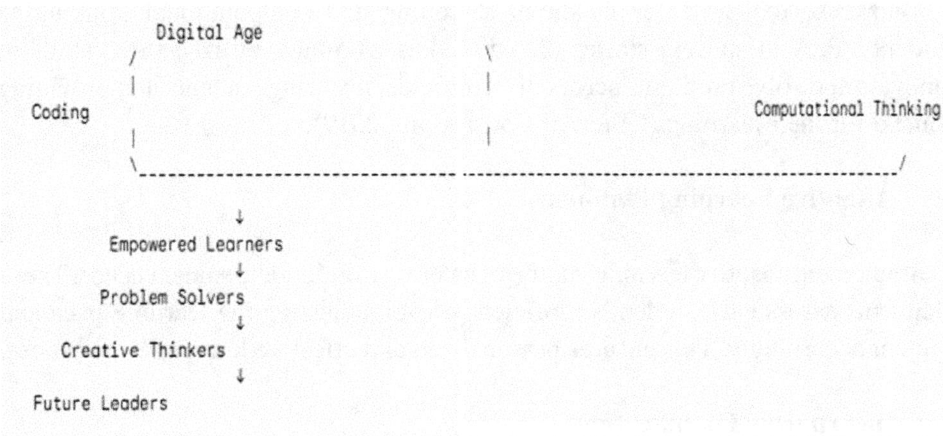

Emphasize project-based learning methods wherein students work on authentic coding projects. This hands-on approach enables students to apply their coding skills in practical scenarios, fostering a profound understanding of computational thinking and problem-solving.

- **Interactive Coding Platforms**:

Introduce students to interactive coding platforms and educational tools specifically designed for them. Platforms providing instant feedback, interactive coding challenges, and gamified features can enhance student engagement and motivation.

- **Multidisciplinary Integration**:

Integrate coding and computational thinking across various subjects, demonstrating how these skills are applicable in mathematics, science, literature, and beyond. This multidisciplinary approach helps students recognize the interconnected nature of knowledge and the versatility of coding skills.

- **Collaborative Learning Environments:**

Cultivate collaborative learning environments where students collaboratively work on coding projects. This mirrors real-world scenarios emphasizing teamwork and collaborative problem-solving. Digital collaboration tools can facilitate remote collaboration, promoting inclusivity.

- **Real-World Applications:**

Showcase real-world applications of coding and computational thinking to students. Present success stories of individuals who have utilized these skills to innovate and solve problems across diverse fields, inspiring students and providing context for their learning (CSforAll Consortium, 2019).

- **Adaptive Learning Platforms:**

Implement adaptive learning platforms catering to individual student needs. These platforms assess each student's proficiency level, adjusting the learning pace and content accordingly. This ensures personalized and effective learning experiences.

- **Incorporate Gamification:**

Integrate gamification elements into coding education, including gamified challenges, rewards, and competitions. Such elements can make the learning process enjoyable, motivating students to actively participate and persist in mastering coding and computational thinking skills.

- **Continuous Assessment and Feedback:**

Establish a system of continuous assessment and feedback. Regular assessments, quizzes, and feedback loops help students monitor their progress, identify areas for improvement, and reinforce their learning. Digital tools streamline this process, providing instant feedback.

- **Professional Development for Educators:**

Provide professional development opportunities for educators to enhance their understanding of coding and computational thinking. Empowering teachers with the necessary skills ensures effective curriculum delivery and promotes a positive learning experience for students.

- **Encourage Independent Exploration:**

Encourage students to explore coding independently. Provide resources, tutorials, and challenges that allow students to pursue coding outside the classroom, fostering curiosity and self-directed learning.

By implementing these methodologies, educators can create an enriched learning environment where students actively engage with coding and computational thinking in the context of the digital age, fostering a generation of technologically literate and creative individuals.

CONCLUSION

The integration of the digital age with coding and computational thinking from the student perspective unfolds as a transformative educational journey. As we navigate this landscape, it becomes evident that empowering students with these essential skills is not merely an adaptation to the times but a proactive strategy to equip them for the challenges and opportunities of the future.

From engaging pedagogies that leverage technology to project-based learning experiences, the methodologies explored in this chapter cater to the evolving needs of digital-age learners. The multidisciplinary integration of coding and computational thinking serves as a bridge between traditional subjects and real-world applications, providing students with a holistic understanding of the interconnected nature of knowledge.

The emphasis on collaborative learning environments mirrors the collaborative nature of the digital age, preparing students for a workforce where teamwork and adaptability are paramount. Real-world applications and success stories showcase the tangible impact of these skills, inspiring students to envision themselves as future innovators and problem solvers.

The incorporation of gamification elements adds a layer of enjoyment to the learning process, fostering motivation and persistence. Adaptive learning platforms and continuous assessment strategies ensure that education is personalized, catering to individual student needs and providing timely feedback for improvement.

As we invest in the professional development of educators, we recognize the pivotal role they play in shaping the educational experience. Their proficiency in coding and computational thinking not only enhances the delivery of the curriculum but also serves as a source of inspiration for students.

Encouraging independent exploration fosters a culture of curiosity and self-directed learning, essential qualities for navigating the ever-evolving digital landscape. In essence, the methodologies outlined in this chapter collectively contribute to the development of empowered learners—individuals equipped with not just technical skills but also a mindset of creativity, adaptability, and collaboration.

As we envision the culmination of these efforts, we see students who not only thrive in the digital age but emerge as architects of positive change. By seamlessly integrating coding and computational thinking into the student perspective, we pave the way for a generation that is not just prepared for the future but actively shaping it. The journey continues, and with each keystroke and algorithm, students embark on a path that leads to a future where their digital fluency becomes a catalyst for innovation, progress, and global connectivity.

REFERENCES

CSforAll Consortium. (2019). *K-12 Computer Science Framework*. CS for All. https://www.csforal.org/framework

Grover, S., & Pea, R. (2013). Computational Thinking in K–12: A Review of the State of the Field. *Educational Researcher*, *42*(1), 38–43. doi:10.3102/0013189X12463051

International Society for Technology in Education. (2016). *ISTE Standards for Students*. ISTE. https://www.iste.org/standards/for-students

Kafai, Y. B., & Burke, Q. (2014). *Connected Code: Why Children Need to Learn Programming*. The MIT Press. doi:10.7551/mitpress/9992.001.0001

National Research Council. (2010). *Report of a Workshop on The Scope and Nature of Computational Thinking*. The National Academies Press.

Papert, S. (1980). *Mindstorms: Children, Computers, and Powerful Ideas*. Basic Books.

Partovi, H. (2017). *Code.org: Inspiring a Generation to Learn Computer Science*. TEDxRainier. https://www.ted.com/tedx

Resnick, M. (2017). *Lifelong Kindergarten: Cultivating Creativity through Projects, Passion, Peers, and Play*. The MIT Press. doi:10.7551/mitpress/11017.001.0001

Wing, J. M. (2006). Computational thinking. *Communications of the ACM*, *49*(3), 33–35. doi:10.1145/1118178.1118215

Wing, J. M. (2011). Research Notebook: Computational Thinking—What and Why? *The Link Magazine*, *26*(2), 27–36.

Chapter 3
Design of Immersive Gamified Ecosystems:
Acceptance of the Methodology and Predictors of Future Implementation

Nerea López-Bouzas
https://orcid.org/0000-0003-0753-0672
University of Oviedo, Spain

Jonathan Castañeda Fernández
University of Oviedo, Spain

M. Esther Del Moral Pérez
https://orcid.org/0000-0002-9143-5960
University of Oviedo, Spain

ABSTRACT

This study arises from an innovation in initial teacher education aimed at designing immersive gamified ecosystems (IGEs), instructional resources where gamification converges with the use of augmented reality and artificial intelligence. The objectives are: a) to analyse university students' opinions on the generated motivation, ease of elaboration, group work, educational value, and future intention of application; b) to identify the level of acceptance of the methodology; and c) to analyse the mediation effect between the different variables. The research is empirical, non-experimental, descriptive, and inferential. A questionnaire adapted from the TAM model was used. The results demonstrate that the level of acceptance of the methodology is very high and is related to high motivation, ease of elaboration, contributions of group work, the educational value assigned to IGE, and the intention to apply it. Finally, this methodology proves suitable for teacher training by confirming its formative potential and increasing the intention to implement IGEs in their classrooms.
DOI: 10.4018/979-8-3693-5370-7.ch003

INTRODUCTION

The Horizon Report, Teaching and Learning Edition (Pelletier et al., 2023), outlines the methodologies that will become consolidated in the educational domain, emphasizing the progressive integration of Augmented Reality (AR) and Virtual Reality (VR) in classrooms. Additionally, it highlights the establishment of the maker culture associated with innovation (Pelletier et al., 2023), aimed at creatively and collaboratively solving problems through the creation of artifacts supported by digital resources (Godhe et al., 2019). This necessitates training teachers to design proposals that engage students in experimentation and collaborative construction of makerspaces to foster creativity (Marsh et al., 2019; Soomro et al., 2023).

On the other hand, gamification incorporates game mechanics, dynamics, and aesthetics, fostering learning through the accomplishment of playful missions or challenges (Lam and Tse, 2022; Ofosu, 2020). Occasionally, this technique relies on the use of devices and digital resources, activating student motivation (Leitão et al., 2022), being applied in language education (Pugh-Opher, 2023), introducing historical thinking (Martínez et al., 2021), enhancing pro-environmental behavior (Ricoy and Sánchez-Martínez, 2022), etc. Moreover, the use of gamification is being hybridized with emerging technologies, creating immersive experiences that combine virtual elements with real ones, promoting interactions with AR (Liao et al., 2023). Others design playful scenarios, inviting users to engage in the story and assist characters in achieving their goals by overcoming educational challenges (Del Moral et al., 2023).

Certainly, the use of AR is consolidating in schools as it offers the opportunity to improve students' attitudes, motivation towards learning, engagement with tasks, participation, knowledge acquisition, interest, and enjoyment (Lampropoulos et al., 2022). Additionally, with the advent of Artificial Intelligence (AI) applications in schools, questions arise about how they can become allies in educational work (Kim et al., 2023). Experiences are emerging where interactions of students with bots are analyzed to perform activities that develop computational and musical language (Ganesh et al., 2022); others evaluate the potential of AI applications to learn scientific content (Heeg and Avraamidou, 2023); stimulate socio-emotional skills, promote multiple literacies prioritizing digital literacy (Krajcik et al., 2023), and more.

In this context, the training of future teachers for the design of gamified resources that integrate AR and AI becomes particularly relevant, contributing to the optimization of the teaching and learning process, as indicated by Manzano et al. (2021). Therefore, the originality of this research lies in the implementation of a teaching innovation aimed at qualifying future Early Childhood Education teachers (ages 3-6) to collaboratively design Immersive Gamified Ecosystems (IGEs) in physical format enriched with AR and AI resources, in line with the maker culture.

INTEGRATING INNOVATIVE METHODOLOGIES IN TEACHER TRAINING

Trends regarding the future of teaching and learning in the higher education framework envision educational innovations that promote the ethical and creative use of AI as a facilitative tool for predictive and personalized learning. Additionally, in response to student disengagement with educational institutions stemming from pandemic-induced isolation, there is a push for innovations that enhance a sense of belonging to a reference group and activate collaborative work (Pelletier et al., 2023).

Specifically, innovations in the context of initial teacher training require implementing educational practices that collectively develop various competencies. These include digital competence focused on handling tools for content creation (Gabarda et al., 2023), socio-collaborative skills, fostering abilities for group work (Bush and Grotjohann, 2020), didactics for designing educational activities adopting gamification techniques (Manzano et al., 2022), and creativity, harmonizing the use of AR and AI apps for educational purposes, going beyond the mere use of commercial or pre-designed tools and opting for the creation of original resources (Neira-Piñeiro and Del Moral, 2021).

In this regard, gamification constitutes an innovative practice that exploits the opportunities of gaming to engage students in their own learning. Gamification necessitates building on a narrative featuring fictional characters placed in physical or virtual settings, incorporating missions or challenges that players must overcome to progress in the game (Valenza et al., 2019). At times, emotionally involving users and turning them into co-protagonists or auxiliary characters in the story. Consequently, the task of designing gamified activities and/or resources involves a certain level of complexity. On one hand, the creation or adaptation of a narrative, and on the other, the development of a physical support that seamlessly integrates it, representing the settings and characters while interspersing challenges that must be overcome to receive rewards upon achieving the game's objective.

Furthermore, the design of gamified proposals enriched with digital and AR resources promotes interactivity through mobile devices (Peláez and Solano, 2023). This necessitates educators to be adept at handling technological tools to apply them to the design of their own resources and be familiar with the functionality of certain AI apps for educational purposes.

Gamification of Narratives With Augmented Reality and Artificial Intelligence

Valencia and Orellana (2019) point out that the main barrier to implementing gamification in the educational field lies in the inherent complexity of designing a coherent gamified strategy. Hence, the need to establish guidelines that allow educational practices to be transformed into games, using immersive narratives as a guiding thread and integrating game mechanics, dynamics, and aesthetics. Additionally, the incorporation of AR and AI resources requires the training of specific skills. On one hand, digital skills, as it involves designing digital, AR, and AI resources in line with the adopted narrative, serving to cohesively connect the plot, characters, and settings (Gurbuz and Celik, 2022).

On the other hand, it also demands ludic-narrative skills, as it requires the development of a coherent storyline and the provision of interactive elements that structure the story (Bayeck, 2020). Furthermore, missions need to be designed that align with educational objectives, incorporate challenges with varying levels of difficulty, provide feedback, and allocate rewards linked to the narrative (Laine and Lindberg, 2020). Similarly, in a collaborative working context, designing these gamified narratives involves activating interpersonal communication, leadership skills, and the development of creativity (Betti et al., 2022).

In this regard, there are studies analyzing the development of skills in the initial teacher training when implementing gamification (Manzano et al., 2022), AR resources (Palamar et al., 2021), and generative AI applications (Montenegro et al., 2023). However, there are scarce investigations describing innovative proposals that qualify future teachers for the design of gamified resources supported by these emerging technologies. Hence, this article presents the results derived from implementing an innovative project in the Early Childhood Education degree, focusing on the collaborative creation of Immersive Gamified Ecosystems (IGEs) supported by digital, AR, and AI resources.

Immersive Gamified Ecosystems: Playful Narratives With Augmented Reality and Artificial Intelligence

The implemented innovation is oriented towards the design of Immersive Gamified Ecosystems (IGE), understood as physical resources crafted with manipulative materials that recreate scenarios, in this case, from children's animated films, adopting their narratives and incorporating educational challenges or playful missions. These challenges facilitate immersion by interacting with AR and AI resources. In particular, the process of creating IGEs, carried out in the initial teacher training, has followed the following phases (Figure 1).

Figure 1. Phases of the IGE design process
(Author's own elaboration)

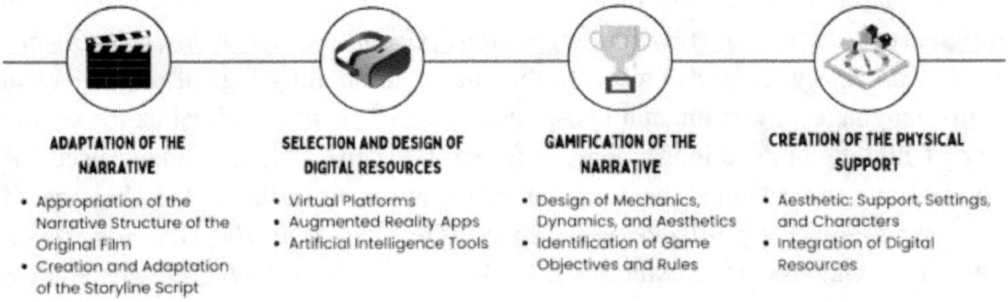

As a result of this process, the university students collaboratively designed 9 IGEs, using the narrative of an animated film as a starting point and recreating its settings on various physical supports (Table 1).

Each support integrates elements designed using digital tools such as *Canva*, *Paint*, Video Maker, etc. Characters, activities, and scenarios were created using Artificial Intelligence applications such as *eBing*, *Remove*, *Scribbel Diffusion*, *Canva AI*, *Leonardo.ai*, *Animated Drawings*, etc. Voiceovers, dialogues, and videos were created using *Voice Forge*, *CapCut*, or *Animaker Voice*. They also recorded their own audio to explain the objective and rules of the game, as well as to provide instructions to the students to progress and overcome the proposed missions. Additionally, the university students enriched the supports by incorporating videos from the movies themselves, as well as from YouTube or created by themselves to weave the narrative.

Table 1. Identification of developed IGEs

ID	Adapted Film (Year)	Studio and Production Company	Physical Support
ID1	Coco (2017)	Pixar Animation Studios	Roulette
ID2	The Lion King (1994)	Walt Disney	Book
ID3	Encanto (2021)	Walt Disney Pictures-Pixar Animation Studios	Board Game
ID4	Despicable Me (2010)	Illumination, Universal Pictures	Model
ID5	Ice Age (2002)	Blue Sky Studios-Century Fox	Board Game
ID6	Inside Out (2015)	Pixar Animation Studios-Walt Disney Pictures	Cube
ID7	Monsters, Inc. (2001)	Pixar Animation Studios-Walt Disney Pictures	Model
ID8	Toy Story (1995)	Pixar Animation Studios	Model
ID9	Moana (2016)	Walt Disney Studios	Model

Source: Author's own elaboration.

Others chose to create complementary physical resources (dice, cards, dolls, doors, boxes, etc.) for hands-on activities.

The playful challenges or missions integrated into the IGEs were created using different platforms, such as *LearningApp*, *Canva*, *Genially*, *Classroom Screen*, *Bouncy Balls*, *Educaplay*, *Scratch*, etc., with the aim of stimulating logical-mathematical skills, language, environmental knowledge, and artistic and musical expression in Early Childhood Education students (3-6 years). Specifically, the students used AR applications and designed their augmented resources according to the objective of each ecosystem. They utilized marker sheets (*Quiver, Chromville, Octagon Studio,* QR code generator, etc.), Merge Cube (*Merge Explorer, Merge Object Viewer,* and *MomentAR*), and holographic 3D modeling (*CoSpaces, JigSpaces, Metaverse, MomentAR, ZapWorks, Word Walls, Catchy Words*, etc.).

Most of them constructed models (Figure 2): in ID4. Despicable Me, the player must navigate through a city populated by minions with different professions, described by themselves in holographic form (*Metaverse*), solving challenges associated with each of them: traveling through space and observing holographic planets (*Space 4D+),* identifying animals on AR cards (*Animal 4D+),* observing the plant growth process with marker sheets (*Quiver* and *Chromville*), etc. In ID7. Monsters, Inc., different monsters holographically provide necessary instructions to players (*Metaverse*) to move through the board squares and return the protagonist to the initial door. AR activities range from observing different parts of the movie (*Merge Cube*), coloring 3D monsters (*Quiver*), etc.

In the case of IGE ID8. Toy Story, the protagonist toys help the player overcome challenges integrated into the narrative through voiceovers and holograms (*ZapWorks*) to find elements hidden around the room. The activities that structure the missions are associated with the role of each character, so: Dino (dinosaur) helps them identify augmented dinosaurs (*Dinosaur 4D+*), Buzz (astronaut) accompanies them on a virtual journey through the Solar System (*Merge Explorer),* Mr. Potato shows them body parts with 3D holograms (*Humanoid 4D+),* etc. On the other hand, ID9. Moana transports the player to a paradise island that they must traverse to overcome various missions to eliminate the curse that corrupts it. To do this, they have to use manipulable resources (wooden blocks), 3D cards (*Animal 4D+),* and AR sheets (*Quiver*) to increase their vocabulary about marine animals, and finally, navigate a virtual space to find a hidden treasure (*CoSpaces*).

Others chose to create board games: in ID3. Encanto, using squares, cards, and dice, the player must navigate a haunted house with rooms that present virtual landscapes alluding to different themes (jungle, space, garden, etc.) (*ZapWorks).* These rooms include challenges that students must overcome to achieve the final objective: finding the doorknob of the only closed door in the house and discovering what is hidden inside. The missions require using digital resources to arrange sentences

Figure 2. IGEs that use models as support
(Students' own elaboration)

(WordWall), change voices (*BouncyBalls*), play a memory game (*Educaplay),* or connect tangrams (*Genially*). As well as AR apps to see jungle animals (*Animal 4D+),* color them (*Quiver*), explore Colombian culture (*MomentAR*), or complete the names of characters in the story (*Catchy Words*). On the other hand, IGE ID5. Ice Age features a squirrel as the protagonist traveling through different natural environments (jungle, desert, and snowy mountain) and needs to overcome challenges to find its precious acorn. They will find it after properly matching images with their names in Spanish (*LearningApps*) and English (*Wordwall*). The player must also use AR apps to navigate the ecosystem map with smart glasses (*CoSpaces*), color the 3D jungle (*Quiver*), and identify elements of each holographic natural space (*Merge Object Viewer* and *MomentAR*).

IEG ID1. Coco presents a roulette divided into six sections, each featuring a character (*Metaverse*) that gives instructions to perform the corresponding mission and collect the elements to attend a party commemorating the Day of the Dead. Each character presents a different challenge using AR: searching for lost costume parts (*ZapWorks*), doing a memory game of 3D objects (*Octagon Studio*), and visualizing the human skeleton (*Merge Object Viewer*). On the other hand, ID2. The Lion King consists of three augmented books in which different wild animals in 3D (*Metaverse*) help the player overcome missions to gather the protagonists of the story. Different challenges linked to digital resources are integrated to complete a puzzle (*LearningApps*) or create a memory game (*WordWall*). AR resources are also included to guess secret words (*Weird Type),* animate drawings (Animate Drawings), color 3D animals (*Quiver*), and answer questions about their characteristics, as well as establish the choreography of a dance (*Merge Cube).*

Finally, ID6. Inside Out uses an augmented cube as support, where each face represents an emotion. Students must solve the challenges associated with each emotion to help the protagonist identify and recognize their own moods. The challenges rely on digital resources aimed at connecting puzzles and memories (*LearningApps*), discriminating the sounds of each one (*BouncyBalls*), ordering letters of words (*Catchy Words*), and connecting them with their meanings (*Wordwall*). Students must use AR resources to see emotions in a holographic way and discover their characteristics (*Metaverse*), use the Merge Cube to discover which image is associated with each one (*MomentAR*), paint different 3D characters according to the actions they perform and their emotional component (*Quiver*).

After completing this innovative practice, the students wanted to know their opinion on the collaborative design process of the IGEs carried out and their level of acceptance of the methodology used to ascertain the extent to which they consider the applicability of this resource in their future teaching work. Therefore, they filled out an online questionnaire that provided relevant data, which is included later on.

METHODOLOGY

This is an empirical, non-experimental, descriptive, and inferential study involving a mediation analysis, how is it defined by Cohen et al. (2011). The objectives of this study are: a) to analyze the opinion of university students about the motivation generated by the design of their IGE, the ease of its elaboration, the contributions of group work, the educational value they assign to the IGE, and their intention to implement it in their future teaching tasks; b) to identify their level of acceptance of the methodology used; and c) to analyze the mediation or interaction effect between the different variables that influence the acceptance of the methodology inherent in the design of the IGE.

Thus, the starting hypotheses are: H1. Future teachers consider that the methodology inherent in the collaborative design of the IGE is motivating, easy, enriching, and useful, predisposing them to use it in their future teaching practice in Early Childhood Education classrooms; H2. The level of acceptance of this methodology is high; H3. Future implementation is conditioned by the educational value they assign to the IGE and mediated by the ease of design, the motivation generated by its elaboration, and the contributions derived from the group work carried out.

Sample

The sampling was intentional, non-probabilistic, with the participation of 32 students from the optional subject "Communication, Child Development, and Education" in the 4th year of the Bachelor's Degree in Early Childhood Education at the University of Oviedo (Spain) (2023/2024), where the teaching innovation project aimed at the collaborative design of Immersive Gamified Ecosystems for Early Childhood Education was carried out.

Procedure

After creating their IGE, students responded to a previously validated questionnaire through exploratory factor analysis to gather their opinions, focusing on different dimensions: motivation, ease of design, contributions of group work, educational value, and intention for future implementation. Subsequently, the construct "*Acceptance of the Methodology Inherent in the Design of the IGE*". Figure 3 shows the convergence of the different dimensions defining the construct.

The level of acceptance of this methodology by the subjects was identified. A mediation analysis was performed to understand the causal relationship between the educational value that students assign to the IGE and the intention to implement them in their future teaching tasks.

Figure 3. Convergent dimensions of the acceptance of this methodology for future implementation
(Author's own elaboration)

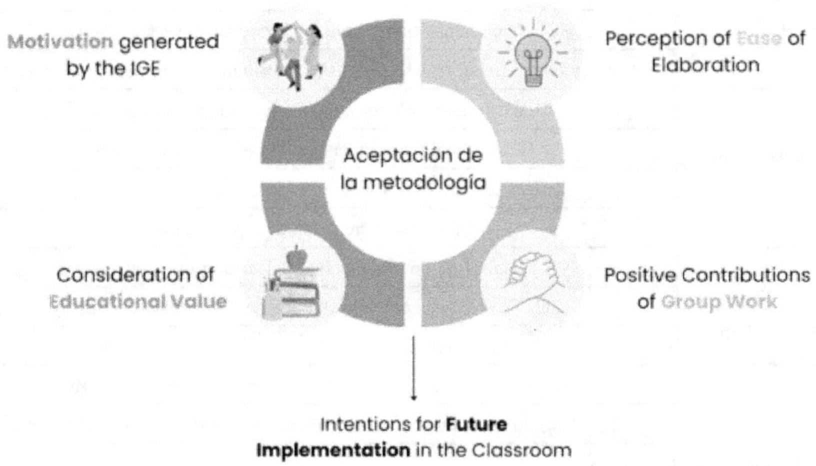

Instrument

The *GAME-DiRA. Gamification Methodology and Digital Resources Acceptance* instrument was designed based on Davis' (1993) *Technology Acceptance Model (TAM)* and Cheng et al.'s (2013) adaptation and it served to determine the level of acceptance of this methodology. For this purpose, the dimensions are identified: motivation generated by the design of the IGE, ease of its elaboration, contributions of group work, educational value granted, and intention for future implementation (Table 2).

To validate the scale, an exploratory factor analysis was conducted. The Bartlett's test of sphericity is significant (p < .000), and the Kaiser-Meyer Olkin (KMO)

Table 2. Dimensions analyzed with the instrument (GAME-DiRA) -adapted from Cheng et al. (2013)-

Dimensions	Items (1=Strongly Disagree; 2=Disagree; 3=Agree; 4=Strongly Agree)
1. Motivation Generated (M)	M1. Gamifying film narratives was enjoyable
	M2. I enjoyed implementing this methodology
	M3. The designed EGI allows learning through play
	M4. Designing resources with AR and AI was enjoyable
2. Ease of EGI Design (ED)	ED1. Integrating and designing digital, AI, and AR resources was easy
	ED2. Establishing game dynamics (narrative, characters, etc.) was easy
	ED3. Integrating game mechanics (missions, rewards, etc.) was easy
	ED4. Weaving the narrative and resources was manageable
	ED5. Creating the physical resource was manageable
3. Group Work Contributions (G)	G1. Collaborating on this project as a group was very enriching
	G2. Contributions from my peers were fundamental
	G3. Communication within the group helped resolve issues
	G4. My commitment to assigned tasks contributed to optimizing the resource
4. Educational Value (EV)	EV1. Enhances learning in Early Childhood Education
	EV2. Facilitates understanding of certain concepts
	EV3. Is useful for learning
	EV4. Will increase student performance
5. Intention for Future Implementation (FI)	FI1. Gamifying narratives makes learning more interesting
	FI2. The EGI can be enjoyable for Early Childhood students
	FI3. The designed EGI can be an optimal learning resource
	FI4. I would like to use this EGI in my future teaching activity
	FI5. I would consider designing another EGI to address different content

Source: Author's own elaboration.

adequacy test shows an acceptable value (KMO=.677). The Unweighted Least Squares (ULS) method was chosen, and the obtained factors are rotated obliquely using the Oblimin method, as suggested by Lloret-Segura et al. (2014), since, despite having variables with sufficient response categories, their distribution is not normalized (Kolmogorov-Smirnov Test<.000). It is observed that 74.7% of the variance is explained by 5 out of the 22 items.

Most items explain a large part of the variability of each variable, as the communalities in the 22 items are close to or higher than .700. The variables are grouped into 5 factors: factor 1 on the ease of EGI design, factor 2 associated with contributions from group work, factor 3 linked to the motivation aroused by its design, factor 4 related to the intention of future implementation, and factor 5 concerning the consideration of the educational value of the EGI (Table 3).

The factorial analysis ensures a good level of validity for the designed instrument. The Cronbach's Alpha coefficient of .911 is high, indicating good reliability of the scale.

For the treatment and analysis of the data collected on the variables under study, descriptive and inferential statistics were applied through the mediation analysis to identify the effect of the interaction of different dimensions. The SPSS-V26 program was used.

RESULTS

University Students' Perception of the EGI Design Task

In a first step, the data related to university students in each of the dimensions that make up the level of acceptance of the methodology inherent in the design of the EGI are analyzed independently. Subsequently, a global score is assigned to the subjects, and their distribution is observed based on different levels of acceptance.

The *motivation* aroused by the activity is inferred from their responses to the items associated with it (Table 4). It is observed that while all the mean values of the indicators are above 3.5, the design of resources with AR and AI reaches a mean close to the maximum value. Additionally, the university students consider that the elaborated resources allow preschoolers to learn through play. In general, they enjoyed the task of gamifying animated children's movies ($\bar{x}$=3.74).

Regarding their perception of the *ease of designing* EGIs, it is observed that the gamification process, the integration of game mechanics ($\bar{x}$=3.84) and dynamics ($\bar{x}$=3.75), along with the design of digital resources ($\bar{x}$=3.75), achieve the highest averages. On the contrary, the creation of physical supports (models, board games, cubes, etc.) has been considered the most complex task, according to their judgment (Table 5).

Table 3. Component grouping

	1	2	3	4	5	Communalities
M1. Gamifying film narratives was enjoyable			**.835**			**.882**
M2. I enjoyed implementing this methodology			.849			.912
M3. The designed EGI allows learning through play			.917			.909
M4. Designing resources with AR and AI was enjoyable			.699			.937
ED1. Integrating and designing digital, AI, and AR resources was easy	.803					.968
ED2. Establishing game dynamics (narrative, characters, etc.) was easy	.750					.790
ED3. Integrating game mechanics (missions, rewards, etc.) was easy	.804					.943
ED4. Weaving the narrative and resources was manageable	.613					.817
ED5. Creating the physical resource was manageable	.607					.699
G1. Collaborating on this project as a group was very enriching		.845				.772
G2. Contributions from my peers were fundamental		.663				.687
G3. Communication within the group helped resolve issues		.758				.729
G4. My commitment to assigned tasks contributed to optimizing the resource					.620	.734
EV1. Enhances learning in Early Childhood Education					.687	.903
EV2. Facilitates understanding of certain concepts					.617	.867
EV3. Is useful for learning					.820	.969
EV4. Will increase student performance					.913	.804
FI1. Gamifying narratives makes learning more interesting				.642		.867
FI2. The EGI can be enjoyable for Early Childhood students				.748		.927
FI3. The designed EGI can be an optimal learning resource				.966		.947
FI4. I would like to use this EGI in my future teaching activity				.615		.944
FI5. I would consider designing another EGI to address different content				.624		.829

Source: Author's own elaboration.

Also, since the development of the EGI required *collaboration* among the different members of each group, they were asked about their opinion on the contributions of group work. They mostly confess that their personal commitment, in assuming

Table 4. Descriptive statistics of the motivation aroused

	1	2	3	4	x̄	DT
Gamifying film narratives was enjoyable	0(0.0)	0(0.0)	11(34.4)	21(65.6)	3.66	0.483
I enjoyed implementing this methodology	0(0.0)	1(3.1)	9(28.1)	22(68.8)	3.66	0.545
The designed EGI allows learning through play	0(0.0)	0(0.0)	7(21.9)	25(78.1)	3.78	0.420
Designing resources with AR and AI was enjoyable	0(0.0)	0(0.0)	4(12.5)	28(87.5)	3.88	0.336
TOTAL	0(0.0)	1(0.8)	31(24.2)	96(75.0)	3.74	0.389

1=Strongly Disagree; 2=Disagree; 3=Agree; 4=Strongly Agree.

Table 5. Ease of design

It has been straightforward:	1	2	3	4	x̄	DT
Integrating and designing digital, AI, and AR resources was easy	0(0.0)	1(3.1)	6(18.8)	25(78.1)	3.75	0.508
Establishing game dynamics (narrative, characters, etc.) was easy	0(0.0)	0(0.0)	8(25.0)	24(75.0)	3.75	0.440
Integrating game mechanics (missions, rewards, etc.) was easy	0(0.0)	1(3.1)	3(9.4)	28(87.5)	3.84	0.448
Weaving the narrative and resources was manageable	0(0.0)	0(0.0)	9(28.1)	23(71.9)	3.72	0.457
Creating the physical resource was manageable	1(3.1)	14(43.8)	11(34.4)	6(18.8)	2.69	0.821
TOTAL	1(0.6)	16(10.0)	37(23.1)	106(66.3)	3.55	0.397

1=Strongly Disagree; 2=Disagree; 3=Agree; 4=Strongly Agree.

the assigned tasks, has allowed increasing the value of the resources developed ($\bar{x}$=3.19). Overall, the students agree that the contributions of their peers have been crucial to successfully create the resource ($\bar{x}$=3.13), as well as considering that intergroup communication has helped resolve contingencies ($\bar{x}$=3.13), and that the group development of the design has been enriching ($\bar{x}$=2.97) (Table 6).

In relation to your opinion regarding the *educational value* of the designed IGEs, you are convinced that they are useful didactic tools for the learning of Early Childhood Education students ($\bar{x}$=3.81). It is emphasized that they facilitate understanding ($\bar{x}$=3.47) and enhance various competencies ($\bar{x}$=3.47). You express a forward-looking perspective, confident that they can improve students' academic performance by emphasizing the value of play ($\bar{x}$=3.31) (Table 7).

On the other hand, we sought your opinion on aspects that may influence your *intention to implement IGEs* in your future teaching tasks in Early Childhood Education classrooms. University students overwhelmingly agree that these resources are enjoyable for this student group ($\bar{x}$=3.91). Furthermore, they believe that narratives

Table 6. Descriptive statistics of contributions from group work

	1	2	3	4	x̄	DT
Collaborating on this project as a group was very enriching	1(3.1)	6(18.8)	18(56.3)	7(21.9)	2.97	0.740
Contributions from my peers were fundamental	1(3.1)	5(15.6)	15(46.9)	11(34.4)	3.13	0.793
Communication within the group helped resolve issues	1(3.1)	3(9.4)	19(59.4)	9(28.1)	3.13	0.707
My commitment to assigned tasks contributed to optimizing the resource	2(6.3)	5(15.6)	10(31.3)	15(46.9)	3.19	0.931
TOTAL	5(3.9)	19(14.8)	62(48.4)	42(32.8)	3.10	0.618

1=Strongly Disagree; 2=Disagree; 3=Agree; 4=Strongly Agree.

Table 7. Descriptive statistics of educational value

	1	2	3	4	x̄	DT
Enhances learning in Early Childhood Education	0(0.0)	2(6.3)	13(40.6)	17(53.1)	3.47	0.621
Facilitates understanding of certain concepts	0(0.0)	1(3.1)	15(46.9)	16(50.0)	3.47	0.567
Is useful for learning	0(0.0)	1(3.1)	4(12.5)	27(84.4)	3.81	0.471
Will increase student performance	1(3.1)	3(9.4)	13(40.6)	15(46.9)	3.31	0.780
TOTAL	1(0.8)	7(5.5)	45(35.2)	75(58.6)	3.52	0.500

1=Strongly Disagree; 2=Disagree; 3=Agree; 4=Strongly Agree.

turned into games make learning more interesting ($\bar{x}$=3.81). They express a desire to use these resources in their future teaching roles ($\bar{x}$=3.75) and contemplate designing other IGEs that address different content areas ($\bar{x}$=3.41) (Table 8).

Figure 4 reflects the means achieved in the dimensions that comprise the variable acceptance of the methodology inherent in the design of IGEs. It is noted that the mean related to their degree of agreement with the positive contributions derived from the collaborative design of the resource is significantly lower than the others.

Thus, the variable acceptance of the methodology inherent in the design of GIEs is constructed from five dimensions: motivation elicited by its design, ease of elaboration, contributions from group work, consideration of its educational value by university students, and future intention to implement it in their teaching tasks. This variable is calculated from the average of the 22 items integrated into the GAME-DiRA instrument, and four levels are established. For each subject, the scores obtained are summed and divided by 22 (total number of items). Since the starting scale consists of four categories (1=Strongly Disagree; 2=Disagree; 3=Agree; 4=Strongly Agree), we chose to maintain the same number of levels, establishing the following intervals: low (1.00-1.74), medium (1.75-2.50), high

Table 8. Descriptive statistics of their intention to implement it in the future

	1	2	3	4	x̄	DT
Gamifying narratives makes learning more interesting	0(0.0)	0(0.0)	6(18.8)	26(81.3)	3.81	0.397
The EGI can be enjoyable for Early Childhood students	0(0.0)	0(0.0)	3(9.4)	29(90.6)	3.91	0.296
The designed EGI can be an optimal learning resource	0(0.0)	1(3.1)	6(18.8)	25(78.1)	3.75	0.508
I would like to use this EGI in my future teaching activity	1(3.1)	0(0.0)	5(15.6)	26(81.3)	3.75	0.622
I would consider designing another EGI to address different content	1(3.1)	3(9.4)	10(31.3)	18(56.3)	3.41	0.798
TOTAL	2(1.3)	4(2.5)	30(18.8)	124(77.5)	3.73	0.409

1=Strongly Disagree; 2=Disagree; 3=Agree; 4=Strongly Agree.

Figure 4. Mean values of the dimensions
(Author's own elaboration)

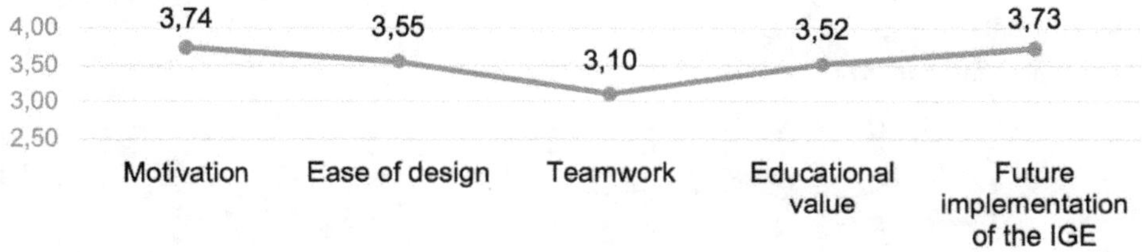

(2.51-3.25), and very high (3.26-4.00), considering the measurement range equal to 3 [Maximum (4) – Minimum (1)] even though there are 4 categories, setting the range of each interval at 0.75 points (3/4=0.75). Thus, university students are distributed as follows, based on their level of acceptance: medium (3.1%), high (12.5%), or very high (84.4%) (Figure 5).

Mediation Analysis

Next, a mediation analysis is conducted -following the guidelines of Hayes (2022)- to examine whether the Educational Value (EV) assigned by university students to the Immersive Gamified Ecosystem (independent variable -X-) is conditioned by the Ease of its Design (ED) (mediator variable 1 -M1-), the Motivation derived from its elaboration (M) (media or variable 2 -M2-), and their perception of the contributions of Group Work (G) (mediator variable 3 -M3). Furthermore, the aim is to determine whether the interaction of these variables influences their intention to implement the IGE in the future (FI) (dependent variable -Y-) (Figure 6).

Figure 5. Distribution of university students according to the level of acceptance of the methodology inherent in the design of IGEs
(Author's own elaboration)

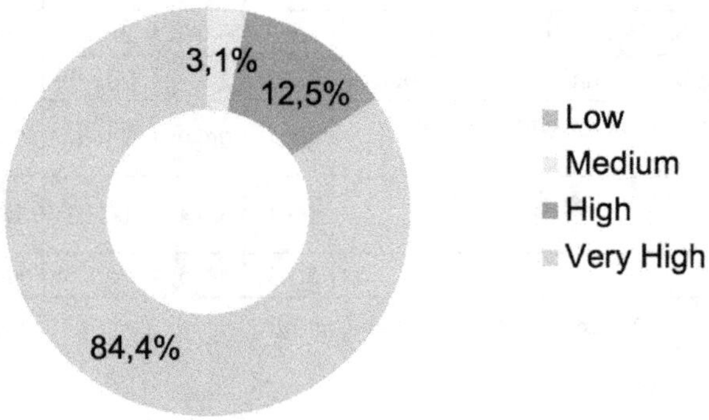

Figure 6. Mediation analysis: Effect of mediator variables on future implementation of the IGE
(Author's own elaboration)

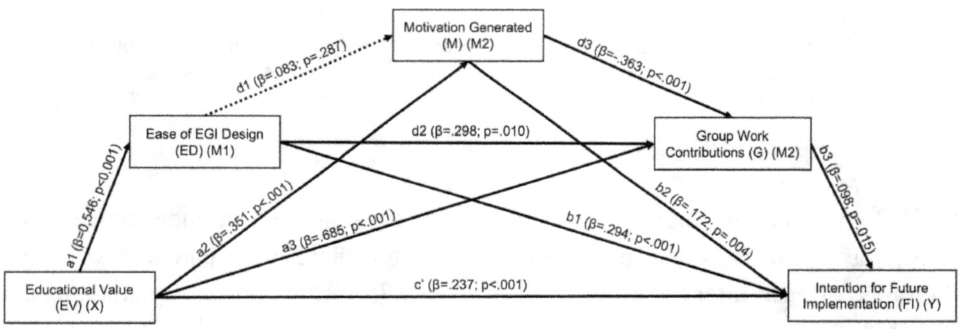

Table 9 presents the results obtained from the mediation analysis. It is evident that the direct effects of their opinion on the educational value of the IGEs are statistically significant for the three mediator variables: ease of design ($\beta=0.546$; $p<.001$), motivation ($\beta=0.351$; $p<.001$), and contributions from group work ($\beta=0.685$; $p<0.001$), as well as for the dependent variable related to the intention to implement the IGE in the future ($\beta=0.237$; $p<.001$). The relationship between the three mediator variables and the dependent variable is also significant (ED Vs IF: $\beta=0.294$; $p<.001$; ME Vs IF: $\beta=0.172$; $p=0.004$; GW Vs IF: $\beta=0.098$; $p=0.015$).

On the other hand, when analyzing the indirect effects of the educational value variable of the IGE on the future implementation variable, mediated by the ease of design variable ($\beta=0.161$; LI=0.059; LS=0.294), or by the motivation derived from the elaboration of the IGE ($\beta=0.060$; LI=0.016; LS=0.103), or by the contributions

Table 9. Results of the mediation analysis with the dependent variable future implementation of the IGE

Effects		Route	β	p	EE	LL	UL
Direct	EV in ED	a1	.546	<.001	.039	.469	.622
	EV in M	a2	.351	<.001	.062	.229	.473
	EV in G	a3	.685	<.001	.097	.494	.876
	ED in FI	b1	.294	<.001	.068	.160	.429
	MO in FI	b2	.172	.004	.060	.054	.290
	G in FI	b3	.098	.015	.040	.020	.176
	EV in FI	c'	.237	<.001	.063	.112	.362
	ED in M	d1	.083	.287	.078	-.070	.237
	ED in G	d2	.298	.010	.114	.072	.523
	MO in G	d3	-.363	<.001	.099	-.557	-.168
Indirect	EV in FI for FD	a1*b1	.161	-	.060	.059	.294
	EV in FI for M	a2*b2	.060	-	.022	.016	.103
	EV in FI for TG	a3*b3	.067	-	.026	.017	.118
	EV in FI for ED and M	-	.008	-	.007	-.004	.023
	EV in FI for ED and G	-	.016	-	.008	.003	.035
	EV in FI for M and G	-	-.012	-	.005	-.023	.003
	EV in FI for ED, M and G	-	-.002	-	.002	-.006	.001
TOTAL	EV in FI for ED, M and G	-	.534	<.001	.042	.453	.616

*β=Coefficient; p=Significance Level; EE=Estimation Error; LL=Lower Limit; UL=Upper Limit;
*Resampling technique has been employed with a number of 10,000 samples.

from group work (β=0.067; LI=0.017; LS=0.118), it is noted that the relationships are statistically significant in all three cases, as the value 0 is not within the interval of the limits. However, the indirect effects of the independent variable along with the three mediators do not yield statistically significant differences in those mediations where the motivation variable is involved. In other words, university students considering the elaboration of the IGE to be enjoyable and having enjoyed it does not necessarily imply that they will carry it out in their future teaching tasks.

Therefore, after acknowledging the limitations associated with the use of the motivation variable, a new mediation analysis was conducted, excluding it. Thus, it was examined whether the educational value (EV) assigned by students to the IGE (independent variable -X-) influences their perception of the ease of its design (ED) (mediator variable 1 -M1-) and their opinion on the contributions of group work (G) (mediator variable 2 -M2-), and in turn, if these influence their intention to implement the IGE in the future (FI) (dependent variable -Y-) (Figure 7).

The direct effects of EV are statistically significant concerning their opinion on the ease of design (ED) (mediator variable) ($\beta=0.546$; $p<.001$) and contributions from group work (G) (mediator variable) ($\beta=0.558$; $p<.001$); as well as regarding their intention to implement it in the future (dependent variable) ($\beta=0.312$; $p<.001$). The relationships between the two mediator variables are also significant ($\beta=0.268$; $p=0.024$), as well as each one of these in relation to their intention to apply the IGE in the future (ED Vs FI: $\beta=0.316$; $p<.001$; G Vs FI: $\beta=0.098$; $p=0.041$) (Table 10).

Figure 7. Variables involved in the mediation analysis with the dependent variable future implementation of the IGE
(Author's own elaboration)

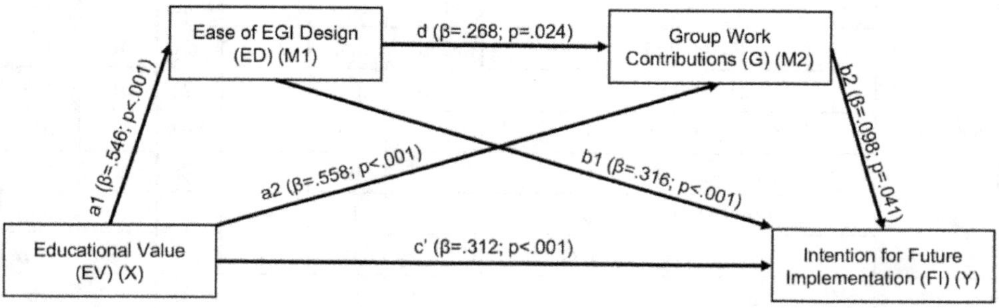

Table 10. Results of the mediation analysis with the dependent variable future implementation of the IGE

Effects		Route	β	p	EE	LL	UL
Direct	EV in FI	a1	.546	<.001	.039	.469	.622
	EV in G	a2	.558	<.001	.093	.374	.741
	ED in FI	b1	.316	<.001	.069	.180	.452
	G in FI	b2	.098	.041	.039	.020	.176
	EV in FI	c'	.312	<.001	.058	.197	.428
	ED in G	d	.268	.024	.117	.036	.499
Indirect	EV in FI for ED	a1*b1	.172	-	.062	.067	.310
	EV in FI for TG	a2*b2	.039	-	.020	.002	.078
	EV in FI for ED and G	-	.018	-	.007	.001	.026
Total	EV in IF for ED and G	-	.534	<.001	.042	.453	.616

*β=Coefficient; p=Significance Level; EE=Estimation Error; LL=Lower Limit; UL=Upper Limit;
*Resampling technique has been employed with a number of 10,000 samples.

Similarly, the indirect effects of the educational value of the IGE towards its future implementation involve considering its design as easy (β=0.172; LI=0.067; LS=0.310) or positively valuing group contributions (β=0.039; LI=0.002; LS=0.078), resulting in both cases statistically significant, as the value 0 is not included in the interval of the limits. Likewise, the indirect effects of the independent variable (EV) along with the two mediator variables (ED and G) also produce statistically significant changes in their intention to implement the IGE in the future (FI) (β=0.018; LI=0.001; LS=0.026).

Therefore, it is logical that the coefficient of determination obtained with the model largely explains the effects on the dependent variable (R2=0.627), etc., on their intention to implement the IGE in their future classrooms. Hence, the total effects present high and significant values (β=0.534; p<.001).

DISCUSSION AND CONCLUSION

The methodology adopted for the design of Immersive Gamified Ecosystems (IGEs) converges gamification with the use of Augmented Reality (AR) and generative Artificial Intelligence (AI) tools in the creation of makerspaces. Specifically, these instructional resources recreate playful scenarios, integrating manipulative and digital elements, structured by narratives adapted from children's animated films, and incorporate challenges or missions that enhance student immersion. This practice has represented an opportunity for the ongoing professional development of the teaching staff, enhancing their digital competence and emphasizing the ethical uses of technology, particularly those related to AI, while avoiding the suppression of their creativity, as noted by Ivcevic and Grandinetti (2024).

Most notably, the supports for the majority of the designed IGEs are models crafted with manipulative materials such as cardboard, clay, wood, fabric, etc., aligning with the maker culture philosophy. The scenarios include original characters from the adapted films, who engage the player to help them achieve their purpose by solving various missions and challenges. These games rely on diverse plots, emphasizing adventure and the quest for characters or magical elements. Additionally, most integrate videos and narrations that engage the player, enhancing immersion in the story. They also incorporate fragments from the original films, akin to cinematics, allowing the narrative to flow, as highlighted by Ferreira and Dos Santos (2021). However, not all VLEs embraced the principles of Universal Design for Learning (UDL) in their design, and as such, formulas should be incorporated to facilitate access for individuals with disabilities, promoting their inclusion, as advocated by Creed et al. (2023).

The integrative capacity of this methodology for IGE design has facilitated future teachers in simultaneously activating various skills. In particular, they have demonstrated proficiency in handling and designing digital resources on various virtual platforms, as well as Augmented Reality resources and using generative AI applications to create elements, scenarios, and characters of the ecosystem. Clearly, this task has allowed the development of the teacher's digital competence (DigComp), as indicated by Mintii et al. (2023) and Palamar et al. (2021), after similar experiences in the initial training of Early Childhood Education teachers. Their ability to apply their didactic knowledge by adapting missions and challenges to the curricular contents of Early Childhood Education, integrating different levels of difficulty, and personalizing the playful experience has also been evident. Nevertheless, to ensure the sustainability of the designed resource, challenges and tasks could be expanded and exchanged, increasing difficulty, addressing various curricular areas, and encompassing diverse languages or cultures, as suggested by MacDowell (2023).

On the other hand, after completing the design process and consulting them on various aspects, the confirmation of H1 is obtained, as the results show that future teachers consider the collaborative development of IGEs to be enriching for their education. They have felt highly motivated by creating AR and AI resources, although the conversion of original films into games posed some difficulty. It would be interesting for them to adapt narratives from different types of films or literary works, not restricting themselves to the same production company. They could also create their own avatars or characters to enhance identification and immersion in the narratives, as suggested by Lee et al. (2023). Modifying the narratives and game objectives to ensure engagement with the proposed tasks, and so forth. However, overall, they declare that this creative gamification practice has been accessible, especially the integration of mechanics, i.e., missions and challenges, along with the assignment of rewards.

Specifically, university students have emphasized the educational value of the created ecosystems as valuable instructional resources for the overall education of the target audience. They also believe that the contributions of collaborative design have been positive, thanks to personal commitment to tasks, achieving mutual enrichment, as described in the studies by Del Moral et al. (2023) and Maier et al. (2021). Undoubtedly, this group creative task has been satisfactory in uniting members of each group to carry out an innovative and original project. It should be noted that this activity has required significant dedication to develop digital and AR resources, as well as manipulative materials. Challenges have been encountered, such as difficulty accessing all the features of certain programs or dealing with unstable online applications.

These facts translate into their expressed intention to implement IGEs in their future teaching activity, considering that their design can contribute to consolidating innovative culture in schools through collaborative projects. Simultaneously, the design of these ecosystems has fostered the sense of belonging of university students to a working group, as well as their connection, creating a motivating learning environment and promoting joint problem-solving and decision-making, similarly to the experience of Zhang and Ouyang (2023).

Likewise, it is concluded that the level of acceptance of the methodology inherent in the design of IGEs is very high (H2), confirmed after noting the high motivation aroused, their conviction of the ease of elaboration, the confirmation of positive contributions derived from group work, the significant educational value assigned, and the expressed intention to apply it in their classrooms in the future. Finally, it is worth noting that their future implementation of IGEs is based on the recognition of the didactic value of the IGE for Early Childhood Education students, the simplicity of its design, and the advantages of collaborative work. However, the motivation aroused by its elaboration is not a predictive factor determining its subsequent use in their future teaching tasks, as indicated in H3.

Future teachers consider that IGEs have significant educational value, are easy to design, and collaborative work in their creation is enriching. All of this influences their intention to implement it in their future professional performance. Undoubtedly, this innovative practice has enabled the creation of gamified resources with high didactic and aesthetic quality, endowed with immersive narratives that can contribute to the engagement of Early Childhood Education students through the interactivity generated by AR and AI. Furthermore, the final products have allowed the training of narrative and digital skills of the university students by creating environments where film characters directly engage with each child. Additionally, didactic, creative, and socio-collaborative skills have been developed by crafting physical resources in line with the philosophy of the maker culture.

With regard to recommendations for implementing these resources in the Early Childhood Education classroom, it is essential to avoid prolonged exposure to the game that may demotivate students by becoming repetitive or create frustration with insurmountable challenges. Additionally, immersion should not lead to a form of alienation or escapism from reality. There should always be an educational component, and their use should be combined with oral expression practices to articulate perceptions, emotional states generated by the game, and promote discovery-based learning.

Ultimately, this methodology has proven to be suitable for implementation in initial teacher education by demonstrating its potential to stimulate teaching skills while increasing the intention to apply IGEs in their classrooms. As limitations of the research, it would be interesting to expand the study sample, analyze the skills enhanced during the design of IGEs, and implement it in other subjects.

REFERENCES

Alves, A., Silva, B., & Silva, M. A. (2021). Análisis del uso de la cultura maker en contextos educativos: Una revisión sistemática de la literatura. *Educatio Siglo XXI*, *39*(2), 143–168. doi:10.6018/educatio.465991

Bayeck, R. Y. (2020). Examining board gameplay and learning: A multidisciplinary review of recent research. *Simulation & Gaming*, *51*(4), 411–431. doi:10.1177/1046878119901286

Betti, A., Biderbost, P., & García, A. (2022). Can active learning techniques simultaneously develop students' hard and soft skills? Evidence from an international relations class. *PLoS One*, *17*(4), e0265408. doi:10.1371/journal.pone.0265408 PMID:35472046

Bush, A., & Grotjohann, N. (2020). Collaboration in teacher education: A cross-sectional study on future teachers' attitudes towards collaboration, their intentions to collaborate and their performance of collaboration. *Teaching and Teacher Education*, *88*, 102968. doi:10.1016/j.tate.2019.102968

Cheng, Y., Lou, S., Kuo, S., & Shih, R. (2013). Investigating elementary school students' technology acceptance by applying digital game-based learning to environmental education. *Australasian Journal of Educational Technology*, *29*(1), 96–110. doi:10.14742/ajet.65

Cohen, L., Manion, L., & Morrison, K. (2011). *Research methods in education*. Routledge.

Creed, C., Al-Kalbani, M., Theil, A., Sarcar, S., & Williams, I. (2023). Inclusive AR/VR: Accessibility barriers for immersive technologies. *Universal Access in the Information Society*, 1–15. doi:10.1007/s10209-023-00969-0

Cruz, I. M., & Cabero, J. (2020). Una experiencia gamificada en el aprendizaje de los triángulos en geometría: grado de aceptación de la tecnología. *Revista Prisma Social, 30,* 65–87. https://revistaprismasocial.es/article/view/3744

Davis, F. (1993). User acceptance of information technology: System characteristics, user perceptions and behavioral impacts. *International Journal of Man-Machine Studies*, *38*(3), 475–487. doi:10.1006/imms.1993.1022

Del Moral, M. E., López-Bouzas, N., & Castañeda, J. (2023). Activating Teacher Competencies Through Designing Gamified Stories With Augmentative Reality. In E. Podovšovnik, T. De Giuseppe, & F. Corona (Eds.), Handbook of Research on Establishing Digital Competencies in the Pursuit of Online Learning(pp. 230-252). IGI Global. doi:10.4018/978-1-6684-7010-7.ch012

Ferreira, J. L., & dos Santos, L. (2021). Design requirements for educational serious games with focus on player enjoyment. *Entertainment Computing*, *38*, 100413. doi:10.1016/j.entcom.2021.100413

Gabarda, V., Marín, D., Vidal, M. I., & Ramón, J. (2023). Digital Competence of Training Teachers: Results of a Teaching Innovation Project. *Education Sciences*, *13*(2), 162. doi:10.3390/educsci13020162

Ganesh, D., Kumar, M. S., Reddy, P. V., Kavitha, S., & Murthy, D. S. (2022). Implementation of AI Pop Bots and its allied Applications for Designing Efficient Curriculum in Early Childhood Education. *International Journal of Early Childhood Special Education*, *14*(3). doi:10.9756/INT-JECSE/V14I3.271

Godhe, A. L., Lilja, P., & Selwyn, N. (2019). Making sense of making: Critical issues in the integration of maker education into schools. *Technology, Pedagogy and Education*, *28*(3), 317–328. doi:10.1080/1475939X.2019.1610040

Gurbuz, S. C., & Celik, M. (2022). Serious games in future skills development: A systematic review of the design approaches. *Computer Applications in Engineering Education*, *30*(5), 1591–1612. doi:10.1002/cae.22557

Hayes, A. (2022). *Introduction to mediation, moderation and conditional process analysis: A regression-based approach*. The Guilford Press.

Heeg, D. M., & Avraamidou, L. (2023). The use of Artificial intelligence in school science: A systematic literature review. *Educational Media International*, *60*(2), 125–150. doi:10.1080/09523987.2023.2264990

Ivcevic, Z., & Grandinetti, M. (2024). Artificial intelligence as a tool for creativity. *Journal of Creativity*, *100079*(2), 100079. Advance online publication. doi:10.1016/j.yjoc.2024.100079

Khaldi, A., Bouzidi, R., & Nader, F. (2023). Gamification of e-learning in higher education: A systematic literature review. *Smart Learning Environments*, *10*(10), 10. doi:10.1186/s40561-023-00227-z

Kim, K., Kwon, K., Ottenbreit-Leftwich, A., Bae, H., & Glazewski, K. (2023). Exploring middle school students' common naive conceptions of Artificial Intelligence concepts, and the evolution of these ideas. *Education and Information Technologies*, *28*(8), 1–28. doi:10.1007/s10639-023-11600-3

Krajcik, J., Schneider, B., Miller, E. A., Chen, I. C., Bradford, L., Baker, Q., Bartz, K., Miller, C., Li, T., Codere, S., & Peek-Brown, D. (2023). Assessing the effect of project-based learning on science learning in elementary schools. *American Educational Research Journal*, *60*(1), 70–102. doi:10.3102/00028312221129247

Laine, T. H., & Lindberg, R. S. (2020). Designing engaging games for education: A systematic literature review on game motivators and design principles. *IEEE Transactions on Learning Technologies*, *13*(4), 804–821. doi:10.1109/TLT.2020.3018503

Lam, P., & Tse, A. (2022). Gamification in everyday classrooms: Observations from schools in Hong Kong. *Frontiers in Education*, *6*, 630666. doi:10.3389/feduc.2021.630666

Lampropoulos, G., Keramopoulos, E., Diamantaras, K., & Evangelidis, G. (2022). Augmented reality and gamification in education: A systematic literature review of research, applications, and empirical studies. *Applied Sciences (Basel, Switzerland)*, *12*(13), 6809. doi:10.3390/app12136809

Lee, H. W., Chang, K., Uhm, J. P., & Owiro, E. (2023). How Avatar Identification Affects Enjoyment in the Metaverse: The Roles of Avatar Customization and Social Engagement. *Cyberpsychology, Behavior, and Social Networking*, *26*(4), 255–262. doi:10.1089/cyber.2022.0257 PMID:37001178

Leitão, R., Maguire, M., Turner, S., & Guimaraes, L. (2022). A systematic evaluation of game elements effects on students' motivation. *Education and Information Technologies*, *27*(1), 1081–1103. doi:10.1007/s10639-021-10651-8

Liao, C. H., Wu, W. C., Gunawan, V., & Chang, T. C. (2023). Using an Augmented-Reality Game-Based Application to Enhance Language Learning and Motivation of Elementary School EFL Students: A Comparative Study in Rural and Urban Areas. *The Asia-Pacific Education Researcher*, 1–13. doi:10.1007/s40299-023-00729-x

Lloret-Segura, S., Ferreres-Traver, A., Hernández-Baeza, A., & Tomás-Marco, I. (2014). El análisis factorial exploratorio de los ítems: Una guía práctica, revisada y actualizada. *Anales de Psicología*, *30*(3), 1151–1169. doi:10.6018/analesps.30.3.199361

Lombardero, X., Murcia, E., Aguiar, F. X., Méndez, A. B., & González, A. (2023). Academic Engagement and Disaffection in Social Work Undergraduates From Spain: The Role of Teaching Styles and Student Motivation. *Journal of Social Work Education*, 1–18. doi:10.1080/10437797.2023.2248225

MacDowell, P. (2023). Teachers designing immersive learning experiences for environmental and sustainability education. In *Immersive education: Designing for learning* (pp. 171–186). Springer International Publishing. doi:10.1007/978-3-031-18138-2_11

Maier, A. M., Eckert, C. M., & Clarkson, P. J. (2021). Factors influencing communication in collaborative design. *Journal of Engineering Design*, *32*(12), 671–702. doi:10.1080/09544828.2021.1954146

Manzano, A., Aguilar, J. M., Rodríguez, J., & Ortiz, A. (2022). Gamification in initial teacher training to promote inclusive practices: A qualitative study. *International Journal of Environmental Research and Public Health*, *19*(13), 8000. doi:10.3390/ijerph19138000 PMID:35805658

Marsh, J., Wood, E., Chesworth, L., Nisha, B., Nutbrown, B., & Olney, B. (2019). Makerspaces in early childhood education: Principles of pedagogy and practice. *Mind, Culture, and Activity*, *26*(3), 221–233. doi:10.1080/10749039.2019.1655651

Martínez, M., Gómez, C. J., & Miralles, P. (2021). The effects of a gamified project based on historical thinking on the academic performance of primary school children. *Humanities & Social Sciences Communications*, *8*(122), 122. Advance online publication. doi:10.1057/s41599-021-00796-9

Mintii, M., Sharmanova, N., Mankuta, A., Palchevska, O., & Semerikov, S. (2023). Selection of pedagogical conditions for training STEM teachers to use augmented reality technologies in their work. In Journal of Physics: Conference Series (Vol. 2611, No. 1, p. 012022). IOP Publishing. doi:10.1088/1742-6596/2611/1/012022

Montenegro, M., Fernández, J., Fernández-Batanero, J. M., & López-Meneses, E. (2023). Impact of the implementation of ChatGPT in education: A systematic review. *Computers*, *12*(8), 153. doi:10.3390/computers12080153

Neira-Piñeiro, M. R., & Del Moral, M. E. (2021). Educación literaria y promoción lectora apoyadas en entornos literarios inmersivos con realidad aumentada. *Ocnos*, *20*(3), 1–19. doi:10.18239/ocnos_2021.20.3.2440

Ofosu, K. (2020). The shift to gamification in education: A review on dominant issues. *Journal of Educational Technology Systems*, *49*(1), 113–137. doi:10.1177/0047239520917629

Palamar, S., Bielienka, G., Ponomarenko, T., Kozak, L., Nezhyva, L., & Voznyak, A. (2021). *Formation of readiness of future teachers to use augmented reality in the educational process of preschool and primary education.* CEUR Workshop. http://ds.knu.edu.ua/jspui/handle/123456789/3775

Peláez, C. A., & Solano, A. (2023). A Practice for the Design of Interactive Multimedia Experiences Based on Gamification: A Case Study in Elementary Education. *Sustainability (Basel), 15*(3), 2385. doi:10.3390/su15032385

Pelletier, K., Robert, J., Muscanell, N., McCormack, M., Reeves, J., Arbino, N., Grajek, S., Birdwell, T., Liu, D., Mandernach, J., Moore, A., Porcaro, A., Rutledge, R., & Zimmern, J. (2023). *EDUCAUSE Horizon Report, Teaching and Learning Edition.* EDUCAUSE. https://www.educause.edu/horizon-report-teaching-and-learning-2023

Pugh-Opher, F. (2023). Teaching and Learning Mandarin Chinese: Gamification and Simulation in an Early Childhood Classroom. In Research Anthology on Early Childhood Development and School Transition in the Digital Era (pp. 157-174). IGI Global.

Ricoy, M. C., & Sánchez-Martínez, C. (2022). Raising ecological awareness and digital literacy in primary school children through gamification. *International Journal of Environmental Research and Public Health, 19*(3), 1149. doi:10.3390/ijerph19031149 PMID:35162171

Romano, M., Díaz, P., & Aedo, I. (2023). Empowering teachers to create augmented reality experiences: The effects on the educational experience. *Interactive Learning Environments, 31*(3), 1546–1563. doi:10.1080/10494820.2020.1851727

Soomro, S. A., Casakin, H., Nanjappan, V., & Georgiev, G. V. (2023). Makerspaces Fostering Creativity: A Systematic Literature Review. *Journal of Science Education and Technology, 32*(4), 1–19. doi:10.1007/s10956-023-10041-4

Valencia, L. I., & Orellana, D. (2019). Barreras en la implementación de la gamificación en educación superior: Revisión de literatura. *InCrescendo, 10*(3), 635–650. doi:10.21895/incres.2019.v10n4.06

Valenza, M. V., Gasparini, I., & da S. Hounsell, M. (2019). Serious game design for children. *Journal of Educational Technology & Society, 22*(3), 19-31. https://www.jstor.org/stable/26896707

Zhang, N., & Ouyang, F. (2023). An integrated approach for knowledge extraction and analysis in collaborative knowledge construction. *International Journal of Educational Technology in Higher Education*, *20*(1), 45. doi:10.1186/s41239-023-00414-5

KEY TERMS AND DEFINITIONS

Artificial Intelligence: A field of computer science that focuses on creating systems capable of performing tasks that typically require human intelligence, such as learning, reasoning, and perception.

Augmented Reality: A set of technologies that allows the visualization of virtual elements within the real world through digital devices that add graphical information through holograms, markers, and 3D elements.

Gamified Narrative: A story that integrates mechanics, dynamics, and aesthetics inherent to games to promote the player's engagement with challenges or missions to achieve the desired objective and enhance immersion in the story.

Immersive Gamified Ecosystems (IGE): Physical resources crafted with manipulative materials that recreate scenarios, in this case, from children's animated movies, adopting their narratives and incorporating playful challenges or educational missions that encourage student immersion by interacting with AR resources.

Mediation Analysis: A statistical technique that enables the understanding of the causal relationship between an independent variable and a dependent variable, identifying the mediating variables that condition it.

Chapter 4
OneLife IoT-Based Self-Monitoring Healthcare System

Ritu Punhani
Amity University, India

Shalini Puri
https://orcid.org/0000-0002-1700-1865
Manipal University Jaipur, India

Vivek Jangra
Amity University, India

Ishika Punhani
UPES, Dehradun, India

ABSTRACT

The health monitoring system has become increasingly popular in recent years due to its unique features and wide range of medical applications. The OneLife IoT-based self-monitoring healthcare system is a smart health monitoring system to detect and predict diseases by monitoring various health-related data such as body temperature, pulse rate, heartbeat, blood pressure, oxygen levels, and sugar levels. It helps track a patient's specific metrics every day and provides analysis for a week, month, and year to predict the patient's condition. It is implemented and tested on two groups of five patients each and achieves accuracy by measuring the general parameters in a controlled environment. It provides the users with the measured results, on LCD including heart rate, blood sugar level, temperature, etc. By incorporating internet of things-based self-monitoring healthcare systems into educational systems, the health of the students can be easily monitored.

DOI: 10.4018/979-8-3693-5370-7.ch004

INTRODUCTION

Ensuring human health is a top priority for a good quality of life. With an increasing number of people suffering from chronic diseases, it is crucial to monitor physiological indicators of health to provide early medical care and potentially save lives. In-patient care costs are on the rise due to the growing demand for modern resources from medical service providers. Additionally, factors such as aging, daily workload, stress, anxiety, and other diseases force people to take medication less frequently, leading to longer recovery times. Patient health monitoring is becoming increasingly important to leverage the resources of current technology. Vital factors, such as pulse rate, body temperature, heart rate, heartbeat, oxygen levels, blood pressure, and sugar, are physiological characteristics that indicate a person's health status. These measures can be used to detect any health problems (Ball et al., 2023; El-Rashid et al., 2020; Harun et al., 2020; Hongru & Goyea, 2020; Hypoxemia, 2020; Lee et al., 2017; Pourhomayoun et al., 2016; Rizzo, 2020; Serpanos & Wolf, 2019; Thailand Medical News, n.d.). The current Internet of Things (IoT) technology and the increasing number of mobile users worldwide enable remote monitoring of a patient's health. Any sensitive patient information must be kept secure in such healthcare systems.

In present days, healthcare systems are frequently utilizing IoT technology. This process involves the collection, storage, and maintenance of sensitive patient data in electronic health record systems through the advantages of IoT networks (Arulananth & Shilpa, 2017; Evans, 2020; Islam et al., 2020; Khan, 2020; Wrist worn pulse oximeter, n.d.). In an IoT environment, biomedical healthcare systems use sensor technologies and microcontroller-based engineering systems to transfer patient data to any remote location. This data is then utilized to monitor the patient's energy levels and notify the doctor or other nurses if anything seems abnormal (Components101., n.d.-c; Pierleoni et al., 2014; Prasath, 2013; Reza et al., 2017; Senith Electronics, n.d.; Srinivasan et al., 2020; Srividya, & Satyanarayana,, 2018; Sutradhar et al., 2019; Tamilselvi, 2020; Yatsenkov, 2018). These proactive technology-assisted self-monitoring measures are aimed at improving the medical services offered by healthcare units.

The IoT-based Health Monitoring System (HMS) involves self-monitoring of the user using a smartphone application to keep track of vital body parameters such as body temperature, pulse rate, blood pressure, heartbeat, heart rate, and sugar levels. The gathered data from sensors is analyzed and processed by the doctor for diagnosis and treatment. Display devices such as Liquid Crystal Displays (LCDs) or Light-Emitting Diodes (LEDs) exhibit the sensor data, which is a part of the IoT system. There are various systems available to monitor chronic illnesses (Components101, n.d.-a; Components101, n.d.-b; Dharmik et al., 2021; Simel et al., 2020). For instance, the Self-Monitoring Healthcare System (SMHS) is used to check the glucose level in diabetes blood. The parameters such as heartbeat, pulse rate, and heart rate are used to determine the state of the heart and how well it is functioning. Additionally, a blood oxygen level test is used to assess lung operation and determine the blood's acid-base balance. Oxygen levels are used to identify underlying health issues. On the other side, the IoT-based self-monitoring healthcare systems play a crucial role in shaping the future of learning as one continues to embrace innovation in education. So, integrating IoT-based self-monitoring healthcare systems into educational settings can improve education in several ways through intelligent systems and data-driven instruction (Dharmik et al., 2021; Gope & Hwang, 2015). Here are a few main benefits:

a. IoT-enabled healthcare solutions provide educators and medical professionals with the ability to identify potential health problems or pressures early on, allowing them to take quick action. For instance, if a patient's heart rate or sleep patterns indicate tension or worry, the system can alert the appropriate staff to offer counseling or relaxation strategies.
b. A program that combines data analysis with health-related areas can promote interdisciplinary learning among patients. Hands-on activities and strategies that combine IoT-based self-monitoring healthcare systems enable patients to explore subjects such as physiology, data science, and health informatics (Prasath et al., 2023; Singh et al., 2023).
c. Self-monitoring healthcare systems allow patients to become more conscious of their health and provide important new information on how lifestyle decisions affect overall health. With this knowledge, they can make lifelong healthy and wellness-promoting decisions and develop lifelong healthy habits that go beyond their school years.
d. Patients may become more motivated and involved in their educational journeys by incorporating health monitoring into educational platforms. Patients can be inspired to adopt healthy habits and take charge of their well-being by receiving real-time feedback on health metrics. This input can also act as a form of accountability and inspiration (Gope & Hwang, 2015).

The chapter presents a OneLife IoT-based self-monitoring healthcare system which is a smart health monitoring mobile app to detect and predict diseases by monitoring several parameters such as body temperature, pulse rate, heartbeat, blood pressure, oxygen levels, and sugar levels. The design of this app is more personalized, engaging, and effective learning that prioritize patients' overall well-being by utilizing intelligent technology and data analytics.

The rest of the chapter is structured as follows. Section 2 elaborates the literature review on the self-monitoring techniques for the existing health care systems. Section 3 presents the proposed OLISMH system along with the design of ESP8266 module and pin layouts and connections. Section 4 describes various components of the OLISMH system including Arduino UNO, oximeter and heart rate monitoring sensor, blood pressure sensor, temperature sensor, blood's glucose monitoring sensor, and the 16 × 2 LCD. Section 5 explains the workflow of the OLISMH system – mobile app. Section 6 presents the experimental results of the proposed system. Section 7 concludes the chapter with future recommendations.

LITERATURE REVIEW

Several self-monitoring systems and applications have been introduced in the health care sector. The healthcare system (Lee et al., 2017) described a wearable device that could monitor glucose levels in sweat. This device also had a module that could administer medicine through the skin. The device's accuracy was improved by using multiple sensors that could detect humidity, pH, and temperature, and the sensors could adjust in real-time accordingly. The device was made up of several layers to improve sweat collection and sensing. Additionally, the device was designed to be disposable, with a strip-style device that uses simple sensors. The device also used temperature-responsive nanoparticles that released medication in response to the patient's glucose level. These nanoparticles were placed on hyaluronic acid hydrogel microneedles to make the drug delivery more precise and multistage.

Another such work (Thailand Medical News, n.d.) provided a collaborative platform to give medical information and resources for Thailand's medical news. The proposed architecture in El-Rashid et al. (2020) consisted of three layers such as the patient layer, the cloud layer, and the hospital layer. In the patient layer, wearable sensors and a mobile app were utilized for patient tracking. To address issues related to data transmission and storage, a fog network design was implemented in the cloud layer. In the hospital layer, a CNN-based deep learning model was utilized for COVID-19 detection using the patient's X-ray scan images and transfer learning. This model demonstrated higher accuracy results of 97.95% compared to the state-of-the-art, with a specificity of 98.85%. The website introduced in Hongru and Goyea (2020) provided details about the center for coronavirus disease in CSSE at Johns Hopkins University (Hongru & Goyea, 2020) and information regarding symptoms, causes, and treatments for Hypoxemia at the level and Clinic (Hypoxemia, 2020).

Another system (Pourhomayoun et al., 2016) proposed an effective predictive analytical approach for the prediction of hospital readmission for Congestive Heart Failure (CHF). The study found that by accessing existing physiological measurements, the system predicted medically unfavorable occurrences for CHF, which could be prevented through early clinical intervention. Thus, a remote HMS could offer a practical means of lowering readmission rates. The architecture and design for IoT systems were defined in Serpanos and Wolf (2019). The complete system architecture, including edge and cloud, was explained. It discussed both the design of IoT nodes and networks after discussing the cyber-physical and industrial control systems. Vital indicators such as temperature, heartbeat, breathing rate, and blood pressure are used to indicate important bodily processes (Ball et al., 2023). Silent hypoxia was a condition where a patient's pulse oximetry reading was lower than expected in the case of a patient who did not seem to be having difficulty breathing. This could occur in various situations but had recently gained attention due to the high frequency with which COVID-19 patients experienced this (Harun et al., 2020; Rizzo, 2020) offered a case study on how pulse oximetry was crucial for the at-home care of COVID-19.

The wrist-worn pulse oximeter (Wrist worn pulse oximeter, n.d.) for extended blood oxygen or pulse rate monitoring along with the Nonin WristOX$_2$ was discussed. High-altitude athletes, such as mountain bikers and sports pilots, as well as individuals receiving home health care who had difficulty breathing due to sleep apnea, asthma, and other lung disorders, often chose a wrist blood oxygen monitor. A method was explained in Evans (2020) to treat coronavirus at home during COVID-19. Another method (Arulananth & Shilpa, 2017) determined the heart rate using an Arduino and a fingertip. It was based on the PhotoPlethysmogGraphy (PPG) principle, which measured the variation in blood volume in tissues using a light source and detector. The blood volume inside the finger artery changed because the heart pumped blood throughout the body. By placing an optical detecting device around the fingertip, the blood fluctuation could be identified. The signal was boosted before being transmitted to Arduino via serial port communication. Heart rate monitoring and counting were done with the use of processing software.

In this study (Khan, 2020), the authors introduced and analyzed the current state and difficulties of IoT-based smart healthcare services for the underprivileged rural population of Bangladesh. The study also reviewed the companies in Bangladesh that offered IoT-based healthcare services and their current standing in this area. To create telemedicine services based on mobile and online applications, healthcare service providers in Bangladesh had employed five sensors - the body temperature sensor, the heartbeat sensor, the room temperature sensor, the CO, and the CO_2 sensor to collect data from the HMS. The research found that IoT-based healthcare service providers were dealing with several newly emerging issues. The devised scheme's error percentage for each scenario was below a predetermined threshold of 5%. Medical professionals received information about the conditions via a portal, which enabled them to process and evaluate the patient's current state. The effectiveness of the system demonstrated how effectively the prototype was suited for healthcare monitoring. The study (Srividya, & Satyanarayana,, 2018) presented a new method of monitoring the respiratory capacity of asthmatics using a portable device powered by Raspberry Pi. The device identified the expiratory part of a spirometry test and its associated parameters.

Another system (Srinivasan et al., 2020) used an Arduino controller to measure the pulse rate at the fingertip based on the principle of PPG. This technique works by analyzing blood pressure differences, detecting fluctuations in blood pressure values, and transmitting the information to the controller. The infrared diode sent infrared light to the fingertip, which passed through the blood inside the finger arteries. The photodiode and infrared LED located in the sensor detected changes in blood volume. The photodiode then analyzed the light signal and sent the controller the value that deviates from the light signal. Another study (Pierleoni et al., 2014) demonstrated that consumer electronics, such as heart rate monitors, had the potential to be used not just for sports purposes but also in medical research and diagnostics. The study developed a system that was simple, accurate, and affordable by using heart rate monitor data. The data was processed on a smartphone, which generated comprehensive reports on the user's (patient) health status, stores report data, initiates emergency calls or SMSs, and connected to a remote telemedicine gateway to send data to an online database. The system detected and categorized episodes of arrhythmia and stress conditions, as well as calculated energy usage.

Another study (Prasath, 2013) discussed the creation of wireless heart rate monitoring using a microcontroller. All ECG signals and heartbeats were recorded on a single computer. A microcontroller was used to first acquire and then process these biological signals. All data were processed before being delivered to a communication interface, which then sent the information to a computer. It was crucial to provide an accurate and speedy diagnosis for the patient who had a cardiac illness. Continuous monitoring of the patient's current heart rate, blood pressure, and ECG signal was necessary for this aim. Furthermore, it used Bluetooth transmission and reception in the hub of any hospital to track the patient's ECG signal. It included several active sensors, including those for eye blinking, temperature, heartbeat, and peripheral-capillary-oxygen-saturation sensors for obtaining the patient's body temperature, eye movement, coronary heart rate, and oxygen saturation. The Arduino UNO board served as the system's microcontroller, and cloud computing was also utilized. The legal person used a cloud server to communicate the patient's vital signs to their smartphones and laptops (Tamilselvi, 2020).

A real-time monitoring system for cardiac health (Reza et al., 2017) was developed with a focus on accuracy, usability, and data security. It was designed to facilitate communication between healthcare providers and provided monitoring services for people with cardiovascular disease outside of a clinical setting. The system consisted of a web portal, an Android handset, and a pulse rate sensor that measured the heartbeat. Its performance analysis demonstrated its reliability and usefulness, as it offered real-time monitoring. The analysis also showed that the proposed solution was both practical and secure. The system also enabled message-based communication between the patient and the healthcare provider. Another study (Sutradhar et al., 2019) was conducted to determine the prevalence and risk factors of Chronic Obstructive Pulmonary Disease (COPD) in Bangladesh. The study used various sources including BANGLAJOL, PubMed, Google Scholar, and Popline. The research was focused on determining the incidence of COPD and/or its risk factors among Bangladeshis. According to the global initiative for chronic obstructive lung disease criteria, the pooled prevalence of COPD among adult Bangladeshis was found to be 12.5%. When considering the lower limit of normalcy criteria, it was 11.9% (95% CI, 11.4-13.6). The study found that males, people from low socioeconomic backgrounds, people who lived in rural areas, and people who used biomass fuel had a greater incidence of COPD. The main risk factors for COPD, based on this study, were age, a history of asthma, exposure to biomass fuel, and smoking.

The cost-efficient Pulse Oximeter MAX30100 / MAX30102, a developer board and an open-source Lua-based firmware called NodeMCU were used for designing an IoT application (Yatsenkov, 2018). The hardware in Components101 (n.d.-c) was based on the ESP-12 module, and the firmware was powered by the ESP8266 Wi-Fi SoC from the ESPRESSIF systems. The LM2596 DC-DC buck converter (Senith Electronics, n.d.) used in the step-down power module featured a high-precision potentiometer and could effectively derived loads up to 2A. If the output current exceeded 1.5 A, a heat sink was installed. Most embedded projects employed 16 × 2 LCD modules since they were inexpensive, readily available, programmer-friendly, and had access to a wealth of educational resources (Components101, n.d.-a).

In Components101 (n.d.-b), the DS18B20, a 1-wire programmable temperature sensor was employed to measure temperature in a range of severe environments, such as chemical solutions, mines, soil, etc. The sensor was easy to install because of the sturdy and waterproof container. It had a good accuracy of 5°C and could measure temperatures from - 55° to +125°. Each sensor had a unique address, so that it could measure temperature at different locations without using up a lot of digital pins on the microcontroller. Additionally, it only needed one MCU pin to relay data from each sensor (Components101, n.d.-b). The study (Simel et al., 2020) explained the concept of the historical perspectives and physical evaluation in the patients. In Dharmik et al. (2021), an IoT-based method for healthcare monitoring was illustrated, whereas the secured IoT-based modern healthcare system (Gope & Hwang, 2015) was explained using body sensor network. In the same direction, the review (Singh et al., 2023) presented the application of IoT in healthcare sector, and the cloud server based intelligent health care (Prasath et al., 2023) was presented using body sensor network. Various machine learning techniques (Punhani et al., 2022; Puri et al., 2023; Puri & Singh, 2019; Puri & Singh, 2020) were explained to handle different types of datasets.

Although several self-monitoring techniques in the healthcare sector have been introduced and implemented successfully to date, but still there is a need of fast, cost-efficient, and space-efficient health care mobile app which can easily be used and for the education and commercial sectors.

THE PROPOSED OLISMH MODEL

The proposed OneLife IoT-Based Self-Monitoring Healthcare (OLISMH) system is a smart health monitoring model based on IoT that detects and predicts diseases by monitoring various health-related data such as body temperature, pulse rate, heartbeat, blood pressure, oxygen levels, and sugar levels. It is lightweight and highly portable, making it easy to integrate with other devices. It helps track a patient's specific metrics every day and provides analysis for a week, month, and year to predict the patient's condition. If the measured sugar level or pulse rate exceeds the normal range, the application notifies the user or patient.

The OLISMH system configuration includes the components such as an Arduino UNO, a pulse sensor, a 16 × 2 LCD, LM355, ESP8266-01, an LED display, a buzzer, a Wi-Fi module, a temperature sensor, a Bluetooth module along with R1, R2 with 2K, R3 with 1K, and R4 with 2K resistors. Its circuit architecture diagram is shown in Figure 1 (a). Figure 1 (b) depicts the block architecture diagram of the OLISMH system including a MAX 30100 pulse oximeter and heart rate monitor sensor, a SON 12 blood pressure sensor, an LM 35 temperature sensor, a glucose sensor, a current transducer, an Arduino UNO, an LCD display, and a power supply. The current transducer takes the inputs from pulse oximeter and heart rate monitor sensor, blood pressure sensor, temperature sensor, and glucose sensor. Its output is further sent to the Arduino UNO, which further sends its output to the LCD display. The power supply is attached to the Arduino UNO and the LCD display. The OLISMH system does not work with higher values than 3.7 V.

Design of ESP8266 Module

An ESP8266 module is a simple and affordable device that provides Internet connectivity to the OLISMH system, as shown in Figure 2. It provides dual functionality as an access point and a station, making it easy to collect data and transmit it to the Internet. It retrieves data from the Internet via Application Programming Interfaces

Figure 1. (a) Circuit architecture of the proposed OLISMH system; (b) Block architecture of the proposed OLISMH system

(a)

(b)

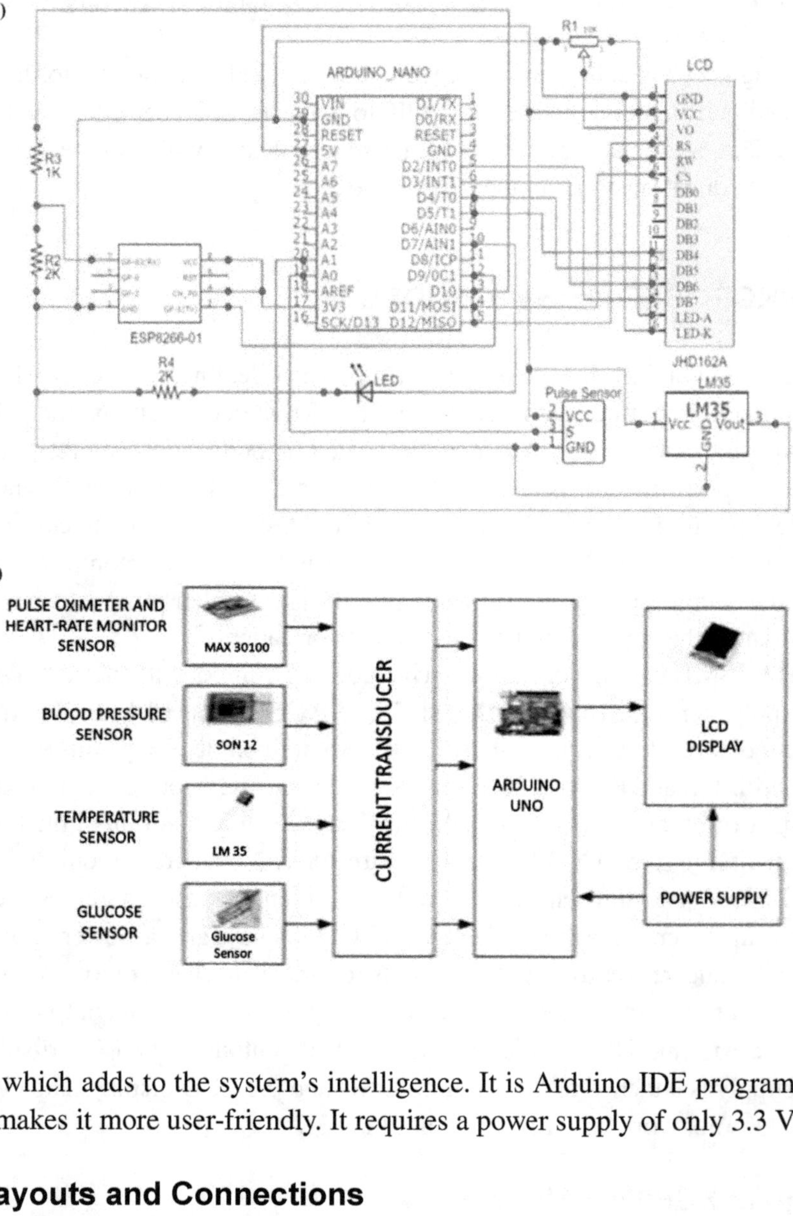

(APIs) which adds to the system's intelligence. It is Arduino IDE programmable, which makes it more user-friendly. It requires a power supply of only 3.3 V.

Pin Layouts and Connections

The circuit architecture of the OLISMH system includes eight pins and have sensor connections, LED connections and LCD connections. Their layout and connection description are given below.

Figure 2. ESP8266 design

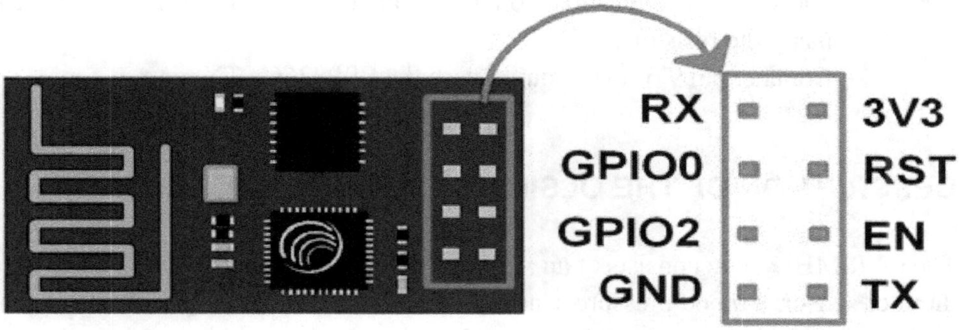

A. Pin Layout
- Pin one is Ground and is connected to the circuit's ground.
- Pin two is TX/GPIO, which is connected to the programmer's RX pin to upload the program.
- Pin three is GPIO for input/output.
- Pin four is the EN which enables the chip,
- Pin five is general purpose Flash/GPIO pin used for input/output.
- Pin six is used to reset the module.
- Pin seven is RX/GPIO which is the General-Purpose Input/Output.
- Pin eight is V_{cc} and is only be connected +3.3 V.

B. Sensor Connections
- Connect Arduino A0 to the pulse sensor output pin, and V_{CC} and GND to the other two pins.
- Connect the Arduino A1 pin to the output pin of the LM35 temperature sensor, and the other two pins to V_{CC} and GND.

C. LED Connection

Connect the LED to Arduino's digital pin seven using a 220-ohm resistor.

D. LCD Connections

- Connect GND to LCD pins 1, 3, 5, and 16.
- Connect V_{CC} to LCD pins 2 and 15.
- Connect pins 4, 6, 11, 12, 13, and 14 of the LCD to digital pins 12, 11, 5, 4, and 3 of the Arduino. However, if the ESP8266's RX pin is connected directly to the Arduino, it does not work since the RX pin runs at 3.3 V. To solve this problem, a voltage divider is constructed using a 2.2 K

and 1 K resistors. This process changes the voltage from 5 V to 3.3 V, allowing the connection from the ESP8266's RX pin to Arduino pin 10 using the resistors.

- Connect pin 9 of the Arduino with the ESP8266's TX pin.

DESCRIPTION OF THE OLSIMH SYSTEM COMPONENTS

The OLISMH system consists of an Arduino UNO, a pulse oximeter and heart rate monitor sensor, a blood pressure sensor, a temperature sensor, a glucose sensor, a current transducer, and an LCD display. It is designed to monitor the heart rate, oxygen saturation in the blood (SpO_2), respiration rate, temperature, blood pressure, and blood glucose level for a wide range of population, including newborns, adults, and elders. It collects the data from the sensors and records it in an app so that doctors, nurses, and others can use them.

Arduino UNO

The OLISMH system uses an Arduino UNO microcontroller board and an ATmega328P microprocessor. The Arduino board includes a 16 MHz ceramic resonator, six analog inputs, six digital I/O pins, a USB port, a power jack, an In-Circuit Serial Programming (ICSP) header, and a reset button. Figure 3 depicts the architecture of the Arduino UNO for the OLISMH system. The Arduino UNO board Additionally, it includes an AC-to-DC adapter or battery to power it and a USB cable to connect it to a computer. After connecting it to the appropriate sensors, it detects several essential parameters of the human body.

Oximeter and Heart Rate Monitoring Sensor

A sensor, referred to as MAX 30100, combines a heart rate monitor and a pulse oximeter in the OLISMH system as shown in Figure 4. It is an optical sensor that emits two wavelengths of light from two LEDs such as red and infrared lights. This specific LED color combination is ideal for using a fingertip to interpret data. The digital output of the device is entirely programmable using software registers and is also stored. Digital communication with a host microcontroller makes use of the I2C interface.

The pulse oximetry subsystem of MAX 30100 consists of an exclusive discrete temporal filter, a 16-bit sigma-delta ADC, and ambient light cancellation. It operates at a very low power, which makes it perfect for battery-operated devices. A power supply that ranges from 1.8 to 3.3 volts is required for MAX 30100. It is a fully

Figure 3. The Arduino UNO

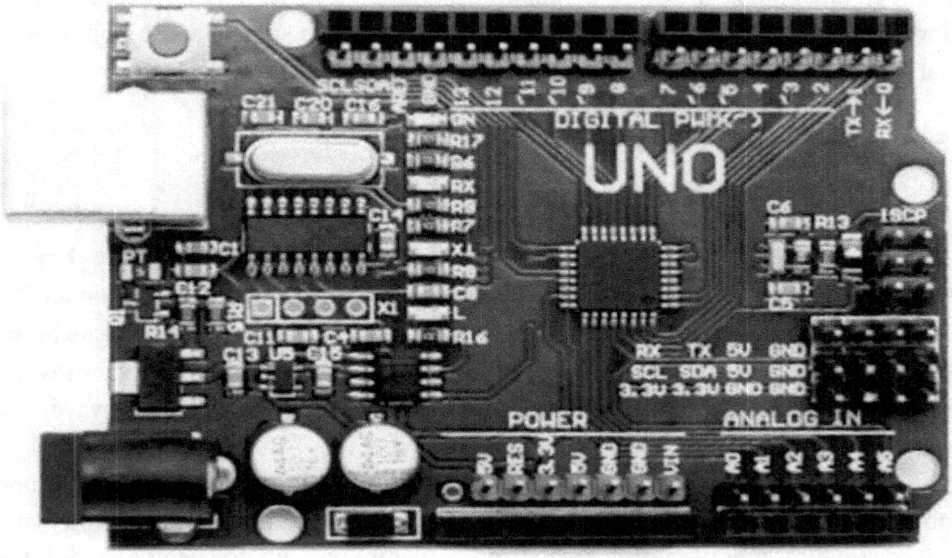

Figure 4. A MAX 3010 oximeter and heart rate monitor sensor

integrated heart rate sensor and pulse oximetry. It combines two LEDs of 660 nm and 940 nm, enhanced optics, a phototransistor that also serves as a detector, and a low-noise analog signal processor to monitor heart rate signals and blood oxygen saturation. The photodetector measures the absorbance of pulsing blood.

Blood Pressure Sensor

The blood pressure sensor module comprises a pulse sensor chip in the OLISMH system that senses and extracts pulse information from the human body through PPG and outputs serial signals such as blood pressure and heart rate via an analog front-end chip and an algorithm chip. Figure 5 depicts the chip diagram of the blood pressure sensor. The blood pressure sensor and monitoring module performs several functions like blood pressure measurement, pulse wave generation, and waveform output selection.

PPG features the cognition and tracking of the changing trend of users' blood pressure. Its important characteristics include high integration and stability and automatic wear identification. Furthermore, it employs a photodetector to track the changes in light intensity as the amount of blood varies. It computes the heart rate, SpO_2, and respiration rate where the respiration rate is four times of the heart rate.

Temperature Sensor

The OLISMH system includes a LM 35 temperature sensor which has a proportional output voltage to Celsius. It is shown in Figure 6. It is designed to function at temperatures ranging from -55°C to +150°C.

Figure 5. Blood pressure sensor chip

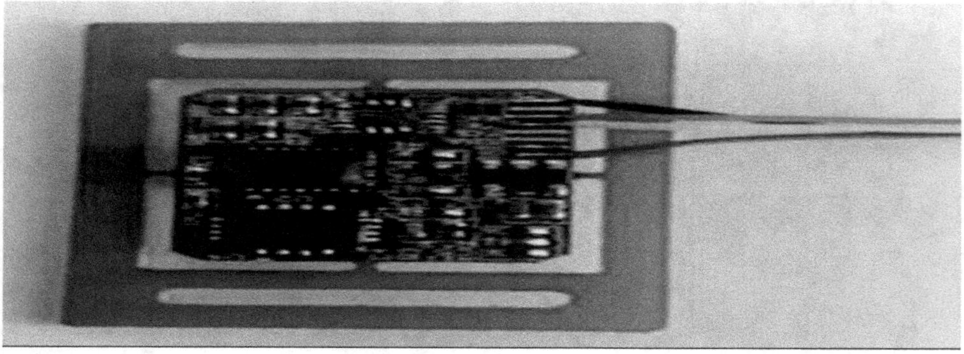

Figure 6. Temperature sensor

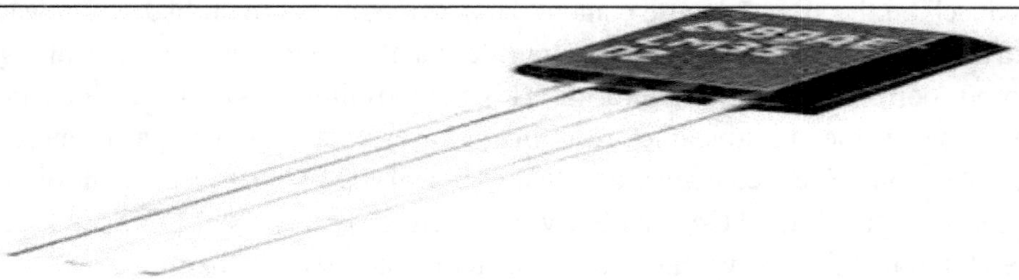

Blood's Glucose Monitoring Sensor

Blood pressure is an essential cardiopulmonary metric that measures the force of blood against the artery wall. It indicates the supply of oxygen to cells and provide indirect information on blood flow during heart contraction and relaxation. It is influenced by various factors, including cardiovascular output, peripheral vascular resistance, blood volume and viscosity, and artery wall flexibility. The OLISMH system includes a glucose monitoring sensor in blood as a component as illustrated in Figure 7. A glucose sensor includes a sweat inlet, sensors, and disposable strip. So, the blood pressure monitoring sensor is a useful tool for tracking high blood pressure, which is a significant contributor to detect the global cardiovascular disease. Such a method allows for multiple measurements throughout the day.

One of the most extensively studied types of sensors is the non-invasive moist-based glucose sensor. Sweat glands produce perspiration, which contains biological macromolecules, electrolytes, metabolites, and trace elements. As sweat carries blood-related indications, so it becomes non-invasive monitoring medium. A patch or band is worn all day, and a combination of various drug-delivery modules help achieve the goal of continuous blood glucose monitoring and intelligent closed-

Figure 7. Glucose monitoring sensor

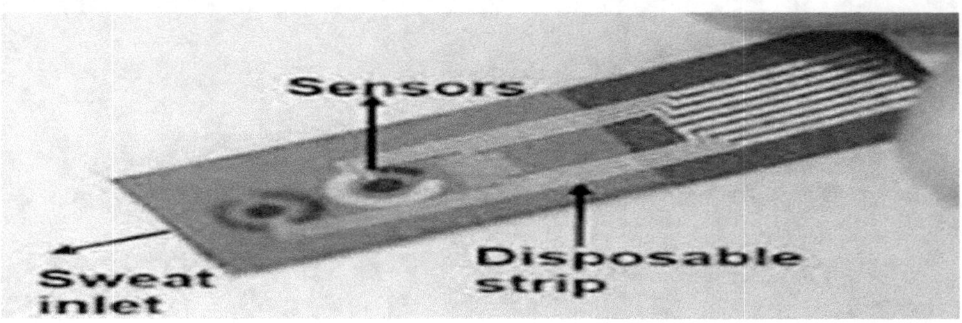

loop treatment. Furthermore, the multi-stage heating and narcotic system receive feedback on the sweat glucose content. Hypoglycemic antimicrobials are released in a timely and efficient manner via a transdermal therapeutic approach, resulting in closed-loop blood glucose monitoring. This method eliminates the pain of injections and bypasses the digestive tract, resulting in lower dosages and no gastrointestinal complications. The method works with the Hitachi HD44780 driver to control LCD panels using the Liquid Crystal library. There are several types of LCD panels, and the 16-pin interface is typically used to differentiate between them.

The 16 × 2 LCD

The OLISMH system applies a 16 × 2 LCD parallel interface along with the microcontroller to control several interface pins simultaneously for running the display. This LCD interface is shown in Figure 8. It consists of several pins, for example register is used to select a pin to determine where data is written in the LCD's memory. There are two types of registers, first is an instruction register that the LCD's controller uses to find additional instructions, and a data register that stores the information displayed on the screen.

The Read/Write pin on the LCD allows the device to distinguish between reading and writing modes. The enable pin helps to write to the registers and the data pins

Figure 8. A 16 × 2 LCD

consist of eight pins from D0 to D7. When one writes to a register, the high or low states of these pins represent the bits which are written, and when one reads from a register, they represent the values which are being read. Additionally, the LCD display can be powered, and the display contrast can be controlled. The LED backlight is turned on and off using the power supply pins (+5V and GND), LED backlight, and display contrast pin (Vo).

PROCEDURAL DETAILS OF THE OLISMH SYSTEM – MOBILE APPLICATION

The OLISMH mobile app is implemented using Java Script, react native, and Firebase backend server. React native is a framework used for developing mobile applications that can run on various platforms such as Android, iOS, macOS, Windows and the web. It combines the react framework with the features of native platform. The firebase backend server is used to store the data. Figure 9 depicts the basic workflow of the proposed OLISMH system-based mobile application. The OBLISMH system - mobile application has six interfaces such as login page, sign up page, services provided, medical historical data of patient, past data of symptoms, and doctor's appointments.

Figure 10 (a) depicts the login UI interface of the mobile application. In this interface, users who have already registered can log in with their credentials, while new users must first register themselves. Figure 10 (b) depicts the signup screen, where new users need to provide their usernames, email addresses, and passwords. After completing the signup procedure, the user's information is kept on the cloud platform Firebase, and the user sees a new interface with a login button. The user signs in to the smartphone application by tapping the login button.

Figure 9. Basic workflow of the proposed OLISMH system-base mobile application

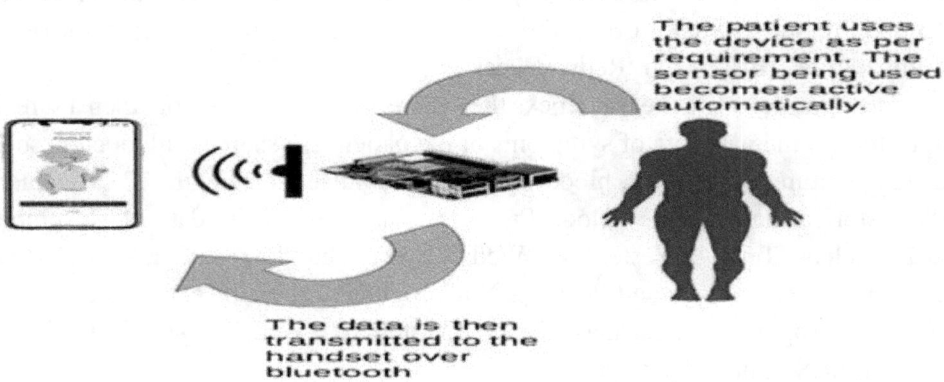

Figure 10. The OLISMH system interface (a) login page (b) sign up page

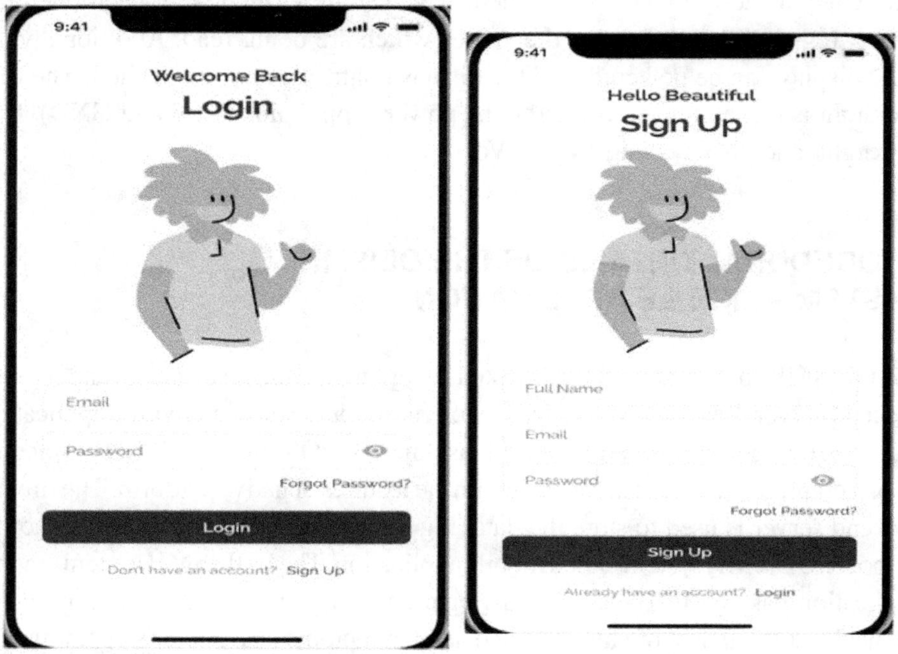

Furthermore, the user gets various service options through interface to measure the general parameters such as 'Your Diet Chart', 'Medical History', 'Lab Results', 'Doctor's Appointment', and 'Finding Yourself'. Figure 11 (a) shows the service options provided by the OLISMH system-mobile app to the user. The system also shows the oxygen saturation and pulse rate values to the user. When the user presses the measure button on the app, then the mobile app establishes a connection with the OLISMH system and shows all the patient's measurements, including temperature, blood sugar level, and pulse rate. Figure 11 (b) shows the medical history of the patient recorded by the OLISMH app. The medical history of the patient includes 'Blood Pressure', 'SpO_2 Level', 'Pulse Rate', 'COVID-19 Test', 'Diabetes', 'Body Temperature', 'ECG', and 'Retina Check'.

Furthermore, when the user clicks the 'Share with Doctor' button, then a screen appears and the past data of symptoms of the patient are shared with doctors such as temperature, sugar level, blood pressure, and pulse rate. Figure 12 (a) depicts the historical data for the 'Blood Pressure' which shows the data of November 2022 such as 'Today', 'Yesterday', 'Wed, 7 Nov', 'Thu, 8 Nov', 'Fri, 9 Nov', 'Sat, 10 Nov', 'Sun, 11 Nov', and 'Mon 12 Nov'. Figure 12 (b) depicts the dates for the 'Doctor's Appointment' such as 'Today', 'Yesterday', 'Wed, 7 Nov', 'Thu, 8 Nov', and 'Fri, 9 Nov' in the year 2022.

Figure 11. OLSIMH mobile app showing (a) service options, and (b) medical history of the patient

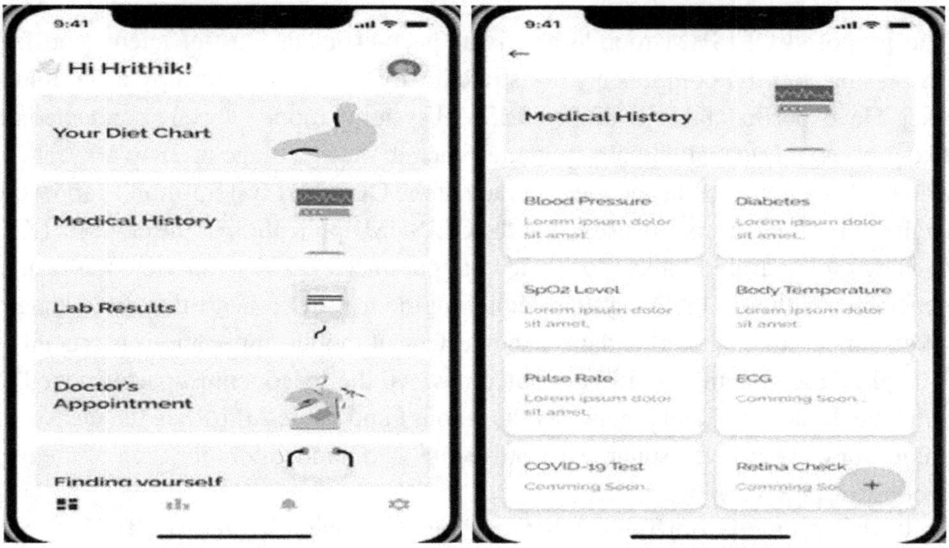

Figure 12. (a) Historical data of blood pressure (b) doctor's appointments

EXPERIMENTAL RESULTS WITH THE OLISMH SYSTEM: MOBILE APP

The proposed OLISHM mobile app is a space-efficient, cost-efficient, and fast processing app. Its components are strategically arranged to occupy a minimum area. The experimental tests of the OLISMH system - mobile app are conducted on two groups of five real humans (patients) each in the age range of 23 to 56 years in a controlled environment and the accuracy of the OLISMH system-mobile app were evaluated. All the users can use either the OLISHM application or the device's LCD to view the measured values for their vital parameters. They can view the results generated by the OLISHM system including the measured heart rate, blood sugar level, temperature, and other data. The interface of mobile applications is crucial as it displays the system's significant outcomes. All the sensors must perform well to generate the accurate and precise results. Table 1 and Table 2 illustrate the measured values for oxygen level, sugar level, pulse rate, and temperature for each of the two groups, respectively.

It was observed from Table 2 that most people's blood sugar levels fall between 140 and 150, close to the recommended levels. The measured pulse rates for both groups were found similar. Different individuals had their physiological data measured. All these measured values were found as accurate when compared to similar commercially available instruments.

Table 1. Group1 test results with the OLISMH system: Mobile application

Patient No.	Oxygen Level	Sugar Level (mg/dl)	Pulse Rate (bpm)	Temperature (C)
Patient 1	95%	140.2	75	37
Patient 2	96%	123.5	73	36
Patient 3	95%	150.6	70	40
Patient 4	94%	135.9	74	37
Patient 5	95%	140.7	75	40

Table 2. Group2 test results with the OLISMH system: Mobile application

Patient No.	Oxygen Level	Sugar Level (mg/dl)	Pulse Rate (bpm)	Temperature (C)
Patient 1	97%	124.7	73	40
Patient 2	95%	133.5	70	37
Patient 3	96%	140.6	75	35
Patient 4	95%	144.9	72	39
Patient 5	94%	146.7	74	36

CONCLUSION AND FUTURE RECOMMENDATIONS

Every day, thousands of people get diagnosed with diseases due to symptoms that either go undiagnosed or are diagnosed too late, leading to a global health disaster. Many efforts have been made to ensure optimal therapy, such as daily monitoring of vital parameters like temperature, blood pressure, sugar level, and pulse rate. The disease rate can be lowered by providing effective treatment when needed. To address these issues, this chapter proposed an IoT-based OLISHM system - mobile app which has several healthcare facilities and can easily be used in the households. It was designed space-efficient, cost-effective, non-invasive, and customizable, making it easy to assess one's health.

This app allowed the users and patients to efficiently monitor their physical and mental conditions from any geographical location and helped them to prevent their health from getting worse by identifying the problems before they became more serious. The pairing of this mobile app with the IoT device made it more comprehensive health monitoring system. It involved an extensive evaluation of all the gadgets and sensors used and their connections as well. It provided data visualization of the patient's health parameters, including historical data of patients with other infections, such as diabetes and chronic obstructive pulmonary disease.

Therefore, it was observed that the OLISHM presented a significant advancement in the education field with the combination of data-driven learning, self-monitoring healthcare systems, and IoT technology. By using sophisticated analytics and intelligent technologies, the educational institutions can create more tailored, interesting, and efficient learning opportunities that prioritize the health and welfare of their students. The proposed mobile app can further be extended by fusing the machine learning paradigm with such health care systems.

REFERENCES

Arulananth, T. S., & Shilpa, B. (2017). *Fingertip based heartbeat monitoring system using embedded systems.* Proc. International Conference of Electronics Communication and Aerospace Technology (ICECA).

Ball, J. W., Dains, J. E., Flynn, J. A., Solomon, B. S., & Stewart, R. W. (2023). Seidel's Guide to Physical Examination 10th ed. St Louis MO: Elsevier.

Components101. (n.d.-a). *16×2 LCD module.* https://components101.com/displays/16x2-lcd-pinout-datasheet

Components101. (n.d.-b). *DS18B20 temperature sensor.* https://components101.com/sensors/ds18b20-temperature-sensor?fbclid=IwAR1h7fnrZYY0OGivtUdqvf14qwTz0MUT4sO-U6pID7Qn4LeHKPQ7Y0OypH4

Components101. (n.d.-c). *NodeMCUESP 8266.* https://components101.com/development- boards/nodemcu-esp8266-pinout-features-and-datasheet

Dharmik, R., Gotarkar, S., Dinesh, P., & Sant Burde, H. (2021). An IoT Framework for Healthcare Monitoring System. *Journal of Physics: Conference Series, 1913*(1), 012145. doi:10.1088/1742-6596/1913/1/012145

El-Rashid, N., El-Sappagh, S., Islam, S. M. R., ElBakry, H. M., & Abdelrazek, S. (2020). End-to-end deep learning framework for coronavirus (COVID-19) detection and monitoring. Academic Press.

Evans, M. (2020). COVID-19: How to Treat Coronavirus at Home. *Patient UK.* https://patient.info/news-and-features/covid-19-how-to-treat-coronavirus-at-home

Gope, P., & Hwang, T. (2015). BSN-Care: A secure IoT-based modern healthcare system using body sensor network. *IEEE Sensors Journal*, *16*(5), 1368–1376. doi:10.1109/JSEN.2015.2502401

Harun, M. A. A., Hossain, M. M., & Bari, M. A. (2020). Bangladesh Journal of Otorhinolaryngology, vol. 26 no. 1 pp. 55–67 Pulse oximetry is essential in-home management of elderly. *COVID*, 19.

Hongru, D., & Goyea, T. (2020). *Novel coronavirus (COVID-19) cases Johns Hopkins University Baltimore Maryland.* JHU. https://coronavirus.jhu.edu/.

Hypoxemia, C. O. (2020). *Symptoms, Causes, Treatments.* Cleveland Clinic. https://my.clevelandclinic.org/health/diseases/17727-hypoxemia

Islam, M. M., Rahmanand, A., & Islam, M. R. (2020). Development of Smart Healthcare Monitoring System in IoT Environment. *SN Computer Science*, *1*(3), 185. doi:10.1007/s42979-020-00195-y PMID:33063046

Khan, M. M. (2020). *IoT based smart healthcare services for rural unprivileged people in Bangladesh: current situation and challenges.* International Electronic Conference on Applied Science MDPI, Switzerland.

Lee, H., Song, C., Hong, Y. S., Kim, M. S., Cho, H. R., Kang, T., Shin, K., Choi, S. H., Hyeon, T., & Kim, D. H. (2017). Wearable/disposable sweat-based glucose monitoring device with multistage transdermal drug delivery module. *Science Advances*, *3*(3), e1601314. doi:10.1126/sciadv.1601314 PMID:28345030

Pierleoni, P., Pernini, L., Belli, A., & Palma, L. (2014). An Android-Based Heart Monitoring System for the Elderly and for Patients with Heart Disease. *International Journal of Telemedicine and Applications, 2014*, 625156. doi:10.1155/2014/625156 PMID:25210513

Pourhomayoun, M., Alshurafa, N., & Dabiri, F. (2016). *Why do we need a remote human- health monitoring system A study on predictive analytics for heart failure.* 11th International Conference on Body Area Networks, Turin, Italy.

Prasath, A. A., Srinivasan, S., Ranganathan, C. S., Latha, N., & Saravanan, K. (2023, August). Cloud Server Based Intelligent Health Care Kit using Body Sensor Network. In *2023 Second International Conference on Smart Technologies For Smart Nation (SmartTechCon)* (pp. 323-327). IEEE. 10.1109/SmartTechCon57526.2023.10391445

Prasath, J.S. (2013). Wireless monitoring of heart rate using micro-controller. *International Journal of Advanced Research in Computer Science and Electronics Engineering, 2.*

Punhani, R., Arora, V. P. S., & Sai Sabitha, A. (2022). K-prototype algorithm for clustering large data sets with categorical values to established product segmentation. In Proceedings of Data Analytics and Management: ICDAM 2021, Volume 1 (pp. 343-353). Springer Singapore.

Puri, S., Dubey, M., & Dubey, S. M. (2023). Breast cancer prognosis and prediction through gene expression analysis and the hybrid model of SVM and logistic regression. *IEEE 2023 World conference on communication and computing (WCONF).* IEEE Press. 10.1109/WCONF58270.2023.10235198

Puri, S., & Singh, S. P. (2019). A hybrid Hindi printed document classification system using SVM and fuzzy: An Advancement. *Journal of Information Technology Research, 12*(4), 107–131. doi:10.4018/JITR.2019100106

Puri, S., & Singh, S. P. (2020). Advanced applications on bilingual document analysis and processing systems. *International Journal of Applied Metaheuristic Computing, 11*(4), 149–193. doi:10.4018/IJAMC.2020100108

Reza, T., Shoilee, S. B. A., Akhand, S. M., & Khan, M. M. (2017). *Development of android based pulse monitoring system.* Second International Conference on Electrical, Computer and Communication Technologies (ICECCT), Coimbatore, India,

Rizzo, A. (2020). *Silent hypoxia and its role in COVID-19 detection.* Chief Medical Officer American Lung Association.

Senith Electronics. (n.d.). *LM2596 DC-DC buck converter step-down power module.* Senith Electronics. http://www.senith.lk/shop/item/1081/lm2596-dc-dc-buck-converter-step-down-power-module

Serpanos, D., & Wolf, M. (2019). *Internet-of-Things (IoT).* Systems Architectures Algorithms Methodologies Springer International Publishing Switzerland.

Simel, D. L., Goldman, L., & Schafer, A.I. (2020). Goldman-Cecil Medicine (26th ed.). Philadelphia PA: Elsevier.

Singh, B., Lopez, D., & Ramadan, R. (2023). Internet of things in healthcare: A conventional literature review. *Health and Technology, 13*(5), 699–719. doi:10.1007/s12553-023-00771-1

Srinivasan, P., Ayub Khan, A., Prabu, T., Manoj, M., & Ranjan, M. (2020). Heartbeat sensor using fingertip through Arduino. *Journal of Critical Review, 7*(7).

Srividya, B. & Satyanarayana, V. (2018). Personal lung function monitoring system for asthma using Internet of things. *International Journal of Research in Electronics and Computer Engineering, 6.*

Sutradhar, I., Das, G. R., Hasan, M., Wazib, A., & Sarker, M. (2019). Prevalence and risk factors of chronic obstructive pulmonary disease in Bangladesh: a systematic review. *Cureus, 11.*

Tamilselvi, V. (2020). *IoT based health monitoring system.* 6th International Conference on Advanced Computing and Communication Systems (ICACCS), Coimbatore, India.

Thailand Medical News. (n.d.). *News.* Thai Medical News. https://www.thailandmedical.news

Wrist worn pulse oximeter. (n.d.). Concord Health Supply. https:// www.concordhealthsupply.com/Wrist-Oximeter-p/75006.html

Yatsenkov, V. (2018). *Pulse oximeterMAX30100/MAX30102-how to fix wrong board.* Reed Paper. https://reedpaper.wordpress.com/2018/08/22/pulse-oximeter-max30100- max30102-how-to-fix-wrong-board/

Chapter 5
Right to Online Education vis a vis Privacy:
A Global Transition of a Basic Human Right Since the COVID-19 Pandemic

Mili Gupta
Reva University, Bengaluru, India

Gagneet Singh
Independent Researcher, India

ABSTRACT

Online learning platforms have accelerated tremendous growth since the inception of the Covid pandemic. Learning platforms such as Khan academy and BYJU's had shown significant rise in the enrolment figures of candidates willing to pursue online education. The Covid-19 pandemic, at one time, depicted a picture that online education is the only future as schools and colleges were forced to shut down. However, accessing online education was not easy for every student due to several hindrances. The right to access online education can be hindered by data packs, electricity etc. The state has to look into the fact that economic, cultural, or social barriers are not restrictions for a child to access online education. Online education has been emphasized in different educational policies; several judicial pronouncements but lack effective mechanism to put it in the right place. The most ignorant part is the collection, storage, and dissemination of students' personal data, as the shift from physical to online mode of education involves data transfer of students either directly or indirectly.

DOI: 10.4018/979-8-3693-5370-7.ch005

INTRODUCTION

A student is subject to privacy risks while accessing the right to online education. Those privacy risks involve on-camera surveillance, eye-tracking software's, data profiling through the background images visible on video classes. In order to curb such issues, the data protection authorities all around the globe owe a duty to lay down certain guidelines to the educational institutions regarding the privacy safeguards while conducting online classes. One such example of it is Hungarian Data Protection Authority which during covid-19 pandemic came out with guidelines regarding privacy concerns in online classes. The authority emphasized on the principles of data minimisation and purpose limitation as envisaged under General Data Protection Regulation.

Data minimisation principle reads as *"adequate, relevant and limited to what is necessary in relation to the purposes for which they are processed"* and in view of this principle, the guidelines states that "*the camera should be set up so that it should show primarily the educator and the teaching instruments (blackboard, projector) used by him and students should be shown if possible only if it is closely related to the presentation of the activities in class and is necessary for the elaboration of the teaching materials (e.g. presentation of the results of solving a task in a small group for the other students)*". Purpose limitation principle reads as "*data collected for specified, explicit and legitimate purposes and not further processed in a manner that is incompatible with those purposes; further processing for archiving purposes in the public interest, scientific or historical research purposes or statistical purposes shall, in accordance with Article 89(1), not be considered to be incompatible with the initial purposes*" and in view of this principle, the guidelines state that "*the classes or lectures streamed should not be recorded or stored because they would not be stored within the framework of traditional education and such recording could be suitable for the abuse of students or educators (for instance, eventual risk of on-line harassment)*".

The government of India in National Education Policy, 2020 had focused on developing digital infrastructure for online learning. Setting up National Education Technology Forum (NETF) to ensure wider reach of online education has been highlighted in the policy (Web Desk, 2020). In reference to physical attendance of children to schools, the state government and local authority in model rules under right to children to free and compulsory education act, 2008 have been entrusted with an obligation that no student should be deprived of access to schooling due to social and cultural factors (Department of Higher Education). India is a signatory to The International Covenant on Economic, Social and Cultural Rights and Article 13 of the said international instrument emphasizes on the right to education. Article 2 of the covenant reads as "*Each State Party to the present Covenant undertakes to take steps, individually and through international assistance and co-operation, especially economic and technical, to the maximum of its available resources, with a view to achieving progressively the full realization of the rights recognized in the present Covenant*"[5]. The phrase "*especially economic and technical, to the maximum of its available resources*" needs to be given due consideration. It suggests that each member country undertakes for economic and technical utilization of resources in order to fully realize the rights.

In view of abovesaid concerns, India demands for separate legislation as similar to that of United States of America for protecting students' online data (Poggi, 2023) or the central government to formulate rules under Section 40 of the Digital Personal Data Protection Act, 2023. Emphasizing more on the data minimisation principle, The Digital Personal Data Protection Act, 2023 also applies to educational institutions. Educational Institutions are generally not aware of the compliances and have a duty to the data principals i.e., students. Educational institutes collecting personal data of the students need to obtain consent with a clear notice specifying the collection of data. Apart from this, recording and circulation of real-time classes without consent is also of utmost concern. The tutor taking the class holds a copyright over his or her recording and any individual involved in dissemination of such educational content should be held legally accountable under the copyright law and data protection law. The rationale behind the same involves some element of privacy. During covid-19 pandemic, a professor was in limelight when his wife kissed her in a moment of love during the class being conducted on zoom platform, (Bartool, 2021). The video was leaked by the participants of the zoom class which raised million views on social media platforms. Despite being an embarrassing moment for the tutor and entertaining content for the class participants, the class participants do not hold any right to disclose and circulate such content without the express authorization of tutor. Commercial benefit of class participant i.e., circulator via views on one hand and suffering from mental agony accompanied with loss of privacy for the tutor remains the outcome. In order to struck a balance between right to online education and privacy, certain guidelines need to be formulated pertaining to the collection of children's personal data.

EDUCATION AS A HUMAN RIGHT FROM PRE TO POST COVID 19 PANDEMIC

Education is a fundamental human right and is indispensable for exercising other human rights and finds its place in several international instruments concerning human rights, (UNESCO, 2020). Three concerns that revolve around right to online education is digital divide, access and privacy, (Kayar, 2022). The Supreme Court had taken cognizance of digital divide by stating that right to education in online mode (Roy, 2021) is also a right that exists and most importantly for the socially and economically underprivileged sections of the society. The court remarked that "*A need of online education for an underprivileged student cannot be denied*"[6]. Continued inequalities and injustice are a sociological concern with technology use in education, (Selwyn, 2014).

Educational Right and its Access in Online Mode

The Constitution of India expressly states that every citizen has a fundamental right to education.[7] The inequality in education was increased in digital divide after Covid 19 pandemic and prior to covid, the obstacles were unconstructed or unlevelled roads, improper transportation facilities etc. Availing a right by a citizen of being educated and in order to being educated, the accessibility of educational right with the limited accessible opportunities is indirectly violating the right to education. Post-covid, when all the educational institutions had shifted to online medium of instruction, the students especially those belonging to economically weaker sections and other poor students lacked sufficient funds to purchase internet data packs, electronic devices etc. In *Action Committee Unaided Recognized Private Schools v. Justice for All*, the Supreme Court[8] stated that *"Access to online education for EWS students cannot be denied and the state has to come forward and finance the resources for online education failing to which the students will take a drop-out from schools in the pandemic"* (Roy, 2021). This situation was after covid but prior to covid-19 pandemic, whether the government was responsible to finance the students in accessing their right to education. Several governments had taken the initiative of supplying basic resources required for accessing the right to education. Akhilesh Yadav distributed laptops to students on his 49th birthday for all the girls who had secured top positions in the class, (Srivastava, 2022). Not only laptops but cycles and other necessary items have been distributed by several state governments to promote girls' education in rural areas.

CHALLENGES IN EXERCISING THE RIGHT TO ONLINE EDUCATION

Inaccessible transportation to school, as well as inaccessible facilities in schools such as drinking water units, mid-day meal areas, and toilets, inappropriate classroom furniture, slippery flooring, and inadequate illumination and ventilation can pose barriers to the education of children with disabilities and the same to a greater extent has led to rise in online education, (UNICEF). Even, if the right to online education is exercisable, the parents and children's are not aware how the information is used as extensive data is open for public view, (Grayson, 1978).

Non-Access to Smartphones

Due to the government initiatives like Mid-day meals and Beti Bachao Beti Padhao; the school was able to record more than 90% attendance of the students but distance learning is a very new concept for everyone which many are not able to understand due to the financial strain upon them, (Shams). In 2020, around 74 percent students in India from private schools had access to smartphone at home for at-home learning while only around 50 percent students from government schools had access to smartphone at home, (Rathore, 2023).

Privacy Risk

the migration to a new learning space has faced several major concerns relating to policy, pedagogy, logistics, socioeconomic factors, technology, and psychosocial factors. In education a person's privacy can be invaded in several ways.

Figure 1. Share of students who have access to smartphone at home in government and private schools in India in 2018 and 2020

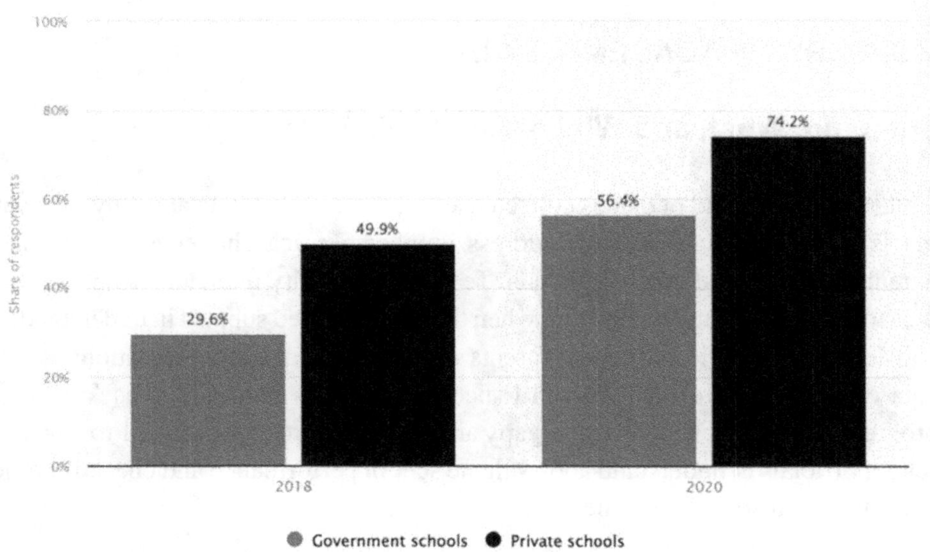

Physical Surveillance of Students

The behaviour of students can be easily put on surveillance through technology. The behaviour can be surveillanced by teachers from schools, online coaching tutors, children counsellors who directly keep a record of student's behaviour.[9]

Sensitive Academic Records of Students

All educational institutions do retain certain data of students including the parent's data. The records include medical data, knowledge evaluation data reports, family background data etc. Further, a student file can also include student opinion, truths and other information.

Need for Centralized Data Repository

Standardization and centralizing educational data shall aid the educational institutions in mitigating privacy risks of student's data. A centralized data repository within the institution shall ensure to link data from the sources and build a link to determine privacy violation. A strong internal data policy for better functioning of centralized data repository is also a necessity, (Best, 2018). Data standardization is the necessity today and the School Interoperability Frame work, developed by the nonprofit education data standards cooperative Access 4 Learning Community, offers an open specification for academic institutions, as well as a system for sharing data between institutions.[10]

HOLDERS OF ACADEMIC DATA

The Who, What, and Why of Academic Data

Under this, what kind of data is collected and who needs the data and why. The data that is collected by schools is age, address, number, physical challenge etc. Teachers, parents, students and school officials. Teachers or faculty members need student's data to analyze and understand that when the students need support in understanding and learning specific concepts, parents or guardians demand educational status data of their child to help the ward succeed. Students require feedback on their progress to take decisions on the gaps and help them to prepare well to succeed, school officials to understand and evaluate school performance and check if proper allocation of resources is done.

Data Access to Faculty Staff

Accessibility of data by faculty members or teachers in educational institutions is a grey area which requires the attention of policy makers and researchers. Accessibility clause in teaching employability contract can be a benefit and can serve several benefits and drafters of employability contract in educational institutions should be well versed with what kind of data is required and only accessibility of that data be given to the newly recruited faculty member out of contractual obligation, (Singh, 2022). In Case, a student data is required; the same can be obtained from the centralized data repository.

NEP: ENABLING ONLINE EDUCATION

National Education Policy: Enabling Online Education

Digital learning has been proposed as an alternative to conventional classroom learning in National Education Policy, 2020. However, implementing digital learning in rural areas would still be a concern, (Sardana, 2021). When compared the urban and rural population of India, it is enviable that rural population is twice that of urban population. A commission named "National Commission on Population" constituted under the Ministry of Health and Family Welfare had provided population projections for the period ranging from 2011 to 2036. According to the population projections, the urban population is predicted to increase rapidly with decrease in rural population, (Agarwal, 2020). Access to internet is exacerbated because of electricity cuts, low household incomes and shortage of signal frequency of towers. *In Faheema Shirin RK v. State of Kerala & Ors*[11], the Supreme Court declared that right to have an access to internet is integral to right to education under article 21, (Satheesh, 2020). Access to internet will enable access to online education.

PRIVACY CONCERNS IN ONLINE EDUCATION

Student's Stored Personal Data With Educational Institutions

From inception of admission to The graduation of a candidate, the educational institutions store the student's personal data. Such data can range from financial, personal to health. In a nutshell, it is necessary to determine whether educational institutions are bound to comply with data protection laws or not. Secondly, whether educational institutions be considered to be a data fiduciary. Upon the enactment of Digital Personal Data Protection Act, 2023; the educational institutions as a data fiduciary have to comply with the enacted data law. Considering educational institutions as data fiduciary, categories of data that they hold are name, age, address, medical history records, birth certificate, educational history records, account details etc, (Sahni, 2020). Not only the personal data of students but also the personal data of faculty members. The five parameters of privacy norms according to Nissenbaum are sender, recipient, information type, subject and transmission principle.

Indian Educational Institutions and Data Protection Law

The educational institutions have been reluctant to follow data protection laws. The educational institutions do collect certain data's which are not relevant and do not carry a legitimate purpose of its collection. It is important to figure out the personal data that an educational institution requires

Demographic Information: Age, gender, disability status, language, socio-economic status

Academic Information: Grades, Attendance Rates, Graduation Rates, teacher observation and evaluation data

Behavioural Information: Suspensions, counselling, peer surveys, parents surveys, discipline records.

On the basis of certain parameters such as demographic information, academic information and behavioural information, educational institutions should work on minimizing the collection of data. They should pre-determine a list of data that they require and accordingly demand the same from students. A student should not be denied admission on the basis of refusal to give any data. Education as a necessity and submission of data contingent upon accessing education.

Collection of Personal Data

Relying on the principle of data minimization mentioned under Article 5 of General Data Protection Regulation also known as data avoidance, the educational institutions should figure out the data that it requires from the students. The regulatory bodies such as University Grants Commission should suo-moto take cognizance of it and direct all universities to follow the data collection guidelines issued by it. Accreditation agencies and affiliation granting bodies can also issue guidelines for colleges in collecting student's data. Each and every kind of data collected by educational institutions is not required for its processing. Name, age, previous educational details and address of the student at the outset appears relevant for an educational institution. Further, if the educational institutions go on collecting any such other information, then such data collection goes against the tenent of Data avoidance. It shall also be difficult to determine which kind of data is justified and lawful for an educational institution to process.

- Is it necessary for an educational institution to collect Student's age? Yes, verification of age as a necessity
- Is it necessary for an educational institution to know the gender of student?
- Is it necessary for an educational institution to know the socio-economic status of student?
- Is it necessary for an educational institution
- Personal data of students collected by educational institutions can be used for very minimal purposes such as examination and other academic tasks. Educational institutions have been mandated by several accreditation agencies which require students details as per their pre-structured proforma and if the universities do not follow the same, it leads to reduction of ranking of university by such accreditation bodies.

Data Storage

Educational institutions after Covid-19 pandemic started storing personal data of students and considering it as one of the reasons; the educational institutions have been brought under the ambit of the Digital Personal Data Protection Act, 2023. With digital learning and Universities providing online degree programs, it becomes important for universities to adopt data protection mechanisms. Storage limitation as one of GDPR principle appears to be ignored by educational institutions. A candidate enrolled with an educational institution has to submit his credentials which are preserved by institutions for the whole lifetime.

Check on Data Protection Principles

The recently passed Digital Personal Data Protection Act, 2023 is in consonance with the European Union's General Data Protection Regulation. The definition of personal data is also in parlance with the GDPR data protection law. The law imposes an obligation on all data fiduciaries including educational institutions to comply with the law. With the emergence of Covid 19 pandemic, both private and public educational institutes started taking a lead in remote learning which results in collection of personal data, (Murthy, 2023).

PROPOSED DATA PROTECTION MODEL FOR EDUCATIONAL INSTITUTIONS

Educational Institutions have to take an initiative of drafting a data protection policy which should include data protection committee and data protection officers. For each faculty or department, one individual can be appointed as data protection officer. The data shall originate from data protection officer and be returned to the same originating destination.

Proposed Personal Data Holder

The authors tend to propose that every educational institution should have a mandatory designation of Data Manager who shall be vested with the responsibility to take care of employee data including the data of individuals who are directly or indirectly associated with the company. Every faculty member joining an educational institution would ipso facto have an access to the student's personal data. Giving access of data to a faculty member as a part of employment would not help in protecting student's data but a way can be figured out of it by giving data access to one person who shall enter into the register, the name of faculty requesting for data against the purpose of data collection. This will ensure accountability of faculty member towards the educational institution for the data that they possess.

CSR TOWARDS SUPPLY OF ONLINE EDUCATIONAL NECESSITIES

In times of Covid-19, CSR expenditure towards education saw a downfall as health was the focal point which can be well-substantiated by the huge number of deaths which required the companies to spend on CSR. CSR expenditure on education reduced from Rs5,718 crore in FY19 to Rs5,244 in FY20, (Shekhar, 2021). Schedule 7 of the Companies Act, 2013 lists the activities on which CSR funds can be utilised by the companies. Digital divide is one of the niche areas where companies can look for investing their CSR amount. Ministry of Corporate Affairs should identify the areas where CSR can be spent. Corporate entities can help the students in achieving the right to education by providing the required resources such as internet data packs, laptop or cell phone etc. CSR expenditure on education has been from a long period of time such as ITC out of each and every notebook is contributing Rupees 1 towards education of poor people. After Covid 19, the shift from physical to online education demands for investing in online education. If the same happens, then companies can aid in the elimination of digital divide.

Aahwahan Foundation Model: A Basis for Corporate Entities in Ensuring Online Education Right

The interesting part of divergence is that Aahwahan foundation initiative has started distributing laptops for the underprivileged students. The aim of this initiative is fulfilling the lack of access to online devices (A. P., 2021). The initiative started distributing laptops which are pre-enabled with access to internet as well. The founder of this Bengaluru based NGO also stated that "Every citizen must come forward and contribute to these students for a viable future of the country and social positive change. I urge the contribution of community groups and corporations through their CSR programmes to enable education for the marginalised groups of the society," (A. P., 2021).

The organisation is aimed at providing scientific and technological education to students from sixth standard to high school. Courses such as personality development, digital marketing and soft skill development are offered. Not only this, courses for competitive exams like JEE and UPSC are also offered. Aahwahan team comprises of six volunteers, six permanent teachers, four volunteers, and part time faculties ranging between seven to eight. Teaching faculties registered with Aahwahan are the ones who have completed their doctorate degrees or master's degree. Some of those faculties have been associated with some institutes for teaching robotics. "We have video conferencing in our buses, which enables our students to get first-hand

Figure 2. Education on wheels bus
(Aahwahan Foundation)

experience of what is being taught in good institutes and universities we have tied up with them," Pradhan adds. The content is either prepared by the teachers or is outsourced from Vedantu, BYJU'S, and WhiteHat Jr. The teachers are present in the bus to supervise and help the students with their problems. The team visits the villages first and registers the students. They are provided with headphones and a computer system to log into their respective online lectures. "We map out village clusters and spend three hours in each village for three days. We usually start by 7:30 am and mostly get over for the day at 8 pm. These buses also visit schools and provide hands-on practical experience to the students," Pradhan explains. Before launching the programme, the NGO conducted extensive research and found that most government schools in India needed more proper infrastructure and qualified teaching faculty, which were significant obstacles for students in their learning journey. The study conducted by the NGO identified various areas that needed to be addressed, including digital, technical, science, and robotics education alongside the issue of girls dropping out of school after 10th grade due to family pressure or financial constraints. "In large schools with a strength of 500+ students, it is possible to build these facilities, but in smaller schools, it is not possible. So we came up with the idea of taking education to their doorstep," Pradhan says.

NGO AND CORPORATE COLLABORATION IN UPHOLDING ONLINE EDUCATION ACCESSIBILITY

INFINERA CSR India supports Aahwahan Foundation\'s HEALTH ON WHEELS, (A. P., 2021). Corporate entities can save expenditure incurred on financial experts who guide them on where and how to spend the CSR Amount. NGO's are organizations working for the betterment of society and corporate entities on the other hand have been casted a mandatory obligation to incur expenditure for betterment of society. NGO's seek donations from the general public for the public good and it would easy if a policy exists where the corporate entities be allowed to give their 2 percent CSR expenditure directly to NGO's who would then use the same with the maximum outreach of the required assistance. For this, schedule 7 should be amended in such a way that a mechanism be brought for transfer of funds from corporate entity to NGO. One of the drawbacks is the accountability of CSR expenditure as CSR return is filed with Ministry of Corporate Affairs. If funds in form of CSR are transferred from Company to NGO, then who shall be liable to generate a expenditure report or whether the company shall be the authority to decide where the CSR funds be utilized. Contrary to this, the main aim of NGO-Company collaboration is NGOs having a better understanding of where the funds have to be invested rather than the company and if company decides everything, then it shall be a setback.

Role of NGO's

NGO's do act as a mediator between the government and the citizens, when the government fails to fulfil the needs of society, then NGOs come forward in two ways. One is by initiating public interest litigations and second is taking up suo-moto action on the social causes and working on the same. Non-governmental organizations such as teach for India, Pratham Education Foundation, Bachpan Bachao Andolan are involved in working towards education but these NGO's are promoting education in terms of organizing classes in rural areas, volunteers for personal teaching etc. The main issue is the transformative role of education which has entered into digital world which demands for resources required to access online education. Whether NGO's can distribute laptops or mobilephones to underprivileged students, whether NGO's can seek donations from corporate entities.

ACCESS TO DIGITAL RESOURCES IN OTHER JURISDICTIONS

Covid-19 pandemic proved us that resources are needed to ensure equitability in right to education. Computers and internet were just tools required for processing, research etc but became an essential tool with the inception of Covid 19 pandemic.

United States of America

The Department of Education, USA has decided to provide 1 lakh devices for remote learning, (McDonald, 2020). According to American Community Survey, the access of internet was found high where the parents had attained a bachelor or higher degree and the access of internet was found low where the parents had less than high school degree. The access of internet is reliant on the educational status of parents, (NCES Blog Editor, 2021) On a similar ground, if the family income is high, then the access to internet remains high. But was completely different in 2019, higher the level of parental education lower the percentage use of smartphone use for internet access. Higher level of family income lower the percentage use of smartphone for internet access. Remaining remote without significant improvements to the education offered this spring could lead to a dramatic decline in student retention and completion, especially among the most disadvantaged students, (Kelly & Columbus, 2020)

United Kingdom

To support the distance learning and ensuring the wide reach of education, the government of United Kingdom in April 2022 had dispatched 1.95 million tablet devices and laptops to local authorities and all educational institutions for supporting the remote learning in the covid-19 pandemic. This scheme initially started to provide laptops and tablets to schools in May 2020 during the Summer term of the 2019/20 academic year and was expanded significantly at the start of 2021, increasing from 562 thousand in December 2020 to more than one million two months later in February 2021.

New Zealand

Eduroam is a network preferred by students as they can use it by approving the device/ login for free. The Aotearoa People's Network Kaharoa (APNK) and Research and Education Advanced Network New Zealand (REANNZ) is working with eduroam for extending the internet network for the benefit of high school students

While the network is currently only available for people in the tertiary/academic sector, eduroam is looking to open up access to students to increase the areas that students can safely access their schoolwork. Schools can enable school devices to connect to the eduroam network using their single sign-in (SSI) so that students can easily get online wherever the network is available.

Figure 3. Cumulative number of laptop or tablet devices delivered from December 2020 to April 2022
(Clark, 2023)

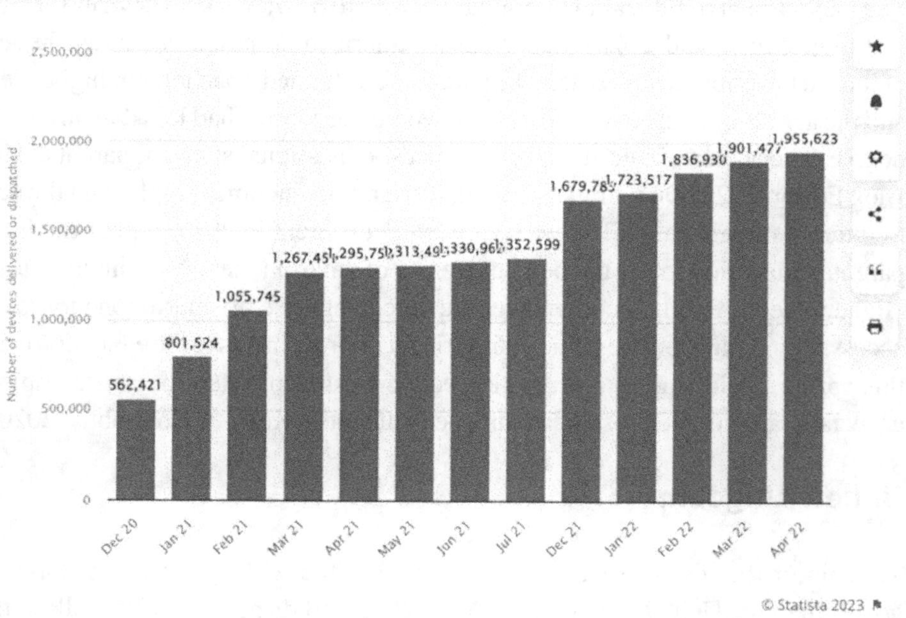

TRANSITION OF EDUCATION BEFORE AND AFTER COVID 19 PANDEMIC

Before Covid-19 Pandemic

- Laptops, mobilephones and tablets were not considered as a necessity for pursuing education. large proportions of the world's population, primarily in developing countries, lack access to a simple mobile phone, let alone much more sophisticated technologies, (Shrier, 2021).
- Having access to internet was immaterial

After Covid-19 Pandemic

Cyber Crime Against Children: NCRB Data

The NCRB data makes it clear that the cyber-crime cases against children have started increasing after Covid 19, (P., 2021). Students should have access to internet but it should also be ensured that internet is safe, open and trusted by all. National Crime Records Bureau in its report titled "Crime in India" published statistical data on crime. Around 1102 cyber-crime cases against children were registered in 2020 as compared to 305 in 2019. Covid 19 which took its pace in the initial months of 2020 forced schools and colleges to shut down.

That is why the government is committed to policies and actions that ensure that Internet in India is always Open, Safe, Trusted and Accountable for all Indians. The National Crime Records Bureau (NCRB) compiles and publishes statistical data on crimes in its publication "Crime in India". The latest published report is for the year 2020. As per data published by NCRB, a total of 305 and 1102 cases of cyber-crime against children were registered during the year 2019 and 2020 respectively.

Social and Economic Division

According to think impact, 33 percent students in poor third world countries don't have access to tools required for digital learning and it becomes difficult for them to cope up with online education growing trends, (Vlasova, 2022). According to a survey, 86% of graduates say the value gained from their online degree exceeds or equals the cost paid for it.[12]

Overall Development of E-Learning Market

By 2026, the global e-learning market is forecast to reach almost 400 billion U.S. dollars. In 2019, the global e-learning market was sized at almost 200 billion U.S. dollars. In the same year, the learning management system (LMS) market generated roughly 18 billion U.S. dollars, (Statista Research Department, 2022).

Additionally, learning management systems (LMS) played a crucial role in managing and delivering educational content. Schools and universities adopted popular LMS platforms like Moodle and Canvas, enabling them to organise coursework, share materials, and track student performance. These platforms provided a centralised space for students to access resources, submit assignments, and engage in discussions, (Sakthi, 2023).

Increase in access to data collecting websites

With more reliance on online education, the students have gained more access to online websites and databases. The more reliance and use of a free service providing website will have an adverse impact. UGC has approved 38 universities to offer full-fledged online degree courses in India. These universities, which include 15 deemed-to-be universities, 13 state universities, three central universities, and three private universities, do not need to get prior approval from University Grants Commission from the same. Jamia Millia Islamia (JMI) will be offering MA (Education) and MA

Figure 4. Size of the global e-learning market in 2019 and 2026, by segment

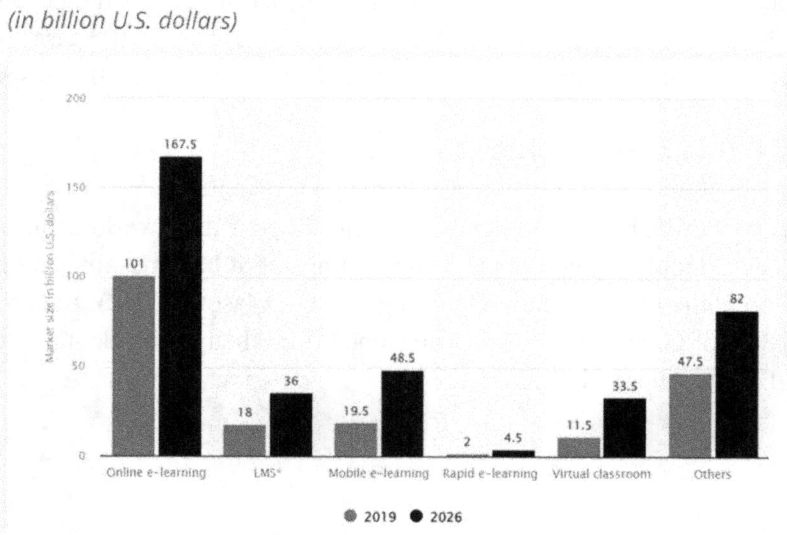

(Public Administration), JNU will offer MA (Sanskrit), while Mizoram University will offer four online degree programmes. Jammu University will offer MA (English) and MCom in online mode (Web Desk, 2021).

CONCLUSION AND SUGGESTIONS

With the drastic shift of education pattern from physical to online, there have been several challenges that are associated with online education. The crucial part of online education is lack of academic policies concerning privacy, no data protection standards of academic data, institutional delays in adopting safeguards or measures for issues in online learning. The shift from physical learning to digital learning has improved access to education with a limitation of digital divide. The judiciary in its several pronouncements has delivered that accessibility of internet is also a fundamental right and if internet access right is violated, it will impact the right to education as well. The educational institutions being a data fiduciary owe a responsibility towards data subject i.e., the students in ensuring appropriate storage mechanism, the check on accessibility of data. The right to education has been a human right and conversion of this right from physical to online shall not preclude the claimors of this right.

REFERENCES

UNESCO. (2020, November 26). *What you need to know about the right to education*. UNESCO. https://www.unesco.org/en/articles/what-you-need-know-about-right-education

A. P. (2021, November 25). *How Aahwahan Foundation's 'Laptop Bank' Is Fulfilling The Online Education Needs Of Underprivileged Students*. SOCIALSTORY. https://yourstory.com/socialstory/2021/11/aahwahan-foundations-laptop-bank-underprivileged-students

A. P. (2021, November 25). *How Aahwahan Foundation's 'Laptop Bank' is Fulfilling the Online Education Needs of Underprivileged Students*. Socialstory. Your Story. https://yourstory.com/socialstory/2021/11/aahwahan-foundations-laptop-bank-underprivileged-students

A. P. (2021, August 4). *INFINERA CSR India supports Aahwahan Foundation\'s HEALTH ON WHEELS*. CSRBOX. https://csrbox.org/India_CSR_news_HEALTH-ON-WHEELS-%E2%80%93-INFINERA-CSR-India-supports-Aahwahan-Foundation-for-the-enhancement-of--healthcare-system-in-Karnataka_1388

Agarwal, K. (2020, August 13). India's Population Will Be 1.52 Billion by 2036, With 70% of Increase in Urban Areas. *The WIRE*. https://thewire.in/government/india-population-growth-government-report-2036-projections-urban-migration

Batool, Z. (2021, February 12). *Oops! Romance Gone Wrong – Professor Shoos Wife Away Kissing Him During Zoom Class*. PARHLO. https://www.parhlo.com/professor-shoos-wife-away-kissing-during-zoom-class/

Best, K. L., & Pane, J. F. (2018). *Privacy and Interoperability Challenges Could Limit the Benefits of Education Technology*. RAND Corporation. https://www.jstor.org/stable/resrep19899

Blog, N. C. E. S. (Ed.). (2021, September 20). Students' Internet Access Before and During the Coronavirus Pandemic by Household Socioeconomic Status. *NCES Blog*. https://nces.ed.gov/blogs/nces/post/students-internet-access-before-and-during-the-coronavirus-pandemic-by-household-socioeconomic-status

Clark, D. (2023, October 11). *Cumulative number of laptop or tablet devices dispatched or delivered by the UK government to education providers in England from December 2020 to April 2022*. Statista. https://www.statista.com/statistics/1263494/educational-digital-devices-delivered-by-uk-government/#:~:text=As%20of%20April%202022%2C%20the%20government%20of%20the,to%20support%20remote%20learning%20during%20the%20coronavirus%20pandemic

Faheema Shirin RK v. State of Kerala & Ors, *WP. No.19716 OF 2019*

Grayson, P. L. (1978). Education, Technology, and Individual Privacy. *Educational Communication and Technology, 26*(3), 197. https://doi.org/http://www.jstor.org/stable/30220912

Shekhar. D. (2021, May 6). Inside the reshaping of CSR in India during Covid-19. *India Forbes*. https://www.forbesindia.com/article/take-one-big-story-of-the-day/inside-the-reshaping-of-csr-in-india-during-covid19/67821/1

McDonald, C. (2020, October 6). *Government to provide 100,000 devices for remote learning*. ComputerWeekly.com. https://www.computerweekly.com/news/252490162/Government-offers-100000-devices-for-remote-learning

Murthy, S. Y. P. (2023, September 22). *How Data Protection Law affects education sector*. TechCircle. https://www.techcircle.in/2023/09/22/how-data-protection-law-affects-education-sector

Nayar, K. P. (2022, April 24). What Happens to the Right to Education, Online? *The WIRE*. https://thewire.in/education/what-happens-to-the-right-to-education-online

P. (2021, November 14). Over 400% rise in cyber-crime cases committed against children in 2020: NCRB data. *The Economic Times*. https://economictimes.indiatimes.com/news/india/over-400-rise-in-cyber-crime-cases-committed-against-children-in-2020-ncrb-data/articleshow/87696995.cms

POGGI. N. (2023, September 28). *Three crucial online student privacy laws*. Prey Project. https://www.indiatoday.in/education-today/featurephilia/story/will-nep-give-a-much-needed-boost-to-online-education-in-india-1713926-2020-08-22

Rathore, M. (2023, July 10). *Share of students who have access to smartphone at home in government and private schools in India in 2018 and 2020*. Statista. https://www.statista.com/statistics/1276401/india-share-of-students-who-have-access-to-smartphone-at-home/

Roy, D. (2021, October 8). *Access to online education for EWS students cannot be denied: Supreme Court issues notice on plea*. Bar and Bench. https://www.barandbench.com/news/litigation/access-to-online-education-for-ews-students-cannot-be-denied-supreme-court-issues-notice-in-plea

Roy, D. (2021, October 8). *Access to online education for EWS students cannot be denied: Supreme Court issues notice on plea*. Bar and Bench. https://www.barandbench.com/news/litigation/access-to-online-education-for-ews-students-cannot-be-denied-supreme-court-issues-notice-in-plea

Sahni, S. (2020, September 18). Personal Data Protection Bill (PDPB) and Educational Institutions. *The Cyber Blog India*. https://cyberblogindia.in/personal-data-protection-bill-pdpb-and-educational-institutions/

Sardana, S. (2021, July 14). Bringing down the barriers. *The Hindu*. https://www.thehindu.com/education/what-are-the-challenges-of-education-in-rural-india-and-how-technology-can-help-overcome-them/article35316970.ece

Satheesh, A. (2020, November 1). *Right to internet fundamental for right to education: faheema shirin r.k. V. State of kerala & ors*. Lawsisto. https://lawsisto.com/legalnewsread/ODU5OA==/Right-to-internet-fundamental-for-right-to-education-Faheema-Shirin-RK-v-State-of-Kerala-Ors

Selwyn, F. N. K. (2014). The sociology of education and digital technology: Past, present and future. *Oxford Review of Education*, *40*(4), 489. https://doi.org/http://www.jstor.org/stable/24736320

Shams, S. (n.d.). *E-Learning And The Fate Of Right To Education In India*. Lexlife India. https://lexlife.in/2021/07/02/e-learning-and-the-fate-of-right-to-education-in-india/

Shrier, D. L. (2021). From Shock to Awe: How the Pandemic Crisis has Opened Up the Dialogue for A True Reinvention of Education. *Horizons: Journal of International Relations and Sustainable Development, 19*, 72. https://www.jstor.org/stable/48617354

Singh, G. M. (2022, December 22). Accessibility to personal data by employees of data fiduciary, and the Digital Personal Data Protection Bill. *The Leaflet*. https://theleaflet.in/accessibility-to-personal-data-by-employees-of-data-fiduciary-and-the-digital-personal-data-protection-bill/

Srivastava, A. (2022, July 1). Akhilesh Yadav distributes laptops to students on his 49th birthday. *India Today*. https://www.indiatoday.in/education-today/news/story/akhilesh-yadav-distributes-laptops-to-students-on-his-49th-birthday-1969017-2022-07-01

Statista Research Department. (2022, July 6). *Size of the global e-learning market in 2019 and 2026, by segment*. Statista. https://www.statista.com/statistics/1130331/e-learning-market-size-segment-worldwide/

Web Desk, I. T. (2020, August 22). Will NEP give a much-needed boost to online education in India? *India Today*. https://www.indiatoday.in/education-today/featurephilia/story/will-nep-give-a-much-needed-boost-to-online-education-in-india-1713926-2020-08-22

Web Desk, I. T. (2021, June 19). 38 universities can offer online degree courses now, says UGC: Check full list with programmes here. *India Today*. https://www.indiatoday.in/education-today/news/story/38-universities-can-offer-online-degree-courses-now-says-ugc-1816919-2021-06-19

ENDNOTES

1. Article 5 1 (c), General Data Protection Regulation
2. Hungarian Data Protection Authority, Information on the data protection and data security aspects of digital distance learning, *Case number NAIH/2020/7127/*

3 Article 5 1 (b), General Data Protection Regulation

4 Supra note 4.

5 Article 2, International Covenant on Economic, Social and Cultural Rights

6 *Ibid.*

7 The Constitution of India, 1950, article 21 A.

8 https://indiankanoon.org/doc/76866560/

9 Supra note 22.

10 *Ibid.*

11 Faheema Shirin RK v. State of Kerala & Ors, *WP. No.19716 OF 2019*

12 *Ibid*

Chapter 6
Perceptions of Remote Teaching by Diverse Student Cohorts in the Kingdom of Bahrain:
Emergency Remote Teaching

Fatema Wali
https://orcid.org/0000-0003-4600-8238
Bahrain Polytechnic, Bahrain

George Toworfe
Regent University College of Science and Technology, Accra, Ghana

Henk Huijser
https://orcid.org/0000-0001-9699-4940
Queensland University of Technology, Australia

ABSTRACT

Like many sectors affected by the Coronavirus (Covid - 19) pandemic, the higher education sector was disrupted globally and needed immediate re-adjustments to provide distance learning solutions. Educational management contingency plans were initiated in many parts of the world to reach out to students isolated due to the pandemic; however, it quickly became clear that one size (or plan) did not fit all, especially with regards to students with online learning constraints. This qualitative research explores the online learning experiences of students during the pandemic in the Kingdom of Bahrain. The study employed an online survey to investigate Bahraini students' perceptions of online learning as a new initiative during the pandemic. The findings of this survey suggest that the digital divide, digital inequities, and differences in e-learning opportunities have been experienced by students through the implementation of online learning. The study also revealed different perceptions of the educational technologies available to students.
DOI: 10.4018/979-8-3693-5370-7.ch006

INTRODUCTION

The academic disruption caused by Covid-19 has influenced both students and academics worldwide (Marinoni at al., 2020), including in the Middle East (Al-Mahadin, 2020; Mohammed & Mudhsh., 2021). Schools and universities experienced an unprecedented shift from traditional face-to-face teaching and learning to distance online learning in response to closures and lockdowns. Authorities in educational institutions initiated e-learning strategies through virtual online learning environments. This has been termed 'emergency remote teaching' (Hodges et al., 2020), and has been defined as "a temporary shift of instructional delivery to an alternate remote delivery mode due to crisis circumstances" (Iglesias-Pradas et al., 2021). In their study of K-12 educators' responses to emergency remote teaching in the US, Trust and Whalen (2020) found that,

"Participants felt overwhelmed and unprepared to use online or remote teaching strategies and tools and they struggled to adapt their pedagogy to fluctuating situations, such as students' unreliable Internet access, changing personal needs, and unclear or shifting educational or governmental directives." (p. 191)

Apart from many educators, some students also faced considerable challenges. In short, not all students or academics had the same level of digital literacy or even digital means, leading to increasing "inequalities and [exacerbating] a pre-existing education crisis" (UNESCO, 2020). According to UNESCO (2020), a minimum of one-third of students globally were excluded from receiving proper distance education due to the lack of connectivity and devices. With the Bahraini government's expectation for teaching and learning to continue through other means than face-to-face, 10 days into the pandemic, educational institutions were confronted with the challenge of how to find innovative ways to connect with students and continue teaching and learning. The reality of the digital divide and consequent digital inequality became more apparent within the higher education sector when the demands to offer online learning came to the fore. For educational institutions, especially in government institutions, the means of delivering virtual lessons was a challenge for both students and teachers. However, many private schools and higher education institutions that already had virtual learning environments, which had been utilisedfor their face-to-face teaching, found the shift less challenging. The challenge for teachers was to provide suitable teaching materials through e-learning tools that would keep students well-engaged and informed at the same time. Yet, some tutors who were not computer or internet-literate were resistant to change and found the demanded changes in their roles traumatic, especially when learning to develop online materials or just navigate through the available online tools (Tadesse

& Muluye, 2020). Furthermore, students also faced digital divide obstacles in accessing technology and relevant digital tools, which affected their learning through the pandemic. For example, not all students had access to the internet and others did not own electronic devices which would allow them to join their online classes (Litchfield et al., 2021). These socio-economic differences resulted in inequalities in accessing online learning. This relates both to accessing technologies and the skills to use them (Mathrani et al., 2022).

Digital Divide and Digital Inequalities

Chan (2021) defines the digital divide as the gap between individuals capable of benefiting from the digital age and those who are not, due to technological and sociocultural factors. Rainford (2021) adds that having the technological infrastructure and the ability to access resources such as technologies and broadband differ from one individual to another. Similarly, Grant and Gedeon (2020) report that educational institutions with traditional teaching suddenly faced the challenge of offering online learning with no pre-existing essential infrastructure or support services to deal with the new teaching situation. Gong (2020) states that having unreliable access to the internet as well as parents' inability to afford to buy devices for their children is another challenge to effective online education (Cranfield et al., 2021). This divide has widened and widening participation has therefore become a focus due to the rapid transition to online outreach during the pandemic (Rainford, 2021). Mathrani et al. (2022) have noted that the gap in access to information and communication technologies (ICTs) in developing countries, between the *haves* (the privileged class) and the *have-nots* (the underprivileged class) is rather wide, and therefore, "when students were forced to suddenly pursue studies from inside their homes, this gap would have had more impact among the *have-nots*" (p. 625). There is a flow-on effect from a lack of access to technology, which then translates into the ability to use technology, or rather a lack of ability to use technology, and in particular technologies for learning. Thus, disadvantage gets exacerbated in an event such as the Covid-19 pandemic. Given the larger numbers of learners with lack of access to technologies that are used for learning in developing countries, the digital divide tends to grow faster in those countries. Of course, there is not a clear binary between 'developed' and 'developing' nations in this respect; it is rather a continuum with highly uneven access *within* some societies (Azubuike et al., 2021). Thus, the digital divide refers to more than access, and includes a range of sociocultural factors that have various degrees of overall impact (Mathrani et al., 2022).

Sociocultural factors involve "computer and network skills, digital literacy and the knowledge of how to make use of the technical tools for personal well-being, learning, self-sufficiency, collaboration and participation in the economy via digital means" (Chan, 2021, p. 4). Liu (2020) claims that low literacy rates and poor economic status of individuals have challenged shifting to online learning which demands investments in devices and infrastructure. This is reinforced by Alajmi and Rorissa (2018) who focused on the Gulf Cooperation Council States, including Bahrain. Rainford (2021) adds that because of the excessive focus on technology and teaching online deliverables, both students or teachers and their individual challenges and barriers should be taken into consideration. Many teachers had to alter their teaching content to suit online delivery with no prior training or support offered (Al-Kumaim et al., 2021) and the same applied to designing and invigilating assessments online (Singh, 2011). Along the same lines, Song et al. (2020) add that the digital divide can occur because of a lack of digital and technological skills and competencies. Overall, Karakose (2021) has noted that "the emergency remote teaching put in place due to the COVID-19 pandemic has led to the widening of the digital divide among higher education students" (p. 53).

The digital divide and digital inequalities are connected. Doud and Log (2011) and DiMaggio et al. (2004) defined digital inequality as the inequality among users of the internet relevant to how they really benefit from their use of internet technology. Digital inequality takes five different forms: inequality in technological means, inequality in the autonomy of use, inequality of skills, inequality in social support and variation in the purposes for which people use the technology (DiMaggio & Hargittai, 2001). Inequality in terms of technical means is related to students' access to hardware and connections to access the internet. Accessing the internet from home, work or school, having monitored or non-monitored internet access, and competing with other users for time online represent inequality in autonomy. Moreover, the differences in individual skills using the internet represent inequality in skills while inequality in social support is shown through how internet users seek support to use it. The fifth inequality type is related to the different objectives people use the technology for. All these five different forms, however, are inextricably linked and in many ways reinforce each other. This should be an important factor in how we move forward in terms of how we design learning in the post-Covid-19 era. Predictions about the post-pandemic future of digital learning vary, but most scholars agree that equity of access should be a key element of designing that future (Guppy et al., 2022). This study contributes to considerations around learning design in a post-pandemic higher education sector.

Purpose

The goal of this study was to investigate the effectiveness of the virtual learning environment as the only means of delivering teaching and learning strategies in higher education institutions in the Kingdom of Bahrain, in terms of the academic outcomes of learners, as well as to evaluate the levels of equity achieved within the digital divide. Due to Covid-19, tutors had to adopt innovative ways of teaching and learning -referred to here as e-learning. This study evaluated learners' perceptions of the virtual learning environment to which they had been exposed over the 24 months since the start of the pandemic, in contrast to the traditional face-to-face sessions. This study sought to provide insights into different perspectives and identify the benefits that students derived from the virtual learning platform as well as the challenges they experienced.

The four main research questions that were addressed in this study are:

1. Has online learning in the Covid 19 era helped students improve their digital literacy?
2. Have there been any significant academic improvements in grades and in students' learning in e-learning mode during the Covid-19 period?
3. Is it easier for students to access learning using online learning facilities compared to face-to-face?
4. Have online learning systems been able to remediate/ fix the challenges of teaching during the Covid 19 era?

METHODOLOGY

This study adopted a mixed-method (qualitative and quantitative) approach in collecting and analysing data. To ascertain the impact of virtual learning/e-learning on learners, we measured the impact of e-learning on learners through a combination of qualitative and quantitative measures.

Although the data collection instrument is quantitative in nature, it also included open-ended questions, thus serving in part as a qualitative data collection tool. The questions were targeted at students/learners who had, throughout the Covid 19 era, taken part in online/virtual learning spanning the past 12 to 24 months. The aim was to receive learners' feedback, impressions and responses based on their experiences with online/virtual teaching and learning platforms during the Covid 19 era. Most of the closed-ended questions however adopted the Likert model. The questionnaire was administered via email to a randomised sample of students/learners from an available large database of students from a number of higher education institutions in the Kingdom of Bahrain, and 631 responded to share their experiences and/ or impressions about virtual/e-learning. These students were enrolled in Bahrain Polytechnic, University of Bahrain, Arab Open University, Ahlia University, Royal College of Surgeons in Bahrain, Kingdom University and University of Technology Bahrain. The researchers did not perceive the number of respondents as enough. The number is merely a sample that represents the views of the participating students in the study. The findings may/ may not have been similar if the researchers of this study had had access to the databases of all universities in Bahrain.

The main objective of this research was to investigate the impact virtual/online learning has had on all categories of learners/students at Higher Education (HE) institutions in the Kingdom of Bahrain. The reality that is currently facing all HE institutions, worldwide, is that all teaching and learning is largely taking place virtually/online or in blended mode, including in all HE institutions in the Kingdom of Bahrain since the COVID-19 pandemic. The objective, therefore, was to show the level of effectiveness of the virtual teaching and learning methodology during the Covid 19 pandemic. Furthermore, the study was expected to be able to point to areas of development in this teaching and learning methodology in order to enable practitioners to derive maximum benefit and enhance the overall teaching and learning experiences of learners into the future.

Results/Findings

The data obtained in the study came from a large number of learners (a total of 631 students) from higher education institutions across the Kingdom of Bahrain. Their responses to the questionnaires have been summarised and presented as charts and tables. The data obtained was imported into Excel and analysed using basic data analysis tools in Excel as well the Descriptive and survey statistical tools. The results include demographics and survey statistics, as well as a thematic analysis of two quasi-open-ended questions (Tables 1 and 2 below, which were part of the survey). The socio-economic factors of the learners were taken into consideration, since they contributed significantly to learners' well-being and impacted their learning during Covid-19. Some of the questions were thus designed to address those factors.

The total number of females who took part in the study was more than 55% compared to the total number of males, which was 281, out of a total of 631 respondents. It is important to indicate that the target population was mainly middle-class and upper-class learners, since they represent the overall population of learners in the Kingdom. Data obtained (Fig 1b) about the age distribution of students who participated in the research clearly shows that the age range of most (99%) of the students who took part in the study was between 18 and 30. .

Evidently, students used mostly laptops to access their online learning, as laptops are more versatile compared to the other electronic devices listed. The least used devices were iPads and mobile phones.

Do you believe that online learning has been useful to you during the Covid-19 period.

Figure 1. Gender and age of learners who participated in the survey

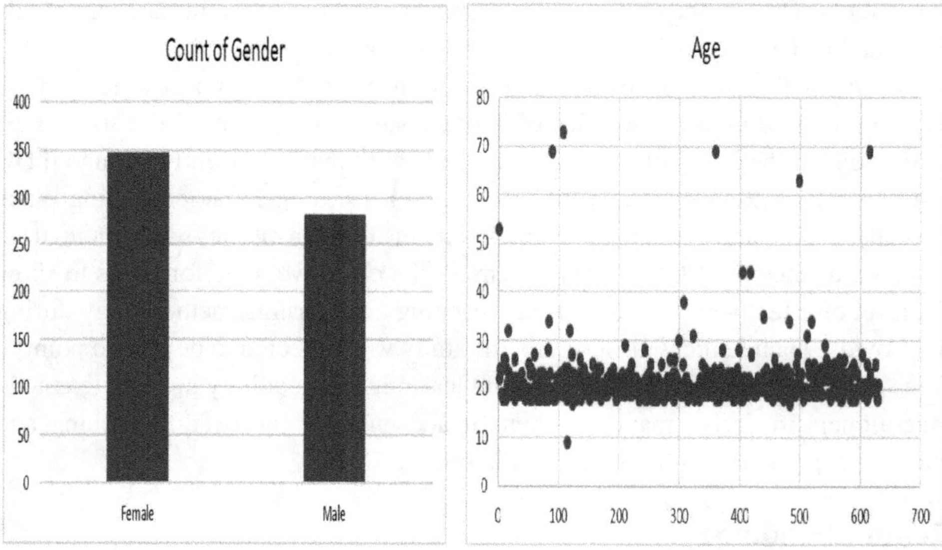

Figure 2. What electronic devices students use to access their online learning (e.g., desktop computer, laptop, etc.) 'Computer' in the graph refers to 'desktop computer'

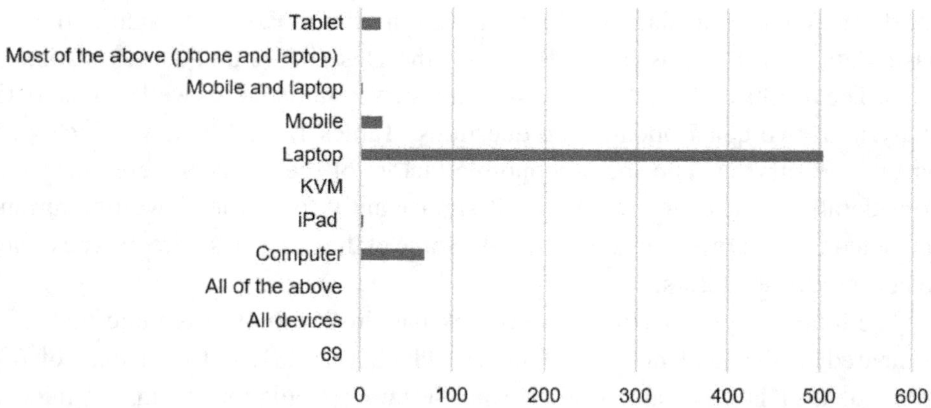

Learners were asked whether they believed that online learning has been useful, in terms of whether it supported their learning during the Covid-19 period. Learners were split in their responses; and the majority neither agreed nor disagreed.

I believe that the features of online learning have been very easy to use.

Students were unanimous in agreeing that the features of online learning were easy to navigate. A very small percentage (8%) of learners, however, strongly disagreed, which may have been due to either access or digital literacy issues.

Figure 3. Belief in the usefulness of online learning during Covid-19 period

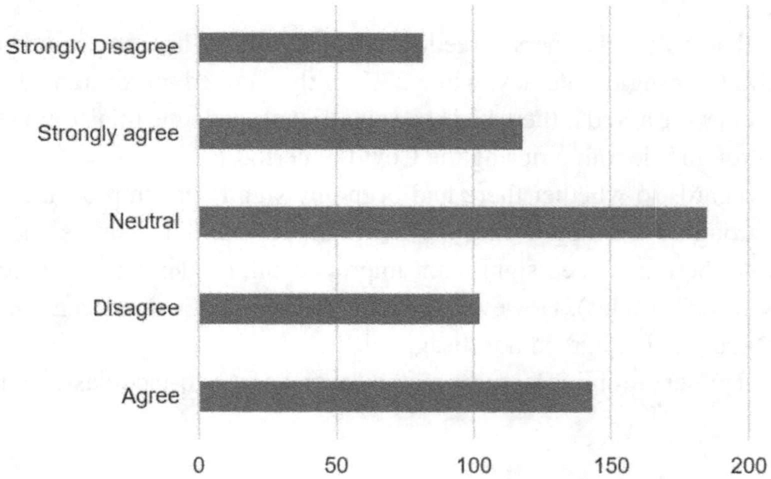

Figure 4. Belief in the ease of use of the online learning features

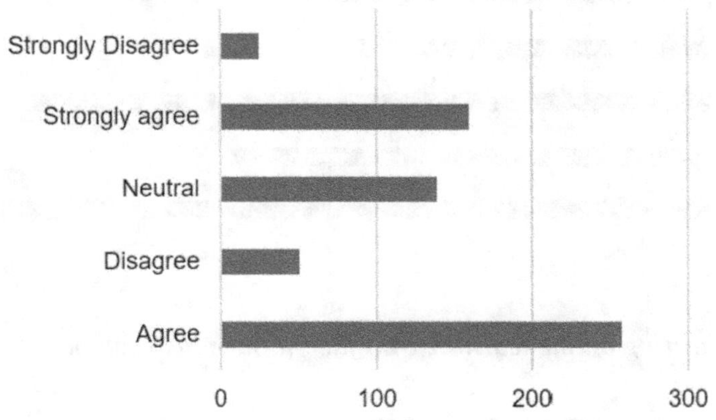

Figure 5. Impact of online learning on the improvement of digital literacy (learning skills)

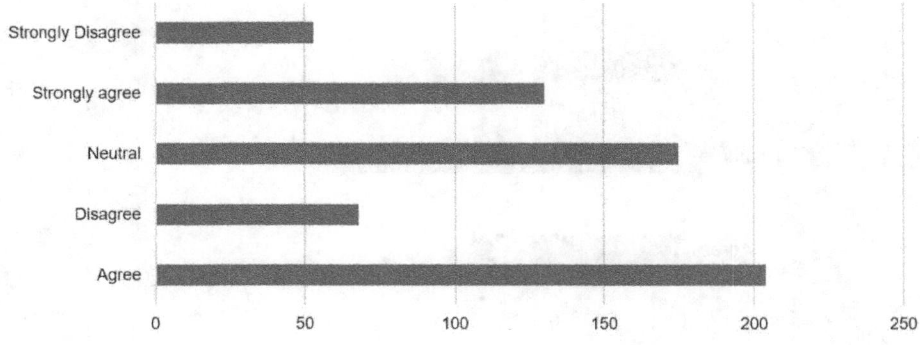

I feel that online learning will help me to improve on my digital literacy (learning skills).

More than 50% of learners agreed that they felt online learning could help them to improve their digital literacy, while 27% neither agreed nor disagreed.

Learners were asked if there had been significant academic improvement in their studies through e-learning during the Covid19 period.

With regards to whether there had been any significant improvement in their studies through e-learning during the Covid 19 period, the students unanimously agreed that there had been significant improvement, academically (evident by an increase in their grades). However, the data showed that a significant percentage, 24%, of them neither agreed nor disagreed.

I think I prefer the online learning method over the face-to-face classroom method.

Figure 6. Students' academic improvement through e-learning during Covid-19

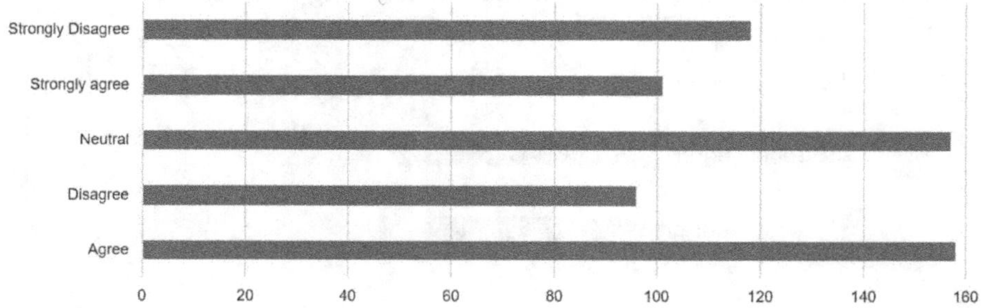

Figure 7. Preferring online learning over face-to-face instruction

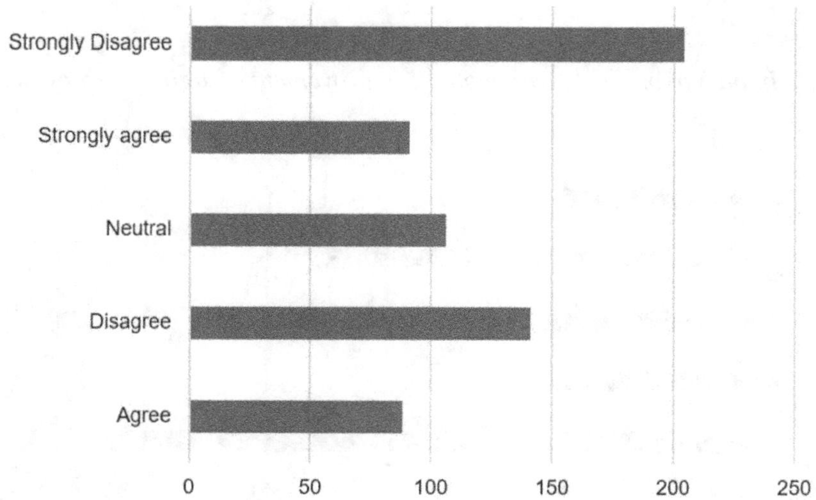

Most respondents disagreed that they *preferred* online learning to a face-to-face (classroom) instruction, implying they would have preferred face-to-face instruction if it had been available. This preference could be explained because Covid 19 just happened and disrupted the entire academic system. Students were therefore not ready to transition into a different teaching and learning strategy.

Are you at ease in using online learning facilities rather than face-to-face?

However, when students were asked whether they were at ease with using online learning facilities rather than face-to-face, the data obtained indicated somewhat of a split in their responses. Thus, this suggests that students were not necessarily happy to transition to a different teaching and learning methodology, even though most felt at ease with it.

Figure 8. Feeling at ease with online learning facilities/face-to-face ones

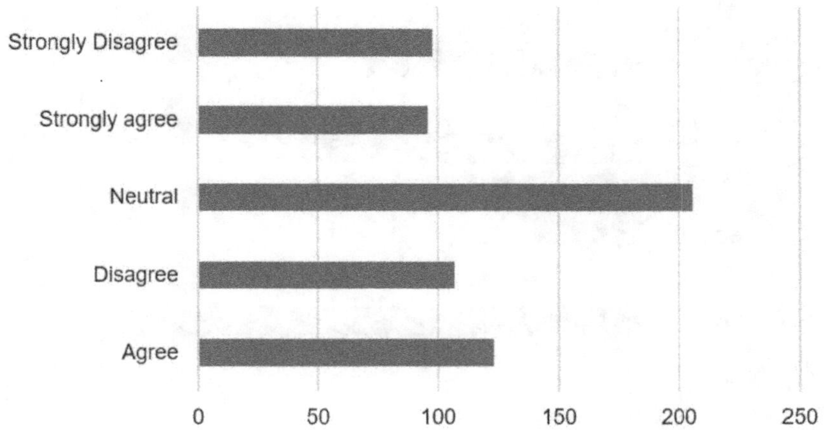

Figure 9. Flexibility in learning

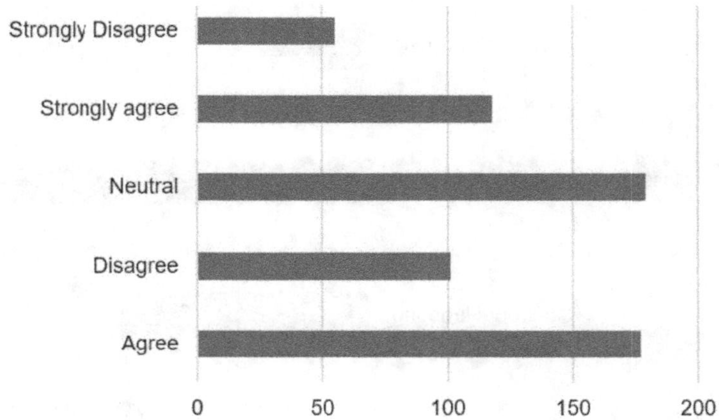

Has online learning provided a lot of flexibility compared to the face-to-face method?

With regards to whether online learning had provided a lot of flexibility compared to the face-to-face method, around 47% were in total agreement (agree and strongly agree), while 26% of the respondents disagreed (Strongly disagree and Disagree). 27% of respondents, however, were neutral in their responses.

In response to one of the key questions about whether online learning systems can remediate or fix the current lockdown challenge in teaching and learning, during this Covid 19 era, over 57% of the respondents agreed while less than 15% disagreed.

Figure 10. Effectiveness of online learning in the face of Covid-19 challenges

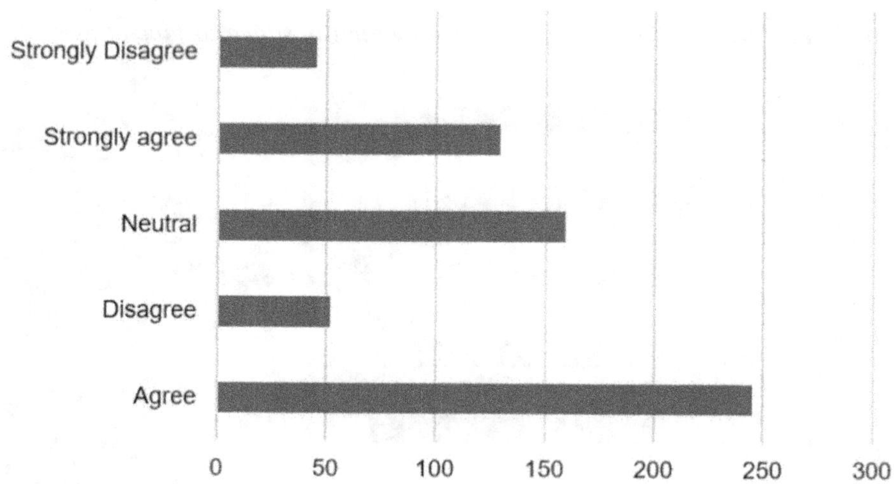

Figure 11. Post-Covid preferences for learning

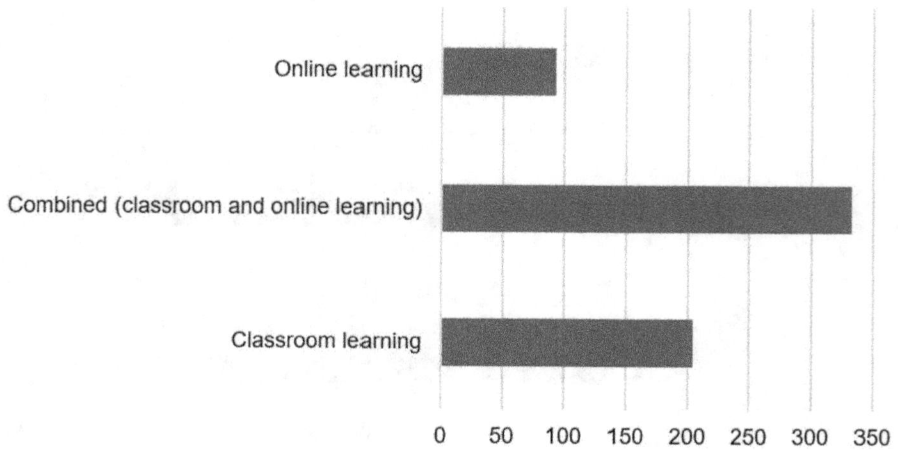

When students were asked what their preferences for learning would be like when the pandemic is over, more than 50% recommended the combined (blended) learning approach, which is a combination of both the face-to-face (classroom) and online/virtual learning.

Learners were asked whether they had sound knowledge of ICT to operate in any online learning platform. Although more than 40% of respondents were neutral on this, over 50% were positive that they had sound knowledge in IT which enabled them to operate on any online learning platform.

To the statement "With my good knowledge of the internet, using online learning platform would not be a problem", learners/students unanimously agreed that having sound background knowledge about the internet was an asset for them when they had to access the online learning platform.

Figure 12. Level of IT knowledge

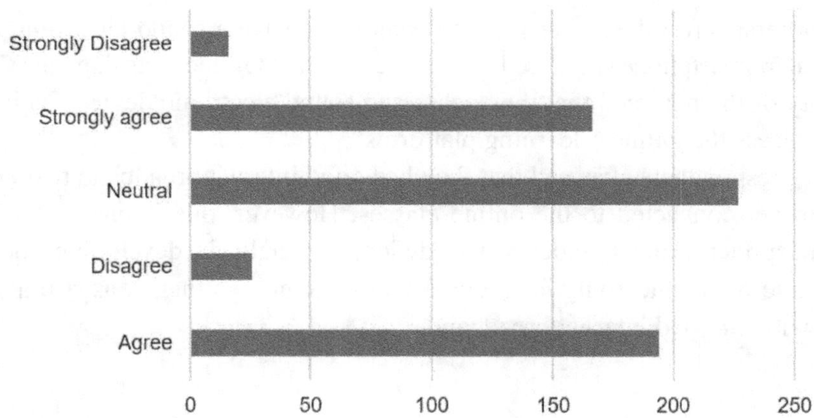

Figure 13. Impact of knowledge of the internet on accessing the online platform

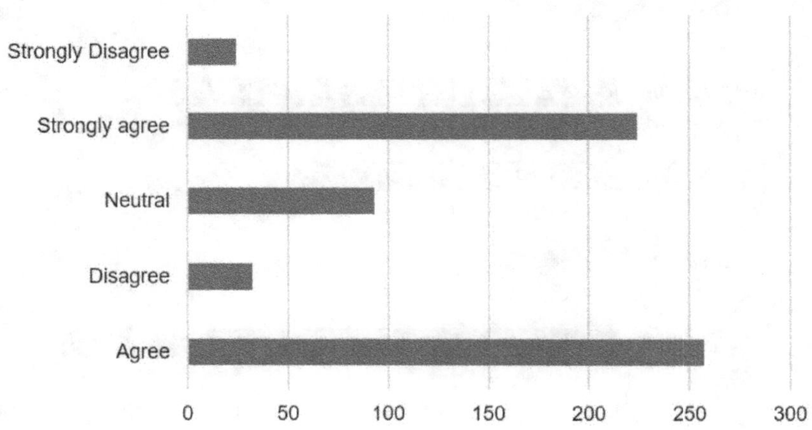

Figure 14. Possession of the relevant electronic devices

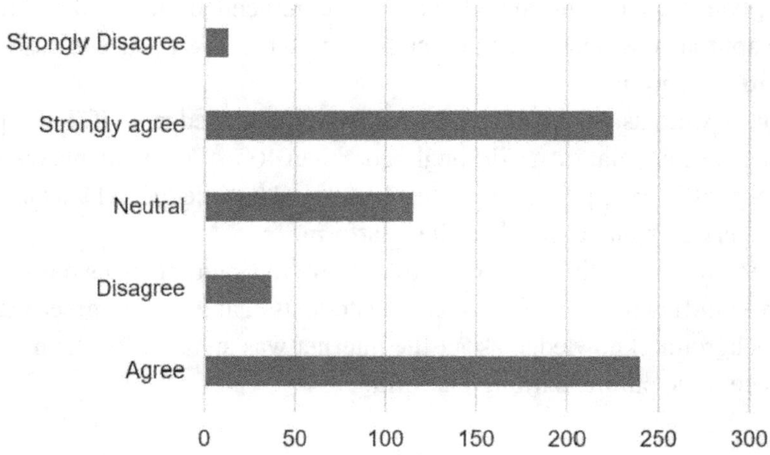

Learners were asked to respond to whether "I have a sound electronic device (computer/smartphone) required to register for an Online learning class". The majority of them agreed that they possessed sound electronic devices which they use to access the online e-learning platforms.

Most respondents affirmed that they had good internet broadband that enabled them to get connected to the online classes. However, this is one of the major challenges facing most students, worldwide, especially in developing countries, where internet connectivity is an unaffordable luxury, so there was still a sizable group without good internet broadband.

Figure 15. Possession of the required internet broadband

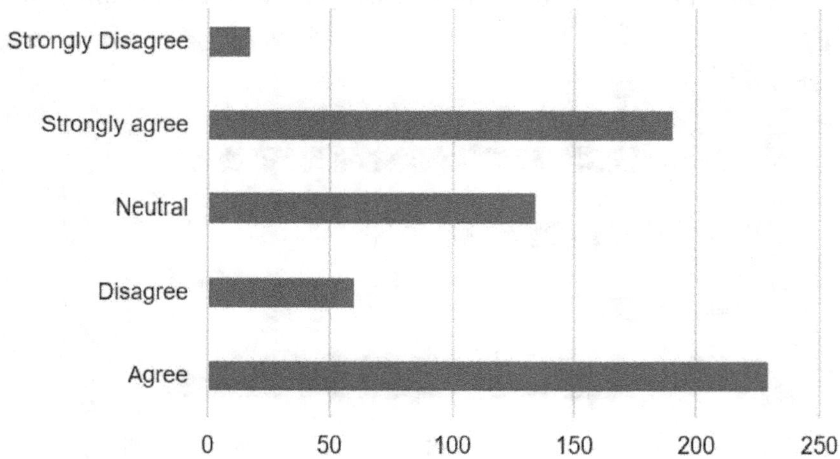

One of the external factors that could potentially impact virtual learning is the availability of power supply. Respondents affirmed that they had a good and regular power supply that enabled them to get connected to the online classes. However, a small percentage disagreed, suggesting they did not have a regular power supply.

Learners were asked whether they faced various forms of distractions while engaged in online learning sessions during the Covid 19 era, and students were diverse in their responses. 30% agreed that they did not face any distractions; while 42% indicated that they faced a lot of distractions. Around 25% of the respondents were neutral. These responses indicate significant challenges in terms of effective learning environments, some related to the digital environment itself, but some related to their learning context at home.

Figure 16. Availability of the power supply

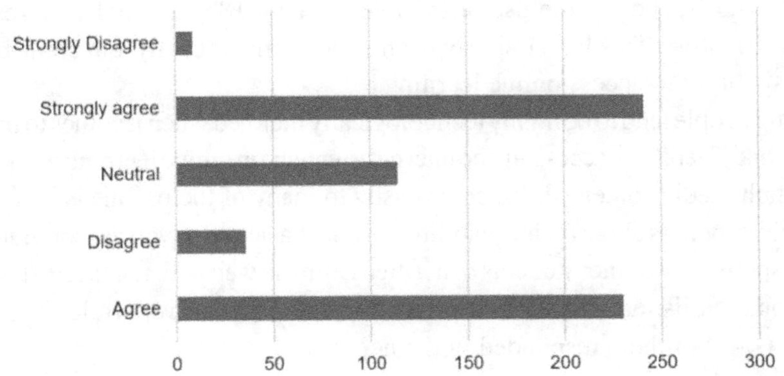

Figure 17. Effective learning environments

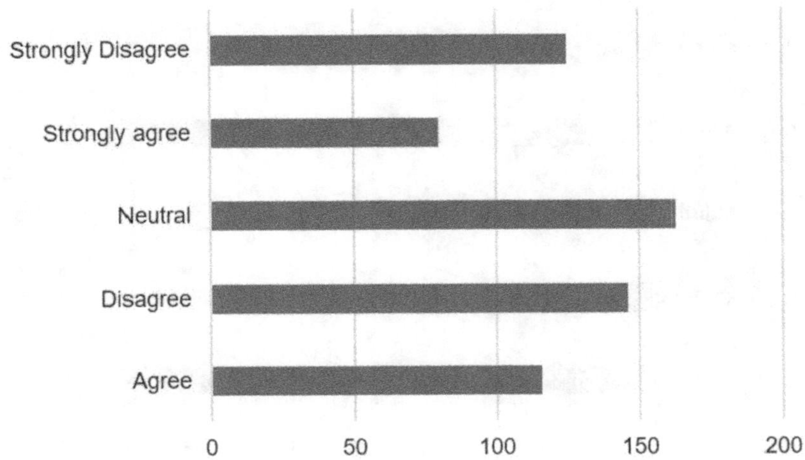

Figure 18. a) Forms of sitraction in online learning, b) Leaners' computer skills

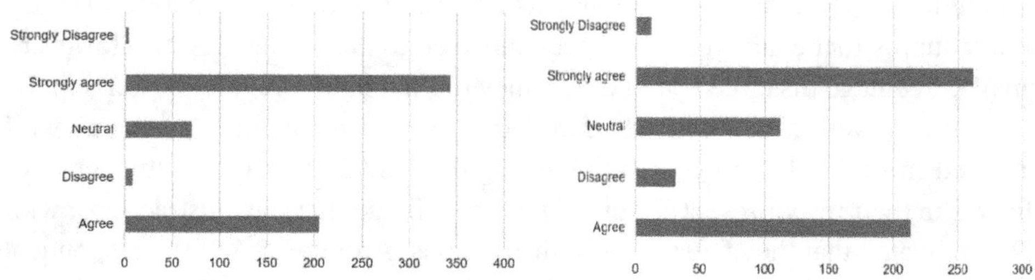

With regards to whether learners had the basic computer skills (e.g., typing and editing), a significant majority (approximately 92%) of learners responded in the affirmative. This has been a major catalyst in contributing to students' ability to access online learning platforms. In response to whether students possessed advanced computer skills, such as the use of the internet (Fig 18b), around 75% responded in the affirmative. This has similarly been another major catalyst in contributing to students' ability to access online learning.

Young people tend to be highly technologically inclined when it comes to managing multimedia. Therefore, accessing the internet to engage in online learning while making use of multimedia content skills, came easily to many of them. This is in agreement with their responses about their capabilities in both basic and advanced computer skills.

In response to whether students benefitted from the web with regards to developing educational skills, around 73% responded in the affirmative, while a very small number (<40) of them responded in the negative.

Figure 19. Use of multimedia

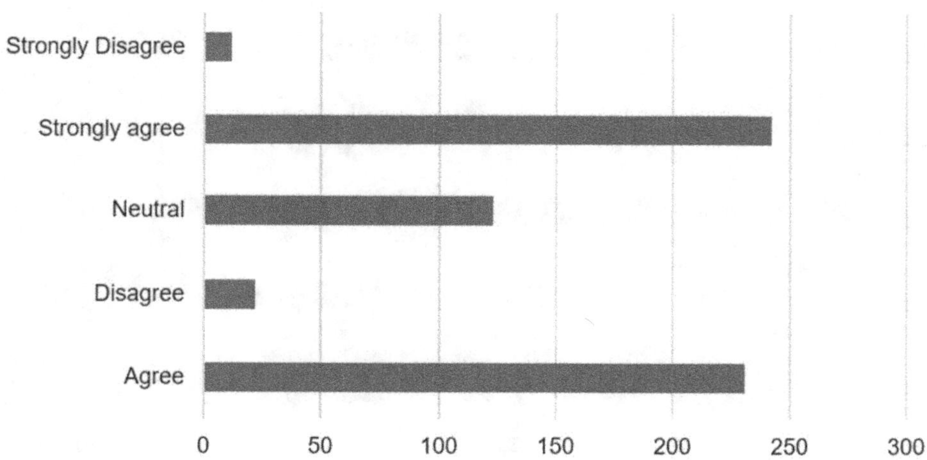

Figure 20.

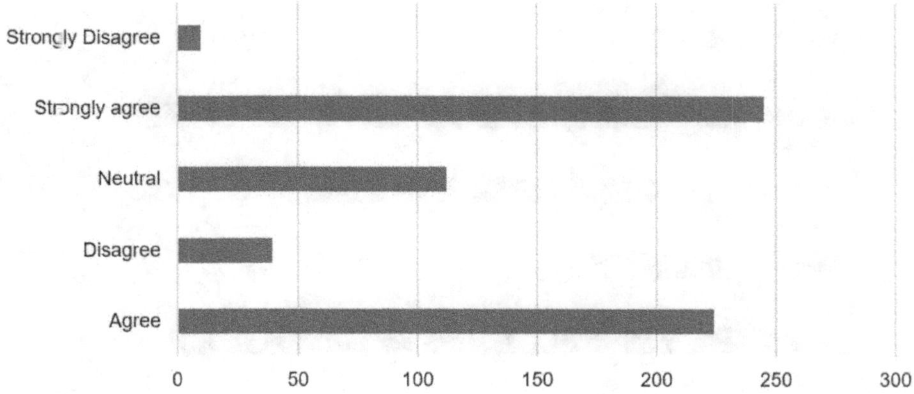

Figure 21. Use of online communication tools

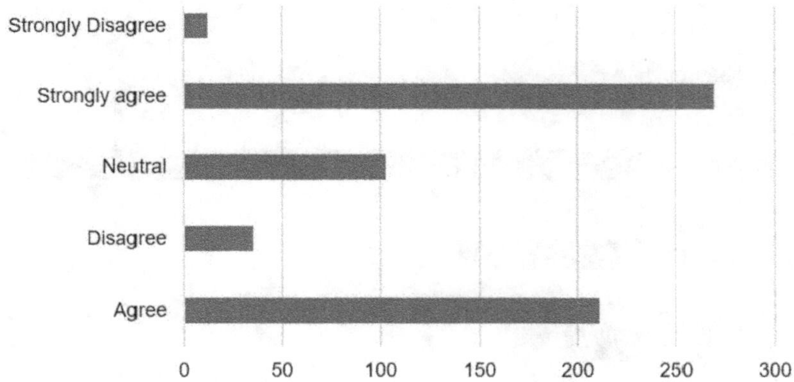

Using online tools in education skills, such as Videochat (e.g. Skype), and Web Video (e.g. YouTube), was relatively easy for them. Therefore, accessing the internet to engage in online learning, in addition to using online communication tools was something they did effortlessly.

The youth of today are highly technologically inclined, when it comes to skills required in dealing with and responding to online content; therefore, accessing the internet to engage in online learning which involved the application of certain online soft skills, was easy for most of them. Only a small percentage of the learners disagreed and were therefore disadvantaged.

With regards to online communication skills, including social media (e.g. Facebook, Twitter, Tik Tok), engaging in online learning was perceived to be fairly easy for them, judging from the percentages of 'agrees'. However, this suggests they may have equated social media use with learning, which is not necessarily warranted.

Figure 22. Using online tools

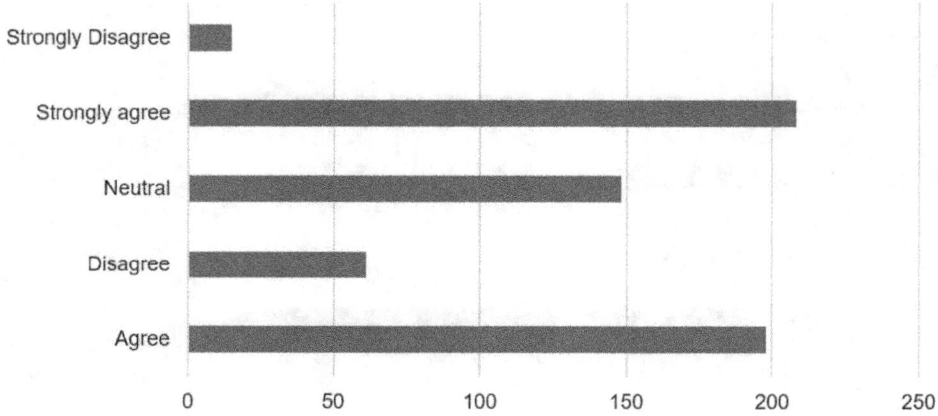

Figure 23. Use of social media

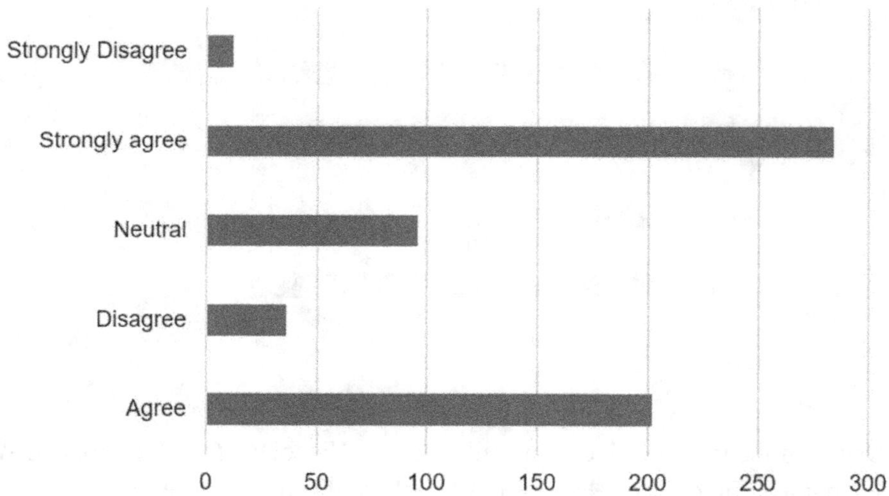

In response to whether students were able to use electronic resources (such as databases, etc.), over 50% responded in the negative. However, these skills were not necessary for learners to have in order to access their online lessons.

One of the key questions was about whether students were able to manage their time while accessing e-learning, and around 47% of the respondents agreed that they could manage their time very well online; 21% disagreed, and 28% were not sure.

Two open-ended questions were included in the questionnaire. However, to avoid complexity in analysing the data, a number of options were provided for students to select from. The first so-called open-ended question was: Based on your own

Figure 24. Use of electronic resources (e.g., databases)

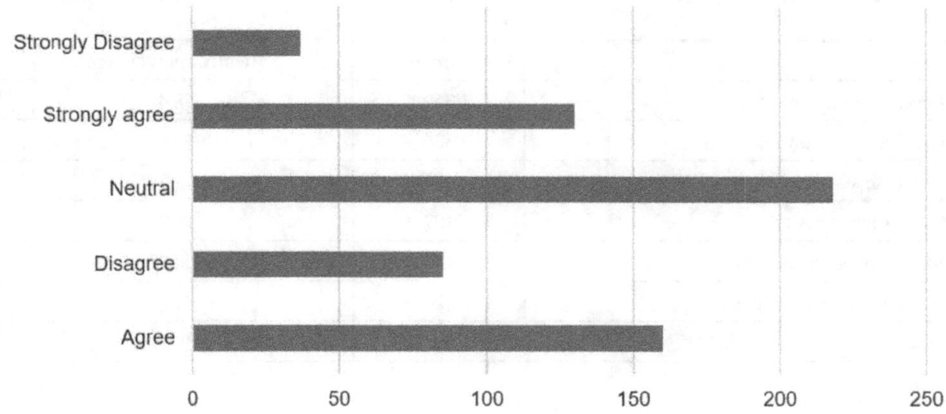

Figure 25. Time management

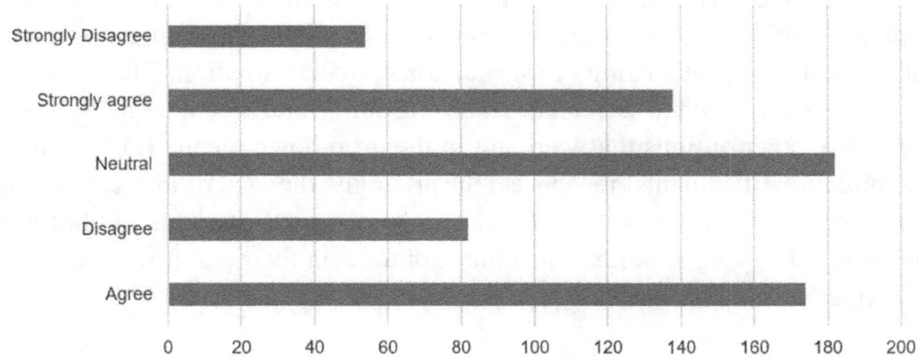

experience, what are the advantages of e-learning? (You can choose more than one). The options provided in this question included: Access to online materials, Learning at your own pace, Ability to stay at home, Class Interactivity, Ability to record a meeting, Comfortable surroundings and Others. Students were allowed to select more than one option and they were allowed to add any other options that were not in the drop-down menu. The table below summarises a compilation of students' responses.

The data obtained indicates that students cared very much about the ability to record the e-learning sessions, probably for future reference/revision of lessons. The second highest response suggested that they love to stay at home in their comfort zones while accessing learning. What they least cared about was class interactivity, perhaps because they get to do this extensively in other social media platforms.

Table 1. Question - Based on your own experience, what are the advantages of e-learning? Total number of respondents = 631. Respondents could select more than 1 option.

	Number	Relative percentage
Access to online materials	369	58.4
Learning at my own pace	326	51.6
Ability to stay at home	420	66.5
Classes interactivity	107	16.9
Ability to record meeting	444	70.3
Comfortable surroundings	326	51.6
Others	41	9.2

The second open-ended question was: Based on your own experience, what are the disadvantages of e-learning? (You can choose more than one). The options provided in this question included: Reduced interaction with the teacher, Technical problems, Lack of interactions with peers, Poor learning conditions, Lack of self-discipline, Ability to stay at home, Social isolation, Others. Again, students were allowed to select more than one option and they were also allowed to add any other options that were not in the drop-down menu. Table 2 shows a compilation of students' responses. Surprisingly, the lack of interaction with their peers was also a challenge for them. As expected, students did not have any problem staying at home, since they got to be in their comfort zones while accessing learning online.

Table 2. Question - Based on your own experience, what are the disadvantages of e-learning? Total number of respondents = 631. Respondents could select more than 1 option.

	Number	Relative percentage
Reduced interaction with the teacher	393	62.2
Technical problems	455	72.0
Lack of interaction with peers	359	56.8
Poor learning conditions	253	40.0
Lack of self discipline	252	39.9
Ability to stay at home	78	12.3
Social Isolation	316	50.0
Others	41	8.7

The data obtained indicates that students were very concerned about the availability of internet access, to enable them to access e-learning uninterrupted. Unfortunately, this assurance could not be guaranteed by the institution, but instead was reliant on the ISP they subscribed to. In addition, technical problems also included the type of technological tools, such as the computer or tablet students used to access the e-learning sessions. The fact that students did not get to directly interact with their teachers was a challenge for most of them, and many of them were concerned about this.

DISCUSSION

This study set out to explore the impact of Covid-19 on the learning experience of higher education students in the Kingdom of Bahrain. To that end, we aimed to survey as many students as possible across all higher education institutions in Bahrain. Given the timing of the survey, the responses relate strongly to the period that has become known for 'emergency remote teaching' (Hodges et al., 2020). In other words, given the sudden shift to online learning and teaching, teachers were forced to adapt almost overnight to what was for many a completely new approach to teaching. Not only did this sudden transition have a strong impact on teachers, including a strong emotional impact in many cases (Taylor et al., 2022), but it also had a strong potential impact on the student experience and student learning outcomes (Stevanović et al., 2021; Yan et al., 2021). The survey data in this study reflects the feedback from a randomised sample of 631 students from across all higher education students in the Kingdom of Bahrain. The results will allow us to reflect on the lessons that could be learned from the initial period of emergency remote teaching, and to explore how we could possibly not only respond better to future crises and prepare teachers better (Lundberg & Stigmar, 2022), but also how we can leverage elements of learning design that worked well for future learning design, and as a part of sustainable learning design into the future. One example of this type of work that is beginning to emerge is a recent study by Cano et al. (2023), who focused on competency-based assessment as part of the lessons they learned from emergency remote teaching, and identified a number of challenges related to staff use of technologies in relation to assessment and the need for assessment literacy in broader terms. Interestingly, these challenges apply to both teachers and students. This example shows how an evaluation of emergency remote teaching can highlight broader learning and teaching issues that can be addressed and thereby improve the student experience in the future. Furthermore, it is important to keep in mind that while there were many challenges, many "educators and students adapted quickly to the shift" (Mutizwa et al., 2023, p. 16), while the main challenge was often connectivity issues, which is reflected in the data in this study as well. Moreover, one of the main findings in this study relates to the issue of connectivity, and in a broader sense to the issue of the digital divide. Indeed, as Azubuike et al. (2021) have asked, "who get to learn in a pandemic?"

Within the Bahraini context, and based on the survey data in this study, the digital divide was definitely a factor during the pandemic, yet not always explicitly so. As noted, the digital divide involves a number of discreet elements, so it can be seen as a broad umbrella term for connectivity issues, access to technology, and digital literacy, with all these three elements potentially being related, but not necessarily so (Rainford, 2021; Tay et al., 2023). For example, when the data tell us that only a small percentage (8%) of respondents strongly disagreed that online learning features were easy to navigate, this seems to suggest digital literacy challenges on their part, but this could at the same time be directly related to lack of access to technology and/or connectivity issues. We then explicitly asked students about digital literacy, and more than 50% thought that the emergency remote learning had helped them improve their digital literacy; however, whether they therefore preferred online learning as a result, is a different question. This was further reflected in the question about preferences, which split this cohort down the middle, with about half of the respondents seemingly preferring online learning in face-to-face contexts, despite also indicating that they were at ease in online environments and despite indicating that online learning provided a lot of flexibility. This apparent contradiction may be due to the sudden change to online learning, and a potential desire to go 'back to normal'. Yet, it does also indicate that there are positive elements of online learning that can possibly be built into learning design in the future.

In terms of preferences, about half of the respondents stated a preference for a blended learning approach, which again suggests that going back 'wholesale' to face-to-face teaching would not be desirable. This also aligns with more than half of the respondents indicating that they thought they had sound technology knowledge that allowed them to operate in online learning platforms, which suggests that their own perceptions were that they had relatively high digital literacy levels, or at least sufficient levels in that respect. This creates a number of issues. Firstly, it indicates relatively high levels of confidence amongst a majority of students in Bahrain, which suggests that the ground is generally fertile for more online learning, or at least blended learning approaches. Conversely however, digital literacy is based on dynamic and ever-changing technologies and the social and professional contexts in which to use those technologies. Thus, confidence by itself is not necessarily a sound indicator of required capabilities, nor is extensive use of, and skills in using, social media. Without critically reflecting on this issue and incorporating that reflection into learning design and learning outcomes, we run the risk of reinforcing what Bhatt and MacKenzie (2019) have called an 'epistemology of ignorance'. In response, they argue that there is a need to develop approaches to counter such ignorance (p. 302). Such responses would rely to an important extent on digital literacy levels amongst teachers who would need to develop such approaches. The need to develop those digital literacy levels seems obvious, but it is a delicate balancing act between acknowledging 'digital anxiety' amongst a certain cohort of teachers, especially during the initial phases of the pandemic, combined with 'change fatigue' on the one hand, and the need for lifelong learning and continuous skills' development on the other. Compton and Gilmour (2022) have referred to this balancing act as 'walking a tightrope', and they suggest there is a need for 'compassionate academic development', to enhance professional agency, expertise and pedagogic approaches' amongst teachers (p. 203).

Even if all teachers have the required digital literacy skills to develop and facilitate engaging blended learning environments and learning experiences, the data in this study show that there would still be a group of students, albeit a relatively small cohort, that would struggle with the online components simply because of insufficient internet connectivity. It is therefore crucial that universal access and connectivity, as well as power supply, amongst all students in the Kingdom of Bahrain be a matter of priority in order to avoid a growing digital divide. While digital divide issues relate to broader equity issues, such as poverty and social marginalisation, this also relates to learning environments. For example, 42% of respondents in this study indicated that they faced a lot of distractions in their home environments. While this may be partly related to the fact that everyone was working from home during the pandemic, it could also point to relative overcrowding in some students' households, reinforcing the importance of good (or at least sufficient) mobile technologies to create more opportunities to find appropriate spaces and times for learning.

CONCLUSION

Covid-19 had a major impact on higher education globally, including in the Kingdom of Bahrain, and it initially threw everyone into emergency online teaching out of necessity. We are now at a stage where we can reflect on that experience and in the process develop plans for sustainable approaches to online and/or blended learning that would have us better placed to deal with similar situations in the future. This study has shown that most students, according to their own perceptions, are sufficiently equipped to study effectively in online environments, but that may not necessarily be backed up by the reality. Furthermore, digital literacy is dynamic and therefore requires constant updating in the form of lifelong learning. Teachers are a central cog in this machine, and continuous professional development of teachers is therefore important. Issues related to digital equity and the digital divide have long been talked about, and while the number of students with accessibility and connectivity issues appears to be relatively small, based on the data in this study, there is still a need to be vigilant in this respect to ensure that everyone has equal access to learning opportunities and learning experiences in digital environments.

This study has a number of limitations. For example, the study is restricted to students in the Kingdom of Bahrain, and could be expanded to other contexts in the Gulf region or beyond. Moreover, the study is restricted to student feedback and perceptions, and future research could incorporate teachers' perceptions instead. A way to delve even deeper into these data sets would be to conduct interviews with both students and teachers, which would allow us to develop a more detailed picture of their ideas, particularly as they relate to digital literacy and digital divide related issues.

REFERENCES

Al-Kumaim, N. H., Alhazmi, A. K., Mohammed, F., Gazem, N. A., Shabbir, M. S., & Fazea, Y. (2021). Exploring the impact of the COVID-19 pandemic on university students' learning life: An integrated conceptual motivational model for sustainable and healthy online learning. *Sustainability (Basel)*, *13*(5), 2546. doi:10.3390/su13052546

Al-Mahadin, S. (2020). Laughing it off: Coronavirus superspreaders, anxiety, and fear in Jordan and Australia. *Psychological Trauma: Theory, Research, Practice, and Policy*, *12*(S1), S45–S46. https://psycnet.apa.org/doi/10.1037/tra0000630. doi:10.1037/tra0000630 PMID:32597676

Alajmi, M. A., & Rorissa, A. (2018). E-environments in the Gulf Cooperation Council States: An analysis of the literature. *IFLA Journal*, *44*(1), 56–73. doi:10.1177/0340035218755167

Azubuike, O. B., Adegboye, O., & Quadri, H. (2021). Who gets to learn in a pandemic? Exploring the digital divide in remote learning during the COVID-19 pandemic in Nigeria. *International Journal of Educational Research Open*, *2*, 100022. doi:10.1016/j.ijedro.2020.100022 PMID:35059664

Bhatt, I., & MacKenzie, A. (2019). Just Google it! Digital literacy and the epistemology of ignorance. *Teaching in Higher Education*, *24*(3), 302–317. doi:10.1080/13562517.2018.1547276

Cano, E., Lluch, L., Grané, M., & Remesal, A. (2023). Competency-based assessment practices in higher education: Lessons from the pandemics. *Trends in Higher Education*, *2*(1), 238–254. doi:10.3390/higheredu2010012

Chan, V. W. (2021). Initiative on reducing the "digital divide". *IEEE Communications Magazine*, *59*(5), 4–5. doi:10.1109/MCOM.2021.9446683

Compton, M., & Gilmour, A. (2022). Walking the tightrope: Enabling mindset and practice transformation at scale through compassionate academic development. *The International Journal for Academic Development*, *27*(2), 203–206. doi:10.1080/1360144X.2022.2066674

Cranfield, D. J., Tick, A., Venter, I. M., Blignaut, R. J., & Renaud, K. (2021). Higher education students' perceptions of online learning during COVID-19: A comparative study. *Education Sciences*, *11*(8), 403. doi:10.3390/educsci11080403

DiMaggio, P., & Hargittai, E. (2001). From the 'digital divide'to 'digital inequality': Studying Internet use as penetration increases (Working papers 47). *Princeton: Center for Arts and Cultural Policy Studies, Woodrow Wilson School, Princeton University, 4*(1), 4-2.

DiMaggio, P., Hargittai, E., Celeste, C., & Shafer, S. (2004). Digital inequality: From unequal access to differentiated use. In K. M. Neckerman (Ed.), *Social inequality* (pp. 355–400). Russell Sage Foundation.

Doud, F., & Log, E. L. (2011). *Digital divide versus digital inequality*. Forrest Doud. https://forrestdoud.wordpress.com/2011/02/07/digital-divide-versus-digital-inequality/

Gong, R. (2020, March 27). Coping with COVID-19: Distance learning and the digital divide. *Kri Views,* 21/20.

Grant, K., & Gedeon, S. (2020). The impact of Covid-19 on university teaching. In D. Remenyi, K. grant & S. Singh (Eds.), The university of the future: Responding to Covid-19. ACPIL.

Guppy, N., Verpoorten, D., Boud, D., Lin, L., Tai, J., & Bartolic, S. (2022). The post-COVID-19 future of digital learning in higher education: Views from educators, students, and other professionals in six countries. *British Journal of Educational Technology*, *53*(6), 1750–1765. doi:10.1111/bjet.13212

Hodges, C., Moore, S., Lockee, B., Trust, T., & Bond, A. (2020, March 27). The difference between emergency remote teaching and online learning. *Educause Review*. https://er.educause.edu/articles/2020/3/the-difference-between-emergency-remote-teaching-and-online-learning

Iglesias-Pradas, S., Hernández-García, Á., Chaparro-Peláez, J., & Prieto, J. L. (2021). Emergency remote teaching and students' academic performance in higher education during the COVID-19 pandemic: A case study. *Computers in Human Behavior*, *119*, 106713. doi:10.1016/j.chb.2021.106713 PMID:34866769

Karakose, T. (2021). Emergency remote teaching due to COVID-19 pandemic and potential risks for socioeconomically disadvantaged students in higher education. *Educational Process*, *10*(3), 53–62. doi:10.22521/edupij.2021.103.4

Litchfield, I., Shukla, D., & Greenfield, S. (2021). Impact of COVID-19 on the digital divide: A rapid review. *BMJ Open*, *11*(10), e053440. doi:10.1136/bmjopen-2021-053440 PMID:34642200

Liu, Y. (2021). *An investigation of the shift to distance education and the widening of the digital divide during the COVID-19 pandemic* [Doctoral dissertation, Auckland University of Technology].

Lundberg, A., & Stigmar, M. (2022). Deliberative academic development with university teachers in times of crisis. *The International Journal for Academic Development*, *27*(2), 163–175. doi:10.1080/1360144X.2022.2084742

Lundberg, A., & Stigmar, M. (2022). University teachers' shifting views of successful learning environments in the future. *Scandinavian Journal of Educational Research*, 1–16. doi:10.1080/00313831.2022.2115127

Marinoni, G., Van't Land, H., & Jensen, T. (2020). The impact of Covid-19 on higher education around the world. *IAU global survey report, 23*, 1-17.

Mathrani, A., Sarvesh, T., & Umer, R. (2022). Digital divide framework: Online learning in developing countries during the COVID-19 lockdown. *Globalisation, Societies and Education*, *20*(5), 625–640. doi:10.1080/14767724.2021.1981253

Mohammed Saeed Mohammed, G., & Mudhsh, A. D. (2021). The effects of COVID-19 on EFL learners' anxiety at the University of Bisha. *Arab World English Journal*. Mutizwa, M. R., Ozdamli, F., & Karagozlu, D. (2023). Smart learning environments during pandemic. *Trends in Higher Education*, *2*(1), 16–28. doi:10.3390/higheredu2010002

Rainford, J. (2021). Moving widening participation outreach online: Challenge or opportunity? *Perspectives*, *25*(1), 2–6. doi:10.1080/13603108.2020.1785968

Singh, J. D. (2011). Higher education in India–Issues, challenges and suggestions. In S. P. Singh & K. L. Dangwal (Eds.), *Higher education (pp* (pp. 93–103). Lambert Academic Publishing.

Song, Z., Wang, C., & Bergmann, L. (2020). China's prefectural digital divide: Spatial analysis and multivariate determinants of ICT diffusion. *International Journal of Information Management*, *52*, 102072. doi:10.1016/j.ijinfomgt.2020.102072

Stevanović, A., Božić, R., & Radović, S. (2021). Higher education students' experiences and opinion about distance learning during the Covid-19 pandemic. *Journal of Computer Assisted Learning*, *37*(6), 1682–1693. doi:10.1111/jcal.12613 PMID:34903902

Tadesse, S., & Muluye, W. (2020). The impact of COVID-19 pandemic on education system in developing countries: A review. *Open Journal of Social Sciences*, *8*(10), 159–170. doi:10.4236/jss.2020.810011

Tay, A. Z., Huijser, H., Dart, S., & Cathcart, A. (2023). Learning technology as contested terrain: Insights from teaching academics and learning designers in Australian higher education. *Australasian Journal of Educational Technology*, 56–70. doi:10.14742/ajet.8179

Taylor, D., Bearman, M., Scarparo, S., & Thomas, M. K. E. (2022). The emotional transition to online teaching: Grief, loss, and implications for academic development. *The International Journal for Academic Development*, *27*(2), 176–190. doi:10.1080/1360144X.2022.2083141

Tinubu Ali, T., & Herrera, M. (2020). *Distance learning during COVID-19: 7 equity considerations for schools and districts*. Southern Education. https://www.southerneducation.org/covid-19-digital-equity/

Trust, T., & Whalen, J. (2020). Should teachers be trained in emergency remote teaching? Lessons learned from the COVID-19 pandemic. *Journal of Technology and Teacher Education*, *28*(2), 189–199. https://www.learntechlib.org/primary/p/215995/

Trust, T., & Whalen, J. (2021). Emergency remote teaching with technology during the COVID-19 pandemic: Using the whole teacher lens to examine educator's experiences and insights. *Educational Media International*, *58*(2), 145–160. doi:10.1080/09523987.2021.1930479

UNESCO. (2020). *School closures caused by Coronavirus (COVID-19)*. UNESCO. https://en.unesco.org/COVID19/educationresponse

Yan, L., Whitelock-Wainwright, A., Guan, Q., Wen, G., Gašević, D., & Chen, G. (2021). Students' experience of online learning during the COVID-19 pandemic: A province-wide survey study. *British Journal of Educational Technology*, *52*(5), 2038–2057. doi:10.1111/bjet.13102 PMID:34219755

Chapter 7
An Investigation Into Primary School Teachers' Perceptions About the Delivery of Physical Education (PE) Lessons Through Distance Learning, in the Republic of Ireland, During the COVID-19 Pandemic

Conn O'Hanlon
St. Etchen's National School, Ireland

Xiuping Li
Ulster University, UK

ABSTRACT

The purpose of this chapter is to present a study based at a primary school at the Republic of Ireland, which investigates the perceptions of primary school teachers about the delivery of PE lessons through distance learning by leveraging technology using Google Classroom (GC) during the COVID-19 pandemic. To achieve the primary objectives of this study, a mixed-method approach was adopted. The research instruments employed include teacher questionnaires and a focus group. The quantitative data was gathered and analysed through Google Forms and the qualitative data was collated and analysed thematically in terms of thematic analysis. The results demonstrate the challenges and strategies during distance learning and indicate the importance of PE teacher training and the significance of leadership. This study concludes with a list of future recommendations derived from the findings concerning the development of practical strategies to resolve PE issues and to effectively support school children with physical health and mental well-being.

DOI: 10.4018/979-8-3693-5370-7.ch007

INTRODUCTION

This chapter aims to share the researchers' insights into the perceptions of primary physical education (PE) teachers about distance learning in light of the findings from a research project. This research project was undertaken to investigate and explore the perceptions of teachers in the Republic of Ireland (ROI), about the delivery of PE lessons through distance learning by using Google Classroom (GC) during the COVID-19 pandemic. To gather quantitative data, 22 teachers working in St Etchen's National School (NS) engaged with an online questionnaire. The data collected was then used to form a focus group with 4 teachers working within the same school to gather qualitative data. The researchers also aimed to include a semi-structured interview with 2 members of the Senior Leadership Team (SLT), however, for some reason, neither of them could participate this time, and the researchers respected their decision given ethical considerations, this will be discussed later in the sections on METHODOLOGY and Ethical Considerations. This study sheds light on the significance of this research, the detailed challenges the PE teachers encountered, and the strategies they developed to effectively support their students. This chapter will provide the information in different sections with headings and subheadings for effective communication, which includes the background information and rationale, the research aims and objectives, the relevant literature, the employed methodology, and the results of the study followed by a conclusion and a list of future recommendations for primary PE teachers and school leaders to advance technology-enhanced learning.

Background Information and Rationale

This research focused on St Etchen's National School (NS), in an urban centre in County Westmeath, the ROI, and the research was undertaken with the PE teachers here, given that it is the largest primary school in that area, and with different types of diversity in the students in terms of race, ethnicity, gender, social and economic backgrounds, religious beliefs; with the PE teachers having experienced the delivery of primary school lessons through distance learning by using GC during the COVID-19 pandemic and they all have wide academic social networks to keep updated and well informed of PE related development. All these situations assured the researchers that this school could be used to provide sufficient data to achieve the research aim and could be representative of all the primary PE teachers in the area of the ROI.

The St Etchen's National School is a non-fee-paying voluntary school for boys and girls. The current pupil enrolment is 447, of which 255 are male and 192 are female, with a teaching staff allocation of 29. There are also 12 Special Needs

Assistants (SNAs) to facilitate 3 Autism Spectrum Disorder (ASD) teaching units and other children with specific learning disorders in mainstream classes. The pupils in the school range from the age of 3 (in the ASA unit), up to 13 years of age, in the 6th class. Within the school, 6 teachers fulfill the role of learning support. This role consists of working with children in a small group setting or 1:1. PE does take place in learning support, often as a means of destressing, providing activity that may be lacking, or simply as an enjoyable break from set lessons and activities. Often while observing these small groups or 1:1 lessons, the first researcher who works at this school views teaching strategies that may be suited to whole-class mainstream classes or even activities that may be too challenging or not challenging enough. All the teachers in St Etchen's had little or no experience of employing distance or blended learning prior to the COVID-19 pandemic, and due to this, no lessons (including PE) had ever been delivered remotely. Google Classroom (GC) was the designated platform used by St Etchen's NS during the school closure.

Within the school, a range of technological devices were used to allow pupils to access online resources and develop their IT skills. These include tablets, chrome books, and laptops. Shortly after the outbreak of COVID-19, the decision was made by school management to allow these devices to be collected by any family that did not have adequate access to appropriate devices. Of the one hundred devices available in the school for child learning, approximately 37 were collected and subsequently returned by families.

In the ROI, two prolonged periods of distance learning occurred due to the COVID-19 pandemic. These periods of distance learning severely altered the way teaching and learning took place as teachers and students moved away from classrooms. This research was directly inspired by the situation in the primary PE setting seeing the challenges of shifting or transferring from classroom-based environments to online learning, leading to the interest in investigating the perceived impact of COVID-19 on primary school children's PE lessons by considering their teachers' perceptions.

Britannica defines distance learning as "form of education in which the main elements include physical separation of teachers and students during instruction and the use of various technologies to facilitate student-teacher and student communication" (Simonson and Berg, 2016, as cited in Masalimova et al., 2022, p. 2). Further, the advantages, challenges and disadvantages of distance learning have also been summarised in the study by Masalimova et al. (2022), but they also argue that prior to the pandemic, interest in distance learning was burgeoning, as it was a unique style of instruction. In the ROI, the schools had to adopt it as there was no other choice due to the disruption of the COVID-19 pandemic.

The rationale for conducting this investigation is multi-faceted. The researchers chose to investigate teachers' perceptions about the delivery of PE through distance learning, which was directly relevant to the first author's (in this chapter it also refers to 'the first researcher) professional context, his knowledge of the PE curriculum, qualifications, and roles in various sports coaching such as Gaelic Football, Hurling, and soccer, and his experience of teaching PE to primary-aged children throughout his teaching career. Also, he attempted to deliver effective PE lessons through the platform for Google Classroom (GC) and other applications during school lockdown and felt that they didn't reach the levels that were achieved while teaching in person in the school setting.

According to Fahey et al. (2005), sports and physical activity play a vital social role in Ireland. Like a lot of aspects of society during the pandemic, however, sport was side-lined, and children had very few outlets to maintain sporting or exercise interests. In the first author's school, the PE policy states that all teachers must adequately provide for the physical, social, emotional, and intellectual development of the child (St Etchen's NS PE Policy, 2022). Like all schools, the child's well-being is at the centre of all that takes place. This includes both physical and mental well-being.

GC is an online platform designed for the field of education. According to Shaharanee et al. (2016), GC has the potential for teaching and learning because of its unique built-in functions that offer pedagogical, social, and technological affordances. Upon the sudden arrival of the COVID-19 pandemic and school closures, online educational platforms such as Edmodo, Seesaw, and GC were adopted. GC was the most popular option and heavily relied upon to deliver distance learning for all subjects. Whilst GC has been an efficient tool for digital communication, its prominence for schools, at least prior to the pandemic, was not considered (Scanlon & Li, 2022).

In the ROI, primary school teachers were expected to deliver lessons in all 11 subjects throughout distance learning. Of all those subjects, PE was one of the most challenging to deliver due to how it is normally taught in school. Structured group lessons where children experience multiple sports, and where large amounts of resources are required. Furthermore, teachers and the teaching style they use have been associated with students' motivation and engagement in the PE settings (De Meyer et al., 2016). With teachers severely limited in how they could deploy this teaching style through distance learning the researchers thought it would be significant to investigate the perceptions of primary school teachers about the delivery of PE throughout distance learning to know how they overcome the challenges and develop the strategies for effective teaching and learning.

Aims and Objectives

The overarching aim of this study is to investigate primary school teachers' perceptions about the delivery of PE lessons through distance learning, in the ROI, during the COVID-19 pandemic. To guide this study, the following objectives were designed:

1. To investigate if teachers were skilled and equipped with the physical requirements and knowledge to utilise a distance learning approach via GC;
2. To investigate the strategies used by teachers to effectively support students during PE lessons throughout distance learning;
3. To investigate the engagement of students during PE lessons throughout distance learning;
4. To investigate senior leadership's role in ensuring appropriate PE lessons were delivered by teachers throughout distance learning.

Research Questions

To address the overall aim, the following research questions have been formulated to carry out the study:

1. Did teachers feel that they held or had been provided with the necessary skills or knowledge to educate learners via GC, and to adequately adopt distance learning?
2. What teaching strategies and ideas did the teachers use throughout distance learning to support the teaching of PE?
3. Were students actively engaged in PE lessons throughout distance learning?
4. Did teachers feel actively supported by senior leadership throughout distance learning?

REVIEW OF THE RELEVANT LITERATURE

This section reviews the existing literature relevant to this research, including the key concepts, theories, and studies concerning PE teaching and physical activity in education during distance learning, and existing gaps in knowledge to shape the purpose of this study.

Key Concepts, Theories, and Studies

The focus of this study is to identify primary school teachers' perceptions toward the teaching of PE through the medium of GC during school closures in the hope of identifying areas of concern for pupils who were subject to that teaching and learning at the time.

Immediately, upon the closure of schools around the world, a race to identify and utilise effective methods of teaching and learning began. To facilitate this teaching and learning, applications or platforms had to be used, in a lot of cases for the first time, by teachers (UNESCO, 2020).

These platforms became numerous and a vast array were used by schools across the world such as SEESAW, Edmodo, and the application which is the focus of this research project, Google Classroom (Sofi-Karim et al., 2023).

The research focused on the two school closures in the ROI, dating March to June 2020, and, Jan to Feb 2021. These are the periods that the teachers delivered distance learning and therefore the theory around the subject and data gathered focused on these exact timings. At these stages of the pandemic, a large number of countries were amid distance learning so therefore recent theory around the subject has begun to be published.

According to Goodyear et al. (2023, p. 1), 'Most children and young people (CYP) worldwide are classified as inactive because they fail to meet the World Health Organisation recommendations for physical activity', the study also indicates that before the pandemic even started inactivity was a huge concern. With this in mind inactivity was a huge concern during distance learning, and, for the most part, still is. Pavlovic et al. (2021) address a lot of similar issues mentioned by the researchers such as, how was physical activity maintained with children throughout distance learning, what resources educators used to deliver the PE curricula, and, the challenges encountered by educators throughout this period.

Of all subjects, perhaps PE was the most unsuited or marginalised to teach through the medium of online applications, and certainly, a lot of teachers would never have envisaged themselves teaching the subject this way (Centeio et al., 2021). Whatever experience a lot of teachers would have had using applications such as GC, it would have been with core subjects such as English, Maths, and in the case of the ROI, Irish. PE certainly was not prioritised to be taught using these applications and therefore with the introduction of distance learning teachers immediately encountered difficulties to overcome.

Classroom teachers were at the centre of delivering effective lessons throughout distance learning, and for the case of this study, in particular, PE lessons. However, the duty to ensure these lessons were, firstly being taught in the first place, and, secondly, being taught to an expected standard, rested with school leadership. Like all education staff, distance learning was new to the members of school leadership, and they encountered plenty of difficulties and issues during the pandemic. Fahy et al. (2020) acknowledge these issues and many more as they attempted to navigate the roles and responsibilities of these leaders such as adapting their staff, and ensuring their school performs, while simultaneously ensuring their own well-being during a very stressful and anxious period.

In addition, a study conducted by Scanlon and Li (2022) explores post-primary school teachers' perceptions about the use of Google Classroom: supporting pupils in remote and blended learning in Northern Ireland during the COVID-19 pandemic. Although the specific focus is on post-primary level teachers, the findings indicate the significance of teacher training, upskilling, and the role of leadership in implementing GC which interested the researchers and as a reference in designing a new study.

Overall, the outbreak of COVID-19 and the resulting pandemic has greatly affected education throughout the world, for the most part, maybe negatively. Delivering a vast array of subjects, 11 in the Irish curriculum, was challenging for all teachers. One of the most tested subjects was PE, due to its holistic and naturally competitive nature. The literature reviewed was expected to inform the study in evaluating the strengths and limits of PE practices during distance learning. It is hoped this study will contribute to the knowledge base in the primary PE field in relation to the impact of the COVID-19 pandemic on PE and also provide useful insights into the experiences of PE teaching and learning when distance learning is needed, as it is a popular form of education, particularly in an era of rapidly changing digital technologies.

The Significance of This Study

In summary, the review of relevant literature revealed numerous studies regarding 2nd level teachers' perceptions towards teaching PE throughout the COVID-19 pandemic and through the medium of distance learning. Kim et al. (2021) explore secondary-level teachers in the USA reporting unfavourable results regarding distance teaching. While Konukman et al. (2022) address the situation in Turkey and how their secondary teachers saw a massive gender imbalance in engagement throughout distance learning. Lastly in Spain, from reading López-Fernández et al. (2021), second-level teachers in Spain found their students showed greater levels of dedication throughout distance learning. Despite the wealth of literature from a second-level perspective, there has been little research carried out to investigate the perceptions of primary school teachers towards the teaching of PE throughout distance learning, and in particular, primary school teachers in Kinnegad, County Westmeath, the ROI. This research was proposed as it aimed to identify the teaching practice that took place concerning PE and address the research gap in knowledge in the literature. It is hoped that this study will provide the most up-to-date, unique, and invaluable insights into teachers' perceptions of how students approached and progressed in PE when distance learning was taking place. The research findings are expected to become the evidence base to recommend the most effective strategies to address any shortcomings that way have developed through distance learning and contribute to the literature locally and globally to support students in similar situations.

METHODOLOGY

This section provides the research methodology and justifies the data collection instruments utilised throughout the study, including the results of the pilot study on each instrument, addressing ethical concerns and adherence to ethical regulations.

Employed Methodology

To achieve the research aim, a Mixed-Methods Research (MMR) approach was employed. The research was designed to be conducted in St Etchen's National School (NS), Kinnegad, Co Westmeth, ROI, where the first author teaches, and 29 teachers teaching PE were invited to participate, for both quantitative and qualitative data through an online questionnaire and a face-to-face focus group consisting of 4-5 participants from those having answered the questionnaire. According to Bulsara (2014, p. 11), "The purpose of this form of research is that both qualitative and quantitative research, in combination, provide a better understanding of a research problem or issue than either research approach alone can". The questionnaire and focus group schedule used in this study are provided in the Appendices at the back of this chapter.

The instruments selected for data collection should be based on their suitability and fitness for purpose (Cohen et al., 2018). This study aims to investigate primary school teachers' perceptions about the delivery of PE lessons through distance learning, in the ROI, during the COVID-19 pandemic. As introduced in the above Introduction section, a primary school: St Etchen's National School (NS) at the ROI, and the teachers involved in primary PE using GC during distance learning were deemed most suitable for conducting this research. The research instruments – questionnaires consisting of closed-ended and open-ended questions and a focus group with open-ended questions were chosen because questionnaires are regarded as a highly valuable and dependable research tool, as noted by Cohen et al. (2018), who emphasise their cost-effectiveness, reliability, validity, and efficiency. A focus group can be defined as a "small group of individuals with similar characteristics selected from a larger population, gathered to elicit insights through moderated discussions" (Menter et al., 2011, p. 148). Much like questionnaires, focus groups serve as an immensely valuable research approach. Given the project's emphasis on understanding teacher perspectives, focus groups offer the most advantageous investigative method. Carey and Asbury (2016, p. 17) emphasise that "focus groups can provide insights into the attitudes and beliefs that underlie behaviour and offer context and perspectives that enable a more holistic understanding of experiences". Focus group discussions were also used to clarify the responses of participants, suggest amendments to the instrumentation, and allow for data triangulation (Scanlon & Li, 2022). As mentioned in the above Introduction section, a semi-structured interview designed with members of the SLT was not able to be carried out as envisaged for some reasons, this proved not to impact the data obtainment as the teachers' responses covered the role of leadership in the context.

The detailed instruments were piloted before implementation with 8 teachers to test the questionnaire and 4 to test the focus group schedule through the medium of Zoom, none of the pilot participants were from the target group. All of them were from a school in the United Arab Emirates where the 1st author worked in the past, but with similar PE teaching backgrounds and experiences, to ascertain comprehension and avoid bias, following Bell's (2005) recommendations. Data from the pilot tests were expected to identify potential problem areas and deficiencies in the research instruments prior to implementation during the full study, to inform necessary changes, and adjustments, enhancing data quality. One of the main advantages of a pilot study was that it gave an advanced warning about where the main research project could fail, where research protocols were not followed, and whether proposed methods or instruments were inappropriate or too complicated (Teijlingen & Hundley, 2001). Put simply, as recommended by De Vaus (1993), not taking the risk, pilot test first. The results of the pilot study proved positive with the focus group suggesting no further action required; the test of the questionnaire suggested only a couple of minor changes such as the option added to two questions to allow for expanded and more detailed answers, the question on teaching methods and difficulty in employing them over GC were changed to allow teachers these options.

In this study, the quantitative data were gathered and analysed through Google Forms which offered an automatic quantitative analysis of the results. The qualitative responses were collated and treated thematically by following the five-step process outlined by LeCompte (2000): Tidying up; Finding items; Creating stable sets of items; Creating patterns and Assembling structures, which is similar to Braun and Clarke's (2006) six-phase approach. One point should be made clear that the researchers had initially proposed the use of NVivo software to support the process of thematic analysis, but later thematic analysis was conducted manually as there was no need for its use due to the smaller size of the data which looked quicker to identify patterns in meaning across the data to derive themes through data coding.

Ethical Considerations

This study had been approved by the School of Education Ethics Filter Committee at Ulster University, UK prior to its implementation. The ethical considerations pervaded the whole process of research (Cohen et al., 2007). The researchers acted in compliance with Ulster University's General Data Protection Regulation (GDPR) and strictly adhered to the ethical research guidelines throughout. When inviting the participants and collecting the data, each participant received a participant information sheet (PIS) and completed a consent form. One example is worth mentioning, the researchers explicitly stated the voluntary nature of research participation stating that participants have the right to withdraw participation at any time and without the need to provide a reason. As discussed in the aforementioned areas, the researchers initially designed and intended to carry out a semi-structured interview with the principal and deputy principal at the school about their views, thoughts, and ideas about implementing GC during distance learning, but later they declined, and the researchers respected their decision. This will be discussed later in this chapter where acknowledging the limitations of the study, although this did not affect achieving the research aims.

RESULTS

This section presents the results of each research instrument employed in this study, with reference to the 4 objectives posed in the above INTRODUCTION section. It deals with the responses which have been collected from the sources stipulated below:

- teacher questionnaires
- focus groups with teachers

The findings are summarised and presented in relation to each of the 4 research questions formulated based on the 4 objectives respectively.

Results of the Teacher Questionnaire

The purpose of the questionnaire was to understand primary teachers' perceptions of their delivery of PE lessons by leveraging GC during COVID-19. Google Forms was the platform used to facilitate the 22 responses received from the 29 invited participants.

This form, containing a full list of questions presented to the participants, can be viewed in Appendix 1. Google Forms offered an automatic quantitative analysis of the results (see Appendix 2). The qualitative responses received from the teacher questionnaire were treated thematically and integrated into the overall results through focus group discussions to develop a more in-depth understanding of teachers' perceptions. The quantitative findings of the questionnaire have been categorised into 5 parts and displayed in 5 different tables which can be viewed as Tables, 1, 2, 3, 4, and 5. The following key points have been deduced from the responses in each table.

Table 1. Year groups of teachers during distance learning

Findings
1. 22% of teachers taught in learning support at the time. 2. The next largest groupings were at 13.6%, and they were the senior infants, third, fifth and sixth class teachers. 3. All main stream year groups are represented in the data. 4. No teachers are represented from the preschool autistic unit. 5. All teachers surveyed were working staff at the time.

- All teachers that partook in the survey were teaching during distance learning (not absent due to maternity or illness etc.), therefore the data collected is extremely applicable.
- The only classes in the school not to deliver distance learning content were the preschool classes. No preschool teachers took the survey so again the data is applicable.
- The majority of teachers surveyed were in learning support, tending to the needs of individual children who require extra support in a range of subjects. Therefore, their delivery of all lessons (including PE) is very individualised.
- The remainder of the mainstream classes have an even spread of teachers, once again making the data for this project applicable.

Table 2. Teacher proficiency pre-Covid-19

Findings
1. 40.9% of teachers had never utilised GC before the introduction of distance learning. 2. Exactly 50% of teachers said they were either not proficient at all or not very proficient in the use of GC prior to the introduction of distance learning. 3. While only 4.5% (1 teacher) stated that they were extremely proficient in the use of GC prior to distance learning. 4. 40.9% of teacher had never utilised a distance learning platform similar to GC prior to the introduction of distance learning. 5. 68.2% had never undertaken any PD to assist them with using GC prior to Distance learning.

- The staff of St Etchen's NS were underprepared in the use of GC or any distance learning application before the outbreak of the COVID-19 pandemic.
- While there was no emphasis or immediate demand to utilise GC, such as a pandemic, no distance learning application was being pushed into usage in the school before distance learning.
- Teachers did not see the need to upskill in the usage of distance learning applications, judging by the choice of Professional Development (PD) courses.

Table 3. Teaching PE during distance learning

Findings
1. 40.9% of teacher taught PE more than twice a week during distance learning.
2. Only 4.5% (1 teacher) stated that they never taught PE.
3. 31.8% stuck with the suggested allocated time in the curriculum of one PE session a week.
4. Skill or activity challenges, daily walks or runs, and self-made obstacle courses formed the basis of a lot of the PE lessons from teachers.
5. These were often modelled using videos teachers found online, and occasionally, videos they created themselves.
6. Teachers found these resources easy, for the most part, to employ using GC.

- PE was delivered consistently by the vast majority of teachers throughout distance learning. However, these lessons did not have a consistent approach in how they were delivered with a lot of varying methods and ideas.
- Teachers did not struggle or find GC difficult when posting or displaying these lessons. However, some did state that the application itself is not best suited for interaction.

Table 4. Student engagement with PE lessons during COVID-19

Findings
1. 52.4% of teachers felt their class adequately engaged with PE lessons during distance learning.
2. No teachers felt that none of the class members engaged during distance learning.
3. 86.4% of teachers believed there was no difference in engagement between the males and females in their class.

- Engagement with PE lessons appears to be for the most part average and in some cases very good during distance learning.
- No teachers felt they experienced poor engagement at the time.
- In the vast majority of cases, teachers believe engagement was equal among girls and boys.

Table 5. Support from senior school leadership

Findings
1. 63.6% of teachers experienced no check in or enquiry from school leadership about delivery of PE lessons. 2. 59.1% stated that no PD was offered to assist with the delivery of lessons during distance learning. 3. 18.2% stated that they were offered PD to assist with the usage of GC. 4. A majority of teachers stated that greater importance was placed on core subjects such as English, Irish and Maths.

- Senior school leadership did not appear to be diligent enough regarding the delivery of PE lessons at the time.
- PD was offered to some teachers and not to others, perhaps suggesting that teachers who enquired about it were offered it and the remaining were not.
- Core subjects were prioritised throughout distance learning, with several teachers stating that PE was seen as a 'bonus'.

Results of Focus Group

The purpose of the focus group was to clarify the results of the questionnaire for triangulation, from the viewpoints of 4 teachers who completed the initial questionnaire, to gain in-depth insights into the perceptions of the primary PE teachers during COVID-19. The focus group schedule is displayed in Appendix 3. The responses in terms of qualitative data were treated thematically relating to the 4 research objectives, similar to the themes of the quantitative data from the questionnaire. The analysis of the data is summarised and presented in 4 tables: Tables 6, 7, 8, and 9. The following tables contain the key points that have been deduced from the participants' direct statements in the face-to-face communication.

Table 6. Teacher ability to utilise GC prior to distance learning

Findings
1. Teachers stated that GC had been introduced to the school several years beforehand but there had been no mandatory insistence to use it by teachers. 2. A junior end teacher stated that it was perceived to be a senior end application. 3. One of the senior teachers detailed how he used it as a tool to upload science, history, and geography projects but not to issue homework or any form of distance learning. 4. All teachers agreed that it was something students did not utilise outside of school hours or at home. 5. One PD workshop had taken place with a principal from another school coming in for a training day. 6. Some of the focus groups had used other distance learning applications such as Edmodo and SEESAW, but again this was casual usage and not embedded in their classrooms.

- Although GC has been introduced to St Etchen's NS the vast majority of staff had either not used it, or, had not used it to its full potential.
- There appeared to be a perception in the school that distance learning applications were only for the older classes.
- St Etchen's NS had undertaken a PD Day on the use of GC but no follow-up or expectation to use it in classrooms followed this.
- Any application usage in the school appears to be undertaken under the mercy of individual teachers and not as a whole school directive.

Table 7. Strategies used to support pe during distance learning

Findings
1. All teachers agreed they posted a lot of physical activity challenges as a means of PE.
2. They also agreed that the fast posting of videos and links was effective at keeping their students active at short notice.
3. Students participated more when the teacher recorded or linked themselves performing the activities, instead of YouTube links or others.
4. Senior school teachers argued that GC is not ideal for facilitating feedback from students and that often the student wished to see each other's videos rather than the teachers, akin to SEESAW.
5. With this in mind, they all agreed GC is not best suited to promote or encourage participation.

- GC as an application is not ideal for promoting discussion and participation among students.
- A personal touch from the teacher facilitated more learning than generic links or uploads.
- It is however structured to facilitate fast posting of ideas and content.
- Uploaded videos and links were the main method of encouraging physical activity among students.

Table 8. Student engagement during distance learning

Findings
1. A middle-class teacher states that it was often hard to judge engagement due to the lack of interaction on GC.
2. An older class teacher stated that participation was not compulsory or that students were rarely followed up on if not participating.
3. A lot of PE participation came down to the children that wanted or wished for it. Those that didn't want it had the option to avoid it.
4. All teachers agreed that they saw no difference between male and female participation levels.

- Teachers in St Etchen's did not strictly enforce participation and rarely followed up on a lack of participation from students.

- Similar to PE lessons in a school setting, sport-enthusiastic children often desired and participated keenly in the PE lessons. Also similar to a school setting, the uninterested children tended to miss out on physical activity.
- Like the quantitative data, teachers did not notice any difference in the participation levels of male and female students.

Table 9. Senior leadership role throughout distance learning

Findings
1. All teachers agreed that there was an emphasis on the core subjects throughout distance learning with little or no inquiries made regarding subjects such as PE, art, and music. 2. One teacher stated that she received an inquiry from senior leadership regarding the subject of PE, at the behest of a parent (the parent wanted to see more PE lessons on the GC page). 3. All teachers also stated that they never had an offer of PD development in the use of GC or any other areas throughout distance learning. 4. One teacher stated that her year partner did ask for PD in GC and received it via Google Meets from another principal proficient in its usage.

- Similar to the quantitative data, it is clear senior leadership clearly emphasised the core subjects of English, Irish and, Maths.
- Senior leadership appears to have only enquired about the teaching of PE when dealing with other issues or agendas.
- PD around GC appears to have been offered to teachers that requested it.

Overall, the methodology designed to gather the data for this research project proved a success, through effective employment and utilisation of research instruments, the aims and objectives of this study have been achieved.

FINDINGS, CONCLUSION, AND RECOMMENDATIONS

Following up on the discussion of results, this section focuses on the key findings by referring to each of the 4 research questions as formulated to guide the research, to conclude this study with recommendations, and limitations and implications will also be included.

Findings in Relation to Research Question One

- Do teachers feel that they hold or have been provided with the necessary skills or knowledge to educate learners via GC, to adequately adopt distance learning?

Both the questionnaire and focus group provided a vast amount of relevant data to help answer this question. Question three of the questionnaire informed the researcher that exactly 50% of the teachers surveyed did not feel in any way proficient using GC. Another 31.8% answered that they were somewhat proficient in its usage. Even working on the basis that similar application skills are transferable, for example, if a teacher had used SEESAW or Edmodo previously, perhaps they were proficient with GC, 40.9% of teachers stated that they had never used any form of distance learning application before COVID-19.

The focus group reinforced these statistics with the teachers stating that even when they did use GC, it was used in a remote or distance learning capacity, but rather as a learning tool within the classroom. Winter et al. (2021), reinforce a similar lack of readiness in their article when describing teachers being at the 'unaware stage' and 'basic stage', when using ICT applications for distance learning. This point is also referenced in the UNESCO (2020) report, that teachers were often using these applications for the first time to try and teach remotely.

The results of this study have echoed the suggestions made by Scanlon and Li (2022), regarding the requirement of teacher training and upskilling.

Findings in Relation to Research Question Two

- What teaching strategies and ideas did you use throughout distance learning to support the teaching of PE?

Through the use of the questionnaire and a focus group, a lot of quantitative data assisted in answering this question. Numerous strategies were mentioned between the two methods, with activity links and uploaded videos, being the two most popular. Skill and activity challenges by celebrities and athletes also formed a considerable amount of content. Although useful from an encouragement perspective, the researchers fail to see how this was teaching or assisting the children to learn in a meaningful, structured way. Filiz and Konukman (2020, p. 48), produce very similar content to what the researchers discovered when they state 'Different teachers used different forms such as online classes with live streaming, recorded videos, tasks for students, projects or just links to follow'. They also mention how this was the norm in both North America and Europe, so much of what is considered the Western World.

The findings of this study would very much consolidate the research that has preceded it when it comes to teaching methods and strategies among primary school teachers delivering PE lessons during distance learning. The different resources used to support PE during distance learning from the responses are summarised in Figure 1 Word Cloud which can be viewed in Appendix 2.

Findings in Relation to Research Question Three

- Were students actively engaged in PE lessons throughout distance learning?

In answering the third research question the researchers mostly relied on the quantitative data as it was extremely conclusive. The researchers did address the topic with the focus group and they reinforced the conclusive data received in the questionnaire. 52.4% of teachers felt their students were engaged during PE lessons, while 23.8% felt they were actively engaged and 9.5% felt they were very engaged. This data shows that the vast majority of children were engaged with the PE lessons throughout distance learning in St Etchen's NS.

Coulter et al. (2023) state that they recorded similar levels of engagement when surveying the use of the 'PE at Home' programmes which were several activity videos run through Facebook and YouTube. They also mention how teachers utilised these 'PE at Home' videos with their classes, just as the teachers in the focus group had mentioned finding online links, videos, and resources to teach PE throughout distance learning.

The findings of this question have been validated through supporting literature where both imply that the students were engaged with and in PE lessons during distance learning.

Findings in Relation to Research Question Four

- Did teachers feel actively supported by senior leadership throughout distance learning?

This was a question that was primarily answered through teacher discussions in the focus group. The four teachers could chat, contrast, and compare their experiences of senior leadership throughout distance learning and COVID-19 in its entirety. All teachers agreed that senior leadership showed little to no interest in the delivery of PE lessons at the time. While also stating that they stressed the importance of the core subjects of English, Irish, and Maths to be delivered proficiently. On a larger scale of teaching all subjects through the medium of GC, they all stated that no PD was provided in an attempt to make them more proficient and improve their ability to teach at the time.

Fahy et al. (2020) acknowledge this in their study when they discuss the burdening workload experienced by leadership, and in particular principals, and how certain tasks and responsibilities got left behind.

In summary, the methodology designed to gather the data for this research project proved a success, all the questions posed were fully answered as evidence to substantiate the key findings and lead to the recommendations.

Summary of Key Findings

- Although some teachers had a certain amount of proficiency and readiness using GC, the vast majority did not;
- Teachers endeavoured to come up with ideas and strategies to teach PE at the time, however, were generally limited to some key methods;
- The levels of engagement with students during PE lessons experienced by teachers was adequate;
- A lack of engagement and monitoring by senior leadership and the availability of Professional Development (PD) meant that the delivery of PE lessons was not strictly enforced and that many teachers remained unskilled in using GC throughout distance learning.

CONCLUSION AND RECOMMENDATIONS

This study investigated the perceptions of primary school teachers about the delivery of PE lessons through Distance learning, during the COVID-19 pandemic. Through the successful employment of research instruments, the overall aim and objectives of this study have been achieved. The responses from the participants' lived PE teaching experiences have substantiated the challenges they faced and strategies they developed, suggesting the need for improvement. The main findings guide the following recommendations, hoping to be of help in enhancing primary PE teaching and learning at present and in the future locally and globally while distance learning is used:

- Leaders should consider the views, thoughts, and ideas from this study and how could translate them into practical policy;
- Ensure that all staff are trained in the use of GC, or any other distance learning application utilised;
- Make the most use of experiences gained during the pandemic, constantly upskill the PE team, and enhance diversity by leveraging more digital technologies to promote the success of teaching and learning;
- Provide PE professional development for ideas and strategies that could be employed or utilised upon the event of the reintroduction of distance learning;

- Bring in or incorporate an attendance or check-in system for pupils while learning through distance learning;
- Senior leadership to ensure teaching timetables are all collected from teachers when distance learning is employed, similar to in-school timetables;
- Senior leadership to regularly check and engage with teachers to ensure ICT and GC skills are proficient to deliver lessons using this medium.

Limitations

As in any other academic research studies, it is important to acknowledge the limitations of the current research. First, the investigation had a small sample with only 22 participants and was limited to one primary school in the area of County Westmeath, the ROI, this study would benefit from a larger sample, but as stated in the Section of Background Information and Rationale, this selected school is the largest primary school in that area and with sufficient data to seek, to be in more detail, this sample size proved effective as these 22 participants at the school were full-time PE teachers and their timetables and experiences proved more favourable to respond the questionnaire, their answers to the questions were broadly reflective of the situations in the ROI; secondly, this sample did not include a higher level, e.g. secondary schools, as the specific focus was on the primary PE teachers as set out, so leaving the study of secondary level PE to the future; thirdly, as discussed in the aforementioned sections, the lack of interviews with senior school leaders about the role of leadership in the implementation of GC during distance learning concerning delivery of PE lessons seems a bit disappointing, but the substantial data collected from the questionnaire and the focus group with the teachers supported the findings concerning this respect and also substantiate the need of leaders' full attention to the PE and support.

Implications

As in any other academic studies, the implications should be explored for further relevant research. In this chapter, the impact of this research on understanding primary PE teachers' lived experiences in distance learning through their perceptions has been signified by way of offering evidence-informed findings and a list of concrete recommendations, hopefully for teachers, school leaders, innovators, educators, and policymakers to consider, to benefit all the stakeholders including parents and children about children's physical and mental well-being. This study suggests a need for further research on some different aspects such as conducting questionnaires or interviews with members of the SLT, administrators, parents, and children to obtain richer and more direct information; investigating the relationship between teacher effectiveness and student outcomes for PE teaching and learning, e.g. by a comparative study at pre-pandemic, during the pandemic and post-pandemic periods, in different modes such as face-to-face, online, or hybrid activities; exploring the perceived self-efficacy of the teachers and students, to understand those who have a resilient sense of self-efficacy in overcoming obstacles and experiencing success, through effort and perseverance, during the post-pandemic era.

Overall, the researchers believe that the studies published in this book were undertaken locally, but the information, findings, and recommendations presented in the book can be applied globally in the educational field at the current and in the future.

The researchers would like to conclude this chapter with the following quotes:

"Adaptability to change is itself a hallmark of successful education." - Peter Hilton (as cited in Gullberg, 1997, p. 17).

"Our greatest hopes could become reality in the future. With the technology at our disposal, the possibilities are unbounded." - Stephen Hawking (The Guardian, 2018).

REFERENCES

Bell, J. (2005). *Doing your research project: A guide for first-time researchers.* McGraw-Hill International.

Braun, V., & Clarke, V. (2006). Using thematic analysis in psychology. *Qualitative Research in Psychology*, *3*(2), 77–101. doi:10.1191/1478088706qp063oa

Bulsara, C. (2014). *Using a Mixed Methods Approach to Enhance and Validate Your Research.* ND. https://www.nd.edu.au/downloads/research/ihrr/using_mixed_methods_approach_to_enhance_and_validate_your_research.pdf

Carey, J. W., & Asbury, J. (2016). *Focus Group Research.* Routledge. doi:10.4324/9781315428376

Centeio, E., Mercier, K., Garn, A., Erwin, H., Marttinen, R., & Foley, J. (2021). The success and struggles of physical education teachers while teaching online during the COVID-19 pandemic. *Journal of Teaching in Physical Education*, *40*(4), 667–673. doi:10.1123/jtpe.2020-0295

Cohen, L., Manion, L., & Morrison, K. (2007). *Research Methods in Education* (6th ed.). Routledge. doi:10.4324/9780203029053

Cohen, L., Manion, L., & Morrison, K. (2018). *Research methods in education* (8th ed.). Routledge.

Coulter, M., Britton, Ú., MacNamara, Á., Manninen, M., McGrane, B., & Belton, S. (2023). PE at Home: Keeping the 'E'in PE while home-schooling during a pandemic. *Physical Education and Sport Pedagogy*, *28*(2), 183–195. doi:10.1080/17408989.2021.1963425

De Meyer, J., Soenens, B., Vansteenkiste, M., Aelterman, N., Van Petegem, S., & Haerens, L. (2016). Do Students with Different Motives for Physical Education Respond Differently to Autonomy-Supportive and Controlling Teaching? *Psychology of Sport and Exercise*, *22*, 72–82. doi:10.1016/j.psychsport.2015.06.001

Fahey, T., Delaney, L., & Gannon, B. (2005). *School children and sport in Ireland.* ESRI.

Fahy, A., Murphy, C., Fu, N., & Nguyen, T. (2020). *Irish Primary School Leadership During COVID-19. Principals' Study Report 2020.* Dublin: Trinity College Dublin. http://www.tara.tcd.ie/handle/2262/92883

Filiz, B., & Konukman, F. (2020). Teaching Strategies for Physical Education during the COVID-19 Pandemic. *Journal of Physical Education, Recreation & Dance*, *91*(9), 48–50. doi:10.1080/07303084.2020.1816099

Goodyear, V. A., Skinner, B., McKeever, J., & Griffiths, M. (2023). The influence of online physical activity interventions on children and young people's engagement with physical activity: A systematic review. *Physical Education and Sport Pedagogy*, *28*(1), 94–108. doi:10.1080/17408989.2021.1953459

Gullberg, J. (1997). *Mathematics: From the Birth of Numbers*. W. W. Norton and Company.

Kim, M., Yu, H., Park, C. W., Ha, T., & Baek, J. H. (2021). Physical education teachers' online teaching experiences and perceptions during the COVID-19 pandemic. *Journal of Physical Education and Sport*, *21*, 2049–2056.

Konukman, F., Filiz, B., & Ünlü, H. (2022). Teachers' perceptions of teaching physical education using online learning during the COVID-19: A quantitative study in Turkey. *PLoS One*, *17*(6), e0269377. doi:10.1371/journal.pone.0269377 PMID:35731742

LeCompte, M. D. (2000). Analyzing qualitative data. *Theory into Practice*, *39*(3), 146–154. doi:10.1207/s15430421tip3903_5

López-Fernández, I., Burgueño, R., & Gil-Espinosa, F. J. (2021). High school physical education teachers' perceptions of blended learning one year after the onset of the COVID-19 pandemic. *International Journal of Environmental Research and Public Health, 18*(21), 11146. doi:10.3390/ijerph182111146 PMID:34769673

Masalimova, A. R., Khvatova, M. A., Chikileva, L. S., Zvyagintseva, E. P., Stepanova, V. V., & Melnik, M. V. (2022). Distance Learning in Higher Education During COVID-19. *Frontiers in Education, 7*, 822958. Advance online publication. doi:10.3389/feduc.2022.822958

Menter, I., Elliot, D., Hulme, M., Lewin, J., & Lowden, K. (2011). *A Guide to Practitioner Research in Education.* SAGE. doi:10.4135/9781473957770

Pavlovic, A., DeFina, L. F., Natale, B. L., Thiele, S. E., Walker, T. J., Craig, D. W., Vint, G. R., Leonard, D., Haskell, W. L., & Kohl, H. W. (2021). Keeping children healthy during and after COVID-19 pandemic: Meeting youth physical activity needs. *BMC Public Health, 21*(1), 1–8. doi:10.1186/s12889-021-10545-x PMID:33706744

Scanlon, J., & Li, X. (2022). An Exploration Into Post-Primary School Teachers' Perceptions About the Use of Google Classroom: Supporting Pupils in Remote and Blended Learning in Northern Ireland During the COVID-19 Pandemic. *Handbook of Research on Teacher and Student Perspectives on the Digital Turn in Education,* 420-452. https://www.igi-global.com/book/teacher-student-perspectives-digital-turn/290031 DOI: doi:10.4018/978-1-6684-4446-7.ch019

Sofi-Karim, M., Bali, A. O., & Rached, K. (2023). Online education via media platforms and applications as an innovative teaching method. *Education and Information Technologies, 28*(1), 507–523. doi:10.1007/s10639-022-11188-0 PMID:35791317

United Nations Educational, Scientific, and Cultural Organization (UNESCO). (2020). COVID-19 educational disruption and response. https://en.unesco.org/COVID19/educationresponse

Winter, E., Costello, A., O'Brien, M., & Hickey, G. (2021). Teachers' use of technology and the impact of COVID-19. *Irish Educational Studies, 40*(2), 235–246. doi:10.1080/03323315.2021.1916559

APPENDIX ONE: TEACHER QUESTIONNAIRE DISTRIBUTED VIA GOOGLE FORMS

Questionnaire

Project Title: An Investigation into Primary School Teachers' Perceptions about the Delivery of Physical Education (PE) Lessons through Distance Learning, in the Republic of Ireland, during the COVID-19 Pandemic

Researcher: Conn O'Hanlon

Initial Question:

What is your class group or setting?

Section 1: To investigate if teachers were skilled and equipped with the physical requirements and knowledge to utilise a distance learning approach via Google Classroom.

Q1: Prior to Covid 19 and the introduction of Distance learning had you ever used or utilised Google Classroom before?

Answers: **Yes No**

Q2: If you had used it prior the introduction of distance learning, how proficient would you say you were at using it?

Answers: **I hadn't used it 1 not very proficient** continued up to **5 extremely proficient**

Q3: Had you used any other distance learning application prior to distance learning such as SEESAW, Edmodo etc?

Answer: **Please list the application**

Q4: Did you engage in any professional development since the beginning of the Covid 19 pandemic to assist you with using Google Classroom. If yes, which course or programme?

Answer: **Yes or No** and **name of course of programme**

Section 2: To investigate the strategies used by teachers to effectively support students during PE lesson during distance learning.

Q1: How frequently did you teach PE or encourage physical activity with your class or designated children during distance learning?

Answer: **Teacher lists time frame in which the taught PE to their class**

Q2: When teaching PE our encouraging physical activity during distance learning, what strategies did you use? For example, uploaded videos modelling activity, active challenges, skill challenges etc

Answer: **Teacher lists strategies used to teach PE during distance learning.**

Q3: Where these strategies easy or difficult to employ using Google Classroom? Why?

Answer: Yes or NO Teacher explains why easy or difficult to employ

Section 3: To investigate the engagement of students during PE lessons throughout distance learning.

Q1: How on a scale 1-5, 1 being not engaged at all, 5 been extremely engaged, how engaged were the children you taught with the PE lessons delivered.

Answer: **Scale 1-5**

Q2: Did you notice a difference in engagement between male and female student and if yes, which engaged more?

Answer: **Yes or No and which engaged more with the PE lessons.**

Q3: If there was an imbalance between male and female students, why do you feel this was?

Answer: **Teacher explain why there might have been an imbalance.**

Section 4: To investigate senior leadership's role in ensuring appropriate PE lessons were delivered by teachers throughout distance learning.

Q1: Did school leadership check or enquire if PE lesson were being delivered throughout your distance learning experience?

Answer: **Yes or no that they checked on the delivery of PE lessons during distance learning.**

Q2: Did school leadership attempt to provide any professional development courses in using or up skilling with Google Classroom throughout distance learning?

Answer: **Yes, they did provide or no they didn't.**

Q3: Would you have utilised or taken part in such courses if they had been offered?

Answer: **Yes, I would have or no I wouldn't.**

Q4: If courses were provided, what was the name of the course and did you find it assisted you with delivering PE lessons during distance learning.

Answer: **Name of courses if undertaken and whether they assisted with the delivery of PE lessons.**

APPENDIX TWO: RESULTS OF THE TEACHER QUESTIONNAIRE VIA GOOGLE FORMS

Figure 1.

What was your class group or setting during distance learning? If you moved class during distance learning please choose a class you spent the longest duration in.
22 responses

Prior to Covid 19 and the introduction of Distance learning, had you ever used or utilised Google Classroom before?
22 responses

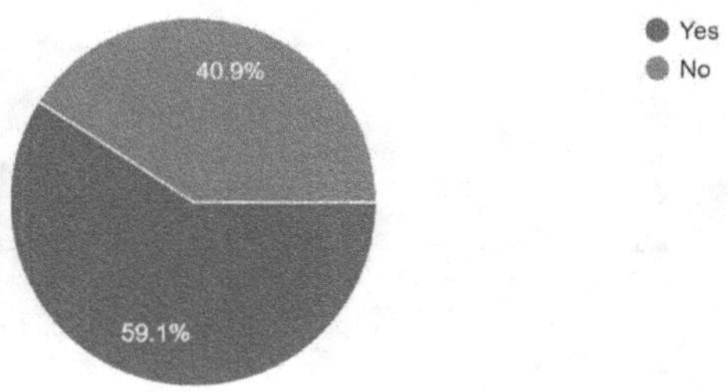

If you had used it prior to the introduction of distance learning, how proficient would you say you were at using it? 1-not proficient 5-extremely proficient
22 responses

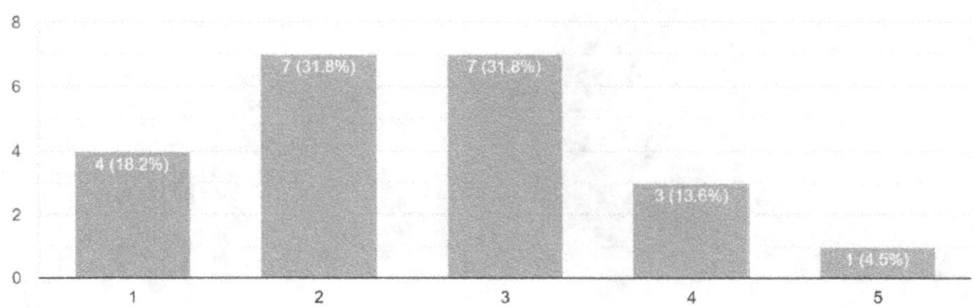

Figure 2.

Prior to the outbreak of Covid-19 had you used any other distance learning application such as SEESAW, Edmodo etc?

22 responses

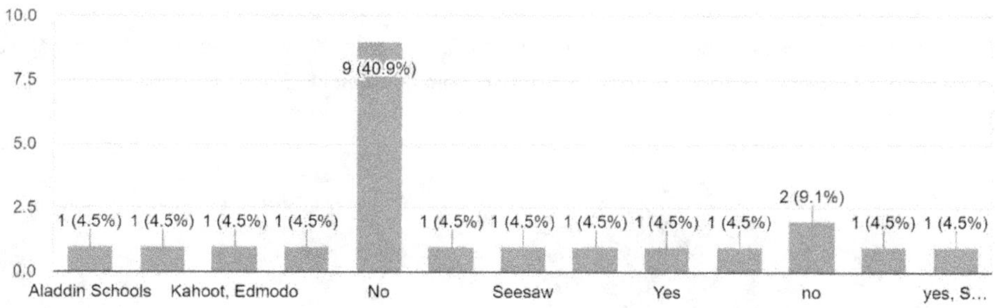

Did you engage in any professional development since the beginning of the Covid 19 pandemic to assist you with using Google Classroom. If yes, which course or programme?

22 responses

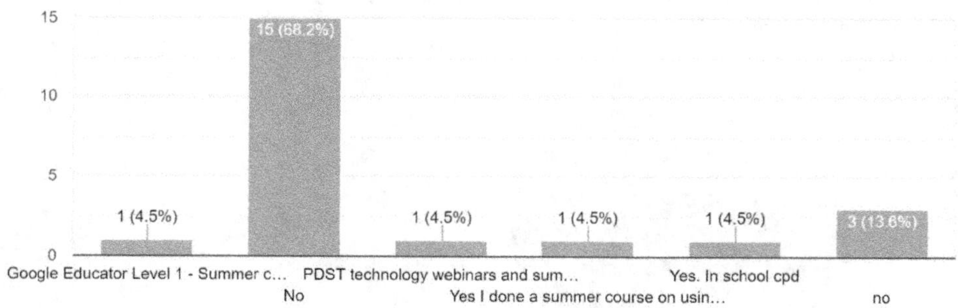

How frequently did you teach PE or encourage physical activity with your class or designated children during distance learning?

22 responses

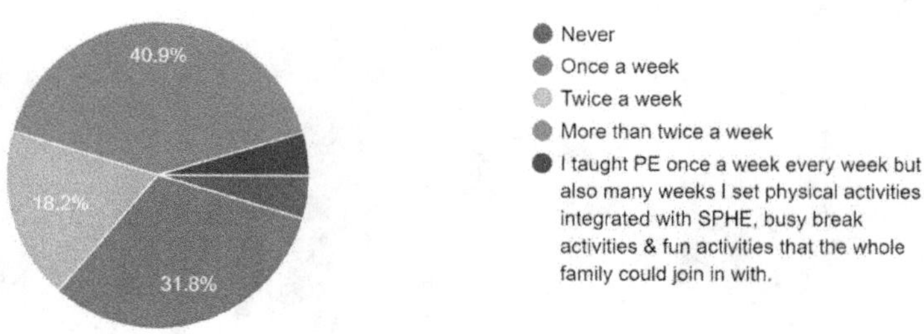

Figure 3.

What do you feel would have prompted you to deliver more regular or consistent PE lessons during distance learning?

22 responses

I encouraged my learning support groups to get outside and play/walk/cycle for their wellbeing

I was using the Aladdin app in senior infants for distance learning (was on mat leave for the second time) and so uploading videos was not option through this portal. It was predominantly used for uploading documents and pictures of work.

Online resource/videos

I encouraged physical activity daily during distance learning.

The idea that the children were more lightly sitting more at screens and in general. They were missing activities with sport's clubs that they would usually be part of as well as missing out on extra activities with friends. I also thought it would be helpful to give parents/guardians ideas of physical games/activities etc. that they could encourage their children to try instead of maybe being 'bored' and that the whole family could do together & enjoy.

Ensure children have less screen time and to keep a level of fitness and get enough exercise

If and when teaching PE or encouraging physical activity during distance learning, what strategies did you use? For example, uploaded videos modelling activity, active challenges, skill challenges etc

22 responses

Uploaded videos

Uploaded links to active challenges provided by RTE 10@10, Joe Wicks workouts, GoNoodle, Cosmic Yoga

Skill Challenges, use YouTube videos e.g. joe wicks, 10 minutes outdoor activity daily scheduled work

Sourced videos and challenges from various sources to promote skills activities, exercise, yoga, challenges, dance etc.

I uploaded videos modelling activities, I shared links to Youtube and other sites with suitable fun activities, games, dances, music to dance along to. I set different challenges and encouraged the children to share their views, successes, videos and photos trialling or completing different activities. I shared pics/videos of teacher doing some activities to encourage the kids and to join the fun.

Video links, initiatives such as busy bees, encouraging challenges amongst families/bubbles

As above- active challenges, Joe wicks videos. I had infants who love these type of activities so the uptake was great. Also youtube dancing videos, go noodle videos

Figure 4.

Did you find the strategies you used easy or difficult to employ using Google Classroom? Why?

22 responses

I kept it simple, with games that the children would really enjoy and would be enthusiastic to try.

Uploading links was the only option for the Aladdin app.

Neither easy or difficult

Activities were pitched to the level and achievable by students. Difficult to ensure that students partook in the activities.

Relatively easy

Difficult as engagement with Google classroom was mixed from different families

Very easy

N/A

Easy, readily available online

On a scale of 1-5, how engaged were the children you taught with the PE lessons?

21 responses

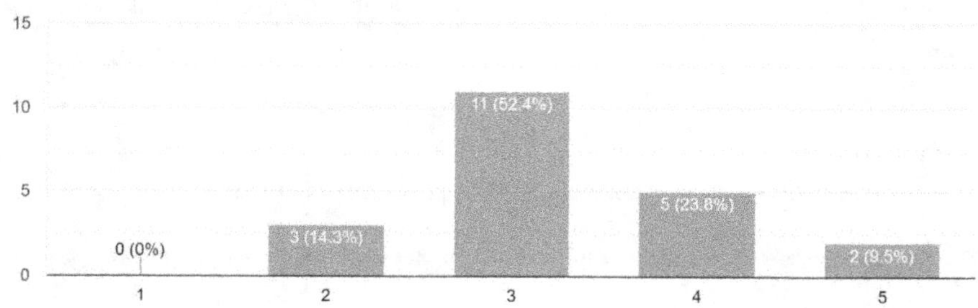

Did you notice a difference in engagement between male and female students, and if yes, who engaged more?

22 responses

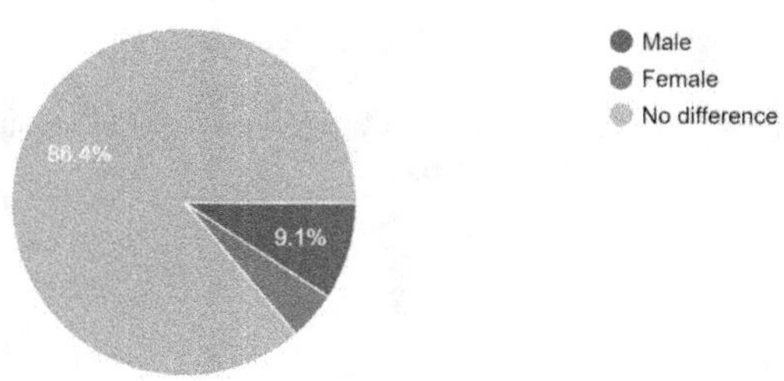

Figure 5.

If there was an imbalance between male and female students, why do you feel this was?
10 responses

N/A

I didn't notice an imbalance

n/a

N/a

I feel female students are more self conscious about their physical abilities and are they are less willing to try and get involved.

Males were outside engaging in their own forms of PE.

N/A

I felt male class members enjoyed the challenges more , espeically at the beginning of distance learning and then again in the summer when we moved outside with the videos and challenges.

Did school leadership check or enquire if PE lessons were being delivered throughout your distance learning experience?
22 responses

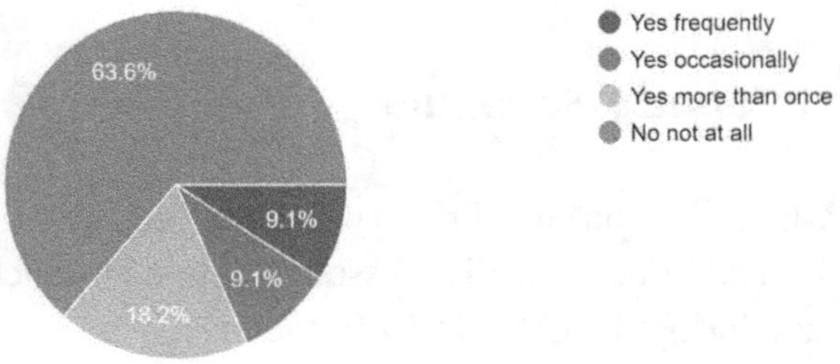

Did school leadership provide any professional development courses in using or up skilling with Google Classroom throughout distance learning?
22 responses

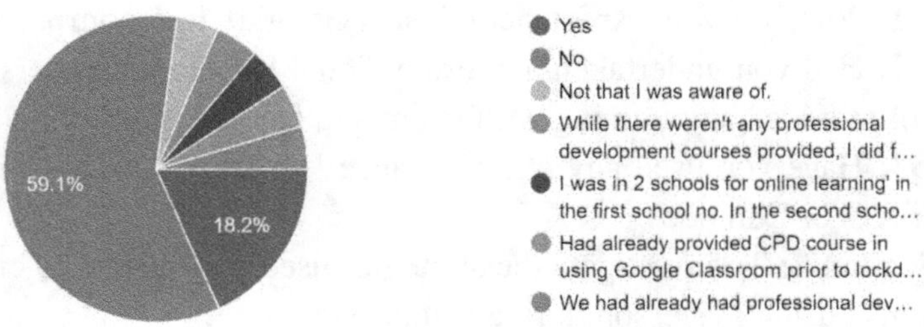

Figure 6.

Did notice a difference in perception from school leadership towards PE in comparison to other subjects, such as English, Maths and Irish?

22 responses

Yes, it was evident that there was an emphasis placed on outdoor activities for the child's wellbeing, they were encouraged to get out and enjoy some physical activities & were encouraged to take breaks during their academic tasks by doing so

Less focus or importance placed on the teaching of PE

Not noticed from leadership but I felt PE more important while distance learning inorder to get children more active and away from screens

School leadership did not mention PE or prioritise any subjects

No. I felt there was trust in my professionalism to teach all areas of the curriculum as expected when in the physical school.

Yes. English and maths were definitely regarded as more important

Yes it was more of a bonus

APPENDIX 3: FOCUS GROUP SCHEDULE

Focus Group Interview Schedule

Project Title: An Investigation into Primary School Teachers' Perceptions about the Delivery of Physical Education (PE) Lessons through Distance Learning, in the Republic of Ireland, during the COVID-19 Pandemic

Thank you for taking part in this focus group. By answering each question, you agree to participate on the above study:

Section 1: To investigate if teachers were skilled and equipped with the physical requirements and knowledge to utilise a distance learning approach via Google Classroom.

Q1: What was your experience of using Google Classroom pre distance learning?

Q2: Had you undertaken any Professional Development personally or had the school provided any training with regards to Google Classroom?

Q3: Have you used any other distance learning platforms in the past such as SEESAW or Edmodo?

Section 2: To investigate the strategies used by teachers to effectively support students during PE lesson during distance learning;

Q1: What teaching strategies did you use or explore during distance learning to deliver PE lesson?

Q2: Where these strategies difficult to employ using Google Classroom?

Q3: Which strategies would you say were most effective, and why?

Section 3: To investigate the engagement of students during PE lessons throughout distance learning.

Q1: Would you say your students were actively engaged when delivering your PE lessons?

Q2: Was there a difference in male and female engagement throughout the delivery of lesson?

Section 4: To investigate senior leadership's role in ensuring appropriate PE lessons were delivered by teachers throughout distance learning.

Q1: Did senior leadership show an interest in how PE was been delivered, in comparison to other subjects, during distance learning?

Q2: Did senior leadership attempt to provide any training on Google Classroom during distance learning?

Summary:

Any additional comments?

Please note, additional questions may be developed by the researcher following responses obtained from the Focus Group.

Thank you for taking the time to answer these questions.

Your response will be incredibly helpful.

APPENDIX FOUR:

Figure 7. Word cloud: resources used by the teachers to support PE during distance learning

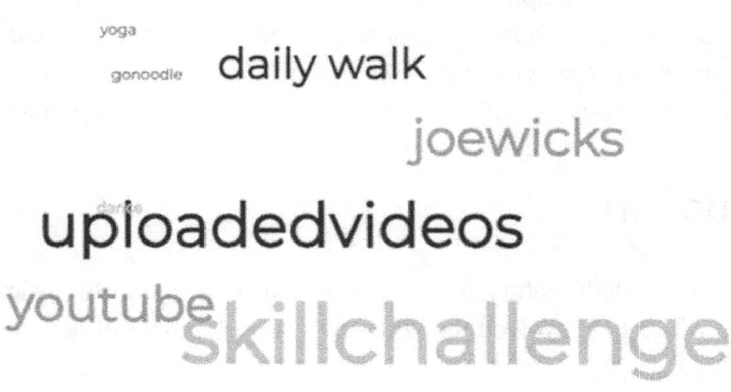

Chapter 8
The Combination of Flipped Classroom and ICTs Towards Effective Instruction in an EFL Environment

Antonio Daniel Juan Rubio
https://orcid.org/0000-0003-3416-0021
Universidad de Granada, Spain

ABSTRACT

Differentiation is one of the major challenges an EFL teacher must face. Learning preferences and styles, readiness, interests, and all the specificities of each student should have an impact on planning instruction and assessment. Innovative educational approaches and methodologies seem to have at their core two fundamental aspects: the integration of ICTs (information and communication technologies) and the acquisition of competences through cooperation. These two key aspects are strongly related to the shift from Teacher-Centred Teaching to Learner-Centred Teaching. When investigating the fields of ICTs, project-based cooperative learning, and the student-centred approach, the concept of flipped learning turned out to be recurrent. In this chapter, the authors are going to expose how flipping the class using ICTs can allow teachers to respond to the diversity of interests, cultural backgrounds, academic readiness, and learning styles in an EFL environment to move away from one-size-fits-all teaching. The authors will also raise awareness on the challenges that had to be faced when flipping the class.

INTRODUCTION

Since the mid-twentieth century, the world has been experiencing the Third Industrial Revolution, which has involved the widespread development of new technologies

DOI: 10.4018/979-8-3693-5370-7.ch008

worldwide. Information and Communication Technologies (ICTs) have had a significant impact on the way we live, work, and communicate. As pointed out by Hwang and Fu when trying to convey the increasing complexity of our globalized world: "New technologies have produced a new dynamic as the training of individuals and groups, scientific and technical advances and modes of cultural expression have been constantly evolving since the mid-twentieth century, notably in the direction of growing interdependence" (2020, p. 5).

In such a hyperconnected world, languages are an essential asset that will help students thrive in their academic, professional, and personal lives, as bonds between countries, organizations, and individuals seem to be endlessly expanding. English is one of the most frequently used languages on the Internet. The term "English as a lingua franca" is often used to convey the undeniable fact that English is the language most chosen to communicate among speakers with different first languages. According to Landeo et al. (2023), only one out of every four users of English in the world are native speakers of the language.

Consequently, teaching English as a foreign language not only offers the knowledge of a new language and culture to our students, but also gives them a crucial tool to interact with the world and to have access to lifelong learning thanks to a higher degree of autonomy. As a global language, English is indispensable for engaging in a constant personal learning process. It is therefore our responsibility as educators to provide students with the basis for learning to learn and to foster motivation to help them acquire goal-directed behaviour that will be vital for their self-development throughout life.

The purposeful use of new technologies and the acquisition of English seem to be a perfect combination to prepare our students to confront the challenges of an uncertain future. Recently, the great disruption unleashed by the COVID-19 pandemic has highlighted the need to re-evaluate the role of educational centres and teachers, and thereby the different teaching approaches and methodologies related to second language acquisition in specific environments, according to Mendoza and Martos (2021).

Considering the knowledge acquired, we can confirm that innovative educational approaches and methodologies have at their core two fundamental aspects: the integration of ICTs and the acquisition of competences through cooperation. These two key aspects are strongly related to the shift from teacher-centred teaching to the learner-centred teaching, which has its roots in the well- acknowledged and thoroughly researched approach developed by the American psychologist Carl Rogers. When investigating the three fields previously mentioned, ICTs, project-based cooperative learning, and the student-centred approach, two didactic concepts turned out to be recurrent: flipped learning and differentiated instruction (Qader and Arslan, 2019).

The challenge as a 21st century educator is to reap the benefits that ICTs combined with flipped learning could bring to each of the students in terms of motivation, involvement, flexibility, and, more importantly, individualization. In our opinion, excellence in education is achieved when an educator manages to tailor instruction to meet individual student's needs. We will then explore how flipping the class using ICTs can allow teachers to respond to the diversity of interests, cultural backgrounds, academic readiness, and learning styles to move away from one-size-fits-all teaching.

LITERATURE REVIEW

The Flipped Classroom

The methodological proposal that we develop adopts, as a frame of reference, the pedagogical principles characteristic of the flipped classroom model in which certain learning processes that facilitate and demand more autonomous work from the student are transferred outside the classroom. In this way, time is freed up to turn the classroom into a dynamic and interactive learning environment in which the teacher becomes the necessary facilitator and guide for students. Awidi and Paynter (2019) reported the impact of a flipped classroom approach of biology students using pre-recorded lectures, online quizzes, and in-class group activities.

The most inspiring and innovative approach we have become acquainted with is the flipped classroom approach. This innovative approach played a central role as we wanted to put it into practice to become aware of its advantages and drawbacks. Within the general framework of the flipped classroom approach, we also used the task-based approach because students had to complete a task at the end of the course (Das et al., 2019).

The flipped classroom is a blended learning modality that facilitates student participation both inside and outside the classroom. The use of this pedagogical model is increasing in schools as teachers seek to innovate the educational process with the support of technological tools and educational web platforms (Barreto et al., 2021). In fact, the flipped classroom replaces the activities conducted in the classroom with the elaboration of individual and collaborative tasks at home; therefore, this pedagogical model allows the creation of educational spaces that increase the motivation of students during the teaching-learning process (Buil et al., 2019).

Before the face-to-face session, students consult multimedia resources from anywhere while, in the classroom, teachers organise creative individual and collaborative activities that facilitate the active role of students. Teachers can innovate school activities inside and outside the classroom and organise new virtual educational spaces through the flipped classroom (Hsiao et al., 2021).

At the beginning of the face-to-face session, the resolution of doubts improved the academic performance. Moreover, students play a leading role in the educational process because of collaborative classroom activities. The flipped classroom promotes the use of technological tools, educational software, and web applications to facilitate the learning process and develop students' competencies (Sosa et al., 2021).

In the 21st century, the flipped classroom has radically changed the roles of participants in the educational process during the organisation and implementation of school activities. For example, teachers are looking for new pedagogical models that facilitate the assimilation of knowledge and development of competencies in students (Moreno et al., 2021). The flipped classroom with the support of new technologies improved teaching-learning conditions, as teachers use pedagogical models and new technologies in the educational field to improve the learning process according to Shahnama et al. (2021).

Amiryousefi (2019) proposed that flipped classroom activities include conducting online discussion forums and quizzes before face-to-face sessions, and collaboratively developing assignments after face-to-face sessions to facilitate the assimilation of knowledge and develop students' competencies.

Many scholars have mentioned the ineffectiveness of teacher-centred lessons and lectures in higher education. In traditional learning environments, the sit-and-listen format is the main method used, although it has been proven to be one of the less effective methods for retaining information and learning (Sánchez et al., 2019). The "learning Pyramid", sometimes referred to as the "cone of learning" suggests that most students only remember about 10% of what they hear from teachers and lecturers (Turan & Akdag, 2019).

With the flipped classroom, it is possible for the students to be more active during the lessons as they have already done the passive part at home learning basic content knowledge. According to Zarrinabadi and Ebrahimi, "the events that have traditionally taken place inside the classroom now take place outside the classroom and vice versa" (2019, p. 270). In fact, the time spent in class is then devoted to activities that involve higher-order thinking skills, such as discussing concepts, investigating questions, solving problems, and creating pieces of work on subjects with which the students have been previously acquainted.

The flipped classroom provides more time to build up knowledge by interacting with other students by doing activities and not just listening to a lecture. Thus, Bloom's taxonomy is at the core of the principles that underpin the organisation of a flipped classroom. In 1956, Bloom created a classification of learning outcomes and objectives that represents the process of learning from lower to higher-order thinking skills.

This hierarchical framework was revised in 2001 by Anderson and Krathwohl, yielding the revised Bloom's Taxonomy, where the stages are represented with verbs

Figure 1. The learning pyramid adapted
(Turan & Akdag, 2019, p. 595)

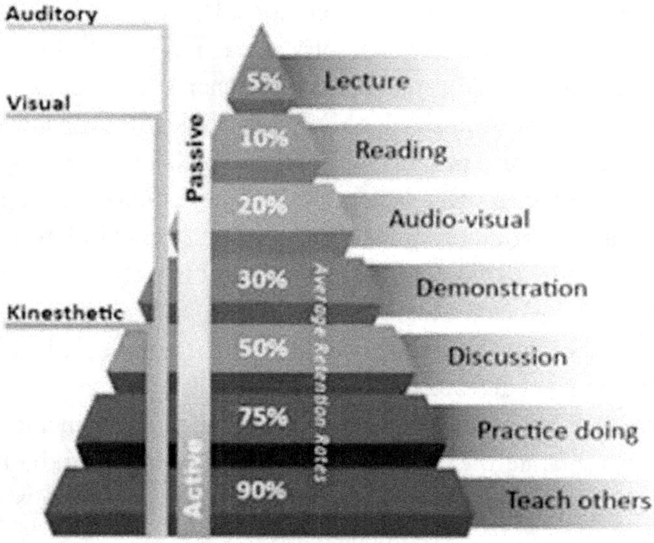

and the highest level is not represented by the concept of "synthesis" anymore but by the verb "creating". This contrast is clearly shown in the following table.

Bloom's revised taxonomy has been used for a wide range of purposes, from framing digital tasks and evaluating apps, to defining objectives, writing questions, and assessments. In education, it has proven useful as a "starting point for many applications, such as school activities, lesson planning, rubric making, or curriculum mapping, among others" (Al-Naabi, 2020, p. 68).

The flipped classroom facilitates the construction of new spaces in which students can learn course topics and develop their skills. Bezzazi's study (2019) recommends the use of the flipped classroom in the educational field because this pedagogical model, together with technology, facilitates the active role of students during the learning process. According to Ghufron and Nurdianningsih (2020), teachers can innovate school activities, improve teaching-learning conditions, encourage student participation, and facilitate knowledge assimilation.

Although there are many positive aspects, there are also some disadvantages to the implementation of this model, such as, having or not having a personal computer or Internet connection, and it also requires greater demand for adaptation compared to traditional teaching (Aguayo et al., 2019). In this sense, both the teacher and student are responsible for the success of the process, with the latter having to work previously on the material provided by the teacher, without which it would not be possible to put it into practice in the classroom.

Table 1. Bloom vs. Anderson/Krathwohl

Bloom's taxonomy (1956)	Anderson and Krathwohl's taxonomy (2001)
Knowledge: remembering or retrieving previously learned material. Examples of verbs that relate to this function are: know, identify, relate, list, define, recall, memorise, repeat, record, name, recognise, acquire.	Remembering: recognising or recalling knowledge from memory. Remembering is when memory is used to produce or retrieve definitions, facts, or lists, or to recite previously learned information.
Comprehension: the ability to grasp or construct meaning from material. Examples of verbs that relate to this function are: restate, locate, report, recognise, explain, express, identify, discuss, describe, review, infer, illustrate, interpret, draw, represent, differentiate, conclude.	Understanding: constructing meaning from different types of functions be they written or graphic messages or activities.
Application: the ability to use learned material, or to implement material in new and concrete situations. Examples of verbs that relate to this function are: apply, relate, develop, translate, use, operate, organise, employ, restructure, interpret, demonstrate, illustrate, practice, calculate, show, exhibit, dramatize.	Applying: carrying out or using a procedure though executing or implementing. Applying relates to or refers to situations where learned material us used through products like models, presentations, interviews, or simulations.
Analysis: the ability to break down or distinguish the parts of materials into its components so that its organizational structure may be better understood. Examples of verbs that relate to this function are: analyse, compare, probe, inquire, examine, contrast, categorise, differentiate, investigate, detect, survey, classify, deduce, experiment, scrutinise, discover, inspect, dissect, discriminate, separate.	Analysing: breaking materials or concepts into parts, determining how the parts relate to one another or how they interrelate, or how the parts relate to an overall structure or purpose. Mental actions included in this function are differentiating, organising, and attributing, as well as being able to distinguish between the components or parts. When one is analysing, he can illustrate this mental function by creating spreadsheets, surveys, charts, diagrams, or graphic representations.
Synthesis: the ability to put parts together to form a coherent or unique new whole. Examples of verbs that relate to this function are: compose, produce, design, assemble, create, prepare, predict, modify, plan, invent, tell, formulate, collect, set up, generalize, document, combine, relate, propose, develop, arrange, construct, organise, originate, derive, write, propose	Evaluating: making judgements based on criteria and standards through checking and critiquing. Critiques, recommendations, and reports are some of the products that can be created to demonstrate the processes of evaluation. In the newer taxonomy, evaluating comes before creating as it is often a necessary part of the precursory behaviour before one creates something.
Evaluation: the ability to judge, check, and even critique the value of material for a given purpose. Examples of verbs that relate to this function are: judge, assess, compare, evaluate, conclude, measure, deduce, argue, decide, choose, select, rate, estimate, validate, consider, appraise, value, criticise, infer.	Creating: putting elements together to form a coherent or functional whole; reorganising elements into a new pattern or structure though generating, planning, or producing. Creating requires users to put parts together in a new way or synthesise parts into something new and different creating a new form or product.

Source: Wilson (2016, p. 4)

Furthermore, the model does not fully consider the cognitive differences of each student and their understanding of the material on the display. Physical spaces, with their traditional layouts and organisation, hinder the exchange between the students themselves and the teacher (Abad & González, 2019).

Figure 2. Bloom's revised taxonomy in the flipped classroom
(Wilson, 2016, p. 5)

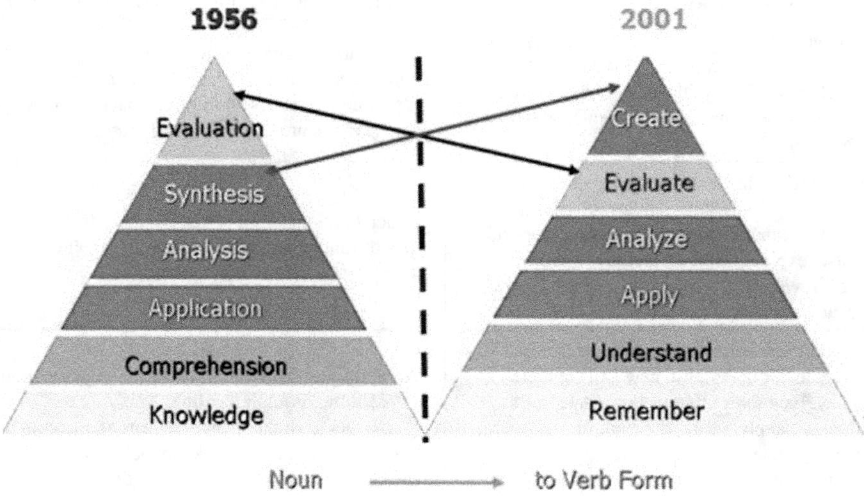

ICTs as a Medium for Teaching EFL

The impact of technology is unquestionable and widespread across all aspects of life. From university students who can search the online archives of any institution in the world to companies who can offer their services to clients across continents via live conferences, all activities on our planet are currently shaped by technology and education cannot be an exception if we want to meet the needs of the future citizens.

Arellano and Andrade (2020) analysed how 25 professors use ICTs in their teaching practice. The results showed prevalence of their own uses of the teaching digital competence (e-skills), above didactic competence and innovation with ICT. According to Casimiro and Torres (2023, p. 181), "it can be an essential path to cultivate a passion for learning and to inspire innovation in young learners who become aware of its boundless possibilities".

At the same time, within the framework of this constant era of change, the rise of ICTs has made greater access to information and knowledge, enhancing people's possibilities to learn new things through the use of new tools. It is in this way that the learning of English as a second language has been boosted by the development of technology and the use of ICTs, which have revolutionised the teaching of this language (Garzón et al., 2023). The results indicated a medium impact on learning gains and a very large impact on motivation to learn. It is concluded that the use of ICT is effective in complementing the educational process in English.

The use of ICTs in the teaching of English is based on different theories and pedagogical approaches that maintain that learning is more effective when it is related to previously acquired concepts and knowledge, occurs through the interaction of the individual with the environment, and is based on the resolution of problems and real situations. Girón et al.'s article (2023) presents an analysis of students' progress in English pronunciation after participating in a collaborative project to generate ICT-mediated audio-visual products.

Nowadays, ICTs have transformed the way English is taught and learned, providing new tools and resources to facilitate the learning process. The use of ICTs as a method of teaching English can be an effective strategy for improving English language learning and promoting greater student participation and motivation (González, 2023). However, according to Lorente and Pulido (2022), the objective is to investigate the digital resources that have been applied in higher education institutions, paying attention to the type and frequency of use of resources.

The application of ICTs in foreign language teaching is progressive, and there are a large number of classes in virtual environments. When working in virtual contexts, the emphasis is generally on written expression, and it is oral production that is weakened, as not all virtual platforms offer specific tools for its development and the teacher does not always make use of the resources available (Rachmalla, 2021).

Similarly, in traditional face-to-face teaching, oral production has been one of the most neglected in language classes. In the face of teaching of grammatical and metalinguistic postulates with regard to reading and writing, teachers focus on complying with the content assigned for the teaching period, and do not always have the time to assess oral production on an individual basis. Quintero and Jaimes (2023) addressed the impact of the use of ICTs on the development of listening, speaking and writing skills in A1 English level students.

Since the Covid-19 pandemic, the impact of technology has reached educational fields such as language teaching and learning, so much so that it has become a recurrent theme in didactic and pedagogical practice. Its inclusion in curricula and classroom work makes it an object of interest for research and a compulsory topic in the most recent training courses, workshops, webinars, videoconferences, and so on. (Mujica, 2021).

Research on the motivational effect of ICTs clearly shows that "students who use ICTs improve their grades and are more motivated. The conclusion was drawn that ICT-based syllabuses highly improve motivation and learning achievement" (Flores, 2022, p. 102). The aim of this research was to describe the adaptability of teachers to virtual environments through the characterisation of the dimensions of their teaching profile.

ICTs tools not only motivate students, but they are also the perfect partners to flip the classroom and eventually try to tailor instruction to meet students' individual needs. Indeed, by presenting a topic through WebQuest, each student can watch videos provided as many times as they need (Galindo, 2021). Furthermore, reading and watching videos can be performed at different locations. Some students do it while travelling, making most of the daily bus trips, for instance. Materials and resources are even more useful and motivating when they help minimize learning difficulties by allowing each student to learn at their own pace (Fundora et al., 2023).

The academic benefits are also worth highlighting according to Mejía and Mejía (2022). First, the use of ICTs facilitates greater student participation and allows for real-time correction and positive reinforcement of daily progress, which has a direct impact on motivation. Second, these digital tools encourage peer-to-peer cooperative learning, facilitating interaction between teachers and students as well as among students themselves, which is a fundamental part of the andragogical methodology.

The use of ICTs in foreign language classrooms is a very motivating method because it stimulates learners because they are attracted to them, and they can be used in different ways. Like all teaching methods, the use of new technologies has both advantages and disadvantages. According to Varona (2022), ICT use in classrooms has the following advantages:

- Interest, motivation. Students are highly motivated when using ICT resources, and motivation is one of the driving forces behind their learning.
- Interaction. Students are permanently active when interacting with the computer.
- Development of initiative. The constant participation of students encourages the development of initiatives.
- Learning from mistakes. Immediate feedback allows students to become aware of their mistakes when they occur.
- Greater communication between teachers and students. The communication channels provided by the Internet facilitate contact between the students and teachers.
- Cooperative learning. The tools provided by ICT facilitate group work and the cultivation of social attitudes, exchange of ideas, and cooperation.
- High degree of interdisciplinarity. Educational tasks carried out with computers allow for a high degree of interdisciplinarity, with different types of treatment of very broad and varied information.
- Digital and audiovisual literacy. These materials provided students with contact with ICT as a means of learning and as a tool for information processing.
- Development of information search and selection skills. This requires the implementation of techniques that help locate and evaluate the necessary information.

- Improvement in expression and creativity skills. The tools provided by ICT (word processors, graphic editors, etc.) facilitate the development of written, graphic, and audiovisual expression skills.

The use of ICTs in the foreign language classroom involves an effort on the part of teachers because they have to constantly update and receive training to be able to use these resources when teaching. According to Vera et al. (2020), digital competences are necessary for today's education, being an important part of the current educational model and constituting an indispensable element for learning. They also determined that ICT, teacher training and English language learning constitute an important part of these topics.

Therefore, ICTs are not a replacement for teachers; it is only a matter of applying them as a source of information in the teaching-learning process. Therefore, teachers must motivate and encourage the use of ICTs during the learning period (Ramírez & Pinochet, 2021). It should be emphasised that the role of the teacher is very important in the use of ICTs, as the teacher is the person who helps students to achieve skills in the use and learning of new technologies. Therefore, it is imperative that all teachers be willing to offer these opportunities to their students.

According to Roys and Franco (2019), the integration of ICTs in the classroom depends on teachers' willingness to make lessons non-traditional. The teacher has to be aware that he/she is a key and important figure in the student's life and must be willing to help the student to learn. Hence, it is important for teachers to use new technologies in classrooms with students.

In summary, the use of digital platforms is an issue that must be considered because education is changing and updating. Both teachers and students must be in tune with the times with respect to new technologies, this being yet another resource for teaching (Carrión et al., 2021). The easy method of teaching was with a blackboard and eraser, but that has changed, and we have to take it on board and apply it to reality. Today's educational model seeks to maximise the use of these technologies to train human resources that meet today's labour competencies.

Differentiated Instruction

Differentiation is undoubtedly one of the major challenges teachers must face. Responding to variance among learners can be very demanding and frustrating if the targeted goals are not reached in terms of creating the best learning experience for all students. As pointed out by Manivannan and Nor: "Recent emphasis on heterogeneity makes the challenge of serving academically diverse learners in regular classrooms seem an inevitable part of a teacher's role." (2020, p. 295).

When trying to give a brief definition of the concept of differentiated instruction, Watts et al. (2022, p. 109), affirm that: "differentiation is responsive teaching rather than one-size-fits-all teaching". In their opinion, the key starting point is all about stopping looking at the class as a group and starting to look at them as individuals to become aware that they come to us with different language backgrounds, different degrees of security, different past experiences at school, different peer relationships, and a thousand more differences that need to be dealt with. Responding to those differences is not something that can be improvised, "it is crucial to acknowledge them and then start working with them as a part of my teaching plan" (Gaitas et al., 2022, p. 9).

According to Gheyssens et al. (2023, p. 678), "differentiated instruction is an approach that aims to meet the learning needs of all students in mixed ability classrooms by establishing maximal learning and differentiating instruction with regard to content, process, and product in accordance with student needs in terms of their readiness, interests, and learning profiles".

To clarify the steps to be taken, differentiated instruction can be broken down into different elements that need to be varied (Ojong, 2023):

- **Content**: it needs to be presented at different levels to meet all students' needs, especially those at the end of the learning spectrum. Teachers should consider different learning styles and present information in a variety of ways so that more students can comprehend the content.
- **Environment:** It is remarkably effective to physically change things by allowing flexible seating. This aspect is crucial for promoting collaborative learning. Teachers should gradually devolve responsibility within the learning process and try to move their students towards independence. This shift implies a change in mindset that will help students set up goals to be achieved and develop their risk-taking skills and independent thinking.
- **Process:** The teacher should try to let go of the need to control the pathways students take to achieve their goals. There are multiple effective methods to obtain the same results. The pace at which students acquire competencies can be extremely diverse.
- **Product:** The product or outcome should be adapted to students' interests, readiness, or profiles. These adjustments could be made by modifying the rubrics to match and extend the students' different levels, or by encouraging students to create original products that contain proof of the competencies to be developed.

Differentiated instruction is an effective strategy that many experts have recommended to teachers. Student-aware teaching recognises and teaches according to learner differences. According to Shareefa et al., "differentiated instruction is defined as an approach that provides students with opportunities for learning while embracing individual differences and needs" (2019, p. 323).

Galora and Salazar (2019) suggested three simple ways to differentiate instruction in the classroom by outcomes, teaching methods, and tasks. Bearing these three aspects in mind in everyday planning, teachers should consider students' needs. It is important to remember that the implementation of differentiated instruction requires major changes in teaching practice and curriculum design.

Differentiated instruction is an instructional method that brings students' potential abilities to the maximum level possible by considering their characteristics. When planning differentiated education, students' characteristics, course elements, and teaching strategies should be carefully evaluated (Safawi & Akay, 2022).

In their book, Letzel-Alt and Pozas (2023) recognised that a promising inclusive teaching approach that aims to meet students' individual learning needs by maximizing educational opportunities is differentiated instruction. Educational equity, inclusion, and high-quality teaching are key elements of global importance. In this context, differentiated instruction can foster those elements in the student body and can be considered as a malleable inclusive teaching strategy that can be used in different educational settings.

Evangelou defines differentiated instruction as "an innovative teaching approach that involves systematic teaching practices by the teacher -adapting and proactively modifying the curriculum, teaching methods, resources, learning activities and children's projects - to respond effectively to the diversity of students in terms of their readiness level, interests and learning profile" (2023, p. 17).

Differentiated instruction appears as a measurement indicator in the quality evaluation system of Hungarian primary and secondary school teachers (Kótay-Nagy, 2023). This suggests that teachers working in Hungarian public education that teach English as a foreign language (EFL) are expected to use differentiated instruction in their lessons. This study intended to explore the perspectives of teachers in a variety of teaching contexts. Kötay-Nagy recorded participants' self-reported practices of differentiated instruction.

METHODOLOGY

Objective

This research aims to determine whether the implementation of an innovative model that includes the use of ICT, such as flipped classroom, can be an efficient alternative to improve foreign language levels and achieve the objectives set out in

Figure 3. Participants' self-reported practices of differentiated instruction
(Kötay-Nagy, 2023, p. 7)

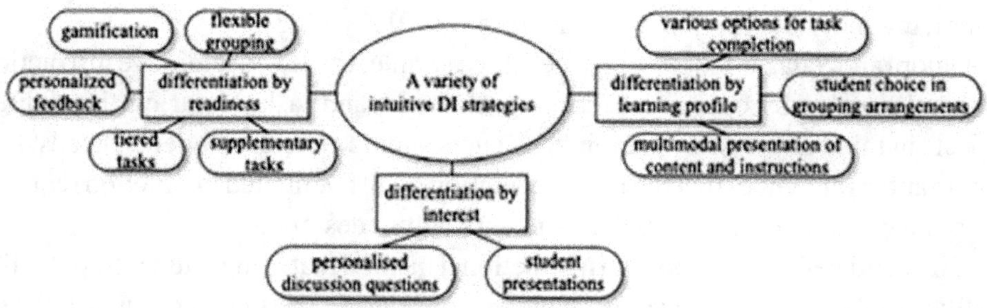

the teaching-learning process. Therefore, the objective was to analyse the influence of the flipped classroom pedagogical model in combination with ICTs on the foreign language learning process.

In accordance with these general objectives, some specific objectives were also established: to apply an academic module based on the flipped classroom model with ICTs; to verify the degree of appropriation of knowledge with the aforementioned methodology; and to determine the effectiveness of the flipped classroom methodology in conjunction with the use of new technologies.

Design

The type of design used in this research is quasi-experimental in nature. This is due to the fact that the data collection and its respective analysis come from the selection of the group of students, in which no random selection was made. This means that the subjects in the study were not randomly assigned to the group since it was already formed before the start of the research process.

In view of the above, the internal validity of the research is achieved by means of comparison since the purpose of this study is to observe the advantages of using the combination of flipped classroom methodology with ICTs on foreign language learning. Anchored to the above, there is equivalence in the group both in numbers and in behavioural and academic characteristics. This equivalence is present from the beginning of the research, during the process until the end. The instruments will be applied in the same way, excluding any kind of flaw in the data collection.

Sample

The research was conducted in a state high school in Spain. The institution has several buildings. Some of these belong to the primary basic education level, and it has a main school which provides basic education and secondary education. The school's mission is to educate autonomous and dynamic, tolerant and respectful, responsible and honest, understanding and reflective people.

The final sample is composed of a group of secondary school students. The number of students is determined by a total of 30 students, 15 boys and 15 girls, in the range of 14-15 years. They all live in the same municipality and their educational level is generally high, though there is a lack of motivation to learn a foreign language.

This is a non-probabilistic sample in the sense that they were chosen by the researcher. This was because a group of students who had not recently completed their secondary school studies was needed. With the sample selected, a long-term projection can be made. This choice was made in a controlled manner so that the problem statement could be constituted. From the above, it can be affirmed that the type of sample was directed and with voluntary subjects, since the subjects were chosen fortuitously and are homogeneous.

Instruments

Throughout this research, basically two instruments were used: a WebQuest, and a Kahoot Quiz.

A WebQuest

The main innovative resource is WebQuest, created using the web page creation tool Google Sites. Originally, WebQuests originated at San Diego State University in the Learning Design and Technology Program, and they were inquiry-oriented lessons used to have students work collaboratively to complete a task. Websites were created to provide students with answers to problems by navigating them.

In this project, WebQuest is used to complement coursebook materials and provide information and input supplied by the Internet. Through the website, students were introduced to the context by reading articles and watching videos on International Women's Day. Moreover, on the same website, they are given the grammar content that they need to write their task and the essential information to prepare to write a narrative, as well as some links to online dictionaries and online bilingual apps and web services.

In fact, the WebQuest designed for this project is more of a website as a means of flipping the classroom. Indeed, once the low order thinking skills, which are *remembering and understanding,* are completed outside the class, students start writing in class and therefore use the thinking skill at the top of the revised version of Bloom's taxonomy: *creating*. Consequently, not only is the task tiered and adapted to different levels and different learning styles as the website contains videos and texts of multiple difficulty levels, but it also enables the teacher to provide more effective support by interacting with the students individually.

The webpage builder Google Sites coupled with the flipped classroom approach represents a fruitful and powerful way of achieving differentiated instruction in an ESP environment. The Website entitled Let us change the world! includes five pages:

- Introduction: some facts about International Women's Day (IWD). The introduction stage is used to provide background information on IWD and introduce key vocabulary and concepts that learners need to understand to complete the tasks involved.
- Inspiring women: Some women's biographies were provided to set up a context to create a powerful piece of writing on a woman who made a difference in history.
- Useful grammar. This part, which is normally called "the process part", introduces lexical areas or grammatical points that are essential to the task. This project introduces the past continuous and the simple past through two videos.
- Online dictionaries and helpful websites. On this page, links to online dictionaries and online bilingual apps and web services are shown to help students gradually acquire a higher degree of autonomy.
- Task description: how to write a narrative? The entire WebQuest is wrapped around this task, which consists of writing a narrative. In this section, students will find hints on the content, structure, and punctuation that should be used to write a narrative. This piece of writing will be related to any kind of event linked to a woman who has made a difference in the fight for human rights or gender equality.

A Kahoot Quiz

Gamification is a new concept that is increasingly being used to increase students' motivation. It involves including game elements in the classroom and has been shown to exponentially increase motivation. As Ribeiro et al. (2018, p. 249) state, "it has become increasingly challenging to engage students in the classroom, gain their attention, and involve them in some activities". Introducing a quiz like Kahoot can be highly beneficial to get the students involved in assessment activities carried out in a more traditional way, which can be stressful and boring for students.

Kahoot, a quiz that can be accessed via a web browser or the Kahoot app, is a game-based learning platform that allows teachers to create, share, and play learning games or trivia quizzes. Kahoot fosters social learning as all players connect using a generated game pin that is shown on a common screen, which is usually the whiteboard in a classroom. The students were required to answer questions created by the teacher using a computer, tablet, or mobile phone. The points each student or group receives are calculated based on how many questions are answered correctly and how long it takes the students to answer. The players can also get a streak, which means they are given more points if they answer the questions correctly in sequence.

Kahoot has a basic version, which is a multiple-choice quiz; however, it can be upgraded. Three extra types of quizzes are offered: the puzzle, which consists of arranging letters or syllables to form a word or to make a sentence; a true or false version; and a type-answer version. Combining the different versions increases focus and concentration and allows the players to work on different skills. The puzzle version, as well as the type-answer version, is a highly efficient way to work on spelling and grammatical structures, whereas the true or false version of the quiz develops reading comprehension skills. Kahoot can be used for formative or summative assessments, or it can also be a motivating starting point to start a unit.

In the designed activities, this trivia quiz is used to review specific characteristics of a narrative, such as its content and structure, as well as the tenses used in it. Its title is "writing". It is, therefore, part of a formative assessment, as while playing it, students evaluate what they have understood about the grammar and text typology of the written task they are to complete. It also allows the teacher to appraise the learning process and makes it possible to detect difficulties, adjust the activities, and provide further explanations. It is important to stop and analyse the results after each question to ensure that all the students understand why their answers were incorrect.

RESULTS

Over the past decades, traditional teaching environments in which the teachers deliver their lessons in a sit-and-listen format have given way to more innovative environments in which approaches such as the Flipped Classroom and Task-Based methodologies place students at the centre of the learning-teaching process. Therefore, the learning-teaching process is nurtured by constant feedback from students to teachers. Several approaches and methodologies on which the lesson plan has been based aim to improve the learning- teaching process:

- **The Flipped Classroom:** In the activities described previously, the teacher is not delivering a lesson. In contrast, the teacher constantly helped the students and monitored their learning process. It is therefore possible for the teacher to adjust practices and differentiate instruction by adapting explanations and providing help on a one-to-one basis.

❖ **Metacognitive strategies:** Metacognition is the ability to critically analyse one's own learning process. When implementing metacognitive strategies in the classroom, the tasks can be divided into three stages, which can be clearly observed in the lesson plan: planning, monitoring, and reviewing. At the beginning of the lesson, the teacher set clear goals. Students are given the objectives and assessment rubrics for them to be aware of what they are expected to achieve. They can then plan (step one) their writing according to the items described in the rubric and the objectives presented by the teacher. During the task, students were asked to monitor (step two) their learning process by using online dictionaries and reflecting on previous mistakes made when completing the exercises set up in WebQuest. Once the writing is finalized, reviewing is a key stage (step three). Using effective revision strategies helps students improve their learning processes and independent learning. The students will also be asked to analyse their learning process via a self-assessment rubric that will help them reflect on their learning process and adjust some steps for future writing tasks. From an emotional point of view, metacognitive strategies can also help students change their self-talk and boost their motivation by developing resilience.

In addition to the feedback obtained from the students' learning processes, the same steps can be applied to teachers performance. The European Centre for Modern Languages of the Council of Europe (ECML) website contains an action-oriented approach that provides teachers with the necessary tools to ensure quality in language teaching: **CEFR QualiMatrix.** One of the main tools is the matrix itself which consists of a self-assessment questionnaire organized around the classic quality assurance circle of planning, implementation, evaluation, and action.

The results of the questionnaire gave the teachers the possibility of diagnosing their planning and teaching performance. Self-assessment for teachers is also an extraordinary way to become aware of one's own weaknesses and strengths. Using this tool, teachers can adjust many aspects of their teaching practices concerning the assessment criteria used as well as their students' motivation. Two examples of the results generated after answering the questions are shown.

In the first stage, guidelines are provided for every dimension. The guidelines for the written dimensions are as follows:

- Students should be able to gradually apply the strategies needed to write a text in different formats, following adequacy, coherence, and consistency standards, using digital tools (correctors, online dictionaries, etc.). Four steps were followed: planning, producing written or multimedia texts, reviewing, amending, and rewriting after the revision.

Figure 4. Analysis of the results of CEFR QualiMatrix questionnaire
(Retrieved June 20,2021 from https://tools.ecml.at/matrix/index.php?id_lng=1&step1=yes)

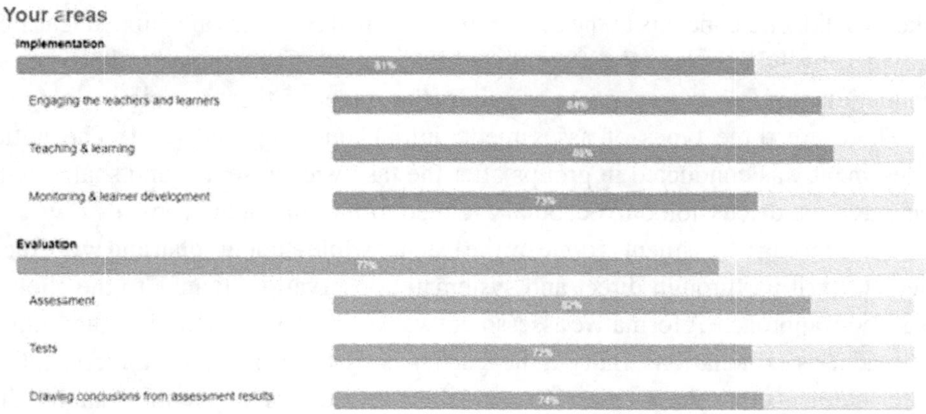

- Students should also be able to write short texts that contain personal information, basic feelings, and opinions.
- Familiar topics and experiences including past and future events in a simple descriptive language.

When practicing writing skills, reflection on grammar and spelling rules must be carried out. Likewise, students should be able to present written and multimedia texts in different formats in a gradually more thorough and autonomous manner. In addition, students should be able to build their personal learning environment (PLE) using web tools to create their digital and personal space as well as portfolios to monitor and assess their learning process. These guidelines are narrowed down into three learning assessment criteria that specify that students should be able to:

- Write formal and informal texts based on appropriate planning and a subsequent revision taking the receiver and context into account and ensuring adequacy, coherence, and consistency standards.
- Write creative texts based on one's experiences or on simulated situations.
- Digital tools are progressively being used in a more autonomous way to write texts, search for information, process it, and enrich it creatively. Sending and receiving digital messages to establish internal and external relationships

DISCUSSION OF RESULTS

The two didactic concepts at the core of the designed activities are flipped learning provided by ICT tools and differentiated instruction. Consequently, the types of evaluation used follow some of the principles that underpin these two methodologies.

There are three types of assessment: initial, ongoing, and final. The initial assessment was conducted in groups after the task was presented and shared with the class in a discussion on vocabulary related to International Women's Day.

The ongoing assessment is done by the teacher while students plan and write their piece of writing through direct and systematic observation, thanks to the flipped classroom approach. A formative assessment was specifically used to check and adjust the teacher's explanations. Indeed, the teacher assesses the students´ understanding of the elements that shape a narrative and the use of tenses by playing Kahoot with all students. While playing the Kahoot quiz, it is crucial that the teacher stops after every question and clarifies some grammar points that might be challenging.

Finally, the first step of summative evaluation is the task itself, as it is through writing that the assessment guidelines specified beforehand are met. Digital competence is evaluated when the first summative evaluation is carried out as the students send their piece of writing via email or by uploading it to Google Classroom.

Peer assessment allows students to assess each other's performance. It involves students taking responsibility for assessing their peers' work while providing feedback. It also transfers some ownership of the assessment process to them, which can be a great opportunity for students to understand assessment criteria and act as evaluators. Students should attempt to provide constructive and encouraging feedback to create a positive group atmosphere. Peer assessment plays a major role in helping students develop judgement skills and self-awareness, as it gives them a deeper insight into their own learning process.

The lesson plan includes collaborative activities that are assessed from a teamwork perspective. In fact, students are to fill a rubric grid to evaluate their peers' attitudes and behaviours during activities accomplished in groups. This kind of assessment is extremely valuable in helping students learn from each other, especially when behaviour is concerned. While receiving feedback from their peers, students can analyse and try to solve relational problems with their classmates. Furthermore, peer assessment develops students' judgment skills and the ability to critically reflect on their own behaviour. Once the assessment grids were filled, a discussion of the evaluation results was conducted among the members of each group.

The discussions led students to provide explanations to justify the grades given to their classmates. It was interesting to observe how different the feedback given, and perceptions of their own attitudes were. We encouraged the students to commit to improving their behaviour for future activities implemented in teams. Students had to specify what particular behaviour they would strive to change and acknowledge their teammates. To allow peer assessment to contribute to the emotional growth of each student, teams should be stable and last over two or three tasks.

Self-assessment allows students to assess their own performance. Self-assessment requires students to judge how well they have performed in relation to the criteria established by the teacher. This allows them to adjust their learning process by taking actions that will have a direct impact on the development of their competencies. This type of assessment is crucial for developing metacognitive strategies in the classroom, as previously described in the section concerning the learning-teaching process results. In addition, it encourages students to be more responsible for their learning processes and to become more aware of their weaknesses and strengths.

Learning becomes a more active process and helps students internalize the assessment criteria and standards that are required. Developing reflective skills is a major benefit of self-assessment. It can also play a major role in helping students become more autonomous by learning to self- regulate their learning process and by providing tools to reflect on what can be done differently to improve them. When filling the self-assessment rubric, students were automatically reflected in their learning process. They must go through the different skills that are to be acquired to write with accuracy regarding grammar, vocabulary, spelling, and punctuation. They must evaluate the process of revision using paper and digital dictionaries, as well as the layout of their writing. It is certainly a good way to increase self-awareness, as they must try to look at their final task objectively. Undoubtedly, self-awareness skills are the cornerstone of lifelong learning.

CONCLUSION

Exploring a wide array of methodologies and approaches has been like travelling through our own experience of language learning and teaching over the last 20 years. Indeed, we started learning English as a foreign language through the memorization of decontextualized lists of vocabulary. During our teaching experience, we have become acquainted with the task- based learning approach and the CLIL approach, which fostered our interest in innovative language methodologies.

We later discovered the flipped classroom, which is a totally unknown and unexplored methodology. Flipping learning, along with some innovative ICT resources, played a central role in the teaching experience. Putting it into practice to become aware of its advantages and drawbacks is a great challenge, as neither teachers nor students are acquainted with this approach. After applying the flipped classroom approach combined with task-based methodology and ICT tools, we analysed some of the advantages for both students and teachers. The advantages of the flipped classroom for students are the following:

- Motivation: Students entered the classroom ready to contribute to and participate, and this attitude enriched the classroom especially when working in teams. They felt motivated because they were tired of traditional lecture formats.
- Higher-order thinking skills developed in the classroom: Students became more actively involved in their work in the classroom as they could apply the knowledge; they were presented by means of videos and articles presented on the website.
- Differentiated instruction: Students who had a slower learning pace had the possibility to rewind videos and read texts as many times as they wanted. On the other hand, students who had the ability to learn at a faster rate had the possibility of going further and deepening their knowledge without getting bored or losing motivation which sometimes leads to disruption.
- Group cohesion: Cohesiveness arose as students interacted more than they used to with the sit-and-listen format. Teamwork created bonds and increased the degree of closeness, as flipping the class gave them more time to help one another.

The advantages of the flipped classroom for the teacher are as follows:

- Individual support was provided to students who needed assistance. The teacher becomes a facilitator, who can work closely with individuals or small groups.
- Managing behaviour became less challenging, especially for the two students who tended to be very disruptive. The flipped classroom organization provides more classroom time and allows the teacher to create bonds with students, which has an extremely positive impact on their behaviour.

Flipping the classroom was an overall positive experience since it transformed tuition into a more adaptable and flexible experience for every student. It also turned out to be a perfect way of modelling, as students became aware of how teachers process information and present it back through technology. Moreover, the flipped classroom promotes equal learning opportunities, regardless of the students' background. In a flipped classroom model, after viewing the assigned content prior to coming to class, all students receive help from their teachers. Indeed, socio-cultural background plays a less crucial role as inequalities are smoothened by the fact that all the students receive help from their teacher while working on higher-order thinking skills. However, the following challenges must be addressed:

- Creating content requires deep knowledge of research methods and technology tools. Considering the rapid advances in ICT and its application in education, regular training of teachers is imperative.
- Creating content that was well connected to the task carried out in class was not an easy goal.
- Schools should provide interventions for students who do not have access to the Internet.
- Some students did not perform their previous work at home and had to navigate the website in class. They ended up not having much time left to work on their assignments in class and had to take them home and do it on their own without help from the teacher or their peers.

Flipping the classroom helps teachers hold students accountable for their actions. Indeed, while students are working on completing high order thinking skills tasks, some students need to watch the videos and read the texts that they were asked to do at home. Therefore, they will have to complete their tasks on their own with no help from their peers or teachers. Consequently, the students become more responsible for their actions and try to avoid repeating the same situation.

REFERENCES

Abad Segura, E., & González Zamar, M. D. (2019). Análisis de las competencias en la educación superior a través de flipped classroom. *Revista Iberoamericana de Educación*, *80*(2), 29–45. doi:10.35362/rie8023407

Aguayo Vergara, M., Bravo Molina, M., Nocetti de la Barra, A., Concha Sarabia, L., & Aburto Godoy, R. (2019). Perspectiva estudiantil del modelo pedagógico flipped classroom o aula invertida en el aprendizaje del inglés como lengua extranjera. *Review of Education*, *43*(1), 90–120. doi:10.15517/revedu.v43i1.31529

Al-Naabi, I. S. (2020). Is it worth flipping? The impact of flipped classroom on EFL students' grammar. *English Language Teaching*, *13*(6), 64–75. doi:10.5539/elt.v13n6p144

Amiryousefi, M. (2019). The incorporation of flipped learning into conventional classes to enhance EFL learners' L2 speaking, L2 listening, and engagement. *Innovation in Language Learning and Teaching*, *13*(2), 147–161. doi:10.1080/17501229.2017.1394307

Arellano Vega, A. I., & Andrade Cázares, R. A. (2020). Competencias digitales docentes en profesores universitarios. *Journal Educational Innovation, 20*(83), 35–53.

Awidi, I. T., & Paynter, M. (2019). The impact of a flipped classroom approach on student learning experience. *Computers & Education, 128*, 269–283. doi:10.1016/j.compedu.2018.09.013

Barreto Huilcapi, M., Aguirre Fernández, R. E. & Serra Valdés, M. A. (2021). Beneficios del método AICLE/CLIL para el aprendizaje de una lengua extranjera a través del aula invertida. *Revista Panamericana de pedagogía*, 32, 197-215. doi:10.21555/rpp.v0i32.2271

Bezzazi, R. (2019). Learning English grammar through flipped learning. *Australian Journal of Applied Linguistics, 6*(2), 170–184.

Buil-Fabregá, M., Martínez, M., Ruiz-Munzón, N., & Filho, W. (2019). Flipped Classroom as an Active Learning Methodology in Sustainable Development Curricula. *Sustainability (Basel), 11*(17), 1–15. doi:10.3390/su11174577

Carrión Candel, E., Pérez Agustín, M. & Giménez De Ory, E. (2021). ICT and gamification experiences with CLIL methodology as innovative resources for the development of competencies in compulsory secondary education. *Digital education review, 39*, 238–256. doi:10.1344/der.2021.39.238-256

Casimiro-Perlaza, L. F., & Torres-Daza, H. F. (2023). Tecnologías disruptivas en la enseñanza del inglés: Un estudio comparativo de las percepciones de profesores. *RECIE. Revista Caribeña de Investigación Educativa, 7*(2), 175–197. doi:10.32541/recie.2023.v7i2.pp175-197

CEFR- QualityMatrix European Centre for Modern Languages of the Council of Europe. https://www.ecml.at/ECML-Programme/Programme2016-2019/QualityassuranceandimplementationoftheCEFR/Tutorial

Council of Europe. (2020). *Common European Framework of Reference for Languages: learning, teaching, assessment*. Council of Europe.

Das, A., Lam, T. K., Thomas, S., Richardson, J., Booi, H. K., Lau, K. H., & Mathews, Z. N. (2019). Flipped classroom pedagogy: Using pre-class videos in an undergraduate business information systems management course. *Education + Training, 61*(6), 756–774. doi:10.1108/ET-06-2018-0133

Evangelou, F. (2023). Differentiated Instruction on a learner-centred form of teaching in Primary Education. *International Journal of Education, 15*(2), 15–34. doi:10.5296/ije.v15i2.21004

Flores-González, N. (2022). El perfil del docente y su adaptabilidad a entornos educativos virtuales. *RECIE. Revista Caribeña de Investigación Educativa*, *6*(2), 99–115. doi:10.32541/recie.2022.v6i2.pp99-115

Fundora Ramírez, P., Rodríguez Fernández, L. R., & Reiné Herrera, Y. (2023). La enseñanza del inglés a través de las plataformas digitales. *Revista Científica de FAREM-Estelí*, *12*(46), 165–182. doi:10.5377/farem.v12i46.16484

Gaitas, S., Carêto, C., Peixoto, F., & Castro Silva, J. (2022). Differentiated instruction: 'to be, or not to be, that is the question'. *International Journal of Inclusive Education*, 1–19. doi:10.1080/13603116.2022.2119290

Galindo Valero, P. (2021). Utilización de plataformas digitales en educación. *Revista de Educación. Innovación y Formación, REIF*, *4*, 7–25.

Galora Moya, N. P., & Salazar Tobar, M. C. (2019). Differentiated Instruction: Productive skills development with high school and university students. *Investigación y Desarrollo*, *11*(1), 67–73. doi:10.29033/id.v11i1.645

Garzón Álvarez, J. F., Monsalve Franco, A. P., & Valencia Valencia, E. Z. (2023). Impacto de las tecnologías de la información en los estudiantes del grado aceleración del aprendizaje en un curso de inglés. *Revista Virtual Universidad Católica del Norte*, *68*, 37-62. https://www.doi.org/10.35575/rvucn.n68a3

Gheyssens, E., Griful-Freixenet, J., & Struyven, K. (2023). Differentiated Instruction as an Approach to Establish Effective Teaching in Inclusive Classrooms. In Effective Teaching around the World (pp. 677-689). Springer. doi:10.1007/978-3-031-31678-4_30

Ghufron, M. A., & Nurdianingsih, f. (2020). Flipped teaching with CALL media in EFL writing course: Indonesian EFL writing teachers' reflection. *Pertanika Journal of Social Science & Humanities*, *28*(2), 1–18.

Girón-Chávez, A., Cruz-Maldonado, E. Y., Bermejo-del Villar, M. M., & Cancino-Zamarrón, R. (2023). Las TIC y el aprendizaje colaborativo para mejorar la pronunciación de inglés de estudiantes universitarios. *Revista Lengua y Cultura*, *5*(9), 1–10. doi:10.29057/lc.v5i9.11531

González Miranda, M. Y. (2023). Aprendizaje del inglés y el uso de las Tics como método de enseñanza en un grupo de estudiantes de la carrera de inglés de la universidad Autónoma de Chiriquí. *Revista Boletín Redipe*, *12*(3), 14–18. doi:10.36260/rbr.v12i3.1946

Hsiao, I. C. V., Hung, S. T. A., & Huang, H. T. D. (2021). The flipped classroom approach in an English for Specific purposes (ESP) course: A quasi-experimental study on learners' self-efficacy, study process, and learning performances. *Journal of Research on Technology in Education*, 1–20. doi:10.1080/15391523.2021.1976329

Hwang, G. J., & Fu, Q. K. (2020). Advancement and research trends of smart learning environments in the mobile era. *International Journal of Mobile Learning and Organisation*, *14*(1), 114–129. doi:10.1504/IJMLO.2020.103911

Kötay-Nagy, A. (2023). Differentiated instruction in the EFL classroom: An interview study on Hungarian primary and secondary school EFL teachers' views and self-reported practices. *Journal of Adult Learning, Knowledge, and Innovation*, *6*(8), 1–14. doi:10.1556/2059.2023.00076

Landeo Chocce, Z. M., Pareja Ballón, A. Y., Muñoz Chocce, C. M., Lazo Montero, G. L., Quispe Loayza, A. E., & Guerreros Blas, P. R. (2023). Las TIC en el aprendizaje del idioma inglés en estudiantes de una universidad pública. *Ciencia Latina Revista Científica Multidisciplinar*, *7*(2), 8029–8039. doi:10.37811/cl_rcm.v7i2.5937

Letzel-Alt, V., & Pozas, M. (2023). *Differentiated instruction around the world: A global inclusive insight*. Waxmann. doi:10.31244/9783830997023

Lorente Rodríguez, M., & Pulido-Montes, C. (2022). Use of Digital Resources in Higher Education during COVID-19: A Literature Review. *Education Sciences*, *12*(612), 1–19. 10.3390

Manivannan, M. L., & Nor, F. (2020). Barriers in differentiated instruction: A systematic review of the literature. *Journal of Critical Reviews*, *7*(6), 293–297. doi:10.31838/jcr.07.06.51

Mejía-Delgado, O. A., & Mejía-Delgado, Y. Y. (2022). Madurez tecnológica de la generación Z: Reto de la transformación digital. *Revista CEA*, *8*(16), 1–22. doi:10.22430/24223182.1913

Mendoza Navas, B. V., & Martos Eliche, F. (2021). El uso de herramientas tecnológicas en entornos virtuales para el desarrollo de la producción oral en inglés. *MLS Educational Research*, *5*(2), 105–119. doi:10.29314/mlser.v5i2.679

Moreno-Guerrero, A. J., Soler-Costa, R., Marín-Marín, J. A., & López Belmonte, J. (2021). Flipped learning y buenas prácticas docentes en educación primaria. *Comunicar*, *29*, 107–117. doi:10.3916/C68-2021-09

Mujica-Sequera, R. (2021). Clasificación de las Herramientas Digitales en la Tecnoeducación. *Revista Tecnológica-Educativa Docentes 2.0, 12*(1), 71–85. https://doi.org/ doi:10.37843/rted.v1i1.257

Ojong, A. S. (2023). Unraveling the Efficacy of Differentiated Instruction in Enhancing Second Language Acquisition: A Comprehensive Review and Future Directions. *International Journal of Linguistics. Literature and Translation*, *6*(6), 75–82. doi:10.32996/ijllt.2023.6.6.8

Qader, R. O., & Arslan, F. Y. (2019). The effect of flipped classroom instruction in writing: A case study with Iraqi EFL learners. *Teaching English with Technology*, *19*(1), 36–55.

Quintero, W. A., & Jaimes Guerrero, C. A. (2023). Incidencia del uso de las TIC en el desarrollo de las habilidades de comprensión y expresión oral y escrita del idioma inglés en estudiantes de nivel A1 de la licenciatura en lenguas extranjeras inglés-francés de la universidad de Pamplona. *Ciencia Latina Revista Científica Multidisciplinar*, *7*(4), 701–716. doi:10.37811/cl_rcm.v7i4.6904

Rachamalla, S. A. (2021). Usage of 'ICT' in English language teaching. *International Journal of Innovative Research in Science and Engineering*, *7*(11), 22–25.

Ramírez, A., & Pinochet, S. (2021). El mundo digital como facilitador de la enseñanza del idioma inglés. *Redipe*, *10*(13), 120–130. doi:10.36260/rbr.v10i13.1733

Ribeiro, L., Leal, T., & Quadrado, A. (2018). Gamification: A methodology to motivate engagement and participation in a higher education environment. *International Journal of Education and Research*, *6*(4), 58–101.

Roys, N., & Franco, A. (2019). Integración de las TIC para mejorar las habilidades de estudiantes de lenguas extranjeras de comunidades vulnerables. *Sophia*, *15*(2), 4–17. doi:10.18634/sophiaj.15v.2i.770

Safawi, S. S., & Akay, C. (2022). The effect of differentiated instruction approach on students' academic achievement and attitudes: A meta-analysis study. *Integrity Journal of Education and Training*, *6*(6), 120–132. doi:10.31248/IJET2022.163

Sánchez-Rivas, E., Sánchez-Rodríguez, J., & Ruiz-Palmero, J. (2019). Percepción del alumnado universitario respecto al modelo pedagógico de clase invertida. *Magis. Revista Internacional de Investigación en Educación*, *11*(23), 151–168. doi:10.11144/Javeriana.m11-23.paur

Shahnama, M., Ghonsooly, B., & Elahi Shirvan, M. (2021). A meta-analysis of relative effectiveness of flipped learning in English as second/foreign language research. *Educational Technology Research and Development*, *69*(3), 1355–1386. doi:10.1007/s11423-021-09996-1

Shareefa, M., Zin, R. H., Abdullah, N. Z., & Hawawi, R. (2019). Differentiated Instruction: Definition and Challenging Factors Perceived by Teachers. *Advances in Social Science, Education and Humanities Research*, *388*, 322–327.

Sosa-Díaz, M., Guerra-Antequera, J., & Cerezo-Pizarro, M. (2021). Flipped classroom in the context of education: Learning, satisfaction, and interaction. *Education Sciences*, *11*(8), 416–433. doi:10.3390/educsci11080416

Turan, Z., & Akdag-Cimen, B. (2019). Flipped classroom in English language teaching: A systematic review. *Computer Assisted Language Learning*, *33*(5), 590–606. doi:10.1080/09588221.2019.1584117

Varona, F. (2022). Perspectivas en la utilización de las tecnologías de información y comunicación de la educación superior. *Revista Visión Antataura*, *6*(2), 170–184.

Vera Ramírez, L. S., Villao Tomalá, D. C., & Granados Romero, J. F. (2020). Competencias digitales en el uso de herramientas digitales para el aprendizaje de inglés. *Ingenio*, *3*(1), 1–14. doi:10.18779/ingenio.v3i1.21

Watts-Taffe, S., Laster, B., Broach, L., Marinak, B., Conner, C., & Walker-Dalhouse, D. (2022). Differentiated Instruction: Making Informed Teacher Decisions. *The Reading Teacher*, *66*(4), 303–314. doi:10.1002/TRTR.01126

Wilson, L. O. (2016). *Anderson and Krathwohl: Bloom's Taxonomy Revised*. Quincy College.

Zarrinabadi, N., & Ebrahimi, A. (2019). Increasing peer collaborative dialogue using a flipped classroom strategy. *Innovation in Language Learning and Teaching*, *13*(3), 267–276. doi:10.1080/17501229.2018.1455688

KEY TERMS AND DEFINITIONS

CEFR QualiMatrix: The Quality Assurance Matrix for CEFR use (CEFR-QualiMatrix) project aims to promote effective language learning by supporting teachers in engaging in curriculum renewal supported by the CEFR vision of teaching and learning.

EFL Environment: English as a foreign language. The study of English by non-native speakers living in a non-English-speaking environment. EFL (English as a Foreign Language) learners are those who are studying English in a non-native country.

Flipped Classroom: A flipped classroom is a pedagogical model that flips traditional lectures and homework. The traditional lecture is viewed at home before class, and homework activities are done in the classroom with the instructor present to guide students in their endeavours.

Information and Communication Technologies: Information and Communication Technologies (ICTs) refer to all communication technologies, including the Internet, wireless networks, cell phones, computers, software, videoconferencing, and social networking.

Instruction: The traditional classroom, or face-to-face instruction, is when the instructor and students are in a place devoted to instruction, and teaching and learning take place at the same time. This allows for direct interaction between the instructor and learners, fostering collaboration, immediate feedback, and personalized guidance.

Kahoot: Kahoot! is a tool that delivers and presents questions to the students. It is a game in which students can play either individually or in groups. Instructors provide students with multiple-choice questions projected on a classroom screen.

Metacognitive Strategies: Metacognitive strategies are techniques to help students develop an awareness of their thinking processes as they learn and understand the way they learn; in other words, it means processes designed for students to 'think' about their 'thinking'.

WebQuest: A WebQuest is an inquiry-oriented lesson format in which most or all the information that learners work with comes from the web. These can be created using various programs, including a simple word processing document that includes links to websites.

Chapter 9
Collaborative Action on a Transmedia Human Rights Program:
A Digital Strategy to Improve the Well-Being of Students Facing Structural Violence

José Luis Figarotti Jiménez
https://orcid.org/0000-0001-6640-0515
Central University of Venezuela, Venezuela

ABSTRACT

Structural violence has a profound psychological impact on Venezuelan college students, leading to increased levels of stress, anxiety, depression, and hopelessness. This study investigated the psychological impact of structural violence on individuals and served as the basis for the collaborative action on transmedia human rights (CATHR) program design as a peaceful disruptive methodology to counteract violence. The CATHR program is an interdisciplinary educational strategy based on a challenge-based learning framework that fosters civic commitment, democratic values, the defense of human rights, and socio-environmental awareness. The study found that the CATHR program was effective in reducing stress, anxiety, depression, and hopelessness in college students. The study also found that the CATHR program empowered learners to resist and overcome the challenges they face. This chapter highlights the importance of addressing structural violence and its psychological consequences to promote the well-being of individuals and communities worldwide.

DOI: 10.4018/979-8-3693-5370-7.ch009

INTRODUCTION

Education is a fundamental human right, yet millions of children and youths around the world are currently deprived of this right due to a wide range of crises, including armed conflicts, dictatorships, and natural disasters. According to UNESCO, an alarming number of more than 127 million children are currently deprived of education and are living in crisis situations. One-quarter of the world's child population lives in countries affected by either armed conflict, dictatorships, or natural disasters (UNESCO, 2019). Venezuela is one such country severely affected by structural violence, which has led to widespread poverty, hunger, and violence, forcing many students to drop out of school. This ethnographic research study provides a comprehensive overview of the challenges faced by Venezuelan students pursuing degrees in Media and Journalism and investigates the impact of the Collaborative Action on Transmedia and Human Rights (CATHR) program on their resilience and attitudes towards international collaboration.

The study's findings suggest that CATHR is an effective intervention for promoting resilience and positive attitudes towards international collaboration. This program empowers students to connect with peers from other countries and cultures, learn about different perspectives, and collaborate with peers from diverse backgrounds. It serves as a catalyst for introspective growth and transformation, empowering students to act as engaged global citizens and make a positive impact in their communities and beyond.

Breaking Barriers is not just a research study; it is a powerful and transformative testament to the transformative power of education. The CATHR program is a peaceful disruptive strategy to counteract structural violence in Venezuela, promoting social justice and peacebuilding, transforming the lives of young people facing complex social issues, and empowering them to overcome adversity and embrace diversity. This study highlights the importance of interventions and support programs that focus on providing financial assistance, emotional support, and academic resources, and creating a more supportive and inclusive environment for students. It is a call to action for policymakers, educators, and community members to work together and help Venezuelan students achieve their dreams and build a better future for themselves and their country.

Aim of the Study

The purpose of this multidisciplinary study was to investigate the impact of the Collaborative Action on Transmedia and Human Rights (CATHR) program on the psychosocial well-being and learning disposition of Venezuelan college students who were facing the complexities of structural violence. The study used an ethnographic approach to collect information. The collected data formed the basis for the design of this comprehensive pedagogical model that fosters awareness, empathy, self-control, and emotional maturity, and encourages individuals to move beyond the restrictions of their prior worldview (Freire, 1970).

The collaborative online learning strategy implemented in Venezuela has been successful in effectively addressing ethical concerns and using science and technology in the service of peace, justice, and human rights, through the application of the United Nations Sustainable Development Goals https://sdgs.un.org/goals. The program's focus on promoting educational strategies that foster civic commitment, democratic values, the defense of human rights, and socio-environmental awareness has produced transformative effects, as evidenced by successful collaborations with multiple universities across the world.

The study also examined an interdisciplinary educational strategy based on a Challenge-Based Learning framework (Wenger, 1998), that was formulated and implemented at a Venezuelan institution of higher education. The objective of this model was to equip journalists with the capacity for discernment, autonomy, and self-governance. Prior to implementing the pedagogical approach, a thorough qualitative and quantitative analysis was conducted to understand the educational needs and constraints of the students. Throughout the study, the pedagogical methodology was implemented and evaluated to determine its effectiveness in promoting civic engagement, democratic values, reverence for human rights, and environmental awareness.

The collected data indicated that the all-encompassing curriculum significantly influenced the target audience by fostering a culture of mutual support, affirming their value, and endorsing sustainable development and human rights frameworks for future generations. The model integrates several pedagogical methodologies, including autonomous, transformative, emancipatory, and conscientization learning, which can serve as guiding principles for future research.

The study also examined the potential of technology in facilitating innovative forms of collaboration and knowledge dissemination among stakeholders, while also exploring solutions to address structural violence. Specifically, the study provides recommendations to universities and other higher education institutions on how to efficiently employ the Collaborative Action on Transmedia and Human Rights (CATHR) program to enhance their efforts in combating systemic violence. This research also advocates for the need to uphold ethical principles in all epistemological and pedagogical practices to ensure equitable opportunities for all learners with respect to varying contexts and cultures.

Through this work, we hope to contribute to the growing body of knowledge on pedagogy and technology, which can help build prosperous, democratic, and sustainable societies worldwide.

Materials and Methods

Assessing students' performance in cross-cultural negotiation simulations requires evaluating their communication and negotiation skills in a complex and dynamic environment. To overcome this challenge, we employed an array of research methods to ensure a comprehensive understanding of the students' experience. Our approach included both quantitative and qualitative measures, such as surveys, focus groups, and interviews, as well as observation, literature review, photographs, videos, and assignment content analysis.

In particular, we focused on assessing students' metacognitive development, which is essential to their academic success. While self-report measures have been a common method of assessing metacognitive development, recent research suggests that qualitative measures, such as open-ended prompts and interviews, provide a more comprehensive understanding of the complex nature of metacognition. Therefore, we used a combination of self-report measures and semi-structured interviews to gain a deeper understanding of the students' metacognitive processes and strategies.

By employing multiple research methods, we were able to triangulate our findings and provide a more nuanced understanding of the students' experiences. This approach allowed us to overcome the limitations of any single method and ensure the validity and reliability of our results. Overall, our methodology provides a robust framework for assessing students' performance in complex and dynamic environments and evaluating their metacognitive development.

Participants

The participants in this study were 2,500 Venezuelan college students aged 17 to 25 years who were facing the complexities of structural violence. The students were enrolled in a variety of programs, including 120 COIL (Collaborative Online International Learning) projects involving peers from 15 different countries and 100 collaborating professors. 200 of the students also participated in the Collaborative Action on Transmedia and Human Rights (CATHR) program as an extension of the COIL methodology.

The control group consisted of 500 students who had not participated in any COIL projects, and the experimental group consisted of students who had participated in at least one COIL project. The control group was studied from 2015 to 2018, and the experimental group was studied from 2019 to 2023.

DISCUSSION

Examining the Impact of Violence on Student Learning

In this section, we will analyze the impact of violence and structural inequality in Venezuela on the welfare of students. The OAS General Secretariat has classified the nation as experiencing a staggering surge of 1,800% in the prices of essential food items and an alarming number of 18,000 extrajudicial executions in recent years (Bachelet, 2021). We investigated the impact of these circumstances on the physical and mental health of students, their psychosocial welfare, and their attitude toward learning, applying the concepts of structural, symbolic, and normalized violence (Rylko-Bauer et al. 2009). These concepts are multifaceted, encompassing both positive and negative outcomes, and can be constructive or destructive.

During the study period, we conducted multiple focus groups and collected testimonies from young participants. Their statements revealed severe instances of trauma resulting from forced removal, morbidity, mortality, insecurity, domestic abuse, and neglect. We employed the Syndemic theory proposed by Merrill Singer to examine the effects of social circumstances on students' mental health. This theory makes a compelling plea to take action toward dismantling the systems that perpetuate human suffering (Singer, 2009).

The prevalence of violence in Venezuela is pervasive and affects every aspect of society, causing significant harm to those who are physically and socially disadvantaged (Hernández and Cadenas, 2018), (Ojeda and Marcano, 2019), (Noguera-Ramírez, O., & Herrera-Vargas, R., 2017), (Wekesser and Caballero, 2020), (ENCOVI 2019-20). Our research indicates a clear correlation between different types of violence and their impact on the physical, and psychosocial well-being, and academic attitude of Venezuelan students. It's crucial to understand that violence is not limited to its physical manifestations, such as the use of force or causing injury. The term also encompasses acts that violate a victim's personal integrity or self-worth.

Focusing only on the physical aspects of violence, such as torture, terror, and aggression, can limit our ability to observe, analyze, and respond to violence, injustice, and suffering more broadly. Therefore, it's necessary to take a holistic approach that recognizes the multiple dimensions of violence and their impacts on the individual and society (Scheper-Hughes and Bourgois 2004).

Nancy Scheper-Hughes and Phillipe Bourgois contend that violence encompasses not only physical harm but also includes assaults on the victim's personhood, dignity, sense of worth, or value (Scheper-Hughes & Bourgois 2004). They assert that the power and significance of violence stem from its social and cultural dimensions. The intricacy of the violence encountered by Venezuelan learners on a regular basis has a significant impact on their welfare (Hernández and Cadenas, 2018),

(Ojeda and Marcano, 2019), (Noguera-Ramírez, O., & Herrera-Vargas, R., 2017), (Wekesser and Caballero, 2020), (ENCOVI 2019-20). The accounts provided by students in this study demonstrate the challenges they face in navigating a variety of difficult circumstances, including food insecurity, aggression from peers, and violence perpetrated by government forces.

Circumstances in Venezuela during the period in which the students pursued their studies in communications were intricate and precarious. The Venezuelan government's use of repression has been acknowledged by international organizations. The Organization of American States (OAS) General Secretariat's report *Promoting Impunity: The Impact of the Absence of an Investigation by the Prosecutor of the International Criminal Court on the possible commission of crimes against humanity in Venezuela* claims that 18,000 extrajudicial executions have been committed since 2014, 15,000 arbitrary arrests and hundreds of cases of torture, and 724 cases of forced disappearance occurred between 2018 and 2019 (Bachelet, 2021). Furthermore, nearly 1,000 fatalities have been documented. Multidimensional poverty affects 64.8% of households and grew 13.8% between 2018 and 2019 (ENCOVI 2019-20).

The commonplace brutality of infant mortality, gradual malnourishment, illness, hopelessness, and degradation frequently goes unnoticed or misidentified. Venezuela is the poorest country and second most unequal in Latin America, with multidimensional poverty affecting 64.8% of households and a Gini coefficient of 51.0 (Bachelet, 2021). Michelle Bachelet estimates that one-third of Venezuelans are living in food insecurity (Bachelet, 2021).

According to a global ranking based on political instability, GDP, and levels of extreme poverty, Venezuela occupies the second position among 12 countries (Bachelet, 2021). Michelle Bachelet contends that the mean salary of a Venezuelan national is less than 1 US dollar per month, while the cost of the essential food basket has surged by 1,800% in the past year (Bachelet, 2021).

To explore the impact of the sociopolitical climate of the nation on the student population, a formative exercise was conducted through focus groups on their significant life events and post-graduation plans. From 2015 to 2023, on designated class days, 2500 students were asked to identify ten significant experiences that influenced their lives, including both positive and negative situations. After completing the exercise, they were invited to voluntarily share one of their experiences in front of the class. Results indicated that only 20% of the participants felt comfortable presenting their personal experiences to their peers.

Of the aforementioned cohort, 70% of the instances reported by the participants were associated with traumatic events. The prevalent themes that emerged from the testimonies were: (1) Coerced displacement resulting in the detachment of individuals from their parents, siblings, kin, and significant others (one of the respondents likened the feeling of detachment to amputation). (2) Grief resulting from the death of a parent, family member, or intimate associate. (3) Insecurity and crime. (4) Domestic violence. (5) Parental abandonment, whether by the father or mother. This activity has not only facilitated the acquisition of knowledge about the learner's context but also furnished a therapeutic experience at both an individual and collective scale. After the conclusion of the activity, students demonstrated a sense of camaraderie and provided support to their fellow classmates, resulting in a greater sense of integration within the group for the remainder of the semester. Acknowledging occurrences of violence can serve as a catalyst for the healing process.

Towards the end of the activity, the participants were instructed to compile a list of ten personal attributes they perceive they possess. On average, 60% of the participants are unable to complete five attributes. When inquired about their plans after graduation, 80% of the population studied indicated a desire to emigrate from the country. Inquiring about their perspectives on the state of affairs in the nation, the participants were posed with the following query: Do you believe that the ongoing conflict in the country will eventually reach a resolution? Ninety percent of the responses indicate that a short-term solution is not visible.

The concept of violence is slippery and multifaceted, characterized by nonlinearity and the ability to both create and destroy (Scheper-Hughes and Bourgois 2004). Additionally, violence has the potential to perpetuate itself through reproduction. Philippe Bourgois posits that the continuum of violence is intricately linked to the unequal distribution of resources and can be categorized into three primary forms: Structural Violence, Symbolic Violence, and Normalized Violence. Paul Farmer's perspective on Structural Violence highlights how deeply rooted political and economic forces have a detrimental impact on the physical well-being of the socially vulnerable. Bourgois argues that Structural Violence is influenced by discernible institutions, relationships, power dynamics, and ideologies. These may include carceral systems, prejudicial legislation, gender disparities, and racial discrimination. The phenomenon is evident in the form of health inequalities that lead to varying levels of morbidity, mortality, and occupational injuries among different social classes, ethnicities, and citizenship statuses (Scheper-Hughes and Bourgois 2004).

The notion of "Symbolic Violence" was formulated by Pierre Bourdieu and pertains to the process by which individuals who are socially subjugated internalize the existing power structures and hold themselves accountable for their own subordination (Bourdieu 2000, 2001; Bourdieu and Wacquant 1992). The term "Normalized Violence" has been derived from Scheper-Hughes's earlier notion of "Everyday Violence" and has been influenced by Franco Basaglia's critical evaluation of treatment protocols in psychiatric institutions (Scheper-Hughes and Lovell 1987). The incidence of brutality and violations of human rights generates a "Zone of Death" that normalizes the act of killing and inflicting pain, while simultaneously suppressing any form of dissent (Taussig 1984; Rylko-Bauer et al. 2009). Michelle

Table 1. Focus group study on significant life events and post-graduation plans among Venezuelan students

Research Findings	Summary
Sampling Method	Focus groups
Sample Size	2500 students
Data Collection	On designated class days from 2015-2023, students were asked to identify ten significant experiences that influenced their lives, including both positive and negative situations. After completing the exercise, they were invited to voluntarily share one of their experiences in front of the class.
Comfort Level with Sharing	Only 20% of the participants felt comfortable presenting their personal experiences
Prevalent Themes (codes) that Emerged from Testimonies	70% of the instances reported by the participants were associated with traumatic events. The prevalent themes that emerged from the testimonies were: (1) Coerced displacement resulting in the detachment of individuals from their parents, siblings, kin, and significant others (one of the respondents likened the feeling of detachment to amputation). (2) Grief resulting from the death of a parent, family member, or intimate associate. (3) Insecurity and crime. (4) Domestic violence. (5) Parental abandonment, whether by the father or mother.
Personal Attributes	On average, 60% of the participants were unable to complete five attributes
Plans after Graduation	80% of the population studied indicates a desire to emigrate from the country
Perspectives on Resolution of Ongoing National Conflict	90% of the responses indicate that a short-term solution is not visible
Impact of Exercise	This activity has facilitated the acquisition of knowledge about the learner's context and furnished a therapeutic experience at both an individual and collective scale, resulting in a greater sense of integration within the group for the remainder of the semester.

Note: The study found that a large majority of participants were unable to complete the personal attribute section, and substantial numbers of reporting instances were centered around traumatic events. This suggests a general lack of confidence in self-awareness and self-assessment among the student population.

Bachelet asserts that a nation's treatment of its most marginalized members, including prisoners, is a measure of its character. She expresses apprehension over accounts of fatalities among Venezuelan detainees caused by malnourishment, tuberculosis, and other illnesses (Bachelet, 2021).

The interrelated nature of these various forms of violence can lead to their continuity and the misidentification of their connections by the wider population. This, in turn, can legitimize oppressive power structures by placing blame on individuals (Singer 1996, 2009; Singer and Clair 2003; Singer, Erickson, et al. 2006), (Rylko-Bauer et al. 2009).

This framework offers a means of examining the impact of social circumstances on students' well-being, with a particular emphasis on the "Syndemic" theory advanced by Merrill Singer. Syndemic theory suggests that the conditions prevalent in hyper-ghettos lead to the accumulation of diseases that are related to infection,

Figure 1. The social and cultural dimensions of violence
Note. *The complexity of the continuum of violence and its impact on individuals' health is depicted in this figure. Physical violence, which is only the visible component, represents only the tip of the iceberg. The continuum of violence is categorized into three main types: Structural Violence, Symbolic Violence, and Normalized Violence.*

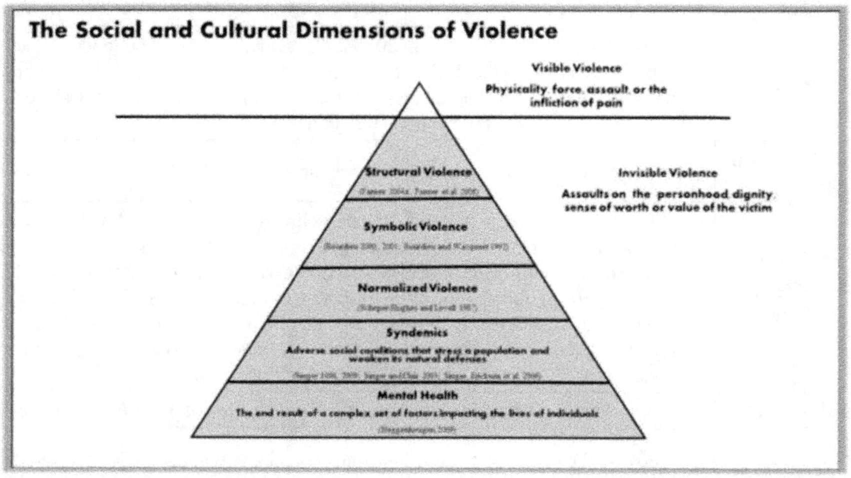

chronic stress, and mental health issues (Singer 1996, 2009; Singer and Clair 2003; Singer, Erickson et al. 2006), (Rylko-Bauer et al. 2009).

Emotional Discomfort and Mental Health

This section delves into the correlation among emotional distress, psychological well-being, and chronic stress, and proposes potential solutions for addressing these issues within educational establishments. By taking into account the intricate array of factors that affect Venezuelans' lives, particularly those related to physiological changes, it is feasible to develop strategies that take into consideration emotional well-being and enhance overall mental health and learning propensity (Hernández and Cadenas, 2018), (Ojeda and Marcano, 2019), (Noguera-Ramírez, O., & Herrera-Vargas, R., 2017), (Wekesser and Caballero, 2020), (ENCOVI 2019-20).

Chronic stress exerts diverse impacts on cognitive processes, encompassing memory, decision-making, and judgment. Chronic stress can lead to atrophy of the brain mass and decrease its weight (Sarahian et al., 2014). The overall impact of stress is a decrease in cognitive function, and several studies have linked chronic stress to both cognitive and affective disorders. Exposure to stress can lead to pathophysiological changes in the brain, which may manifest as behavioral, cognitive, and affective disturbances (Lupien et al., 2009). Stress can have both immediate and long-term effects on cognitive function that are contingent upon the type, timing, severity, and duration of the stressor (Sandi, 2013). These effects can vary from decreased reaction time and improved cognition and memory to reduced neuronal production and destruction of neurons along with other stimulatory neurotransmitters.

Stress can cause functional and structural changes in the hippocampus section of the brain (McEwen, 1999). These structural changes include atrophy and neurogenesis disorders (Lupien and Lepage, 2001). The reactions to this stress can vary from minor disruptions in physiological equilibrium to severe consequences that may jeopardize life, and in some cases, result in fatality (Liu & Alloy, 2010). Individuals who experience stress are at an increased risk of developing various mental disorders, as it can serve as a catalyst or exacerbate existing pathological conditions. The correlation between stressful life events and psychiatric illness is stronger than the correlation with medical or physical illness (Kessler et al., 1997).

The relationship of psychiatry with social determinants of health is seen in the most obvious form in the interaction between unconscious and conscious aspects of personality and environmental stressors (Kessler et al., 1997). Psychiatrists may consider both biological and psychosocial factors in understanding how trauma, stress, and demographic variables lead to different clinical presentations in patients with mental illness. Stressful life events have consistently been identified as potential antecedents to a wide range of psychological and physical disorders, including depression, anxiety, posttraumatic stress disorder, and cardiovascular disease (Liu & Alloy, 2010). Stress is thought to have a biological basis of multiple pathways leading to physiological arousal and alterations in the immune system, which can precipitate or exacerbate existing pathological conditions and increase susceptibility to health problems (Liu & Alloy, 2010).

The present study reveals that a considerable number of individuals, from the 2.500 studied, suffer from mental health disorders, including but not limited to depression, anxiety, and panic attacks, which significantly affect their daily functioning. The chronic stress experienced by college students in Venezuela has a significant impact on both their emotional and physical well-being. This research points out that, on average, five students out of 40 openly manifest experiencing anxiety, depression, or panic attacks. Additionally, several other students privately express their emotional distress and the use of psychotropic medications.

Research has shown that prolonged stress can lead to various complications, such as increased levels of interleukin-6 (IL-6) and plasma cortisol, as well as decreased levels of cAMP-responsive element binding protein and brain-derived neurotrophic factor (BDNF). These changes are similar to those observed in individuals with depression and mood disorders, who often experience a range of cognitive impairments (Song et al., 2006). Furthermore, there exists a physiological connection between stress and cognitive disorders that are based on mood. This is evidenced by the elevated levels of inflammatory markers, including interleukins and TNF- (which are known to contribute significantly to the onset of cognitive disorders) (Solerte et al., 2000; Marsland et al.).

Stress, Cognition, and Learning

In scholarly communities, there is a prevalent belief that moderate levels of stress can enhance cognitive abilities, especially in the domains of verbal and visual memory. Sometimes, under special conditions, stress can actually improve memory (McEwen and Lupien, 2002). However, when stress surpasses an individual's threshold, which varies among individuals, it can result in cognitive impairments, particularly those that impact memory and decision-making abilities (Song et al., 2006). The impact of stress on memory and decision-making is mediated by the hippocampus and prefrontal cortex (Sandi, 2013). According to Gould and Tanapat (1999 and Köhler et al. (2010), stress has been shown to hinder or interrupt the process of neurogenesis in the dentate gyrus region of the hippocampus. This particular region represents one of the few areas in the adult brain where neurogenesis takes place (1999 and Köhler et al. (2010).

Cognition is a crucial component of brain functionality. The field of cognition encompasses a range of cognitive processes, including but not limited to learning, decision-making, attention, and judgment. The aforementioned processes entail the reception and subsequent processing of stimuli that are received (Sandi, 2013). Depending on the severity, duration, source, and magnitude of the stressor, there are various effects on cognitive performance (Sandi, 2013). Prolonged elevations in plasma concentrations of glucocorticoids can result in hippocampal atrophy, which can subsequently cause deficits in memory. MRI scans of individuals diagnosed with post-traumatic stress disorder (PTSD) have revealed a reduction in the volume of the hippocampus, a brain region associated with memory and emotion regulation (Bremner, 1999). The hippocampus, amygdala, and temporal lobe play a critical role in cognitive development, particularly in memory formation (McEwen & Sapolsky, 1995).

One example of this is the biphasic impact of adrenal hormones on the cognitive and memory retrieval functions of the hippocampus (McEwen and Sapolsky, 1995). In addition, these individuals exhibit neurophysiological impacts, including impaired verbal memory. Stress can have adverse effects on both learning and the process of long-term potentiation (LTP) (McEwen and Sapolsky, 1995). The memory consolidation process during stressful periods is modulated by two pivotal factors: noradrenaline and corticosteroids. The concentration of cortisol and memory displays a negative correlation, in which increased levels of plasma cortisol due to prolonged stress result in a deterioration of memory (McEwen and Sapolsky, 1995).

The hippocampus, amygdala, and temporal lobe are the principal brain regions implicated in the physiological and behavioral responses to stress. Co-administration of steroids with other excitatory neurotransmitters may lead to neuronal apoptosis during prolonged periods of stress (Sandi, 2013). Research has demonstrated that being exposed to stress can have an adverse impact on cognitive abilities that are associated with the hippocampus, particularly spatial memory (Borcel et al., 2008; Sandi et al., 2003).

Emotional turmoil and chronic stress have an adverse impact on the cognitive faculties, memory consolidation, aptitude for learning, ability to make sound decisions, and discernment of university students (Song et al., 2006). Stress also has negative effects on learning. Results from hippocampus-dependent loading data demonstrate that subjects are not as familiar with a new environment after having been exposed to chronic stress (Bremner, 1999). A significant proportion of Venezuelan students experience mental health issues. Specifically, 12.5% of the surveyed students in this research reported openly experiencing symptoms of anxiety, depression, or panic attacks, while several others privately disclosed experiencing emotional distress. High levels of glucocorticoids in the brain, which are secreted in response to stress, can cause atrophy of the hippocampus, resulting in cognitive deficits. Moreover, adrenal steroids lead to alteration in long-term potentiation (LTP), which is an important process in memory formation (Bliss and Lømo, 1973).

When developing comprehensive pedagogical methodologies, it is crucial to possess a profound comprehension of the psycho-social circumstances that influence learners' lives. It is also essential to devise strategies that consider the emotional well-being of individuals in educational institutions. Given the detrimental effects of stress on cognitive abilities, it is widely acknowledged that the implementation of behavioral interventions aimed at reducing stress levels can lead to an enhancement in cognitive function (Scholey et al., 2014). This approach can contribute to the overall welfare of communities that are significantly affected by violence.

The findings of this research can be used to improve the well-being of students in several ways:

- Creating a safe and supportive environment: The research findings highlight the prevalence of traumatic events in students' lives and the fact that many students may not feel comfortable sharing their experiences. Thus, creating a safe and supportive environment in schools where students can feel comfortable expressing themselves and seeking support is crucial for their well-being.
- Providing access to mental health resources: Traumatic experiences can have a significant impact on mental health. Schools can provide access to mental

health resources such as counseling services, support groups, and other interventions to help students cope with the effects of traumatic events.

- Building resilience: The findings also highlight the importance of building resilience in students. This can be achieved through various interventions such as teaching coping skills, providing opportunities for positive experiences, and promoting social support networks.
- Addressing systemic issues: The research findings also suggest that many students may have plans to emigrate from the country, indicating a lack of confidence in the future. Addressing systemic issues such as social inequality, crime, and violence can help create a more stable and positive environment for students, which is essential for their well-being.

In summary, the findings of this research can be used to improve the well-being of students by creating a safe and supportive environment, providing access to mental health resources, building resilience, and addressing systemic issues.

Reimagining Possibilities: Subjective Reframing for Learner and Societal Transformation

This segment delineates the pedagogical notion of transformative learning, which refers to a process that encompasses critical consciousness, effective communication, and purposeful action. Through the implementation of effective educational leadership, critical reflection, and discourse, educators can establish a safe and nurturing learning environment that fosters the development of learners' awareness, empathy, self-regulation, and emotional maturity. Robert Kegan's constructive developmental theory has been employed to examine the concepts of transformative learning within the realm of education and assess the impact of a supportive setting on individual growth and development.

Robert Kegan's constructive developmental theory (CDT) is a prominent framework for understanding the cognitive and psychological development of adults. The theory draws from research in developmental psychology, philosophy, and education to describe a model of adult maturity that emphasizes the complexity of thinking and the ability to handle paradoxical or conflicting perspectives (Eriksen, 2020). According to Kegan, individuals go through a series of five developmental stages that build upon each other, from an embedded stage where they rely on external authority and social norms to a self-authoring stage where they create their own values and identities based on internal principles (Kegan, 1982).

Revitalizing education is a crucial undertaking in times of humanitarian crises, and universities have a responsibility to create programs that effectively manage human resources and promote personal growth (Goleman et al. 2002). Educators ought to devise tactics to instruct individuals who possess conscientiousness and can spearhead transformative initiatives in their communities and societies by leveraging their personal and social competencies. The duty of contemporary university leaders today is to prioritize the cultivation of personal attributes that are essential for effective leadership, such as self-awareness, attentive listening, empathy, candor, ethical principles, consistency, and proficiency in collaborative work (Astin & Astin, 2000; Rubino & Amat, 2001).

Facilitating the capacity of young individuals to exercise discernment and act with freedom, autonomy, and reflective critical thinking is essential for fostering the growth of transcendent individuals. It is imperative to encourage learners to reposition themselves concerning the perceived issues. John Dewey argued that education plays a crucial role in promoting social progress and initiating reform (Dewey, 1897). According to Rennick (2015), Dewey recognized the connection between education and participatory democracy. He stressed the significance of the correlation between personal experience and learning.

Active learning is a combination of pedagogical guidance and skill acquisition that enables learners to autonomously navigate their educational journey. Active learning is a fusion of pedagogical guidance and the acquisition of skills that empower the learner to independently manage their educational journey. The main goal of competency-based learning is to promote metacognitive reflection, which can lead to personal and societal transformation. According to Alexander W. Astin, educational leadership plays a crucial role in fostering social competencies among students, which in turn have a positive impact on their communities, schools, and both public and private organizations. As a result, students develop a sense of civic responsibility and self-reflection during the learning process (Astin, 1993).

"Transformative learning" refers to a pedagogical methodology that has the potential to establish a new educational paradigm. The methodology emphasizes impactful learning and is distinguished by hands-on, cooperative, dynamic, and captivating techniques. Education has the potential to bring about a revolution in the individual learner, and as a result, in the community in which they live. According to Jones (2015), transformative learning serves as an exemplar of a pedagogical strategy that can be employed to establish the groundwork for a paradigm shift in education. The philosophy developed by Jack Mezirow extends beyond the mere memorization of information and encompasses both individual and social dimensions and implications. Rennick contends that this pedagogical approach places emphasis on high-impact learning, characterized by experiential, collaborative, active, and engaging methods. When students are consciously engaged, they develop a sense of global citizenship and become dedicated to the greater goals of humanity (Rennick, 2015). This approach possesses the potential to revolutionize the student and, consequently, the community in which the student resides (Taylor & Cranton,

2012). The complete realization of human potential for transformative learning is contingent upon values such as liberty, parity, acceptance, impartiality, civic duty, and education (Taylor & Cranton, 2012).

Transformative learning is a profound cognitive and affective process that enables students to become aware of the fundamental assumptions that shape their ideas and emotions. It also helps them recognize the need for change. The concept of critical consciousness, which was first introduced by Paulo Freire, is an essential component in the quest for liberation. Mezirow utilizes Freire's notions of conscientization and emancipatory learning to contend that genuine liberty encompasses not only the aspiration and comprehension to bring about transformation but also the capability to act towards accomplishing one's objectives. The final phase of the transformation process entails a willingness to put into practice newly acquired understanding through the cultivation of qualities such as mindfulness, empathy, self-control, and psychological growth. Freire argued that the only way to achieve liberation is through "praxis, " which involves both reflection and action to bring about transformative changes in the world.

Transformative learning is a crucial process that involves resolving personal dilemmas, expanding consciousness, and integrating pre-existing and novel patterns of behavior. The acquisition of knowledge requires a readiness to contemplate alternative perspectives, an ability to be receptive to emotions, and a commitment to self-reflection and analytical evaluation. Through this process, individuals can gain a deeper understanding of themselves, their interpersonal relationships, and their perspectives on social equity and harmony.

The educational approach presented in this paper is grounded in the Transformative Learning pedagogical theory and encompasses four interrelated areas of focus for journalism and communication courses, which have been carefully developed and put into practice. The strategy focuses on the production of high-impact projects based on the UN's Human Rights Declaration that provide solutions for the 17 Sustainable Development Goals from the Agenda 2030 and working with local Non-Govermental Organizations, civil associations, and citizens. The pedagogical strategy has proved that Venezuelan students develop awareness, empathy, self-control, and emotional maturity while fostering camaraderie and collaboration in the classroom.

The duty of the educator is to facilitate this transformative learning within the classroom by cultivating critical reflection, inquiry, and discourse. In order To accomplish this, during the courses assessed in this study, professors have set objectives that encompass critical thinking and promote a culture of trust and compassion. To augment the critical thinking abilities of students, educators provided learners with occasions to recognize various frames of reference and reframe problems from diverse viewpoints. Academic discourse requires the reassessment of convictions and principles and was promoted through various methods, including concept mapping, raising awareness, and examining life histories. Professional development was an essential component for educators to achieve authenticity and engage in critical reflection.

Assessment of the Collaborative Action on Transmedia and Human Rights (CATHR) program has shown that a favorable environment that is conducive to growth and development is crucial for facilitating transformation. Through the creation of a safe and secure social environment, educators were able to openly discuss "disorienting dilemmas." This approach has proven successful in constructing new frames of reference and effectively integrating learning into their teaching practices.

Breaking Barriers: The Collaborative Action on Transmedia and Human Rights (CATHR) Program

In today's digital era, educators must empower students to personalize their learning experience by choosing their preferred virtual learning systems. Access to cutting-edge technology and resources beyond the classroom can facilitate problem-solving skills and creativity, preparing students for their professional lives. The Collaborative Action on Transmedia and Human Rights (CATHR) program is a 15-week international program that empowers Venezuelan students to resist and combat structural violence, promote social justice, and create a more informed, engaged, and just world. The program integrates pedagogical methods that prioritize self-efficacy and resilience, as well as the development of transmedia literacy skills. It has been successful in promoting critical thinking, professional ethics, collaborative work, and citizen participation among students, as well as producing high-quality digital journalism.

The program aims to equip individuals with the necessary skills to excel in the realm of digital journalism. The task at hand is to create an informative Transmedia Narrative Universe, centered around a particular article from the Universal Declaration of Human Rights and proposing solutions to one or more of the UN's Sustainable Development Goals. Throughout the execution of these initiatives, students engage in online collaborations with counterparts from esteemed universities worldwide. They acquire team leadership competencies, establish shared objectives, and cultivate a notion of civic duty and self-reflection on their beliefs and principles.

This approach to learning aligns with the United Nations' Sustainable Development Goals, which aim to end poverty, protect the planet, and ensure prosperity for all. By engaging in online collaborations and utilizing technology to interact with others in a global setting, students acquire the necessary skills to contribute to a sustainable future. CATHR offers a promising framework for empowering individuals to resist and combat structural violence and promote social justice. It is a valuable investment in the future of our society, as it empowers students to create and share their own content, thereby creating a more informed, engaged, and just world.

Findings

The study's findings are particularly relevant in the context of Venezuela, where structural violence has had a devastating impact on the country's education system. The study found that students at both institutions faced a range of challenges, including:

- Economic hardship: Many students reported struggling to afford tuition, textbooks, and other essential expenses.
- Political instability: The ongoing political crisis in Venezuela has created a climate of uncertainty and fear, which has made it difficult for students to focus on their studies.
- Violence and insecurity: Students reported feeling unsafe on campus and in their communities.
- Discrimination: Students from low-income backgrounds and from marginalized groups reported experiencing discrimination from faculty, staff, and other students.

Despite these challenges, the study found that many students were resilient and determined to succeed. They reported finding strength in their relationships with their peers, professors, and family members. They also reported finding inspiration in their work, which they saw as a way to make a difference in the world.

The study's findings suggest that there is a need for interventions and support programs that can help Venezuelan students overcome the challenges they face. These programs should focus on providing financial assistance, emotional support, and academic resources. They should also work to create a more supportive and inclusive environment for students.

The study's findings are a call to action for policymakers, educators, and community members. By working together, we can help Venezuelan students achieve their dreams and build a better future for themselves and their country.

The following are some specific recommendations for interventions and support programs:

- Financial assistance: Scholarships and financial aid can help students afford tuition, textbooks, and other essential expenses.
- Emotional support: Counseling and support groups can help students cope with the stress of economic hardship, political instability, violence, and discrimination.
- Academic resources: Tutoring and other academic support services can help students succeed in their studies.

Creating a more supportive and inclusive environment: Educators and administrators can create a more supportive and inclusive environment by addressing issues of discrimination and harassment, and by promoting a culture of respect and understanding.

In addition, the research investigated the impact of the Collaborative Action on Transmedia and Human Rights (CATHR) program on the resilience and attitudes toward the international collaboration of Venezuelan college students who were facing the complexities of structural violence. CATHR is a unique and innovative program, conceived in a Venezuelan university to empower students to resist and combat structural violence. By promoting social justice and creating a more informed, engaged, and just world, CATHR helps students to develop the skills and knowledge necessary to make a positive impact in their communities and beyond. Derived from the Collaborative Online International Learning methodology, CATHR is a Venezuelan-designed pedagogy that has the potential to transform the lives of young people facing complex social issues.

The study found that CATHR had a positive impact on both resilience and attitudes toward international collaboration. Specifically, the study found that:

- Students who participated in CATHR reported significantly higher levels of resilience than students who did not participate in CATHR.
- Students who participated in CATHR reported significantly more positive attitudes toward international collaboration than students who did not participate in CATHR.

The study's findings suggest that CATHR can be an effective intervention for promoting resilience and positive attitudes towards international collaboration among Venezuelan college students who are facing the complexities of structural violence. The study also suggests that CATHR may be a valuable tool for promoting social justice and peacebuilding in Venezuela and other countries that are experiencing structural violence.

Some of the reasons why CATHR may have had a positive impact on the resilience and attitudes towards the international collaboration of Venezuelan college students are:

- CATHR provided students with the opportunity to connect with peers from other countries and cultures. This can help students to develop a more global perspective and to see themselves as part of a larger community.
- CATHR provided students with the opportunity to learn about different cultures and perspectives. This can help students to become more open-minded and to develop a greater appreciation for diversity.

- CATHR provided students with the opportunity to collaborate on projects with peers from other countries. This can help students to develop teamwork skills and to learn how to work effectively with people from different backgrounds.

The Collaborative Action on Transmedia and Human Rights (CATHR) program serves as a catalyst for introspective growth and transformation by provoking critical self-reflection, challenging assumptions, and facilitating the development of empathy and adaptive skills. This introspective growth transforms students' perceptions of themselves and the world, empowering them to overcome adversity and embrace diversity.

The core category that emerged from this research is the idea of CATHR as a catalyst - a stimulus that provokes and accelerates internal changes. During the process of collecting data students described how learning new ideas and perspectives through education:

- Provoked critical self-reflection that challenged their assumptions and worldviews, leading them to gain new insights about themselves and society.
- Fostered the development of empathy, communication skills, and other adaptive capacities that allowed them to understand better and connect with others.
- Equipped them with resilience, support systems, and self-determinacy to overcome obstacles and adversities in their lives.
- Helped them gain a more inclusive perspective that embraced diverse backgrounds and experiences as resources for learning and enrichment.

These internal changes - the introspective growth - transformed students' self-perception and perception of the world, empowering them to act as engaged global citizens. Education served as the catalyst that sparked this introspective process of growth and transformation.

CONCLUSION

The CATHR pedagogical approach fosters an environment where individuals can engage in discussions about civic responsibilities, self-reflection, and critical thinking. Through their involvement in high-impact projects, students can take action based on their acquired knowledge and overcome preconceived notions to develop mindfulness, compassion, self-regulation, and emotional development. This research has shown that students who were exposed to nature while accomplishing their tasks experienced significant improvements in their health, including enhanced psychological well-being and increased cognitive function. When connecting with nature, individuals communicated with each other through openness, acceptance, active listening, and solidarity.

Furthermore, this approach enables individuals to transcend the savior/victim mentality and instead develop a deep understanding of their civic responsibilities. The experiences of the learner during the process extend beyond the mere memorization of facts and have personal as well as social implications. Students exhibit their pursuit of knowledge by conversing with their peers from diverse cultural backgrounds in a collaborative setting, demonstrating a critical reassessment of their psychological and emotional responses to the experience. As individuals acquire new knowledge and undergo novel experiences, they may come to realize that their preconceived notions have been disproven.

Overall, the CATHR pedagogical approach provides an effective framework for promoting critical thinking, civic engagement, and personal growth. By incorporating nature and collaborative learning, this approach can enhance students' health, cognitive function, and interpersonal skills, enabling them to become well-rounded and responsible citizens of the world.

REFERENCES

Anderson, L. W., Krathwohl, D. R., Airasian, P. W., Cruikshank, K. A., Mayer, R. E., Pintrich, P. R., Raths, J., & Wittrock, M. C. (2000). *A Taxonomy for Learning, Teaching, and Assessing: A revision of Bloom's Taxonomy of Educational Objectives*. Pearson, Allyn & Bacon.

Astin, A. W. (1993). How are students affected? *Change*, *25*(2), 44–50. doi:10.1080/00091383.1993.9940617

Astin, A. W., & Astin, H. S. (2000). *Leadership Reconsidered: Engaging Higher Education in Social Change*. W.K. Kellogg Foundation.

Bachelet, M. (2021). *Statement by the United Nations High Commissioner for Human Rights on Venezuela. 46th session of the Human Rights Council*. Geneva. https://www.ohchr.org/EN/NewsEvents/Pages/DisplayNews.aspx?NewsID=26874&LangID=E

Ball, J., & Haque, S. (2016). Ethnographic research in disaster-affected communities: A review of the literature. *Disasters*, *40*(2), 433–453.

Baron-Cohen, S. (2002). The extreme male brain theory of autism. *Trends in Cognitive Sciences*, *6*(6), 248–254. doi:10.1016/S1364-6613(02)01904-6 PMID:12039606

Bauer-Clapp, H. (2010). REVIEW: Global Health in Times of Violence. *Landscapes of Violence*, *1*(1), 8.

Bernal, J. L. (2000). Cuestionario sobre liderazgo transformacional. Aportaciones desde una investigación. En Liderazgo y organizaciones que aprenden, 441-459. Ediciones Mensajero.

Bliss, T. V., & Lømo, T. (1973). Long-lasting potentiation of synaptic transmission in the dentate area of the anaesthetized rabbit following stimulation of the perforant path. *The Journal of Physiology*, *232*(2), 331–356. doi:10.1113/jphysiol.1973.sp010273 PMID:4727084

Bloom, B. S. (1956). *Taxonomy of Educational Objectives, Handbook I: The Cognitive Domain*. David McKay Co. Inc.

Boler, M., & Zembylas, M. (2003). Discomforting truths: The emotional terrain of understanding difference. In P. Trifonas (Ed.), *Pedagogies of difference: Rethinking education for social justice* (pp. 23–45). Routledge.

Borcel, E., Pérez-Alvarez, L., Herrero, A. I., Brionne, T., Varea, E., Berezin, V., Bock, E., Sandi, C., & Venero, C. (2008). Chronic stress in adulthood followed by intermittent stress impairs spatial memory and the survival of newborn hippocampal cells in aging animals: Prevention by FGL, a peptide mimetic of neural cell adhesion molecule. *Behavioural Pharmacology*, *19*(1), 41–49. doi:10.1097/FBP.0b013e3282f3fca9 PMID:18195593

Bourdieu, P. (1977). Cultural Reproduction and Social Reproduction. In J. Karabel & A. H. Halsey (Eds.), *Power and Ideology in Education* (pp. 487–511). Oxford University Press.

Bourdieu, P. (2000). *Cuestiones de Sociología*. Istmo.

Bourdieu, P. (2001). *Masculine Domination*. Polity Press.

Bourdieu, P., & Wacquant, L. (1994). *Per a una sociología reflexiva*. Herder.

Bourgois, P. (2008). *Neoliberal Lumpen Abuse in the 2000s; A 25-Year Ethnographic Retrospective of Violence in the Americas*. Presented at the Conference, Violence and Citizenship in Post-Authoritarian Latin America, Princeton University.

Bremner, J. D. (1999). Does stress damage the brain? *Biological Psychiatry*, *45*(7), 797–805. doi:10.1016/S0006-3223(99)00009-8 PMID:10202566

Casero-Ripollés, A. (2012). Transmedia strategies in news outlets: An approach to the Spanish media panorama. *Communicatio Socialis*, *25*(1), 29–53.

Coppedge, M., & Bitar, S. (Eds.). (2020). *Crises of democracy and the prospect of renewal*. Johns Hopkins University Press.

Dewey, J. (1897, January). My Pedagogic Creed. *School Journal*, *54*, 77–80.

Eriksen, K. (2020). Robert Kegan's constructive developmental theory: An overview and implications for practice. *Journal of Adult Development*, *27*(2), 79–89. doi:10.1007/s10804-019-09353-1

Europa World Plus. (2018). *Venezuela: Social media and political polarization*. Europa World Plus. https://search.proquest.com/docview/2068108154

Farmer, P. (2003). *Pathologies of Power: Health, Human Rights, and the New War on the Poor*. University of California Press.

Farmer, P. (2004). An Anthropology of Structural Violence. *Current Anthropology*, 45.

Farmer, P., Nizeye, B., Stulac, S., & Keshavjee, S. (2006). Structural Violence and Clinical Medicine. *PLoS Medicine*, *3*(10), e449. doi:10.1371/journal.pmed.0030449 PMID:17076568

Freire, P. (1970). *Pedagogy of the oppressed*. Herder and Herder.

Freire, P. (2005). *Pedagogy of the oppressed* (M. Bergman Ramos, Trans.). Continuum. (Original work published 1970)

Freitez, A., España, L., Correa, G., Di Brienza, M., & Ponce, M. (Equipo Coordinador). (2020). *Encuesta Nacional de Condiciones de Vida 2019-20 (ENCOVI'2019-20)*. Caracas. UCAB-USB-UCV.

Galtung, J. (1969). Violence, Peace, and Peace Research. *Journal of Peace Research*, *6*(3), 167–191. doi:10.1177/002234336900600301

Gay, G. (2002). Preparing for culturally responsive teaching. *Journal of Teacher Education*, *53*(2), 106–116. doi:10.1177/0022487102053002003

General Secretariat, O. A. S. (2020). *Fomentando la impunidad: El impacto de la ausencia de una investigación de la Fiscal de la Corte Penal Internacional sobre la posible comisión de crímenes de lesa humanidad en Venezuela (preparado por Jared Genser)*. OAS. https://www.oas.org/es/centro_noticias/comunicado_prensa.asp?sCodigo=C-122/20

Gómez, D. (2019). *Personal communication*. Research Gate.

Gonzalez, Á. P., & Sanchez, P. (2005). What do we know about how students learn in the college? In *Chamorro Plaza, M. C. y Sánchez Delgado, P., Iniciación a la docencia universitaria. Manual de ayuda* (pp. 11–44). Instituto de Ciencias de la Educación, Universidad Complutense.

Gould, E., & Tanapat, P. (1999). Stress and hippocampal neurogenesis. *Biological Psychiatry*, *46*(11), 1472–1479. doi:10.1016/S0006-3223(99)00247-4 PMID:10599477

Gutiérrez, K. D., & Rogoff, B. (2003). Cultural ways of learning: Individual traits or repertoires of practice. *Educational Researcher*, *32*(5), 19–25. doi:10.3102/0013189X032005019

Hernández, A., & Cadenas, L. (2018). The economic crisis and its impact on student dropout rates in higher education in Venezuela. International Journal of Learning. *Teaching and Educational Research*, *17*(3), 185–203.

Human Rights Watch. (2017). *Venezuela: The supreme court's attack on democracy.* HRW. https://www.hrw.org/report/2017/05/26/venezuela-supreme-courts-attack-democracy

Human Rights Watch. (2020). *Venezuela: Dire Conditions for Children.* Human Rights Watch. https://www.hrw.org/news/2020/02/26/venezuela-dire-conditions-children

Jenkins, H. (2009). *Confronting the challenges of participatory culture: Media education for the 21st century*. MIT Press. doi:10.7551/mitpress/8435.001.0001

Jones, P. (2015). Transformative learning theory: Addressing new challenges in social work education. *Exploring Learning & Teaching in Higher Education*, 267-286.

Kegan, R. (1982). *The Evolving Self: Problem and Process in Human Development*. Harvard University Press. doi:10.4159/9780674039414

Kessler, R. C., Davis, C. G., & Kendler, K. S. (1997). Childhood adversity and adult psychiatric disorder in the US National Comorbidity Survey. *Psychological Medicine*, *27*(5), 1101–1119. doi:10.1017/S0033291797005588 PMID:9300515

Kezar, A., & Moriarty, D. (2000). Expanding our understanding of student leadership development: A study exploring gender and ethnic identity. *Journal of College Student Development*, *41*, 55–68.

Köhler, S., Thomas, A. J., Lloyd, A., Barber, R., Almeida, O. P., & O'Brien, J. T. (2010). White matter hyperintensities, cortisol levels, brain atrophy and continuing cognitive deficits in late-life depression. *The British Journal of Psychiatry*, *196*(2), 143–149. doi:10.1192/bjp.bp.109.071399 PMID:20118461

Koyama, J. (2019). *Structural Violence and Education: The Impact on Student Success. University of California*. Center for the Study of Democracy.

Lewis, L. A. (2018). Institutional Betrayal, Cultural Violence, and Structural Violence: Examples from the Educational System. [This article discusses how institutional betrayal, cultural violence, and structural violence perpetuate inequalities in education, particularly for marginalized communities.]. *Journal of Interpersonal Violence*, *35*(1), 66–90.

Liu, R. T., & Alloy, L. B. (2010). Stress generation in depression: A systematic review of the empirical literature and recommendations for future study. *Clinical Psychology Review*, *30*(5), 582–593. doi:10.1016/j.cpr.2010.04.010 PMID:20478648

Lupien, S. J., & Lepage, M. (2001). Stress, memory, and the hippocampus: Can't live with it, can't live without it. *Behavioural Brain Research*, *127*(1-2), 137–158. doi:10.1016/S0166-4328(01)00361-8 PMID:11718889

Lupien, S. J., McEwen, B. S., Gunnar, M. R., & Heim, C. (2009). Effects of stress throughout the lifespan on the brain, behavior, and cognition. *Nature Reviews. Neuroscience*, *10*(6), 434–445. doi:10.1038/nrn2639 PMID:19401723

Masten, A. S. (2014). Global Perspectives on Resilience in Children and Youth. *Child Development*, *85*(1), 6–20. doi:10.1111/cdev.12205 PMID:24341286

McEwen, B., & Lupien, S. (2002). Stress: hormonal and neural aspects. In V. S. Ramachandran (Ed.), *Encyclopedia of the human brain* (pp. 463–474). Elsevier. doi:10.1016/B0-12-227210-2/00333-2

McEwen, B. S. (1999). Stress and hippocampal plasticity. *Annual Review of Neuroscience*, *22*(1), 105–122. doi:10.1146/annurev.neuro.22.1.105 PMID:10202533

McEwen, B. S., & Sapolsky, R. M. (1995). Stress and cognitive function. *Current Opinion in Neurobiology*, *5*(2), 205–216. doi:10.1016/0959-4388(95)80028-X PMID:7620309

Mendenhall, E. (2012). *Syndemic Suffering: Social Distress, Depression, and Diabetes among Mexican Immigrant Women*. Left Coast Press, Inc.

Merrill, S. (2009). *Introducing Syndemics: A Critical Systems Approach to Public and Community Health*. Jossey-Bass.

Mezirow, J. (1978). Perspective transformation. *Adult Education*, *28*(2), 100–110. doi:10.1177/074171367802800202

Mezirow, J. (1991). *Transformative dimensions of adult learning*. Jossey-bass.

Mezirow, J. (1997). Transformative Learning: Theory to Practice. *New Directions for Adult and Continuing Education*, *1997*(74), 5–12. doi:10.1002/ace.7401

Mezirow, J., & ... (Eds.). (2000). *Learning as transformation*. Jossey Bass.

Naím, M., & Toro, F. (2020). Socioeconomic and political roots of Venezuela's crisis. In F. Coppedge & S. Bitar (Eds.), *Crises of democracy and the prospect of renewal* (pp. 137–152). Johns Hopkins University Press.

Noguera-Ramírez, O., & Herrera-Vargas, R. (2017). Human rights education and social justice in higher education: Perspectives from Venezuela. *Higher Education for the Future*, *4*(1), 82–95.

O'Sullivan, E. (1999). *Transformative learning: Educational vision for the 21st. Century*. Zed Books.

Ojeda, D. A., & Marcano, M. (2019). Access to higher education in Venezuela: Challenges and opportunities for socio-economic mobility. *International Journal of Development and Sustainability*, *8*(8), 763–778.

Paulo Freire Institute. (n.d.). *Structural Violence, Education and Freedom*. PFI. http://www.paulofreireinstitute.org/pdf/StructuralViolenceEducationandFreedom.pdf

Rennick, J. (2015). Learning that Makes a Difference: Pedagogy and Practice for Learning Abroad. Teaching & Learning Inquiry. The ISSOTL Journal, 3(2), 71-88.

Robledo, K., & Atarama, T. (2016). Periodismo político transmedia. Estrategias para el desarrollo de la profesión en el actual ecosistema mediático. *Correspondencias & Análisis*, (6), 31–45. doi:10.24265/cian.2016.n6.02

Rubin, J. (2017). *Embedding Collaborative Online International Learning (COIL) at Higher Education Institutions An Evolutionary Overview with Exemplars*. UIC. https://studyabroad.uic.edu/wp-content/uploads/sites/256/2020/08/Rubin-Embedding-Collaborative-Online-International-Learning-at-Higher-Education-Institutions.pdf

Rubin, J., & Guth, S. (2022). *The Guide to COIL Virtual Exchange*. Stylus Publishing.

Ruiz, S., Hernández, S., García, A., & Chacón, J. (2021). Educational innovation in times of crisis: learner voices from the Albany-Caracas COIL exchange. In Satar, Müge (Ed.), Virtual exchange: towards digital equity in internationalization (pp. 131-138). Research-publishing.net. doi:10.14705/rpnet.2021.53.1295

Rylko-Bauer, B., Whiteford, L., & Farmer, P. (Eds.). (2009). *Global Health in Times of Violence*. School of Advanced Research Press.

Sandi, C. (2013). Stress and cognition. *Wiley Interdisciplinary Reviews: Cognitive Science*, *4*(3), 245–261. doi:10.1002/wcs.1222 PMID:26304203

Sarahian, N., Sahraei, H., Zardooz, H., Alibeik, H., & Sadeghi, B. (2014). Effect of memantine administration within the nucleus accumbens on changes in weight and volume of the brain and adrenal gland during chronic stress in female mice. *Modares J Med Sci: Pathobiology.*, *17*, 71–82.

Scheper-Hughes, N. (1996). Small Wars and Invisible Genocides. *Social Science & Medicine*, *43*(5), 889–900. doi:10.1016/0277-9536(96)00152-9 PMID:8870153

Scheper-Hughes, N., & Bourgois, P. (Eds.). (2003). *Violence in War and Peace: An Anthology*. Blackwell Publishers.

Scheper-Hughes, N., & Bourgois, P. (2004). Introduction: Making Sense of Violence. In *Violence in War and Peace: An Anthology*. Blackwell Publishing.

Scheper-Hughes, N., & Lovell, A. (1987). *Psychiatry Inside Out: Selected Writings of Franco Basaglia*. Columbia University Press.

Scholey, A., Gibbs, A., Neale, C., Perry, N., Ossoukhova, A., Bilog, V., Kras, M., Scholz, C., Sass, M., & Buchwald-Werner, S. (2014). Anti-stress effects of lemon balm-containing foods. *Nutrients*, *6*(11), 4805–4821. doi:10.3390/nu6114805 PMID:25360512

Scolari, C. (2008). *Hipermediaciones: elementos para una teoría de la comunicación digital interactiva*. Gedisa.

Singer, M. (1996). A dose of drugs, a touch of violence, a case of AIDS: Conceptualizing the SAVA syndemic. *Free Inquiry in Creative Sociology*, *24*, 99–110.

Singer, M. (2009). *Introduction to Syndemics: A Systems Approach to Public and Community Health*. Jossey-Bass.

Singer, M., & Clair, S. (2003). Syndemics and public health: Reconceptualizing disease in bio-social context. *Medical Anthropology Quarterly*, *17*(4), 423–441. doi:10.1525/maq.2003.17.4.423 PMID:14716917

Singer, M., Erickson, P. I., Badiane, L., Diaz, R., Ortiz, D., Abraham, T., & Nicolaysen, A. M. (2006). Syndemics, sex, and the city: Understanding sexually transmitted diseases in social and cultural context. *Social Science & Medicine*, *63*(8), 2010–2021. doi:10.1016/j.socscimed.2006.05.012 PMID:16782250

Smilde, D., & Ulmer, A. (2018). Repression, resistance, and democratic backsliding in Venezuela. *Annual Review of Political Science*, *21*, 201–216. doi:10.1146/annurev-polisci-050317-070836

Solerte, S., Cravello, L., Ferrari, E., & Fioravanti, M. (2000). Overproduction of IFN-γ and TNF-α from natural killer (NK) cells is associated with abnormal NK reactivity and cognitive derangement in Alzheimer's disease. *Annals of the New York Academy of Sciences*, *917*(1), 331–340. doi:10.1111/j.1749-6632.2000.tb05399.x PMID:11268360

Song, L., Che, W., Min-Wei, W., Murakami, Y., & Matsumoto, K. (2006). Impairment of spatial learning and memory induced by learned helplessness and chronic mild stress. *Pharmacology, Biochemistry, and Behavior*, *83*(2), 186–193. doi:10.1016/j.pbb.2006.01.004 PMID:16519925

Suh, S. A. (2017). Structural Violence and the Possibility of Transformative Education. *Journal of Transformative Education*, *15*(2), 106–120.

SUNY COIL Center. (2020). *What is COIL?* Suny. https://online.suny.edu/introtocoil/suny-coil-what-is/

Taussig, M. (1984). Culture of Terror-Space of Death: Roger Casement's Putumayo Report and the Explanation of Torture. *Comparative Studies in Society and History*, *26*(3), 467–497. doi:10.1017/S0010417500011105

Taussig, M. (1992). *The Nervous System*. Routledge.

Taylor, E. W., & Cranton, P. (2012). Learning to think like an adult: Core concepts of transformation theory. In E. W. Taylor & P. Cranton (Eds.), *The handbook of transformative learning: Theory, research and practice*. Jossey-Bass.

UNESCO. (2019). *Education in Emergencies and Crises: a State-of-the-Art Review of Management, Programming, and Evidence*. UNESCO. https://unesdoc.unesco.org/images/0026/002614/261424e.pdf

UNESCO. (2020). *Global Education Monitoring Report 2020: Inclusion and education: All means all.* Paris: UNESCO. https://en.unesco.org/gem-report/sites/gem-report/files/2020-06/GEM-Report-2020.pdf

UNICEF. (2019). *Out of School Children in Venezuela: A Call for Action*. UNICEF. https://www.unicef.org/venezuela/en/media_71964.html

UNICEF. (2019). *Venezuela's Children and Adolescents in Crisis*. UNICEF. https://www.unicef.org/venezuela/venezuela-crisis-children-and-adolescents

United Nations. (1948). *Universal Declaration of Human Rights*. UN. https://www.un.org/en/about-us/universal-declaration-of-human-rights

United Nations. (2015). *Transforming Our World: The 2030 Agenda for Sustainable Development*. New York: UN Publishing. https://sdgs.un.org/goals

Vázquez-Montilla, E., Martín-Blas, T., & Sánchez-Elvira Paniagua, A. (2020). Attention and working memory in young people with Internet Gaming Disorder: A systematic review. *Adicciones*, *32*(2), 126–139. doi:10.20882/adicciones.1271

Villamizar, G. (2019). *Personal communication*, November 15, 2019.

Wade, C. (2019). *The state of Venezuelan democracy: The role of international actors*. Routledge.

Wekesser, L. J., & Caballero, J. (2020). The state of academic freedom in Venezuela: An analysis. Exchange. *The Journal of Public Diplomacy*, *1*(1), 17–24.

World Health Organization (WHO). (2020). *Violence Prevention Alliance (VPA) - Learning to Live Together - Promote Resilience in Children and Youth*. WHO. https://www.who.int/violenceprevention/alliance/advocacy/Learning.pdf

Yaribeygi, H., Panahi, Y., Sahraei, H., Johnston, T. P., & Sahebkar, A. (2017, July 21). The impact of stress on body function: A review. *EXCLI Journal*, *16*, 1057–1072. doi:10.17179/excli2017-480 PMID:28900385

Chapter 10
Socially Connected Learning Harnessing Digital Platforms for Educational Engagement

Dhiraj Gupta
Greater Noida Institute of Technology, India

Arbaaz Ali Khan
Greater Noida Institute of Technology, India

Abhishek Kumar
Greater Noida Institute of Technology, India

Manoj Singh Baghel
Greater Noida Institute of Technology, India

Ayush Tiwar
Greater Noida Institute of Technology, India

ABSTRACT

The chapter commences by examining the evolving role of social media in the digital age and its pervasive influence on communication, collaboration, and information dissemination. It navigates through a diverse array of social media platforms, exploring their unique features and potential applications within educational contexts. A critical focus of the chapter lies in the pedagogical implications of incorporating social media into teaching strategies. It discusses how educators can leverage these platforms to foster interactive and collaborative learning environments, empowering students to actively participate in knowledge creation and dissemination. The exploration extends to the cultivation of digital literacy skills, emphasizing the importance of guiding students in navigating the complexities of online information.

DOI: 10.4018/979-8-3693-5370-7.ch010

INTRODUCTION

In the rapidly evolving landscape of contemporary education, the infusion of social media has catalysed a paradigm shift, fundamentally redefining the dynamics of teaching and learning. This book chapter embarks on an exploration through the intricate intersections of education and digital connectivity, delving into the transformative potential of integrating social media platforms to elevate engagement and enrich the learning experience.

As the digital age continues to unfold, the role of social media in shaping communication, collaboration, and information dissemination is undeniably pivotal. Its omnipresence in the lives of students and educators alike presents a compelling opportunity to reimagine traditional educational practices. This chapter serves as a guiding compass, navigating the expansive terrain of digital platforms and unveiling the myriad ways in which they can be harnessed to foster meaningful engagement in educational settings.

The exploration commences by unraveling the multifaceted tapestry of social media, examining its diverse array of platforms and functionalities. From the instantaneous connectivity of Twitter to the visual narratives of Instagram and the collaborative potential of platforms like Facebook and LinkedIn, each holds a unique promise for transforming the educational landscape. This exploration lays the foundation for understanding how these tools can be strategically employed to cultivate interactive and participatory learning environments (Lai et al., 2013).

A central focus of our journey is the pedagogical implications of integrating social media into educational strategies. We delve into the ways educators can harness these platforms to not only disseminate information but, more crucially, to empower students as active contributors to the educational discourse. From collaborative project work to global connections, the chapter illuminates the transformative power of social media in shaping students into informed and engaged digital citizens.

However, this integration is not without its challenges. Privacy concerns, digital citizenship, and ethical considerations demand careful navigation. The chapter critically examines these issues, fostering a nuanced understanding of responsible social media usage within educational contexts.

Real-world examples and case studies punctuate our exploration, offering tangible instances of successful social media integration across diverse educational settings. These stories serve as beacons, guiding educators and institutions toward effective practices that transcend traditional boundaries (Bao, 2020).

As we journey through this exploration, we also recognize the evolving role of educators as facilitators of digital discourse. The chapter underscores the importance of ongoing professional development to equip teachers with the skills needed to navigate the digital realm effectively, ensuring that they can guide their students through this dynamic landscape.

In essence, this chapter lays the groundwork for a comprehensive understanding of the integration of social media in education. It is an invitation to educators, administrators, and stakeholders to embark on a transformative odyssey that holds the promise of reinvigorating classrooms, enhancing collaboration, and preparing students for the demands of the digital age.

COMPONENTS OF INTEGRATION OF SOCIAL MEDIA IN EDUCATION

- The Changing Educational Landscape

This section provides an overview of the transformative shifts in the educational landscape brought about by the digital age. It explores the challenges and opportunities arising from increased connectivity and technology's influence on evolving learning methodologies.

- Understanding Social Media Engagement Psychology

Examine the psychological dimensions of social media engagement within the educational context. Discuss how platforms leverage principles of gamification, user experience design, and behavioural psychology to enhance student participation and motivation.

- Effective Practices for Social Media Integration

Offer a comprehensive guide to best practices for incorporating social media into educational settings. This section includes insights on platform selection, content creation, fostering online communities, and addressing privacy concerns (Heilporn et al., 2021). It provides practical tips for educators to implement in their classrooms.

- Global Collaboration Case Studies

Highlight specific case studies showcasing successful global collaborations facilitated by social media in education. Explore examples of international projects, joint initiatives, and cross-cultural exchanges that have enriched the educational experience for students.

- Social Media Analytics for Educational Enhancement

Discuss the role of analytics in measuring the effectiveness of social media integration. Explore how data-driven insights can inform educators about student engagement, identify areas for improvement, and contribute to evidence-based decision-making.

- Promoting Digital Citizenship Education

Delve into the importance of incorporating digital citizenship education alongside social media integration. Discuss strategies for teaching students responsible online behaviour, critical thinking, and ethical considerations in the digital space.

- Addressing Challenges in Social Media Integration

Examine common challenges associated with integrating social media in education, such as cyberbullying, information overload, and distraction. Provide practical solutions and strategies for educators to effectively mitigate these challenges.

- Future Trends and Innovations in Education

Explore emerging trends and innovations in social media and technology likely to impact education in the future. Discuss the potential of augmented reality, virtual classrooms, and other advancements in shaping the next phase of educational engagement (Gamage et al., 2022).

- Continuous Professional Development for Educators

Detail the importance of ongoing professional development for educators in the realm of digital literacy and social media integration. Provide resources and recommendations for educators to stay updated on the latest trends and tools.

- Student Perspectives on Social Media Integration

Include a section that captures the voices and perspectives of students who have experienced social media integration in education. Share testimonials, interviews, or student-created content reflecting their thoughts on the impact of these initiatives as shown in Fig 1.

Figure 1. Components of integration of social media in education

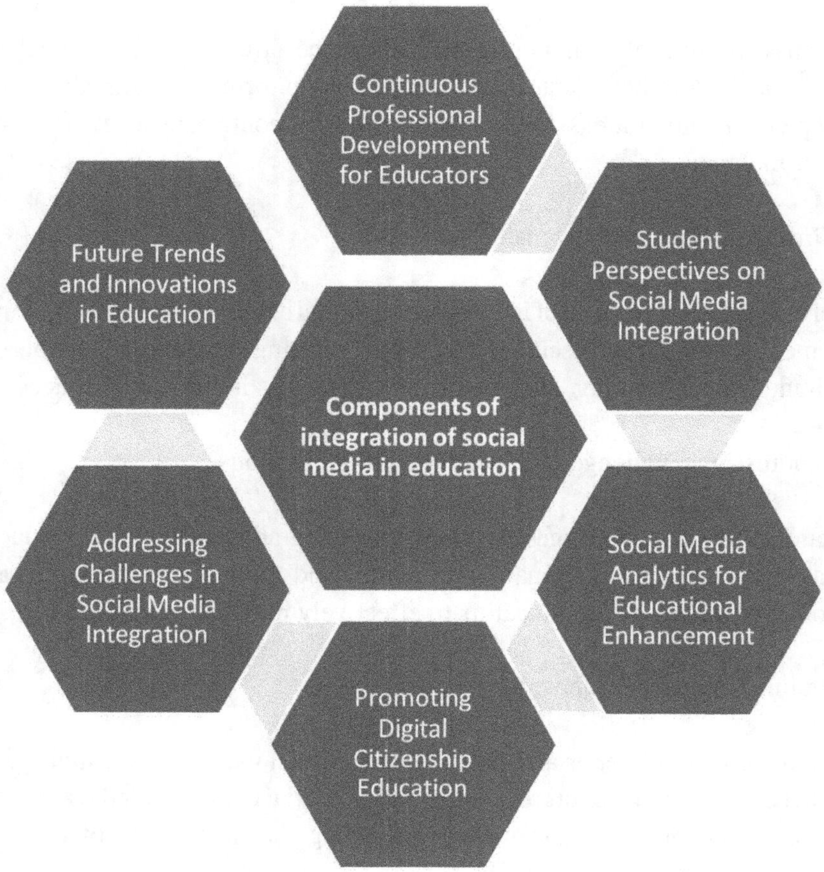

BACKGROUND

The educational landscape is currently undergoing a profound transformation in response to the digital age, characterized by unprecedented technological advancements and the ubiquitous presence of social media. Conventional methods of teaching and learning are undergoing revaluation as educators actively seek innovative approaches to engage students in an increasingly interconnected world (Sistermans, 2020).

The proliferation of social media platforms such as Facebook, Twitter, Instagram, and LinkedIn have become a defining aspect of modern communication. These platforms have transcended their initial purpose of facilitating personal interactions, evolving into potent tools for information dissemination, collaboration, and community building. Recognizing the profound role that social media plays in the lives of students, educators are exploring ways to harness these digital platforms to enrich the educational experience.

The integration of social media in education is driven by a desire to align teaching practices with the communication preferences and technological fluency of contemporary learners. The interactive and dynamic nature of social media provides unique opportunities to establish engaging learning environments, empowering students to actively participate, collaborate, and contribute to knowledge construction.

However, as we delve into this integration, it is imperative to consider both the potential benefits and challenges associated with employing digital platforms for educational purposes. While the prospect of heightened student engagement, global collaboration, and the cultivation of digital literacy skills motivates educators to explore innovative pedagogical approaches, concerns related to privacy, digital citizenship, and the effective use of these tools within an educational context demand careful consideration (Sistermans, 2020).

This background lays the foundation for a comprehensive exploration of the integration of social media in education. It endeavours to comprehend the motivations behind this shift, evaluate the pedagogical implications, and anticipate the potential impact on student engagement and learning outcomes. As educators navigate this digital terrain, their role extends beyond embracing technological tools to fostering a responsible and empowering digital environment for the succeeding generation of learners.

Revolutionizing Education: A Comprehensive Exploration of Integrating Social Media for Enhanced Learning Experiences

- Shifting Educational Paradigms

The transition towards incorporating social media into education signifies a departure from conventional instructional methods. This section examines the evolving paradigm in education, emphasizing not only the dissemination of information but also the creation of interactive and collaborative learning experiences. Social media, with its real-time communication and multimedia capabilities, aligns seamlessly with the dynamic nature of knowledge creation in the digital age.

- The Digital Natives and Their Learning Preferences

A pivotal driver for integrating social media is the prevalence of digital natives—students who have grown up surrounded by digital technologies. Recognizing their learning preferences and communication styles is essential for educators. Social media platforms, being an integral part of their daily lives, naturally extend their learning environment, catering to their preference for instant access to information and interactive communication.

- Social media as Educational Tools

Social media platforms can function as effective educational tools. From microblogging for quick information sharing to collaborative document creation, the versatility of these platforms offers educators a spectrum of possibilities. Case studies and examples are incorporated to illuminate successful instances where educators seamlessly integrated social media tools into their teaching methodologies.

- Enhancing Student Engagement and Participation

A primary objective of integrating social media in education is to enhance student engagement. This section explores strategies for leveraging digital platforms to capture students' attention, foster active participation, and encourage meaningful contributions to the educational discourse. The interactive nature of social media facilitates a transition from passive learning to active engagement (Aldhafeeri & Alotaibi, 2022).

- Navigating Privacy and Ethical Considerations

While the potential benefits of social media integration are significant, it is crucial to address ethical considerations and privacy concerns inherent in these platforms. This section discusses how educators can establish guidelines, promote digital citizenship, and create a secure online space for students. Discussions around responsible use and the implications of sharing information in a public digital domain are central to this exploration.

- Professional Development for Educators

As educators embark on the journey of integrating social media into their teaching practices, ongoing professional development becomes paramount. This section emphasizes the importance of equipping educators with the necessary digital literacy skills, providing resources for continuous learning, and fostering a community of practice where educators can share experiences and insights.

- Measuring Impact and Learning Outcomes

An essential aspect of the integration process is evaluating the impact on learning outcomes. For measuring the effectiveness of social media integration, encompassing qualitative and quantitative assessment tools. It explores how analytics and feedback mechanisms can inform educators about the success of their strategies and areas for improvement.

- Future Trends in Social Media Integration

Exploring future trends in the integration of social media in education. This encompasses emerging technologies, innovative pedagogical approaches, and potential advancements that could further enhance the educational experience. By staying attuned to these trends, educators can proactively adapt their strategies to meet the evolving needs of learners in the digital age as shown in Fig 2.

Role of Social Media for Enhanced Learning Experiences

In the current era of pervasive digital connectivity, the integration of social media in education signifies a transformative shift, poised to revolutionize traditional learning

Figure 2. Revolutionizing education

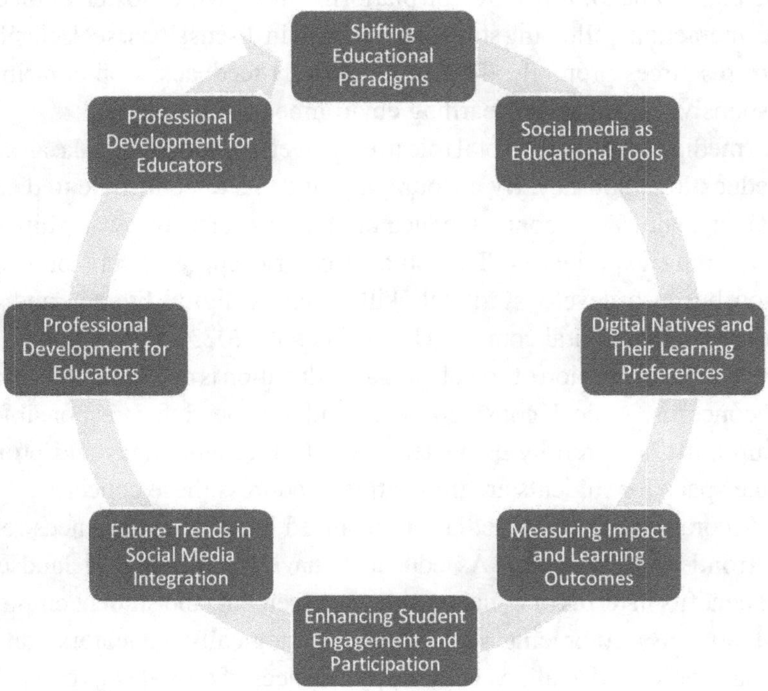

methodologies. Social media platforms like Facebook, Twitter, Instagram, and LinkedIn have transcended their initial roles as tools for personal communication, evolving into dynamic mediums with the potential to profoundly impact educational experiences. This transformation is underlined by the acknowledgment of social media's significant role in the lives of contemporary students. As digital natives, these students have grown up immersed in technology, making social media a natural extension of their daily lives. The potential of social media in education lies in its capacity to foster collaboration, facilitate real-time communication, and create vibrant online communities that transcend geographical boundaries (Ramzan et al., 2023).

One of the primary advantages of integrating social media into educational settings is its ability to cultivate collaborative learning environments. Traditional instructional methods are being revaluated as educators recognize the power of social media to break down physical barriers and promote global collaboration. Students are no longer confined to the limitations of the traditional classroom; instead, they engage in collaborative projects, share insights, and participate in discussions in virtual spaces facilitated by these platforms. This shift towards collaborative learning not only enhances the depth of understanding but also nurtures essential skills such as teamwork, communication, and critical thinking.

Furthermore, the interactive nature of social media enables the creation of engaging learning experiences. Educators can utilize multimedia content, including videos, infographics, and interactive quizzes, to cater to diverse learning styles. The real-time communication features of platforms like Twitter foster immediate and dynamic interactions, allowing students to engage in discussions, seek clarifications, and share resources promptly. This instantaneous feedback loop contributes to a more responsive and adaptive learning environment.

Social media also plays a pivotal role in empowering students to take an active role in their educational journey. By encouraging students to contribute to discussions, share insights, and create content, educators foster a sense of ownership and pride in their learning experiences. This student-centric approach not only enhances motivation but also develops critical skills such as digital literacy and effective communication in a digital context (Holovnia et al., 2023).

However, the integration of social media in education is not without its challenges. Privacy concerns, ethical considerations, and the need for responsible digital citizenship must be carefully navigated. Establishing guidelines and promoting a safe online space for students are imperative to address these concerns.

The exploration of social media for enhanced learning experiences reflects an exciting frontier in education. As educators navigate this digital landscape, the potential benefits in terms of collaboration, engagement, and student empowerment are substantial. By embracing social media strategically, educators can create a learning environment that aligns with the preferences of digital natives and prepares students for active participation in the interconnected, technologically-driven world (Zhong, Zheng, & Zhan, 2023).

Block Diagram of Social Media for Enhanced Learning Experiences

This activity diagram represents the sequential steps involved in integrating social media for enhanced learning experiences. Each step is represented by an activity, and the arrows indicate the flow of the process as shown in Figure 3.

Figure 3. Social media for enhanced learning experiences

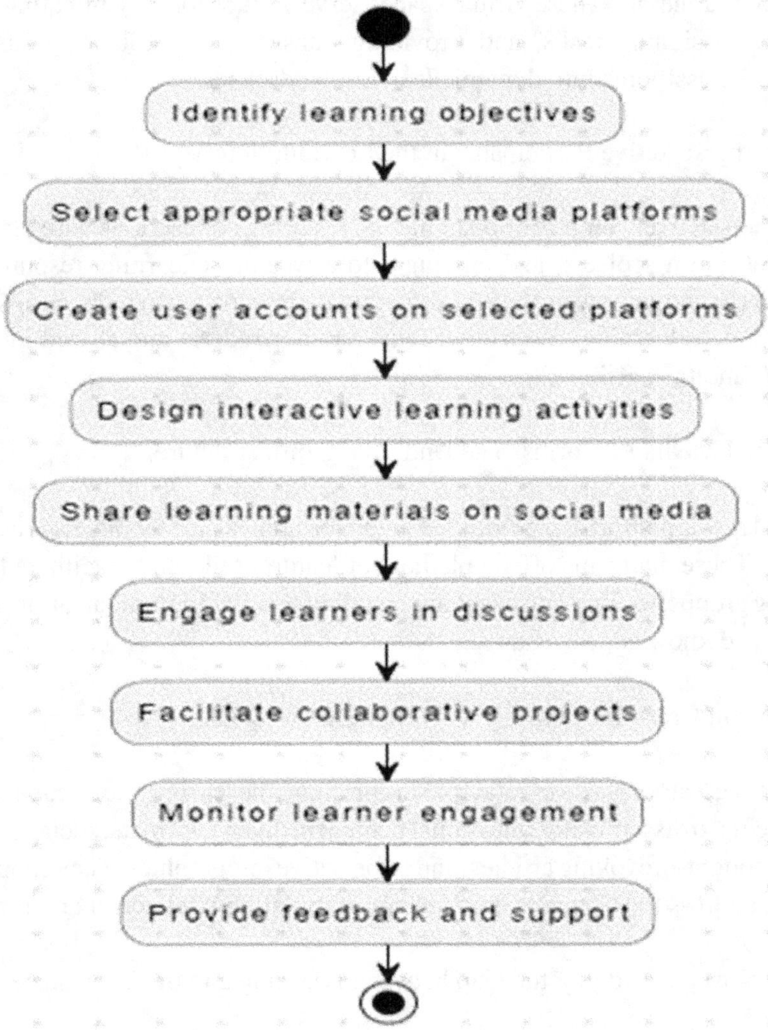

Fostering Enhanced Learning Experiences Through Social Media: A Collaborative Ecosystem

In the dynamic realm of education, social media has emerged as a transformative force, revolutionizing the way knowledge is imparted and acquired. This powerful tool, when harnessed effectively, fosters a collaborative ecosystem where diverse actors play instrumental roles in shaping enriched learning experiences.

- Educators at the Helm:

Educators serve as the guiding lights, leveraging social media to establish vibrant online communities where students can engage with peers and interact with the instructor seamlessly. These virtual spaces serve as hubs for disseminating learning resources, assigning tasks, and providing constructive feedback, transforming traditional classrooms into dynamic learning landscapes.

- Learners: Active Participants in the Learning Journey:

Learners actively embrace social media, fostering connections with classmates, collaborating on projects, and tapping into a wealth of learning resources. This digital landscape empowers them to showcase their work, seek feedback, and engage in peer-to-peer learning, fostering a sense of camaraderie and shared intellectual growth (Pandita & Kiran, 2023).

- Social Media Platforms: The Underlying Infrastructure:

Social media platforms provide the foundation upon which this intricate ecosystem operates. These platforms offer a plethora of features tailored to facilitate learning, including groups, forums, and hashtags, enabling seamless communication, resource sharing, and knowledge exchange.

- Content Creators: Curating a World of Knowledge:

Content creators play a pivotal role in enriching the learning landscape, utilizing social media to disseminate educational content in diverse formats, such as engaging videos, thought-provoking articles, and informative infographics. They connect with learners, address their queries, and foster a stimulating intellectual environment.

- Employers: Bridging the Gap between Learning and the Workplace:

Employers harness the power of social media to identify and nurture talent, utilizing these platforms to connect with potential candidates, provide training opportunities, and stay abreast of industry trends. Social media enables them to foster partnerships and expand their professional networks.

- Envisioning Social Media-Driven Learning in Action:

The transformative impact of social media on learning manifests in innovative pedagogical approaches:

- Flipped Classroom: Redefining the Learning Journey:

In the flipped classroom model, students engage with pre-recorded lectures or online readings asynchronously, utilizing class time for interactive discussions, project work, and collaborative problem-solving. Social media serves as a conduit for sharing learning materials, facilitating discussions, and fostering a vibrant class community.

- Online Courses: Expanding Access to Education:

Online courses transcend geographical boundaries, empowering learners to pursue knowledge acquisition at their own pace and from the comfort of their homes. Social media bridges the physical distance, enabling students to connect with peers, engage with instructors, and cultivate a sense of belonging within the virtual learning environment.

- Professional Development: Unleashing Lifelong Learning:

Social media empowers professionals to embark on continuous learning journeys. Through these platforms, individuals connect with industry experts, stay updated on emerging trends, and share their expertise, cultivating a dynamic network of professional peers.

Social media, when harnessed effectively, transforms the learning landscape into a collaborative ecosystem where educators, learners, social media platforms, content creators, and employers converge to foster enriched learning experiences. This digital tapestry empowers individuals to acquire knowledge, connect with peers, and achieve their educational and professional goals (Zhong, Zheng, & Zhan, 2023).

Merger of Digital Platforms for Educational Engagement

Merging Digital Platforms for Educational Engagement signifies a holistic approach to leveraging various online tools and technologies to create a comprehensive and interactive educational experience. Below is suggested content that delves into the key aspects of this approach:

- The Digital Transformation in Education

In the digital age, education is undergoing a profound transformation. The introduction sets the stage by highlighting the shift towards online and technology-integrated learning environments. It emphasizes the need for a cohesive strategy in merging diverse digital platforms to enhance educational engagement.

- The Landscape of Digital Platforms

Diversity of Platforms: Explore the various digital platforms available for educational use, ranging from Learning Management Systems (LMS) to collaboration tools, video conferencing, and interactive content creation platforms.

Strengths and Weaknesses: Discuss the strengths and weaknesses of different platforms, emphasizing the importance of a balanced and integrated approach.

- Creating a Seamless Learning Experience

Integration Strategies: Examine strategies for seamlessly integrating different digital platforms to create a unified learning experience.

User-Friendly Interfaces: Emphasize the importance of user-friendly interfaces for both educators and students, ensuring accessibility and ease of navigation.

- Enhancing Collaboration through Digital Tools

Virtual Classrooms: Explore the benefits of virtual classrooms, highlighting how platforms like Zoom, Microsoft Teams, or Google Meet can facilitate real-time interactions.

Collaborative Document Editing: Discuss the collaborative features of platforms like Google Workspace or Microsoft 365 for simultaneous document editing and group projects.

- Interactive Content Creation

Engaging Multimedia: Showcase the role of multimedia platforms in creating engaging content, including videos, podcasts, and interactive presentations.

Gamification: Explore the integration of gamification elements through platforms like Kahoot! or Quizizz to enhance student engagement.

- Adapting to Different Learning Styles

Personalized Learning Platforms: Discuss the significance of platforms that support personalized learning paths to cater to diverse learning styles.

AI-Powered Adaptive Learning: Explore the role of Artificial Intelligence in adapting content delivery based on individual student progress.

- Ensuring Data Security and Privacy

Data Security Measures: Address the importance of robust security measures when merging various platforms, ensuring the safety of student data (Jiang et al., 2023).

Compliance with Regulations: Highlight the need for compliance with educational data protection regulations and standards.

- Professional Development for Educators

Training Programs: Advocate for ongoing professional development programs to equip educators with the skills needed to navigate and integrate diverse digital platforms effectively.

Community of Practice: Encourage the formation of a community of practice where educators can share experiences and best practices.

- Measuring Success and Continuous Improvement

Analytics and Feedback: Discuss the use of analytics tools to measure engagement and effectiveness across digital platforms.

Iterative Strategies: Emphasize the iterative nature of the approach, encouraging educators to adapt and improve strategies based on feedback and evolving educational needs.

- Challenges and Considerations

Digital Divide: Address the challenges related to the digital divide and propose strategies to ensure equitable access to digital platforms.

Technological Hurdles: Discuss potential technological challenges and propose solutions to overcome them.

A Unified Educational EcosystemEmphasizing the transformative potential of merging digital platforms for educational engagement. Conclude with a vision of a unified educational ecosystem that maximizes the benefits of diverse digital tools to create a rich and interactive learning environment.

The educational landscape is undergoing a profound shift with the integration of various digital platforms, aiming to create a more comprehensive and engaging learning experience. In this era of technological advancement, educators are no longer confined to traditional teaching methods, having a plethora of digital tools and platforms at their disposal, each offering unique strengths. From Learning Management Systems (LMS) facilitating content delivery to virtual classrooms fostering real-time interactions, the diversity of these platforms provides an opportunity for educators to craft a seamless learning journey. Emphasizing user-friendly interfaces ensures accessibility and navigation ease, enhancing the overall user experience. Moreover, the merging of digital platforms allows the creation of collaborative spaces where students can actively participate in group projects, engage in discussions, and collectively shape their learning environment. Interactive content creation through multimedia platforms and gamification elements further transforms the learning process, appealing to diverse learning styles. However, with these opportunities come challenges, such as ensuring data security, addressing the digital divide, and navigating technological hurdles. Nevertheless, the vision is clear – a unified educational ecosystem where the amalgamation of various digital platforms creates a dynamic and enriched learning experience, preparing students for the demands of the digital age.

METHODOLOGY

The methodology for implementing social media for enhanced learning experiences involves a strategic and systematic approach. Below is a suggested methodology:

Needs Assessment and Goal Setting

Objective Definition: Clearly define the educational objectives and goals you aim to achieve through the integration of social media.

Audience Analysis: Understand the characteristics and preferences of the target audience (students) to tailor the approach accordingly.

Selection of Appropriate Platforms

Platform Analysis: Evaluate different social media platforms in terms of features, privacy settings, and suitability for educational purposes.

Alignment with Goals: Choose platforms that align with your educational objectives and the preferences of your students.

Educator Training and Development

Digital Literacy Training: Provide educators with training on digital literacy, focusing on using social media for educational purposes.

Pedagogical Training: Educators should understand how to integrate social media into pedagogical strategies effectively.

Creating a Safe Online Environment

Privacy Guidelines: Establish clear guidelines on privacy and ethical use of social media within the educational context.

Online Etiquette: Educate both educators and students on responsible online behavior and digital citizenship.

Development of Collaborative Learning Spaces

Online Communities: Create virtual communities where students can collaborate, share resources, and engage in discussions.

Collaborative Projects: Design collaborative projects that leverage the strengths of social media for group work and knowledge exchange.

Content Creation and Sharing

Multimedia Content: Encourage the creation and sharing of multimedia content such as videos, infographics, and presentations.

Interactive Quizzes and Discussions: Use features like polls, quizzes, and discussion forums to enhance interactivity.

Monitoring and Moderation

Continuous Monitoring: Implement tools and procedures for monitoring student activities on social media to ensure a safe and secure learning environment.

Moderation Policies: Establish moderation policies for content shared within the educational community.

Assessment and Feedback Mechanisms

Feedback Surveys: Collect feedback from both educators and students on their experiences with social media integration.

Assessment of Learning Outcomes: Evaluate the impact of social media on learning outcomes through both qualitative and quantitative methods.

Adaptation and Improvement

Continuous Evaluation: Regularly assess the effectiveness of the social media integration, considering evolving educational needs and technological advancements.

Adaptation Strategies: Based on feedback and assessment results, adapt strategies and make improvements to optimize the learning experience.

Documentation and Best Practices

Documentation of Processes: Document the methodology, guidelines, and best practices to create a reference for future implementations.

Sharing Success Stories: Share success stories and case studies within the educational community to inspire and guide others.

CONCLUSION

The exploration of Socially Connected Learning and the utilization of digital platforms for educational engagement underscores a transformative journey within the educational landscape. The dynamic integration of social media has not only redefined traditional paradigms but has also opened avenues for collaborative and engaging learning experiences.

The significance of this approach lies in its ability to align education with the evolving preferences of today's learners—digital natives who thrive in interconnected, technology-driven environments. Socially Connected Learning capitalizes on the strengths of digital platforms to foster collaboration, enrich content delivery, and empower students to actively participate in their educational journey.

As we reflect on the journey, it is evident that the benefits extend beyond the immediate realm of academics. The cultivation of online communities and collaborative projects not only enhances subject matter understanding but also nurtures essential life skills such as communication, teamwork, and digital literacy.

However, this journey is not without its considerations. Privacy concerns, ethical use of digital platforms, and the need for responsible digital citizenship necessitate careful navigation. It is imperative to establish clear guidelines, educate stakeholders on online etiquette, and create a safe online space for meaningful interactions.

The ongoing success of Socially Connected Learning relies on adaptability and continuous improvement. Regular assessments, feedback mechanisms, and the willingness to embrace emerging technologies ensure that the educational experience remains relevant, engaging, and responsive to the needs of both educators and students.

In essence, Socially Connected Learning represents not just a pedagogical shift but a cultural transformation in education. It empowers learners to be active contributors, fosters a sense of community, and prepares them for the demands of an interconnected world. As we move forward, let this exploration serve as an inspiration for educators, administrators, and policymakers to embrace the potential of Socially Connected Learning, creating an educational landscape that is not only academically enriching but also socially and digitally empowering.

REFERENCES

Aldhafeeri, F. M., & Alotaibi, A. A. (2022). Effectiveness of digital education shifting model on high school students' engagement. *Education and Information Technologies, 27*(5), 6869–6891. doi:10.1007/s10639-021-10879-4 PMID:35103044

Bao, W. (2020). COVID-19 and online teaching in higher education: A case study of Peking University. *Human Behavior and Emerging Technologies, 2*(2), 113–115. doi:10.1002/hbe2.191 PMID:32510042

Gamage, K. A., Gamage, A., & Dehideniya, S. C. (2022). Online and hybrid teaching and learning: Enhance effective student engagement and experience. *Education Sciences, 12*(10), 651. doi:10.3390/educsci12100651

Heilporn, G., Lakhal, S., & Bélisle, M. (2021). An examination of teachers' strategies to foster student engagement in blended learning in higher education. *International Journal of Educational Technology in Higher Education, 18*(1), 1–25. doi:10.1186/s41239-021-00260-3 PMID:34805484

Holovnia, O. S., Shchur, N. O., Sverchevska, I. A., Bailiuk, Y. M., & Pokotylo, O. A. (2023, March). Interactive surveys during online lectures for IT students. In *CTE Workshop Proceedings* (Vol. 10, pp. 185-206). 10.55056/cte.556

Jiang, L., Wang, Y., Xie, S., Wu, J., Yin, M., & Wang, J. (2023). Which courses to choose? Recommending courses to groups of students in online tutoring platforms. *Applied Intelligence*, *53*(10), 11727–11736. doi:10.1007/s10489-022-03993-4

Lai, K. W., Khaddage, F., & Knezek, G. (2013). Blending student technology experiences in formal and informal learning. *Journal of Computer Assisted Learning*, *29*(5), 414–425. doi:10.1111/jcal.12030

Pandita, A., & Kiran, R. (2023). The Technology Interface and Student Engagement Are Significant Stimuli in Sustainable Student Satisfaction. *Sustainability (Basel)*, *15*(10), 7923. doi:10.3390/su15107923

Ramzan, M., Javaid, Z. K., & Fatima, M. (2023). Empowering ESL students: Harnessing the potential of social media to enhance academic motivation in higher education. *Global Digital & Print Media Review*, *VI*(II), 224–237. doi:10.31703/gdpmr.2023(VI-II).15

Sahni, J. (2019). Does blended learning enhance student engagement? Evidence from higher education. *The Journal of Learning in Higher Education*, *2019*, 1–14. doi:10.5171/2019.121518

Sistermans, I. J. (2020). Integrating competency-based education with a case-based or problem-based learning approach in online health sciences. *Asia Pacific Education Review*, *21*(4), 683–696. doi:10.1007/s12564-020-09658-6

Xiao, J., Sun-Lin, H. Z., & Cheng, H. C. (2019). A framework of online-merge-offline (OMO) classroom for open education: A preliminary study. *Asian Association of Open Universities Journal*, *14*(2), 134–146. doi:10.1108/AAOUJ-08-2019-0033

Zhong, B., Zheng, J., & Zhan, Z. (2023). An exploration of combining virtual and physical robots in robotics education. *Interactive Learning Environments*, *31*(1), 370–382. doi:10.1080/10494820.2020.1786409

Chapter 11
Embedding Social Media in Education:
Cultivating Engagement and Collaboration in the Digital Learning Environment

Arti Kumari
Greater Noida Institute of Technology, India

Mohd Sahil
Greater Noida Institute of Technology, India

Mohd Jarjis Raza
Greater Noida Institute of Technology, India

ABSTRACT

The abstract delves into strategies employed to effectively incorporate social media tools, highlighting their transformative role in improving student participation and interaction. Emphasizing the dynamic nature of social learning, the chapter navigates through practical examples and case studies, illustrating how educators can leverage these platforms to create an interactive and inclusive educational environment. It addresses the challenges and opportunities associated with integrating social media, taking into account privacy concerns and the necessity for digital literacy skills. Furthermore, the abstract explores the impact of social media on fostering a sense of community and collaboration among students, transcending geographical boundaries. Ultimately, this chapter aims to furnish educators with insights, methodologies, and best practices for successfully integrating social media into their teaching strategies, promoting a more engaging and interconnected educational experience in the rapidly evolving landscape of digital education.

DOI: 10.4018/979-8-3693-5370-7.ch011

INTRODUCTION

The rise of digital technologies has profoundly reshaped the educational landscape, marking an era where social media assumes a crucial role in shaping the dynamics of contemporary classrooms. This chapter delves into the intricate integration of social media into educational frameworks, scrutinizing its far-reaching impact on student engagement and collaborative learning experiences within the digital domain.

As conventional teaching methods adapt to the needs of a technologically progressive society, educators find themselves at the crossroads of pedagogy and digital advancement. This introduction establishes the groundwork for a thorough exploration of how social media platforms can be strategically leveraged to enrich the educational journey. From fostering dynamic interactions among students to dismantling geographical barriers, the integration of social media presents a spectrum of opportunities and challenges for educators(Dabbagh, N., & Kitsantas, 2021).

Embarking on a journey through practical examples and case studies, we navigate the diverse landscape of social learning. The chapter elucidates nuanced strategies educators can employ to seamlessly integrate social media tools, recognizing the transformative potential of these platforms in cultivating a more interactive and inclusive learning environment. Furthermore, we scrutinize essential considerations, including privacy concerns and the imperative for digital literacy skills, that arise with the integration of social media into educational practices.

In essence, this chapter aims to equip educators with a comprehensive understanding of the role social media can play in education, offering insights, methodologies, and best practices to navigate this evolving terrain and harness its potential for fostering engagement and collaboration.

Metrics and Assessment in Social Media Integration in Education

In the dynamic landscape of contemporary education, the infusion of social media into learning environments has emerged as a transformative force, reshaping the way educators engage with students and disseminate information. As educational institutions navigate the integration of these digital platforms, there arises a pressing need to evaluate the effectiveness of this integration, seeking tangible metrics to measure the impact on student engagement and learning outcomes.

This chapter delves into the critical realm of metrics and assessment within the context of social media integration in education. By scrutinizing the quantitative and qualitative dimensions of student interaction and academic achievements facilitated by these platforms, educators can gain valuable insights into the efficacy of their pedagogical approaches.

As the educational landscape continues to evolve, the significance of understanding key metrics becomes increasingly apparent. This introduction sets the stage for a comprehensive exploration of the various parameters that contribute to effective social media integration assessment. From measuring student engagement to evaluating the tangible influence on learning outcomes, educators are presented with a roadmap for navigating the complexities of assessing the impact of social media in education.

In the chapters that follow, we will delve into defining and measuring key metrics, assessing student engagement, evaluating learning outcomes, exploring qualitative assessment approaches, and addressing ethical considerations. Real-world case studies, challenges, and solutions will be examined, providing a holistic understanding of how metrics and assessment contribute to optimizing the integration of social media in education. Ultimately, this chapter aims to empower educators with the tools and knowledge needed to make informed decisions, fostering an enriched educational experience in the digital age(Bedford,2019).

Continuous improvement strategies are essential for optimizing the integration of social media in education. As educational landscapes evolve in response to dynamic digital advancements, educators must adopt iterative approaches to maximize the effectiveness of social media integration. This chapter is dedicated to outlining practical strategies for continuous improvement, ensuring that the benefits of social media in education are continually enhanced.

1. Establishing Baseline Metrics:

Begin by setting baseline metrics to assess the current state of social media integration.Identify key performance indicators (KPIs) related to engagement, collaboration, and learning outcomes.

2. Regular Assessment Cycles:

Implement regular assessment cycles to systematically evaluate the impact of social media.Conduct assessments at defined intervals, allowing for the collection of data over time.

3. Data-Driven Decision Making:

Emphasize the importance of making decisions based on data.Use assessment data to inform adjustments and improvements in social media integration strategies.

4. Feedback Loops:

Establish feedback loops involving students, educators, and administrators. Encourage open communication to gather insights, suggestions, and concerns related to social media integration.

5. Professional Development Initiatives:

Provide ongoing professional development opportunities for educators. Offer training sessions and resources to enhance digital literacy and effective use of social media platforms.

6. Collaboration and Knowledge Sharing:

Foster a culture of collaboration among educators and institutions.Facilitate knowledge-sharing sessions to exchange best practices and lessons learned.

7. Responsive Content Creation:

Continuously assess the relevance and effectiveness of content shared on social media.Modify content creation strategies based on student feedback and evolving educational goals.

8. Flexibility and Adaptability:

Cultivate a mindset of flexibility and adaptability.

Be willing to adjust strategies based on emerging trends, technological advancements, and changing educational needs(Rennie, F., & Morrison,2013).

9. Technology Upgrades and Integration:

Stay informed about technological advancements in social media and educational tools.

Integrate new technologies aligning with educational objectives and enhancing the learning experience.

10. Celebrating Successes and Learning from Failures:

Acknowledge and celebrate successes in social media integration.

Embrace failures as opportunities for learning and improvement, fostering a culture of continuous growth.

11. Community Involvement:

Engage with the educational community, involving parents, students, and other stakeholders.

Solicit input and perspectives to ensure a comprehensive understanding of the impact of social media integration.

12. Regular Policy Review:

Periodically review and update policies related to social media use in education.

Ensure that policies align with best practices, legal considerations, and evolving educational goals.

By implementing these continuous improvement strategies, educators can enhance the integration of social media in education and cultivate an adaptive and responsive learning environment that meets the evolving needs of students and the educational community.

Metrics and Assessment in Social Media Integration in Education

In the ever-evolving landscape of modern education, the integration of social media into learning environments stands as a revolutionary force, transforming the dynamics of how educators interact with students and convey information. As educational institutions navigate the integration of these digital platforms, there is a crucial need to assess the effectiveness of this incorporation, actively seeking concrete metrics to gauge the impact on student engagement and learning outcomes(McLoughlin, C., & Lee, M. J.,2010).

This chapter delves into the vital realm of metrics and assessment within the context of social media integration in education. By examining both the quantitative and qualitative aspects of student interaction and academic achievements facilitated by these platforms, educators can extract valuable insights into the effectiveness of their teaching methods.

As the educational landscape undergoes continuous evolution, the importance of comprehending key metrics becomes increasingly evident. This introduction lays the foundation for an in-depth exploration of the various parameters contributing to effective social media integration assessment. From measuring student engagement to evaluating tangible influences on learning outcomes, educators are provided with a roadmap for navigating the intricacies of assessing the impact of social media in education.

The assessment of student engagement, evaluation of learning outcomes, exploration of qualitative assessment approaches, and consideration of ethical considerations. The inclusion of real-world case studies, challenges, and solutions will offer a comprehensive understanding of how metrics and assessments collectively contribute to optimizing the integration of social media in education. Ultimately, this chapter strives to equip educators with the tools and knowledge necessary to make well-informed decisions, fostering an enriched educational experience in the digital age(Archambault, L., et, al, 2022)..

Role of Social Media in Education

The role of social media in education encompasses diverse positive impacts on teaching and learning, fostering enhanced communication, collaboration, and global connectivity. Social media platforms provide a direct channel for students and teachers to communicate openly, promoting accessibility and engagement.

Global learning communities thrive on social media, enabling students to connect globally and gain exposure to diverse perspectives. Moreover, these platforms serve as repositories for educational resources, facilitating the sharing of articles, videos, and other content, accessible at any time.

Incorporating interactive elements such as polls and quizzes enhances student engagement, motivating learners through informal and collaborative learning experiences. Additionally, social media platforms contribute to professional development for educators, allowing them to participate in Professional Learning Networks (PLNs) and collaborate globally.

Students benefit from social media as a tool for self-expression, empowering them to share thoughts and opinions. It also teaches digital citizenship, promoting responsible online behavior and ethical technology use(O'Connell, J., 2016).

Real-time feedback and peer review processes are facilitated through social media, supporting ongoing assessment and improvement. Furthermore, the integration of social media prepares students for the digital age, fostering digital literacy skills and adaptability to emerging technologies.

Despite these benefits, addressing challenges like privacy concerns and potential distractions is imperative. Educators should employ responsible strategies to maximize the positive impact of social media in education while mitigating potential drawbacks.

BACKGROUND

The backdrop of "Embedding Social Media in Education: Cultivating Engagement and Collaboration in the Digital Learning Environment" revolves around the transformative influence of social media on education, emphasizing the imperative to leverage its potential for enhancing engagement and collaboration in the contemporary digital learning landscape.

- Introduction to the Digital Learning Landscape:

The educational arena is undergoing a profound transformation with the integration of digital technologies. The onset of the digital era has prompted a shift in pedagogical approaches, compelling educators to explore innovative methods to involve students in the learning process.

- Evolution of Social Media in Education:

Social media platforms have emerged as potent tools for communication, collaboration, and information dissemination. Over time, educators and institutions have increasingly acknowledged the potential of social media to augment traditional teaching methods and create dynamic, interactive learning environments(Yu, 2010)

- Rationale for Embedding Social Media:

The decision to integrate social media into education is grounded in the acknowledgment of its ability to foster engagement and collaboration among students. Social media offers a space where students can connect, share ideas, and participate in collaborative learning experiences that go beyond conventional classroom boundaries.

- Importance of Engagement and Collaboration:

Engagement and collaboration are pivotal components of effective learning. The integration of social media in education is perceived as a strategic initiative to cultivate these aspects, encouraging active participation, knowledge exchange, and the development of a sense of community among students.

- Digital Literacy and 21st Century Skills:

In an era dominated by digital information, developing digital literacy skills is crucial for students' success. The integration of social media aligns with the cultivation of 21st-century skills, preparing students to navigate a digital world and participate in collaborative, knowledge-driven economies.

- Educational Technology Trends:

The background acknowledges the broader context of educational technology trends, emphasizing the role of social media as a catalyst in the ongoing evolution of teaching and learning methodologies. It recognizes social media as a key player in the digital toolkit of educators adapting to the demands of contemporary education.

While recognizing the benefits, the background also acknowledges the challenges associated with embedding social media in education, including privacy concerns, digital literacy gaps, and potential distractions. However, it emphasizes that with thoughtful implementation and strategic planning, these challenges can be addressed to unlock the full potential of social media in education(Gikas, 2018).

Cultivating Engagement and Collaboration in the Digital Learning Environment

This explores the intricacies of creating an interactive and collaborative educational experience within the digital realm. In this chapter, we delve into the dynamic landscape of digital learning, emphasizing its transformative impact on traditional educational paradigms. Understanding the pivotal role of engagement in effective learning, we dissect practical strategies for capturing and maintaining students' attention in a digital setting. Exploring collaborative learning, we define its significance and showcase digital tools and platforms that facilitate group activities and project work, fostering a sense of community and interconnectedness among learners. Furthermore, we explore the integration of social media as a powerful conduit for discussions, knowledge sharing, and collaborative projects, unlocking new dimensions of interactive learning. The chapter also examines technology's role as a facilitator of collaboration, with a focus on video conferencing, collaborative document creation, and messaging apps. Addressing challenges inherent to digital engagement, we propose effective solutions and strategies for overcoming obstacles. Additionally, we discuss metrics and assessment methods for measuring engagement and collaboration, utilizing analytics and feedback mechanisms for continuous improvement. Recognizing the importance of ongoing professional development for educators in the digital age, we highlight training programs and resources to enhance their digital pedagogy skills. Throughout, real-world case studies and success stories illustrate the practical implementation of strategies, providing a comprehensive guide for educators navigating the evolving landscape of digital learning(Evans et al., 2023).

Methodology for Integrating Social Media to Education

Integrating social media into education requires careful planning and strategic implementation to harness its benefits effectively. Here are methods to seamlessly incorporate social media into the educational environment:

- **Define Clear Objectives:**

Establish specific educational goals and outcomes for integrating social media. Align these objectives with broader educational goals and curricular requirements.

- **Choose Appropriate Platforms:**

Identify social media platforms that align with the educational objectives.Select platforms based on the target audience, content type, and desired level of interaction.

- **Develop Guidelines and Policies:**

Create clear guidelines and policies for the responsible use of social media. Communicate expectations regarding communication etiquette, privacy, and digital citizenship.

- **Provide Professional Development:**

Conduct training sessions for educators on effective social media use in education.Focus on digital literacy, best practices, and integrating social media into teaching strategies.

- **Create Dedicated Educational Accounts**:

Establish separate social media accounts specifically for educational purposes. Distinguish between personal and educational content to maintain a professional online presence.

- **Integrate Social Media in Lesson Plans:**

Design lesson plans that incorporate social media for collaborative learning. Develop assignments and projects that leverage the interactive features of social media platforms.

- **Encourage Collaboration and Discussion:**

Foster collaborative learning by using social media for group discussions and collaborative projects.Create designated spaces for students to share ideas, resources, and engage in meaningful conversations.

- **Utilize Multimedia Content:**

Leverage the multimedia capabilities of social media platforms for diverse content types.Incorporate videos, images, and interactive content to enhance the learning experience.

- **Implement Live Sessions and Webinars:**

Use live sessions and webinars on social media platforms for real-time interaction. Conduct virtual guest lectures, Q&A sessions, or interactive workshops.

- **Facilitate Student Engagement:**

Encourage students to actively participate by sharing their insights and creations. Use polls, quizzes, and surveys to gauge student understanding and opinions.

- **Monitor and Evaluate:**

Regularly assess the effectiveness of social media integration in achieving educational objectives.Collect feedback from students and educators to make informed adjustments.

- **Promote Digital Citizenship:**

Integrate lessons on digital citizenship, responsible online behavior, and ethical use of social media.Empower students to navigate the digital landscape responsibly.

- **Celebrate Achievements:**

Recognize and celebrate achievements, projects, and collaborations facilitated through social media.Showcase success stories to inspire and motivate both educators and students.

- **Stay Informed about Platform Updates:**

Stay updated on changes and updates to social media platforms.Adapt strategies based on new features and functionalities introduced by the platforms.By employing these methods, educators can effectively integrate social media into education, creating an engaging and collaborative digital learning environment.

- **Trends integrating Social Media to Education**

As of my last knowledge update in January 2022, several trends were influencing the integration of social media into education. Please note that trends in technology and education can evolve rapidly. Here are some noteworthy trends in incorporating social media into education:

- **Microlearning through Social Media:**

The emergence of short, targeted learning experiences on social media platforms. Microlearning content, such as brief videos or infographics, is shared to enhance engagement.

- **Integration with Learning Management Systems (LMS):**

Social media features becoming part of existing learning platforms.Learning Management Systems incorporating discussion forums, collaborative spaces, and content sharing through social media-like interfaces.

- **Educational Influencers and Online Communities**:

The rise of educational influencers and communities on platforms like YouTube and Instagram.Educators leveraging social media to share insights, lesson plans, and innovative teaching practices.

- **Live Streaming for Virtual Classes:**

The use of live streaming features on platforms like Facebook, Instagram, and YouTube for virtual classes.Real-time interaction, Q&A sessions, and collaborative activities through live video.

- **Increased Use of Educational Hashtags:**

The creation and use of educational hashtags to categorize and share educational content.Facilitates content discovery and community building among educators and students.

- **Digital Storytelling and Content Creation:**

Students and educators using social media for digital storytelling.Platforms like TikTok and Instagram being leveraged for creative expression and project sharing.

- **Authentic Assessment through Social Media:**

The use of social media for authentic assessment, allowing students to showcase their skills in a real-world context.Assessment through blogs, podcasts, or multimedia projects shared on social platforms.

- **Global Collaborative Projects:**

Facilitation of global collaborative projects through social media.Students connecting with peers worldwide for joint assignments, discussions, and cultural exchange.

- **Emphasis on Digital Citizenship and Online Safety:**

Integration of social media into digital citizenship education.Emphasis on responsible online behavior, privacy, and navigating social media safely.

- **Augmented Reality (AR) and Virtual Reality (VR) Integration:**

Exploration of AR and VR features within social media for immersive learning experiences.Virtual field trips, 360-degree videos, and AR-enhanced educational content.

- **Social Media Analytics for Educational Insights:**

Use of analytics tools to track student engagement and assess the effectiveness of social media integration.Educators leveraging data to make informed decisions and optimize teaching strategies.

- **Integration of AI and Chatbots:**

• Use of AI-driven tools and chatbots for personalized learning experiences. Automated responses and support for students within social media environments.

PLATFORMS OF SOCIAL MEDIA FOR EDUCATION

Central Hub

Learning Management System (LMS): Remains the foundation, housing crucial materials, announcements, and streamlined communication.

Social Media Management Tool: If managing multiple platforms, consider a tool for scheduling and monitoring posts(Haythornthwaite, 2010).

Social Media Platforms

Enriching Content Delivery

Multimedia Platforms (YouTube, Vimeo): Engage learners with educational videos, lectures, and presentations.

Visual Assets (Instagram, Pinterest): Create appealing infographics, image-based explanations, and visual aids.

Microblogging (Twitter): Share bite-sized updates, news relevant to the curriculum, and spark instant discussions.

Fostering Collaborative Learning

Private Groups (Facebook Groups): Establish closed groups for focused discussions, project collaboration, and peer learning.

Real-time Interaction (Discord): Facilitate live Q&A sessions, ongoing study groups, and dynamic interactions.

Open Discourse (Blogs, Forums): Host discussions, debates, peer review activities, and promote knowledge exchange.

Building a Vibrant Community

Professional Networking (LinkedIn): Connect with experts, alumni, guest speakers, and industry professionals.

Interactive Sessions (Twitter Chats, Facebook Live): Organize live discussions, interviews, and engaging events.

Shared Identity (Class Social Media Account): Foster a sense of belonging, showcase student work, and celebrate achievements.

Bridging the Gaps

Embed social media content directly into the LMS for easy access.Leverage LMS discussion forums to weave in social media interactions.Encourage responsible sharing of relevant social media content.Utilize social media platforms to promote LMS activities and resources.

- Privacy & Security: Establish clear guidelines for responsible online behavior and data protection for all participants.
- Digital Citizenship: Integrate lessons on ethical online interaction, critical thinking skills, and fact-checking abilities.
- Inclusive Access: Ensure all social media activities are accessible and cater to diverse learning styles and needs.
- Meaningful Assessment: Integrate social media activities seamlessly into formative and summative assessments.

Challenges in Integrating Social Media with Education Framework

Integrating social media into education is accompanied by a range of challenges and issues that educators must navigate. These concerns span from privacy considerations to potential distractions, and it is essential to address them thoughtfully:

Privacy Concerns

Student Privacy: Safeguarding the privacy of students is paramount, especially when sharing educational content on public platforms.

Data Security: Ensuring the secure handling of student data when utilizing third-party social media platforms(Dabbagh., 2011).

Digital Literacy Gaps

Varied Skill Levels: Students may possess differing levels of digital literacy, resulting in an uneven ability to effectively navigate and utilize social media for educational purposes.

Educator Training: Some educators may lack the necessary skills to seamlessly integrate social media into their teaching methods(Zaglia, 2011)

Cyberbullying and Misuse

Inappropriate Behavior: Social media platforms can become avenues for cyberbullying and inappropriate conduct among students.

Monitoring Challenges: Educators may encounter difficulties in effectively monitoring and addressing instances of cyberbullying or misuse.

Distractions and Information Overload

Potential Distractions: The allure of non-educational activities on social media can distract students during class time(Tess.2013)

Information Overload: The abundance of information on social media may overwhelm students, hindering their ability to focus on relevant educational content.

Equity and Access Issues

Access Disparities: Inequities in device or internet access may hinder some students from fully participating in social media-based learning(Sandy, M. G., & Franco, Z. E,2014).

Socioeconomic Barriers: Students from lower socioeconomic backgrounds might face challenges accessing and utilizing social media platforms.

Digital Divide

Inequitable Technology Access: Disparities in technology access contribute to a digital divide, amplifying existing educational inequalities.

Authenticity and Reliability of Information

Ensuring Accuracy: Students may struggle to discern between accurate and inaccurate information on social media(Cochrane, T., & Antonczak, L. 2015).

Teaching Information Literacy: Educators play a crucial role in teaching information literacy skills to help students critically evaluate online content.

Platform Reliability and Changes

Unpredictable Changes: Frequent updates to social media platforms may lead to uncertainty in the tools available for educational use.

Potential Platform Shutdowns: Platforms may cease operations or modify their terms, impacting the continuity of educational initiatives.

Overreliance on Social Media

Balancing Traditional Methods: The risk of overreliance on social media should be acknowledged, with a need to balance these methods with traditional teaching approaches when appropriate.

Legal and Ethical Considerations

Intellectual Property Issues: Intellectual property concerns arise when students and educators share content on social media.

Ensuring Fair Use: Adhering to copyright laws and ensuring fair use of materials shared on social media are critical considerations.

Addressing these challenges requires careful planning, ongoing training for educators, and continuous evaluation of the impact of social media integration on both student learning and well-being.

REFERENCES

Archambault, L., Leary, H., & Rice, K. (2022). Pillars of online pedagogy: A framework for teaching in online learning environments. *Educational Psychologist*, *57*(3), 178–191. doi:10.1080/00461520.2022.2051513

Bedford, L. (2019). Using Social Media as a Platform for a Virtual Professional Learning Community. *Online Learning : the Official Journal of the Online Learning Consortium*, *23*(3), 120–136. doi:10.24059/olj.v23i3.1538

Cochrane, T., & Antonczak, L. (2015). Connecting the theory and practice of mobile learning: A framework for creative pedagogies using mobile social media. *Medical Education*, *6*(2), 248–269.

Dabbagh, N., & Kitsantas, A. (2012). Personal Learning Environments, social media, and self-regulated learning: A natural formula for connecting formal and informal learning. *The Internet and Higher Education*, *15*(1), 3–8. doi:10.1016/j.iheduc.2011.06.002

Dabbagh, N., Kitsantas, A., Al-Freih, M., & Fake, H. (2015). Using social media to develop personal learning environments and self-regulated learning skills: A case study. *International Journal of Social Media and Interactive Learning Environments*, *3*(3), 163–183. doi:10.1504/IJSMILE.2015.072300

Evans, M., Trolli, E., Pierson, A., & Tilak, S. (2023). Designing courses with sustainable virtual learning communities: A STEM teacher candidate course that extends beyond higher education. *Journal of Computing in Higher Education*, 1–23. doi:10.1007/s12528-023-09391-0

Gikas, J., & Grant, M. M. (2013). Mobile computing devices in higher education: Student perspectives on learning with cellphones, smartphones & social media. *The Internet and Higher Education*, *19*, 18–26. doi:10.1016/j.iheduc.2013.06.002

Haythornthwaite, C., Andrews, R., Kazmer, M. M., Bruce, B. C., Montague, R. A., & Preston, C. (2007). Theories and models of and for online learning. *First Monday*. Advance online publication. doi:10.5210/fm.v12i8.1976

McLoughlin, C., & Lee, M. J. (2010). Personalised and self regulated learning in the Web 2.0 era: International exemplars of innovative pedagogy using social software. *Australasian Journal of Educational Technology*, *26*(1). Advance online publication. doi:10.14742/ajet.1100

O'Connell, J. (2016). Networked participatory online learning design and challenges for academic integrity in higher education. *International Journal for Educational Integrity*, *12*(1), 1–15. doi:10.1007/s40979-016-0009-7

Rennie, F., & Morrison, T. (2013). *E-learning and social networking handbook: Resources for higher education*. Routledge. doi:10.4324/9780203120279

Sandy, M. G., & Franco, Z. E. (2014). Grounding Service-Learning in the Digital Age: Exploring a Virtual Sense of Geographic Place through Online Collaborative Mapping and Mixed Media. *Journal of Higher Education Outreach & Engagement*, *18*(4), 201–232.

Tess, P. A. (2013). The role of social media in higher education classes (real and virtual)–A literature review. *Computers in Human Behavior*, *29*(5), A60–A68. doi:10.1016/j.chb.2012.12.032

Yu, A. Y., Tian, S. W., Vogel, D., & Kwok, R. C. W. (2010). Can learning be virtually boosted? An investigation of online social networking impacts. *Computers & Education*, *55*(4), 1494–1503. doi:10.1016/j.compedu.2010.06.015

Zaglia, M. E. (2013). Brand communities embedded in social networks. *Journal of Business Research*, *66*(2), 216–223. doi:10.1016/j.jbusres.2012.07.015 PMID:23564989

Compilation of References

A. P. (2021, August 4). *INFINERA CSR India supports Aahwahan Foundation\'s HEALTH ON WHEELS*. CSRBOX. https://csrbox.org/India_CSR_news_HEALTH-ON-WHEELS-%E2%80%93-INFINERA-CSR-India-supports-Aahwahan-Foundation-for-the-enhancement-of--healthcare-system-in-Karnataka_1388

A. P. (2021, November 25). *How Aahwahan Foundation's 'Laptop Bank' Is Fulfilling The Online Education Needs Of Underprivileged Students*. SOCIALSTORY. https://yourstory.com/socialstory/2021/11/aahwahan-foundations-laptop-bank-underprivileged-students

A. P. (2021, November 25). *How Aahwahan Foundation's 'Laptop Bank' is Fulfilling the Online Education Needs of Underprivileged Students*. Socialstory. Your Story. https://yourstory.com/socialstory/2021/11/aahwahan-foundations-laptop-bank-underprivileged-students

Abad Segura, E., & González Zamar, M. D. (2019). Análisis de las competencias en la educación superior a través de flipped classroom. *Revista Iberoamericana de Educación*, *80*(2), 29–45. doi:10.35362/rie8023407

Agarwal, K. (2020, August 13). India's Population Will Be 1.52 Billion by 2036, With 70% of Increase in Urban Areas. *The WIRE*. https://thewire.in/government/india-population-growth-government-report-2036-projections-urban-migration

Aguayo Vergara, M., Bravo Molina, M., Nocetti de la Barra, A., Concha Sarabia, L., & Aburto Godoy, R. (2019). Perspectiva estudiantil del modelo pedagógico flipped classroom o aula invertida en el aprendizaje del inglés como lengua extranjera. *Review of Education*, *43*(1), 90–120. doi:10.15517/revedu.v43i1.31529

Akhtar, R., Zulkhairi, M. H., Raza, A., & Khairi, K. M. (2019). Cultural Competence Training Simulator: Virtual Reality Application for Inclusive Education. In *IEEE International Symposium on Mixed and Augmented Reality (ISMAR)* (pp. 346-349). IEEE.

Alajmi, M. A., & Rorissa, A. (2018). E-environments in the Gulf Cooperation Council States: An analysis of the literature. *IFLA Journal*, *44*(1), 56–73. doi:10.1177/0340035218755167

Aldhafeeri, F. M., & Alotaibi, A. A. (2022). Effectiveness of digital education shifting model on high school students' engagement. *Education and Information Technologies*, *27*(5), 6869–6891. doi:10.1007/s10639-021-10879-4 PMID:35103044

Al-Kumaim, N. H., Alhazmi, A. K., Mohammed, F., Gazem, N. A., Shabbir, M. S., & Fazea, Y. (2021). Exploring the impact of the COVID-19 pandemic on university students' learning life: An integrated conceptual motivational model for sustainable and healthy online learning. *Sustainability (Basel), 13*(5), 2546. doi:10.3390/su13052546

Al-Mahadin, S. (2020). Laughing it off: Coronavirus superspreaders, anxiety, and fear in Jordan and Australia. *Psychological Trauma: Theory, Research, Practice, and Policy, 12*(S1), S45–S46. https://psycnet.apa.org/doi/10.1037/tra0000630. doi:10.1037/tra0000630 PMID:32597676

Al-Naabi, I. S. (2020). Is it worth flipping? The impact of flipped classroom on EFL students' grammar. *English Language Teaching, 13*(6), 64–75. doi:10.5539/elt.v13n6p144

Alves, A., Silva, B., & Silva, M. A. (2021). Análisis del uso de la cultura maker en contextos educativos: Una revisión sistemática de la literatura. *Educatio Siglo XXI, 39*(2), 143–168. doi:10.6018/educatio.465991

Amiryousefi, M. (2019). The incorporation of flipped learning into conventional classes to enhance EFL learners' L2 speaking, L2 listening, and engagement. *Innovation in Language Learning and Teaching, 13*(2), 147–161. doi:10.1080/17501229.2017.1394307

Anderson, L. W., Krathwohl, D. R., Airasian, P. W., Cruikshank, K. A., Mayer, R. E., Pintrich, P. R., Raths, J., & Wittrock, M. C. (2000). *A Taxonomy for Learning, Teaching, and Assessing: A revision of Bloom's Taxonomy of Educational Objectives*. Pearson, Allyn & Bacon.

Archambault, L., Leary, H., & Rice, K. (2022). Pillars of online pedagogy: A framework for teaching in online learning environments. *Educational Psychologist, 57*(3), 178–191. doi:10.1080/00461520.2022.2051513

Arellano Vega, A. I., & Andrade Cázares, R. A. (2020). Competencias digitales docentes en profesores universitarios. *Journal Educational Innovation, 20*(83), 35–53.

Arulananth, T. S., & Shilpa, B. (2017). *Fingertip based heartbeat monitoring system using embedded systems.* Proc. International Conference of Electronics Communication and Aerospace Technology (ICECA).

Astin, A. W. (1993). How are students affected? *Change, 25*(2), 44–50. doi:10.1080/00091383.1993.9940617

Astin, A. W., & Astin, H. S. (2000). *Leadership Reconsidered: Engaging Higher Education in Social Change*. W.K. Kellogg Foundation.

Awidi, I. T., & Paynter, M. (2019). The impact of a flipped classroom approach on student learning experience. *Computers & Education, 128*, 269–283. doi:10.1016/j.compedu.2018.09.013

Azubuike, O. B., Adegboye, O., & Quadri, H. (2021). Who gets to learn in a pandemic? Exploring the digital divide in remote learning during the COVID-19 pandemic in Nigeria. *International Journal of Educational Research Open, 2*, 100022. doi:10.1016/j.ijedro.2020.100022 PMID:35059664

Bachelet, M. (2021). *Statement by the United Nations High Commissioner for Human Rights on Venezuela. 46th session of the Human Rights Council*. Geneva. https://www.ohchr.org/EN/NewsEvents/Pages/DisplayNews.aspx?NewsID=26874&LangID=E

Ball, J. W., Dains, J. E., Flynn, J. A., Solomon, B. S., & Stewart, R. W. (2023). Seidel's Guide to Physical Examination 10th ed. St Louis MO: Elsevier.

Ball, J., & Haque, S. (2016). Ethnographic research in disaster-affected communities: A review of the literature. *Disasters*, *40*(2), 433–453.

Bao, W. (2020). COVID-19 and online teaching in higher education: A case study of Peking University. *Human Behavior and Emerging Technologies*, *2*(2), 113–115. doi:10.1002/hbe2.191 PMID:32510042

Baron-Cohen, S. (2002). The extreme male brain theory of autism. *Trends in Cognitive Sciences*, *6*(6), 248–254. doi:10.1016/S1364-6613(02)01904-6 PMID:12039606

Barreto Huilcapi, M., Aguirre Fernández, R. E. & Serra Valdés, M. A. (2021). Beneficios del método AICLE/CLIL para el aprendizaje de una lengua extranjera a través del aula invertida. *Revista Panamericana de pedagogía*, 32, 197-215. doi:10.21555/rpp.v0i32.2271

Batool, Z. (2021, February 12). *Oops! Romance Gone Wrong – Professor Shoos Wife Away Kissing Him During Zoom Class*. PARHLO. https://www.parhlo.com/professor-shoos-wife-away-kissing-during-zoom-class/

Bauer-Clapp, H. (2010). REVIEW: Global Health in Times of Violence. *Landscapes of Violence*, *1*(1), 8.

Bayeck, R. Y. (2020). Examining board gameplay and learning: A multidisciplinary review of recent research. *Simulation & Gaming*, *51*(4), 411–431. doi:10.1177/1046878119901286

Bedford, L. (2019). Using Social Media as a Platform for a Virtual Professional Learning Community. *Online Learning : the Official Journal of the Online Learning Consortium, 23*(3), 120–136. doi:10.24059/olj.v23i3.1538

Bell, J. (2005). *Doing your research project: A guide for first-time researchers*. McGraw-Hill International.

Bernal, J. L. (2000). Cuestionario sobre liderazgo transformacional. Aportaciones desde una investigación. En Liderazgo y organizaciones que aprenden, 441-459. Ediciones Mensajero.

Best, K. L., & Pane, J. F. (2018). *Privacy and Interoperability Challenges Could Limit the Benefits of Education Technology*. RAND Corporation. https://www.jstor.org/stable/resrep19899

Betti, A., Biderbost, P., & García, A. (2022). Can active learning techniques simultaneously develop students' hard and soft skills? Evidence from an international relations class. *PLoS One*, *17*(4), e0265408. doi:10.1371/journal.pone.0265408 PMID:35472046

Bezzazi, R. (2019). Learning English grammar through flipped learning. *Australian Journal of Applied Linguistics*, *6*(2), 170–184.

Bhatt, I., & MacKenzie, A. (2019). Just Google it! Digital literacy and the epistemology of ignorance. *Teaching in Higher Education*, *24*(3), 302–317. doi:10.1080/13562517.2018.1547276

Bliss, T. V., & Lømo, T. (1973). Long-lasting potentiation of synaptic transmission in the dentate area of the anaesthetized rabbit following stimulation of the perforant path. *The Journal of Physiology*, *232*(2), 331–356. doi:10.1113/jphysiol.1973.sp010273 PMID:4727084

Blog, N. C. E. S. (Ed.). (2021, September 20). Students' Internet Access Before and During the Coronavirus Pandemic by Household Socioeconomic Status. *NCES Blog*. https://nces.ed.gov/blogs/nces/post/students-internet-access-before-and-during-the-coronavirus-pandemic-by-household-socioeconomic-status

Bloom, B. S. (1956). *Taxonomy of Educational Objectives, Handbook I: The Cognitive Domain*. David McKay Co. Inc.

Boler, M., & Zembylas, M. (2003). Discomforting truths: The emotional terrain of understanding difference. In P. Trifonas (Ed.), *Pedagogies of difference: Rethinking education for social justice* (pp. 23–45). Routledge.

Borcel, E., Pérez-Alvarez, L., Herrero, A. I., Brionne, T., Varea, E., Berezin, V., Bock, E., Sandi, C., & Venero, C. (2008). Chronic stress in adulthood followed by intermittent stress impairs spatial memory and the survival of newborn hippocampal cells in aging animals: Prevention by FGL, a peptide mimetic of neural cell adhesion molecule. *Behavioural Pharmacology*, *19*(1), 41–49. doi:10.1097/FBP.0b013e3282f3fca9 PMID:18195593

Bourdieu, P. (1977). Cultural Reproduction and Social Reproduction. In J. Karabel & A. H. Halsey (Eds.), *Power and Ideology in Education* (pp. 487–511). Oxford University Press.

Bourdieu, P. (2000). *Cuestiones de Sociología*. Istmo.

Bourdieu, P. (2001). *Masculine Domination*. Polity Press.

Bourdieu, P., & Wacquant, L. (1994). *Per a una sociología reflexiva*. Herder.

Bourgois, P. (2008). *Neoliberal Lumpen Abuse in the 2000s; A 25-Year Ethnographic Retrospective of Violence in the Americas*. Presented at the Conference, Violence and Citizenship in Post-Authoritarian Latin America, Princeton University.

Bower, M., & Sturman, D. (2015). VR Education: A Historical Perspective. In M. Bower & D. Sturman (Eds.), *Virtual Reality for Teaching and Learning* (pp. 1–16). Springer.

Bowman, D. A., & McMahan, R. (2007). Virtual reality: How much immersion is enough? *IEEE Computer Graphics and Applications*, *27*(6), 16–22.

Braun, V., & Clarke, V. (2006). Using thematic analysis in psychology. *Qualitative Research in Psychology*, *3*(2), 77–101. doi:10.1191/1478088706qp063oa

Bremner, J. D. (1999). Does stress damage the brain? *Biological Psychiatry*, *45*(7), 797–805. doi:10.1016/S0006-3223(99)00009-8 PMID:10202566

Buil-Fabregá, M., Martínez, M., Ruiz-Munzón, N., & Filho, W. (2019). Flipped Classroom as an Active Learning Methodology in Sustainable Development Curricula. *Sustainability (Basel)*, *11*(17), 1–15. doi:10.3390/su11174577

Bulsara, C. (2014). *Using a Mixed Methods Approach to Enhance and Validate Your Research*. ND. https://www.nd.edu.au/downloads/research/ihrr/using_mixed_methods_approach_to_enhance_and_validate_your_research.pdf

Bush, A., & Grotjohann, N. (2020). Collaboration in teacher education: A cross-sectional study on future teachers' attitudes towards collaboration, their intentions to collaborate and their performance of collaboration. *Teaching and Teacher Education*, *88*, 102968. doi:10.1016/j.tate.2019.102968

Cano, E., Lluch, L., Grané, M., & Remesal, A. (2023). Competency-based assessment practices in higher education: Lessons from the pandemics. *Trends in Higher Education*, *2*(1), 238–254. doi:10.3390/higheredu2010012

Carey, J. W., & Asbury, J. (2016). *Focus Group Research*. Routledge. doi:10.4324/9781315428376

Carrión Candel, E., Pérez Agustín, M. & Giménez De Ory, E. (2021). ICT and gamification experiences with CLIL methodology as innovative resources for the development of competencies in compulsory secondary education. *Digital education review, 39*, 238–256. doi:10.1344/der.2021.39.238-256

Casero-Ripollés, A. (2012). Transmedia strategies in news outlets: An approach to the Spanish media panorama. *Communicatio Socialis*, *25*(1), 29–53.

Casimiro-Perlaza, L. F., & Torres-Daza, H. F. (2023). Tecnologías disruptivas en la enseñanza del inglés: Un estudio comparativo de las percepciones de profesores. *RECIE. Revista Caribeña de Investigación Educativa*, *7*(2), 175–197. doi:10.32541/recie.2023.v7i2.pp175-197

CEFR- QualityMatrix European Centre for Modern Languages of the Council of Europe. https://www.ecml.at/ECML-Programme/Programme2016-2019/QualityassuranceandimplementationoftheCEFR/Tutorial

Centeio, E., Mercier, K., Garn, A., Erwin, H., Marttinen, R., & Foley, J. (2021). The success and struggles of physical education teachers while teaching online during the COVID-19 pandemic. *Journal of Teaching in Physical Education*, *40*(4), 667–673. doi:10.1123/jtpe.2020-0295

Chan, V. W. (2021). Initiative on reducing the "digital divide". *IEEE Communications Magazine*, *59*(5), 4–5. doi:10.1109/MCOM.2021.9446683

Cheng, Y., Lou, S., Kuo, S., & Shih, R. (2013). Investigating elementary school students' technology acceptance by applying digital game-based learning to environmental education. *Australasian Journal of Educational Technology*, *29*(1), 96–110. doi:10.14742/ajet.65

Clark, D. (2023, October 11). *Cumulative number of laptop or tablet devices dispatched or delivered by the UK government to education providers in England from December 2020 to April 2022*. Statista. https://www.statista.com/statistics/1263494/educational-digital-devices-delivered-by-uk-government/#:~:text=As%20of%20April%202022%2C%20the%20government%20of%20the,to%20support%20remote%20learning%20during%20the%20coronavirus%20pandemic

Cochrane, T., & Antonczak, L. (2015). Connecting the theory and practice of mobile learning: A framework for creative pedagogies using mobile social media. *Medical Education*, *6*(2), 248–269.

Cohen, L., Manion, L., & Morrison, K. (2007). *Research Methods in Education* (6th ed.). Routledge. doi:10.4324/9780203029053

Cohen, L., Manion, L., & Morrison, K. (2011). *Research methods in education*. Routledge.

Columbia University. (2017). *The Body VR*. Columbia University. https://www.columbiaradiology.org/research/3d-virtual-reality-vr-human-body

Components101. (n.d.-a). *16×2 LCD module*. https://components101.com/displays/16x2-lcd-pinout-datasheet

Components101. (n.d.-b). *DS18B20 temperature sensor*. https://components101.com/sensors/ds18b20-temperature-sensor?fbclid=IwAR1h7fnrZYY0OGivtUdqvf14qwTz0MUT4sO-U6pID7Qn4LeHKPQ7Y0OypH4

Components101. (n.d.-c). *NodeMCU ESP 8266*. https://components101.com/development- boards/nodemcu-esp8266-pinout-features-and-datasheet

Compton, M., & Gilmour, A. (2022). Walking the tightrope: Enabling mindset and practice transformation at scale through compassionate academic development. *The International Journal for Academic Development*, *27*(2), 203–206. doi:10.1080/1360144X.2022.2066674

Coppedge, M., & Bitar, S. (Eds.). (2020). *Crises of democracy and the prospect of renewal*. Johns Hopkins University Press.

Coulter, M., Britton, Ú., MacNamara, Á., Manninen, M., McGrane, B., & Belton, S. (2023). PE at Home: Keeping the 'E'in PE while home-schooling during a pandemic. *Physical Education and Sport Pedagogy*, *28*(2), 183–195. doi:10.1080/17408989.2021.1963425

Council of Europe. (2020). *Common European Framework of Reference for Languages: learning, teaching, assessment*. Council of Europe.

Cranfield, D. J., Tick, A., Venter, I. M., Blignaut, R. J., & Renaud, K. (2021). Higher education students' perceptions of online learning during COVID-19: A comparative study. *Education Sciences*, *11*(8), 403. doi:10.3390/educsci11080403

Creed, C., Al-Kalbani, M., Theil, A., Sarcar, S., & Williams, I. (2023). Inclusive AR/VR: Accessibility barriers for immersive technologies. *Universal Access in the Information Society*, 1–15. doi:10.1007/s10209-023-00969-0

Cruz, I. M., & Cabero, J. (2020). Una experiencia gamificada en el aprendizaje de los triángulos en geometría: grado de aceptación de la tecnología. *Revista Prisma Social, 30,* 65–87. https://revistaprismasocial.es/article/view/3744

CSforAll Consortium. (2019). *K-12 Computer Science Framework.* CS for All. https://www.csforal.org/framework

Dabbagh, N., & Kitsantas, A. (2012). Personal Learning Environments, social media, and self-regulated learning: A natural formula for connecting formal and informal learning. *The Internet and Higher Education, 15*(1), 3–8. doi:10.1016/j.iheduc.2011.06.002

Dabbagh, N., Kitsantas, A., Al-Freih, M., & Fake, H. (2015). Using social media to develop personal learning environments and self-regulated learning skills: A case study. *International Journal of Social Media and Interactive Learning Environments, 3*(3), 163–183. doi:10.1504/IJSMILE.2015.072300

Das, A., Lam, T. K., Thomas, S., Richardson, J., Booi, H. K., Lau, K. H., & Mathews, Z. N. (2019). Flipped classroom pedagogy: Using pre-class videos in an undergraduate business information systems management course. *Education + Training, 61*(6), 756–774. doi:10.1108/ET-06-2018-0133

Davis, F. (1993). User acceptance of information technology: System characteristics, user perceptions and behavioral impacts. *International Journal of Man-Machine Studies, 38*(3), 475–487. doi:10.1006/imms.1993.1022

de la Fuente, M. J., Ortega-Múnez, J., & Amado-Salvatierra, H. R. (2020). Virtual Reality in Teacher Education: A Systematic Review. *International Journal of Educational Technology in Higher Education, 17*(1), 1–28.

De Meyer, J., Soenens, B., Vansteenkiste, M., Aelterman, N., Van Petegem, S., & Haerens, L. (2016). Do Students with Different Motives for Physical Education Respond Differently to Autonomy-Supportive and Controlling Teaching? *Psychology of Sport and Exercise, 22,* 72–82. doi:10.1016/j.psychsport.2015.06.001

Del Moral, M. E., López-Bouzas, N., & Castañeda, J. (2023). Activating Teacher Competencies Through Designing Gamified Stories With Augmentative Reality. In E. Podovšovnik, T. De Giuseppe, & F. Corona (Eds.), Handbook of Research on Establishing Digital Competencies in the Pursuit of Online Learning(pp. 230-252). IGI Global. doi:10.4018/978-1-6684-7010-7.ch012

Dewey, J. (1897, January). My Pedagogic Creed. *School Journal, 54,* 77–80.

Dharmik, R., Gotarkar, S., Dinesh, P., & Sant Burde, H. (2021). An IoT Framework for Healthcare Monitoring System. *Journal of Physics: Conference Series, 1913*(1), 012145. doi:10.1088/1742-6596/1913/1/012145

DiMaggio, P., & Hargittai, E. (2001). From the 'digital divide'to 'digital inequality': Studying Internet use as penetration increases (Working papers 47). *Princeton: Center for Arts and Cultural Policy Studies, Woodrow Wilson School, Princeton University, 4*(1), 4-2.

DiMaggio, P., Hargittai, E., Celeste, C., & Shafer, S. (2004). Digital inequality: From unequal access to differentiated use. In K. M. Neckerman (Ed.), *Social inequality* (pp. 355–400). Russell Sage Foundation.

Doud, F., & Log, E. L. (2011). *Digital divide versus digital inequality*. Forrest Doud. https://forrestdoud.wordpress.com/2011/02/07/digital-divide-versus-digital-inequality/

El-Rashid, N., El-Sappagh, S., Islam, S. M. R., ElBakry, H. M., & Abdelrazek, S. (2020). End-to-end deep learning framework for coronavirus (COVID-19) detection and monitoring. Academic Press.

Eriksen, K. (2020). Robert Kegan's constructive developmental theory: An overview and implications for practice. *Journal of Adult Development*, *27*(2), 79–89. doi:10.1007/s10804-019-09353-1

Europa World Plus. (2018). *Venezuela: Social media and political polarization*. Europa World Plus. https://search.proquest.com/docview/2068108154

Evangelou, F. (2023). Differentiated Instruction on a learner-centred form of teaching in Primary Education. *International Journal of Education*, *15*(2), 15–34. doi:10.5296/ije.v15i2.21004

Evans, M. (2020). COVID-19: How to Treat Coronavirus at Home. *Patient UK*. https://patient.info/news-and-features/covid-19-how-to-treat-coronavirus-at-home

Evans, M., Trolli, E., Pierson, A., & Tilak, S. (2023). Designing courses with sustainable virtual learning communities: A STEM teacher candidate course that extends beyond higher education. *Journal of Computing in Higher Education*, 1–23. doi:10.1007/s12528-023-09391-0

Faheema Shirin RK v. State of Kerala & Ors, *WP. No.19716 OF 2019*

Fahey, T., Delaney, L., & Gannon, B. (2005). *School children and sport in Ireland*. ESRI.

Fahy, A., Murphy, C., Fu, N., & Nguyen, T. (2020). *Irish Primary School Leadership During COVID-19. Principals' Study Report 2020*. Dublin: Trinity College Dublin. http://www.tara.tcd.ie/handle/2262/92883

Farmer, P. (2003). *Pathologies of Power: Health, Human Rights, and the New War on the Poor*. University of California Press.

Farmer, P. (2004). An Anthropology of Structural Violence. *Current Anthropology*, 45.

Farmer, P., Nizeye, B., Stulac, S., & Keshavjee, S. (2006). Structural Violence and Clinical Medicine. *PLoS Medicine*, *3*(10), e449. doi:10.1371/journal.pmed.0030449 PMID:17076568

Ferreira, J. L., & dos Santos, L. (2021). Design requirements for educational serious games with focus on player enjoyment. *Entertainment Computing*, *38*, 100413. doi:10.1016/j.entcom.2021.100413

Filiz, B., & Konukman, F. (2020). Teaching Strategies for Physical Education during the COVID-19 Pandemic. *Journal of Physical Education, Recreation & Dance*, *91*(9), 48–50. doi:10.1080/07303084.2020.1816099

Flores-González, N. (2022). El perfil del docente y su adaptabilidad a entornos educativos virtuales. *RECIE. Revista Caribeña de Investigación Educativa*, *6*(2), 99–115. doi:10.32541/recie.2022.v6i2.pp99-115

Freire, P. (1970). *Pedagogy of the oppressed.* Herder and Herder.

Freitez, A., España, L., Correa, G., Di Brienza, M., & Ponce, M. (Equipo Coordinador). (2020). *Encuesta Nacional de Condiciones de Vida 2019-20 (ENCOVI 2019-20).* Caracas. UCAB-USB-UCV.

Fundora Ramírez, P., Rodríguez Fernández, L. R., & Reiné Herrera, Y. (2023). La enseñanza del inglés a través de las plataformas digitales. *Revista Científica de FAREM-Estelí*, *12*(46), 165–182. doi:10.5377/farem.v12i46.16484

Gabarda, V., Marín, D., Vidal, M. I., & Ramón, J. (2023). Digital Competence of Training Teachers: Results of a Teaching Innovation Project. *Education Sciences*, *13*(2), 162. doi:10.3390/educsci13020162

Gaitas, S., Carêto, C., Peixoto, F., & Castro Silva, J. (2022). Differentiated instruction: 'to be, or not to be, that is the question'. *International Journal of Inclusive Education*, 1–19. doi:10.1080/13603116.2022.2119290

Galindo Valero, P. (2021). Utilización de plataformas digitales en educación. *Revista de Educación. Innovación y Formación, REIF*, *4*, 7–25.

Galora Moya, N. P., & Salazar Tobar, M. C. (2019). Differentiated Instruction: Productive skills development with high school and university students. *Investigación y Desarrollo*, *11*(1), 67–73. doi:10.29033/id.v11i1.645

Galtung, J. (1969). Violence, Peace, and Peace Research. *Journal of Peace Research*, *6*(3), 167–191. doi:10.1177/002234336900600301

Gamage, K. A., Gamage, A., & Dehideniya, S. C. (2022). Online and hybrid teaching and learning: Enhance effective student engagement and experience. *Education Sciences*, *12*(10), 651. doi:10.3390/educsci12100651

Ganesh, D., Kumar, M. S., Reddy, P. V., Kavitha, S., & Murthy, D. S. (2022). Implementation of AI Pop Bots and its allied Applications for Designing Efficient Curriculum in Early Childhood Education. *International Journal of Early Childhood Special Education*, *14*(3). doi:10.9756/INT-JECSE/V14I3.271

Garzón Álvarez, J. F., Monsalve Franco, A. P., & Valencia Valencia, E. Z. (2023). Impacto de las tecnologías de la información en los estudiantes del grado aceleración del aprendizaje en un curso de inglés. *Revista Virtual Universidad Católica del Norte*, *68*, 37-62. https://www.doi.org/10.35575/rvucn.n68a3

Gay, G. (2002). Preparing for culturally responsive teaching. *Journal of Teacher Education*, *53*(2), 106–116. doi:10.1177/0022487102053002003

General Secretariat, O. A. S. (2020). *Fomentando la impunidad: El impacto de la ausencia de una investigación de la Fiscal de la Corte Penal Internacional sobre la posible comisión de crímenes de lesa humanidad en Venezuela (preparado por Jared Genser).* OAS. https://www.oas.org/es/centro_noticias/comunicado_prensa.asp?sCodigo=C-122/20

Gheyssens, E., Griful-Freixenet, J., & Struyven, K. (2023). Differentiated Instruction as an Approach to Establish Effective Teaching in Inclusive Classrooms. In Effective Teaching around the World (pp. 677-689). Springer. doi:10.1007/978-3-031-31678-4_30

Ghufron, M. A., & Nurdianingsih, f. (2020). Flipped teaching with CALL media in EFL writing course: Indonesian EFL writing teachers' reflection. *Pertanika Journal of Social Science & Humanities*, *28*(2), 1–18.

Gikas, J., & Grant, M. M. (2013). Mobile computing devices in higher education: Student perspectives on learning with cellphones, smartphones & social media. *The Internet and Higher Education*, *19*, 18–26. doi:10.1016/j.iheduc.2013.06.002

Girón-Chávez, A., Cruz-Maldonado, E. Y., Bermejo-del Villar, M. M., & Cancino-Zamarrón, R. (2023). Las TIC y el aprendizaje colaborativo para mejorar la pronunciación de inglés de estudiantes universitarios. *Revista Lengua y Cultura*, *5*(9), 1–10. doi:10.29057/lc.v5i9.11531

Godhe, A. L., Lilja, P., & Selwyn, N. (2019). Making sense of making: Critical issues in the integration of maker education into schools. *Technology, Pedagogy and Education*, *28*(3), 317–328. doi:10.1080/1475939X.2019.1610040

Gómez, D. (2019). *Personal communication*. Research Gate.

Gong, R. (2020, March 27). Coping with COVID-19: Distance learning and the digital divide. *Kri Views*, 21/20.

González Miranda, M. Y. (2023). Aprendizaje del inglés y el uso de las Tics como método de enseñanza en un grupo de estudiantes de la carrera de inglés de la universidad Autónoma de Chiriquí. *Revista Boletín Redipe*, *12*(3), 14–18. doi:10.36260/rbr.v12i3.1946

Gonzalez, Á. P., & Sanchez, P. (2005). What do we know about how students learn in the college? In *Chamorro Plaza, M. C. y Sánchez Delgado, P., Iniciación a la docencia universitaria. Manual de ayuda* (pp. 11–44). Instituto de Ciencias de la Educación, Universidad Complutense.

Goodyear, V. A., Skinner, B., McKeever, J., & Griffiths, M. (2023). The influence of online physical activity interventions on children and young people's engagement with physical activity: A systematic review. *Physical Education and Sport Pedagogy*, *28*(1), 94–108. doi:10.1080/17408989.2021.1953459

Gope, P., & Hwang, T. (2015). BSN-Care: A secure IoT-based modern healthcare system using body sensor network. *IEEE Sensors Journal*, *16*(5), 1368–1376. doi:10.1109/JSEN.2015.2502401

Gould, E., & Tanapat, P. (1999). Stress and hippocampal neurogenesis. *Biological Psychiatry*, *46*(11), 1472–1479. doi:10.1016/S0006-3223(99)00247-4 PMID:10599477

Grant, K., & Gedeon, S. (2020). The impact of Covid-19 on university teaching. In D. Remenyi, K. grant & S. Singh (Eds.), The university of the future: Responding to Covid-19. ACPIL.

Grayson, P. L. (1978). Education, Technology, and Individual Privacy. *Educational Communication and Technology, 26*(3), 197. https://doi.org/http://www.jstor.org/stable/30220912

Grover, S., & Pea, R. (2013). Computational Thinking in K–12: A Review of the State of the Field. *Educational Researcher*, *42*(1), 38–43. doi:10.3102/0013189X12463051

Gullberg, J. (1997). *Mathematics: From the Birth of Numbers*. W. W. Norton and Company.

Guppy, N., Verpoorten, D., Boud, D., Lin, L., Tai, J., & Bartolic, S. (2022). The post-COVID-19 future of digital learning in higher education: Views from educators, students, and other professionals in six countries. *British Journal of Educational Technology*, *53*(6), 1750–1765. doi:10.1111/bjet.13212

Gurbuz, S. C., & Celik, M. (2022). Serious games in future skills development: A systematic review of the design approaches. *Computer Applications in Engineering Education*, *30*(5), 1591–1612. doi:10.1002/cae.22557

Gutiérrez, K. D., & Rogoff, B. (2003). Cultural ways of learning: Individual traits or repertoires of practice. *Educational Researcher*, *32*(5), 19–25. doi:10.3102/0013189X032005019

Harun, M. A. A., Hossain, M. M., & Bari, M. A. (2020). Bangladesh Journal of Otorhinolaryngology, vol. 26 no. 1 pp. 55–67 Pulse oximetry is essential in-home management of elderly. *COVID*, 19.

Hayes, A. (2022). *Introduction to mediation, moderation and conditional process analysis: A regression-based approach*. The Guilford Press.

Haythornthwaite, C., Andrews, R., Kazmer, M. M., Bruce, B. C., Montague, R. A., & Preston, C. (2007). Theories and models of and for online learning. *First Monday*. Advance online publication. doi:10.5210/fm.v12i8.1976

Heeg, D. M., & Avraamidou, L. (2023). The use of Artificial intelligence in school science: A systematic literature review. *Educational Media International*, *60*(2), 125–150. doi:10.1080/09523987.2023.2264990

Heilporn, G., Lakhal, S., & Bélisle, M. (2021). An examination of teachers' strategies to foster student engagement in blended learning in higher education. *International Journal of Educational Technology in Higher Education*, *18*(1), 1–25. doi:10.1186/s41239-021-00260-3 PMID:34805484

Hernández, A., & Cadenas, L. (2018). The economic crisis and its impact on student dropout rates in higher education in Venezuela. International Journal of Learning. *Teaching and Educational Research*, *17*(3), 185–203.

Hodges, C., Moore, S., Lockee, B., Trust, T., & Bond, A. (2020, March 27). The difference between emergency remote teaching and online learning. *Educause Review*. https://er.educause.edu/articles/2020/3/the-difference-between-emergency-remote-teaching-and-online-learning

Holovnia, O. S., Shchur, N. O., Sverchevska, I. A., Bailiuk, Y. M., & Pokotylo, O. A. (2023, March). Interactive surveys during online lectures for IT students. In *CTE Workshop Proceedings* (Vol. 10, pp. 185-206). 10.55056/cte.556

Hongru, D., & Goyea, T. (2020). *Novel coronavirus (COVID-19) cases Johns Hopkins University Baltimore Maryland.* JHU. https://coronavirus.jhu.edu/.

Hsiao, I. C. V., Hung, S. T. A., & Huang, H. T. D. (2021). The flipped classroom approach in an English for Specific purposes (ESP) course: A quasi-experimental study on learners' self-efficacy, study process, and learning performances. *Journal of Research on Technology in Education*, 1–20. doi:10.1080/15391523.2021.1976329

Human Rights Watch. (2017). *Venezuela: The supreme court's attack on democracy.* HRW. https://www.hrw.org/report/2017/05/26/venezuela-supreme-courts-attack-democracy

Human Rights Watch. (2020). *Venezuela: Dire Conditions for Children.* Human Rights Watch. https://www.hrw.org/news/2020/02/26/venezuela-dire-conditions-children

Hwang, G. J., & Fu, Q. K. (2020). Advancement and research trends of smart learning environments in the mobile era. *International Journal of Mobile Learning and Organisation, 14*(1), 114–129. doi:10.1504/IJMLO.2020.103911

Hypoxemia, C. O. (2020). *Symptoms, Causes, Treatments.* Cleveland Clinic. https://my.clevelandclinic.org/health/diseases/17727-hypoxemia

Iglesias-Pradas, S., Hernández-García, Á., Chaparro-Peláez, J., & Prieto, J. L. (2021). Emergency remote teaching and students' academic performance in higher education during the COVID-19 pandemic: A case study. *Computers in Human Behavior, 119*, 106713. doi:10.1016/j.chb.2021.106713 PMID:34866769

International Society for Technology in Education. (2016). *ISTE Standards for Students.* ISTE. https://www.iste.org/standards/for-students

Islam, M. M., Rahmanand, A., & Islam, M. R. (2020). Development of Smart Healthcare Monitoring System in IoT Environment. *SN Computer Science, 1*(3), 185. doi:10.1007/s42979-020-00195-y PMID:33063046

Ivcevic, Z., & Grandinetti, M. (2024). Artificial intelligence as a tool for creativity. *Journal of Creativity, 100079*(2), 100079. Advance online publication. doi:10.1016/j.yjoc.2024.100079

Jenkins, H. (2009). *Confronting the challenges of participatory culture: Media education for the 21st century.* MIT Press. doi:10.7551/mitpress/8435.001.0001

Jiang, L., Wang, Y., Xie, S., Wu, J., Yin, M., & Wang, J. (2023). Which courses to choose? Recommending courses to groups of students in online tutoring platforms. *Applied Intelligence, 53*(10), 11727–11736. doi:10.1007/s10489-022-03993-4

Johnson, C. (2016). *Virtual Classroom: A Platform for Teacher Training.* Stanford Press. https://online.stanford.edu/programs/virtual-classroom-platform-teacher-training

Jones, P. (2015). Transformative learning theory: Addressing new challenges in social work education. *Exploring Learning & Teaching in Higher Education*, 267-286.

Kafai, Y. B., & Burke, Q. (2014). *Connected Code: Why Children Need to Learn Programming*. The MIT Press. doi:10.7551/mitpress/9992.001.0001

Karakose, T. (2021). Emergency remote teaching due to COVID-19 pandemic and potential risks for socioeconomically disadvantaged students in higher education. *Educational Process*, *10*(3), 53–62. doi:10.22521/edupij.2021.103.4

Ke, F., & Im, T. (2013). Virtual-Reality-Based Social Interaction Training for Children with High-Functioning Autism. *The Journal of Educational Research*, *106*(6), 441–461. doi:10.1080/00220671.2013.832999

Kegan, R. (1982). *The Evolving Self: Problem and Process in Human Development*. Harvard University Press. doi:10.4159/9780674039414

Kemp, J., & Issroff, K. (2016). The potential of virtual reality for teacher education. *Journal of Computer Assisted Learning*, *32*(4), 311–320.

Kessler, R. C., Davis, C. G., & Kendler, K. S. (1997). Childhood adversity and adult psychiatric disorder in the US National Comorbidity Survey. *Psychological Medicine*, *27*(5), 1101–1119. doi:10.1017/S0033291797005588 PMID:9300515

Kezar, A., & Moriarty, D. (2000). Expanding our understanding of student leadership development: A study exploring gender and ethnic identity. *Journal of College Student Development*, *41*, 55–68.

Khaldi, A., Bouzidi, R., & Nader, F. (2023). Gamification of e-learning in higher education: A systematic literature review. *Smart Learning Environments*, *10*(10), 10. doi:10.1186/s40561-023-00227-z

Khan, M. M. (2020). *IoT based smart healthcare services for rural unprivileged people in Bangladesh: current situation and challenges*. International Electronic Conference on Applied Science MDPI, Switzerland.

Kim, K., Kwon, K., Ottenbreit-Leftwich, A., Bae, H., & Glazewski, K. (2023). Exploring middle school students' common naive conceptions of Artificial Intelligence concepts, and the evolution of these ideas. *Education and Information Technologies*, *28*(8), 1–28. doi:10.1007/s10639-023-11600-3

Kim, M., Yu, H., Park, C. W., Ha, T., & Baek, J. H. (2021). Physical education teachers' online teaching experiences and perceptions during the COVID-19 pandemic. *Journal of Physical Education and Sport*, *21*, 2049–2056.

Köhler, S., Thomas, A. J., Lloyd, A., Barber, R., Almeida, O. P., & O'Brien, J. T. (2010). White matter hyperintensities, cortisol levels, brain atrophy and continuing cognitive deficits in late-life depression. *The British Journal of Psychiatry*, *196*(2), 143–149. doi:10.1192/bjp.bp.109.071399 PMID:20118461

Konukman, F., Filiz, B., & Ünlü, H. (2022). Teachers' perceptions of teaching physical education using online learning during the COVID-19: A quantitative study in Turkey. *PLoS One*, *17*(6), e0269377. doi:10.1371/journal.pone.0269377 PMID:35731742

Kötay-Nagy, A. (2023). Differentiated instruction in the EFL classroom: An interview study on Hungarian primary and secondary school EFL teachers' views and self-reported practices. *Journal of Adult Learning, Knowledge, and Innovation*, *6*(8), 1–14. doi:10.1556/2059.2023.00076

Koyama, J. (2019). *Structural Violence and Education: The Impact on Student Success. University of California*. Center for the Study of Democracy.

Krajcik, J., Schneider, B., Miller, E. A., Chen, I. C., Bradford, L., Baker, Q., Bartz, K., Miller, C., Li, T., Codere, S., & Peek-Brown, D. (2023). Assessing the effect of project-based learning on science learning in elementary schools. *American Educational Research Journal*, *60*(1), 70–102. doi:10.3102/00028312221129247

Kreijns, K., Kirschner, P. A., & Jochems, W. (2003). Identifying the Pitfalls for Social Interaction in Computer-Supported Collaborative Learning Environments: A Review of the Research. *Computers in Human Behavior*, *19*(3), 335–353. doi:10.1016/S0747-5632(02)00057-2

Lai, C., & Bower, M. (2018). Virtual reality in education: A review of the literature. *Computers & Education*, *122*, 109–122.

Lai, K. W., Khaddage, F., & Knezek, G. (2013). Blending student technology experiences in formal and informal learning. *Journal of Computer Assisted Learning*, *29*(5), 414–425. doi:10.1111/jcal.12030

Laine, T. H., & Lindberg, R. S. (2020). Designing engaging games for education: A systematic literature review on game motivators and design principles. *IEEE Transactions on Learning Technologies*, *13*(4), 804–821. doi:10.1109/TLT.2020.3018503

Lam, P., & Tse, A. (2022). Gamification in everyday classrooms: Observations from schools in Hong Kong. *Frontiers in Education*, *6*, 630666. doi:10.3389/feduc.2021.630666

Lampropoulos, G., Keramopoulos, E., Diamantaras, K., & Evangelidis, G. (2022). Augmented reality and gamification in education: A systematic literature review of research, applications, and empirical studies. *Applied Sciences (Basel, Switzerland)*, *12*(13), 6809. doi:10.3390/app12136809

Landeo Chocce, Z. M., Pareja Ballón, A. Y., Muñoz Chocce, C. M., Lazo Montero, G. L., Quispe Loayza, A. E., & Guerreros Blas, P. R. (2023). Las TIC en el aprendizaje del idioma inglés en estudiantes de una universidad pública. *Ciencia Latina Revista Científica Multidisciplinar*, *7*(2), 8029–8039. doi:10.37811/cl_rcm.v7i2.5937

LeCompte, M. D. (2000). Analyzing qualitative data. *Theory into Practice*, *39*(3), 146–154. doi:10.1207/s15430421tip3903_5

Lee, H. W., Chang, K., Uhm, J. P., & Owiro, E. (2023). How Avatar Identification Affects Enjoyment in the Metaverse: The Roles of Avatar Customization and Social Engagement. *Cyberpsychology, Behavior, and Social Networking*, *26*(4), 255–262. doi:10.1089/cyber.2022.0257 PMID:37001178

Lee, H., Song, C., Hong, Y. S., Kim, M. S., Cho, H. R., Kang, T., Shin, K., Choi, S. H., Hyeon, T., & Kim, D. H. (2017). Wearable/disposable sweat-based glucose monitoring device with multistage transdermal drug delivery module. *Science Advances*, *3*(3), e1601314. doi:10.1126/sciadv.1601314 PMID:28345030

Leitão, R., Maguire, M., Turner, S., & Guimaraes, L. (2022). A systematic evaluation of game elements effects on students' motivation. *Education and Information Technologies*, *27*(1), 1081–1103. doi:10.1007/s10639-021-10651-8

Letzel-Alt, V., & Pozas, M. (2023). *Differentiated instruction around the world: A global inclusive insight*. Waxmann. doi:10.31244/9783830997023

Lewis, L. A. (2018). Institutional Betrayal, Cultural Violence, and Structural Violence: Examples from the Educational System. [This article discusses how institutional betrayal, cultural violence, and structural violence perpetuate inequalities in education, particularly for marginalized communities.]. *Journal of Interpersonal Violence*, *35*(1), 66–90.

Liao, C. H., Wu, W. C., Gunawan, V., & Chang, T. C. (2023). Using an Augmented-Reality Game-Based Application to Enhance Language Learning and Motivation of Elementary School EFL Students: A Comparative Study in Rural and Urban Areas. *The Asia-Pacific Education Researcher*, 1–13. doi:10.1007/s40299-023-00729-x

Litchfield, I., Shukla, D., & Greenfield, S. (2021). Impact of COVID-19 on the digital divide: A rapid review. *BMJ Open*, *11*(10), e053440. doi:10.1136/bmjopen-2021-053440 PMID:34642200

Liu, Y. (2021). *An investigation of the shift to distance education and the widening of the digital divide during the COVID-19 pandemic* [Doctoral dissertation, Auckland University of Technology].

Liu, R. T., & Alloy, L. B. (2010). Stress generation in depression: A systematic review of the empirical literature and recommendations for future study. *Clinical Psychology Review*, *30*(5), 582–593. doi:10.1016/j.cpr.2010.04.010 PMID:20478648

Lloret-Segura, S., Ferreres-Traver, A., Hernández-Baeza, A., & Tomás-Marco, I. (2014). El análisis factorial exploratorio de los ítems: Una guía práctica, revisada y actualizada. *Anales de Psicología*, *30*(3), 1151–1169. doi:10.6018/analesps.30.3.199361

Lombardero, X., Murcia, E., Aguiar, F. X., Méndez, A. B., & González, A. (2023). Academic Engagement and Disaffection in Social Work Undergraduates From Spain: The Role of Teaching Styles and Student Motivation. *Journal of Social Work Education*, 1–18. doi:10.1080/10437797.2023.2248225

López-Fernández, I., Burgueño, R., & Gil-Espinosa, F. J. (2021). High school physical education teachers' perceptions of blended learning one year after the onset of the COVID-19 pandemic. *International Journal of Environmental Research and Public Health*, *18*(21), 11146. doi:10.3390/ijerph182111146 PMID:34769673

Lorente Rodríguez, M., & Pulido-Montes, C. (2022). Use of Digital Resources in Higher Education during COVID-19: A Literature Review. *Education Sciences*, *12*(612), 1–19. 10.3390

Lundberg, A., & Stigmar, M. (2022). Deliberative academic development with university teachers in times of crisis. *The International Journal for Academic Development*, *27*(2), 163–175. doi:10.1080/1360144X.2022.2084742

Lundberg, A., & Stigmar, M. (2022). University teachers' shifting views of successful learning environments in the future. *Scandinavian Journal of Educational Research*, 1–16. doi:10.1080/00313831.2022.2115127

Lupien, S. J., & Lepage, M. (2001). Stress, memory, and the hippocampus: Can't live with it, can't live without it. *Behavioural Brain Research*, *127*(1-2), 137–158. doi:10.1016/S0166-4328(01)00361-8 PMID:11718889

Lupien, S. J., McEwen, B. S., Gunnar, M. R., & Heim, C. (2009). Effects of stress throughout the lifespan on the brain, behavior, and cognition. *Nature Reviews. Neuroscience*, *10*(6), 434–445. doi:10.1038/nrn2639 PMID:19401723

MacDowell, P. (2023). Teachers designing immersive learning experiences for environmental and sustainability education. In *Immersive education: Designing for learning* (pp. 171–186). Springer International Publishing. doi:10.1007/978-3-031-18138-2_11

Maier, A. M., Eckert, C. M., & Clarkson, P. J. (2021). Factors influencing communication in collaborative design. *Journal of Engineering Design*, *32*(12), 671–702. doi:10.1080/09544828.2021.1954146

Manivannan, M. L., & Nor, F. (2020). Barriers in differentiated instruction: A systematic review of the literature. *Journal of Critical Reviews*, *7*(6), 293–297. doi:10.31838/jcr.07.06.51

Manzano, A., Aguilar, J. M., Rodríguez, J., & Ortiz, A. (2022). Gamification in initial teacher training to promote inclusive practices: A qualitative study. *International Journal of Environmental Research and Public Health*, *19*(13), 8000. doi:10.3390/ijerph19138000 PMID:35805658

Marinoni, G., Van't Land, H., & Jensen, T. (2020). The impact of Covid-19 on higher education around the world. *IAU global survey report, 23*, 1-17.

Marsh, J., Wood, E., Chesworth, L., Nisha, B., Nutbrown, B., & Olney, B. (2019). Makerspaces in early childhood education: Principles of pedagogy and practice. *Mind, Culture, and Activity*, *26*(3), 221–233. doi:10.1080/10749039.2019.1655651

Martínez, M., Gómez, C. J., & Miralles, P. (2021). The effects of a gamified project based on historical thinking on the academic performance of primary school children. *Humanities & Social Sciences Communications*, *8*(122), 122. Advance online publication. doi:10.1057/s41599-021-00796-9

Masalimova, A. R., Khvatova, M. A., Chikileva, L. S., Zvyagintseva, E. P., Stepanova, V. V., & Melnik, M. V. (2022). Distance Learning in Higher Education During COVID-19. *Frontiers in Education*, *7*, 822958. Advance online publication. doi:10.3389/feduc.2022.822958

Masten, A. S. (2014). Global Perspectives on Resilience in Children and Youth. *Child Development*, *85*(1), 6–20. doi:10.1111/cdev.12205 PMID:24341286

Mathrani, A., Sarvesh, T., & Umer, R. (2022). Digital divide framework: Online learning in developing countries during the COVID-19 lockdown. *Globalisation, Societies and Education*, *20*(5), 625–640. doi:10.1080/14767724.2021.1981253

McDonald, C. (2020, October 6). *Government to provide 100,000 devices for remote learning*. ComputerWeekly.com. https://www.computerweekly.com/news/252490162/Government-offers-100000-devices-for-remote-learning

McEwen, B. S. (1999). Stress and hippocampal plasticity. *Annual Review of Neuroscience*, *22*(1), 105–122. doi:10.1146/annurev.neuro.22.1.105 PMID:10202533

McEwen, B. S., & Sapolsky, R. M. (1995). Stress and cognitive function. *Current Opinion in Neurobiology*, *5*(2), 205–216. doi:10.1016/0959-4388(95)80028-X PMID:7620309

McEwen, B., & Lupien, S. (2002). Stress: hormonal and neural aspects. In V. S. Ramachandran (Ed.), *Encyclopedia of the human brain* (pp. 463–474). Elsevier. doi:10.1016/B0-12-227210-2/00333-2

McLoughlin, C., & Lee, M. J. (2010). Personalised and self regulated learning in the Web 2.0 era: International exemplars of innovative pedagogy using social software. *Australasian Journal of Educational Technology*, *26*(1). Advance online publication. doi:10.14742/ajet.1100

Mejía-Delgado, O. A., & Mejía-Delgado, Y. Y. (2022). Madurez tecnológica de la generación Z: Reto de la transformación digital. *Revista CEA*, *8*(16), 1–22. doi:10.22430/24223182.1913

Mendenhall, E. (2012). *Syndemic Suffering: Social Distress, Depression, and Diabetes among Mexican Immigrant Women*. Left Coast Press, Inc.

Mendoza Navas, B. V., & Martos Eliche, F. (2021). El uso de herramientas tecnológicas en entornos virtuales para el desarrollo de la producción oral en inglés. *MLS Educational Research*, *5*(2), 105–119. doi:10.29314/mlser.v5i2.679

Menter, I., Elliot, D., Hulme, M., Lewin, J., & Lowden, K. (2011). *A Guide to Practitioner Research in Education*. SAGE. doi:10.4135/9781473957770

Merrill, S. (2009). *Introducing Syndemics: A Critical Systems Approach to Public and Community Health*. Jossey-Bass.

Mezirow, J. (1978). Perspective transformation. *Adult Education*, *28*(2), 100–110. doi:10.1177/074171367802800202

Mezirow, J. (1991). *Transformative dimensions of adult learning*. Jossey-bass.

Mezirow, J. (1997). Transformative Learning: Theory to Practice. *New Directions for Adult and Continuing Education*, *1997*(74), 5–12. doi:10.1002/ace.7401

Mezirow, J., & ... (Eds.). (2000). *Learning as transformation*. Jossey Bass.

Minocha, S., & Roberts, D. (2018). An Evaluation of VR for Learning Maths and Spatial Awareness in Primary School. In S. Minocha & D. Roberts (Eds.), *Interaction Design and Virtual Reality* (pp. 39–66). Springer.

Mintii, M., Sharmanova, N., Mankuta, A., Palchevska, O., & Semerikov, S. (2023). Selection of pedagogical conditions for training STEM teachers to use augmented reality technologies in their work. In Journal of Physics: Conference Series (Vol. 2611, No. 1, p. 012022). IOP Publishing. doi:10.1088/1742-6596/2611/1/012022

Mohammed Saeed Mohammed, G., & Mudhsh, A. D. (2021). The effects of COVID-19 on EFL learners' anxiety at the University of Bisha. *Arab World English Journal*. Mutizwa, M. R., Ozdamli, F., & Karagozlu, D. (2023). Smart learning environments during pandemic. *Trends in Higher Education*, *2*(1), 16–28. doi:10.3390/higheredu2010002

Montenegro, M., Fernández, J., Fernández-Batanero, J. M., & López-Meneses, E. (2023). Impact of the implementation of ChatGPT in education: A systematic review. *Computers*, *12*(8), 153. doi:10.3390/computers12080153

Moreno-Guerrero, A. J., Soler-Costa, R., Marín-Marín, J. A., & López Belmonte, J. (2021). Flipped learning y buenas prácticas docentes en educación primaria. *Comunicar*, *29*, 107–117. doi:10.3916/C68-2021-09

Mujica-Sequera, R. (2021). Clasificación de las Herramientas Digitales en la Tecnoeducación. *Revista Tecnológica-Educativa Docentes 2.0, 12*(1), 71–85. https://doi.org/ doi:10.37843/rted.v1i1.257

Murthy, S. Y. P. (2023, September 22). *How Data Protection Law affects education sector*. TechCircle. https://www.techcircle.in/2023/09/22/how-data-protection-law-affects-education-sector

Naím, M., & Toro, F. (2020). Socioeconomic and political roots of Venezuela's crisis. In F. Coppedge & S. Bitar (Eds.), *Crises of democracy and the prospect of renewal* (pp. 137–152). Johns Hopkins University Press.

National Research Council. (2010). *Report of a Workshop on The Scope and Nature of Computational Thinking*. The National Academies Press.

Nayar, K. P. (2022, April 24). What Happens to the Right to Education, Online? *The WIRE*. https://thewire.in/education/what-happens-to-the-right-to-education-online

Neira-Piñeiro, M. R., & Del Moral, M. E. (2021). Educación literaria y promoción lectora apoyadas en entornos literarios inmersivos con realidad aumentada. *Ocnos*, *20*(3), 1–19. doi:10.18239/ocnos_2021.20.3.2440

Noguera-Ramírez, O., & Herrera-Vargas, R. (2017). Human rights education and social justice in higher education: Perspectives from Venezuela. *Higher Education for the Future*, *4*(1), 82–95.

O'Connell, J. (2016). Networked participatory online learning design and challenges for academic integrity in higher education. *International Journal for Educational Integrity*, *12*(1), 1–15. doi:10.1007/s40979-016-0009-7

O'Sullivan, E. (1999). *Transformative learning: Educational vision for the 21st. Century*. Zed Books.

Ofosu, K. (2020). The shift to gamification in education: A review on dominant issues. *Journal of Educational Technology Systems*, *49*(1), 113–137. doi:10.1177/0047239520917629

Ojeda, D. A., & Marcano, M. (2019). Access to higher education in Venezuela: Challenges and opportunities for socio-economic mobility. *International Journal of Development and Sustainability*, *8*(8), 763–778.

Ojong, A. S. (2023). Unraveling the Efficacy of Differentiated Instruction in Enhancing Second Language Acquisition: A Comprehensive Review and Future Directions. *International Journal of Linguistics. Literature and Translation*, *6*(6), 75–82. doi:10.32996/ijllt.2023.6.6.8

P. (2021, November 14). Over 400% rise in cyber-crime cases committed against children in 2020: NCRB data. *The Economic Times*. https://economictimes.indiatimes.com/news/india/over-400-rise-in-cyber-crime-cases-committed-against-children-in-2020-ncrb-data/articleshow/87696995.cms

Palamar, S., Bielienka, G., Ponomarenko, T., Kozak, L., Nezhyva, L., & Voznyak, A. (2021). *Formation of readiness of future teachers to use augmented reality in the educational process of preschool and primary education.* CEUR Workshop. http://ds.knu.edu.ua/jspui/handle/123456789/3775

Pandita, A., & Kiran, R. (2023). The Technology Interface and Student Engagement Are Significant Stimuli in Sustainable Student Satisfaction. *Sustainability (Basel)*, *15*(10), 7923. doi:10.3390/su15107923

Papert, S. (1980). *Mindstorms: Children, Computers, and Powerful Ideas*. Basic Books.

Partovi, H. (2017). *Code.org: Inspiring a Generation to Learn Computer Science*. TEDxRainier. https://www.ted.com/tedx

Paulo Freire Institute. (n.d.). *Structural Violence, Education and Freedom*. PFI. http://www.paulofreireinstitute.org/pdf/StructuralViolenceEd ucationandFreedom.pdf

Pavlovic, A., DeFina, L. F., Natale, B. L., Thiele, S. E., Walker, T. J., Craig, D. W., Vint, G. R., Leonard, D., Haskell, W. L., & Kohl, H. W. (2021). Keeping children healthy during and after COVID-19 pandemic: Meeting youth physical activity needs. *BMC Public Health*, *21*(1), 1–8. doi:10.1186/s12889-021-10545-x PMID:33706744

Peláez, C. A., & Solano, A. (2023). A Practice for the Design of Interactive Multimedia Experiences Based on Gamification: A Case Study in Elementary Education. *Sustainability (Basel)*, *15*(3), 2385. doi:10.3390/su15032385

Pelletier, K., Robert, J., Muscanell, N., McCormack, M., Reeves, J., Arbino, N., Grajek, S., Birdwell, T., Liu, D., Mandernach, J., Moore, A., Porcaro, A., Rutledge, R., & Zimmern, J. (2023). *EDUCAUSE Horizon Report, Teaching and Learning Edition*. EDUCAUSE. https://www.educause.edu/horizon-report-teaching-and-learning-2023

Pierleoni, P., Pernini, L., Belli, A., & Palma, L. (2014). An Android-Based Heart Monitoring System for the Elderly and for Patients with Heart Disease. *International Journal of Telemedicine and Applications*, *2014*, 625156. doi:10.1155/2014/625156 PMID:25210513

Plass, J. L., Homer, B. D., & Kinzer, C. K. (2015). The effects of virtual reality on learning: A meta-analysis. *Journal of Educational Psychology*, *107*(3), 525–546.

POGGI. N. (2023, September 28). *Three crucial online student privacy laws*. Prey Project. https://www.indiatoday.in/education-today/featurephilia/story/will-nep-give-a-much-needed-boost-to-online-education-in-india-1713926-2020-08-22

Pourhomayoun, M., Alshurafa, N., & Dabiri, F. (2016). *Why do we need a remote human- health monitoring system A study on predictive analytics for heart failure*. 11th International Conference on Body Area Networks, Turin, Italy.

Prasath, A. A., Srinivasan, S., Ranganathan, C. S., Latha, N., & Saravanan, K. (2023, August). Cloud Server Based Intelligent Health Care Kit using Body Sensor Network. In *2023 Second International Conference on Smart Technologies For Smart Nation (Smart Tech Con)* (pp. 323-327). IEEE. 10.1109/SmartTechCon57526.2023.10391445

Prasath, J.S. (2013). Wireless monitoring of heart rate using micro-controller. *International Journal of Advanced Research in Computer Science and Electronics Engineering, 2.*

Pugh-Opher, F. (2023). Teaching and Learning Mandarin Chinese: Gamification and Simulation in an Early Childhood Classroom. In Research Anthology on Early Childhood Development and School Transition in the Digital Era (pp. 157-174). IGI Global.

Punhani, R., Arora, V. P. S., & Sai Sabitha, A. (2022). K-prototype algorithm for clustering large data sets with categorical values to established product segmentation. In Proceedings of Data Analytics and Management: ICDAM 2021, Volume 1 (pp. 343-353). Springer Singapore.

Puri, S., Dubey, M., & Dubey, S. M. (2023). Breast cancer prognosis and prediction through gene expression analysis and the hybrid model of SVM and logistic regression. *IEEE 2023 World conference on communication and computing (WCONF)*. IEEE Press. 10.1109/WCONF58270.2023.10235198

Puri, S., & Singh, S. P. (2019). A hybrid Hindi printed document classification system using SVM and fuzzy: An Advancement. *Journal of Information Technology Research*, *12*(4), 107–131. doi:10.4018/JITR.2019100106

Puri, S., & Singh, S. P. (2020). Advanced applications on bilingual document analysis and processing systems. *International Journal of Applied Metaheuristic Computing*, *11*(4), 149–193. doi:10.4018/IJAMC.2020100108

Qader, R. O., & Arslan, F. Y. (2019). The effect of flipped classroom instruction in writing: A case study with Iraqi EFL learners. *Teaching English with Technology*, *19*(1), 36–55.

Quintero, W. A., & Jaimes Guerrero, C. A. (2023). Incidencia del uso de las TIC en el desarrollo de las habilidades de comprensión y expresión oral y escrita del idioma inglés en estudiantes de nivel A1 de la licenciatura en lenguas extranjeras inglés-francés de la universidad de Pamplona. *Ciencia Latina Revista Científica Multidisciplinar*, *7*(4), 701–716. doi:10.37811/cl_rcm.v7i4.6904

Rachamalla, S. A. (2021). Usage of 'ICT' in English language teaching. *International Journal of Innovative Research in Science and Engineering*, *7*(11), 22–25.

Rainford, J. (2021). Moving widening participation outreach online: Challenge or opportunity? *Perspectives*, *25*(1), 2–6. doi:10.1080/13603108.2020.1785968

Ramírez, A., & Pinochet, S. (2021). El mundo digital como facilitador de la enseñanza del idioma inglés. *Redipe*, *10*(13), 120–130. doi:10.36260/rbr.v10i13.1733

Ramzan, M., Javaid, Z. K., & Fatima, M. (2023). Empowering ESL students: Harnessing the potential of social media to enhance academic motivation in higher education. *Global Digital & Print Media Review*, *VI*(II), 224–237. doi:10.31703/gdpmr.2023(VI-II).15

Rathore, M. (2023, July 10). *Share of students who have access to smartphone at home in government and private schools in India in 2018 and 2020*. Statista. https://www.statista.com/statistics/1276401/india-share-of-students-who-have-access-to-smartphone-at-home/

Rennick, J. (2015). Learning that Makes a Difference: Pedagogy and Practice for Learning Abroad. Teaching & Learning Inquiry. The ISSOTL Journal, 3(2), 71-88.

Rennie, F., & Morrison, T. (2013). *E-learning and social networking handbook: Resources for higher education*. Routledge. doi:10.4324/9780203120279

Resnick, M. (2017). *Lifelong Kindergarten: Cultivating Creativity through Projects, Passion, Peers, and Play*. The MIT Press. doi:10.7551/mitpress/11017.001.0001

Reza, T., Shoilee, S. B. A., Akhand, S. M., & Khan, M. M. (2017). *Development of android based pulse monitoring system*. Second International Conference on Electrical, Computer and Communication Technologies (ICECCT), Coimbatore, India,.

Ribeiro, L., Leal, T., & Quadrado, A. (2018). Gamification: A methodology to motivate engagement and participation in a higher education environment. *International Journal of Education and Research*, *6*(4), 58–101.

Ricoy, M. C., & Sánchez-Martínez, C. (2022). Raising ecological awareness and digital literacy in primary school children through gamification. *International Journal of Environmental Research and Public Health*, *19*(3), 1149. doi:10.3390/ijerph19031149 PMID:35162171

Rizzo, A. (2020). *Silent hypoxia and its role in COVID-19 detection*. Chief Medical Officer American Lung Association.

Robledo, K., & Atarama, T. (2016). Periodismo político transmedia. Estrategias para el desarrollo de la profesión en el actual ecosistema mediático. *Correspondencias & Análisis*, (6), 31–45. doi:10.24265/cian.2016.n6.02

Rohit, K. (2022). Digital leadership in 21st century education. *International Journal for Research Trends and Innovation, 7*(7).

Romano, M., Díaz, P., & Aedo, I. (2023). Empowering teachers to create augmented reality experiences: The effects on the educational experience. *Interactive Learning Environments, 31*(3), 1546–1563. doi:10.1080/10494820.2020.1851727

Roy, D. (2021, October 8). *Access to online education for EWS students cannot be denied: Supreme Court issues notice on plea*. Bar and Bench. https://www.barandbench.com/news/litigation/access-to-online-education-for-ews-students-cannot-be-denied-supreme-court-issues-notice-in-plea

Roys, N., & Franco, A. (2019). Integración de las TIC para mejorar las habilidades de estudiantes de lenguas extranjeras de comunidades vulnerables. *Sophia, 15*(2), 4–17. doi:10.18634/sophiaj.15v.2i.770

Rubin, J. (2017). *Embedding Collaborative Online International Learning (COIL) at Higher Education Institutions An Evolutionary Overview with Exemplars*. UIC. https://studyabroad.uic.edu/wp-content/uploads/sites/256/2020/08/Rubin-Embed ding-Collaborative-Online-International-Learning-at-Higher-Education-Institutions.pdf

Rubin, J., & Guth, S. (2022). *The Guide to COIL Virtual Exchange*. Stylus Publishing.

Ruiz, S., Hernández, S., García, A., & Chacón, J. (2021). Educational innovation in times of crisis: learner voices from the Albany-Caracas COIL exchange. In Satar, Müge (Ed.), Virtual exchange: towards digital equity in internationalization (pp. 131-138). Research-publishing.net. doi:10.14705/rpnet.2021.53.1295

Rylko-Bauer, B., Whiteford, L., & Farmer, P. (Eds.). (2009). *Global Health in Times of Violence*. School of Advanced Research Press.

Sadiq, S., & Nosrati, A. (2019). The role of virtual reality in teacher education: A systematic review of the literature. *Computers & Education, 132*, 132–145.

Safawi, S. S., & Akay, C. (2022). The effect of differentiated instruction approach on students' academic achievement and attitudes: A meta-analysis study. *Integrity Journal of Education and Training*, *6*(6), 120–132. doi:10.31248/IJET2022.163

Sahni, S. (2020, September 18). Personal Data Protection Bill (PDPB) and Educational Institutions. *The Cyber Blog India*. https://cyberblogindia.in/personal-data-protection-bill-pdpb-and-educational-institutions/

Sahni, J. (2019). Does blended learning enhance student engagement? Evidence from higher education. *The Journal of Learning in Higher Education*, *2019*, 1–14. doi:10.5171/2019.121518

Sánchez-Rivas, E., Sánchez-Rodríguez, J., & Ruiz-Palmero, J. (2019). Percepción del alumnado universitario respecto al modelo pedagógico de clase invertida. *Magis. Revista Internacional de Investigación en Educación, 11*(23), 151–168. doi:10.11144/Javeriana.m11-23.paur

Sandi, C. (2013). Stress and cognition. *Wiley Interdisciplinary Reviews: Cognitive Science, 4*(3), 245–261. doi:10.1002/wcs.1222 PMID:26304203

Sandy, M. G., & Franco, Z. E. (2014). Grounding Service-Learning in the Digital Age: Exploring a Virtual Sense of Geographic Place through Online Collaborative Mapping and Mixed Media. *Journal of Higher Education Outreach & Engagement, 18*(4), 201–232.

Sarahian, N., Sahraei, H., Zardooz, H., Alibeik, H., & Sadeghi, B. (2014). Effect of memantine administration within the nucleus accumbens on changes in weight and volume of the brain and adrenal gland during chronic stress in female mice. *Modares J Med Sci: Pathobiology., 17*, 71–82.

Sardana, S. (2021, July 14). Bringing down the barriers. *The Hindu.* https://www.thehindu.com/education/what-are-the-challenges-of-education-in-rural-india-and-how-technology-can-help-overcome-them/article35316970.ece

Satheesh, A. (2020, November 1). *Right to internet fundamental for right to education: faheema shirin r.k. V. State of kerala & ors.* Lawsisto. https://lawsisto.com/legalnewsread/ODU5OA==/Right-to-internet-fundamental-for-right-to-education-Faheema-Shirin-RK-v-State-of-Kerala-Ors

Scanlon, J., & Li, X. (2022). An Exploration Into Post-Primary School Teachers' Perceptions About the Use of Google Classroom: Supporting Pupils in Remote and Blended Learning in Northern Ireland During the COVID-19 Pandemic. *Handbook of Research on Teacher and Student Perspectives on the Digital Turn in Education,* 420-452. https://www.igi-global.com/book/teacher-student-perspectives-digital-turn/290031 DOI: doi:10.4018/978-1-6684-4446-7.ch019

Scheper-Hughes, N. (1996). Small Wars and Invisible Genocides. *Social Science & Medicine, 43*(5), 889–900. doi:10.1016/0277-9536(96)00152-9 PMID:8870153

Scheper-Hughes, N., & Bourgois, P. (2004). Introduction: Making Sense of Violence. In *Violence in War and Peace: An Anthology.* Blackwell Publishing.

Scheper-Hughes, N., & Bourgois, P. (Eds.). (2003). *Violence in War and Peace: An Anthology.* Blackwell Publishers.

Scheper-Hughes, N., & Lovell, A. (1987). *Psychiatry Inside Out: Selected Writings of Franco Basaglia.* Columbia University Press.

Scholey, A., Gibbs, A., Neale, C., Perry, N., Ossoukhova, A., Bilog, V., Kras, M., Scholz, C., Sass, M., & Buchwald-Werner, S. (2014). Anti-stress effects of lemon balm-containing foods. *Nutrients, 6*(11), 4805–4821. doi:10.3390/nu6114805 PMID:25360512

Scolari, C. (2008). *Hipermediaciones: elementos para una teoría de la comunicación digital interactiva.* Gedisa.

Selwyn, F. N. K. (2014). The sociology of education and digital technology: Past, present and future. *Oxford Review of Education*, *40*(4), 489. https://doi.org/http://www.jstor.org/stable/24736320

Senith Electronics. (n.d.). *LM2596 DC-DC buck converter step-down power module.* Senith Electronics. http://www.senith.lk/shop/item/1081/lm2596-dc-dc-buck-converter-step-down-power-module

Serpanos, D., & Wolf, M. (2019). *Internet-of-Things (IoT).* Systems Architectures Algorithms Methodologies Springer International Publishing Switzerland.

Shahnama, M., Ghonsooly, B., & Elahi Shirvan, M. (2021). A meta-analysis of relative effectiveness of flipped learning in English as second/foreign language research. *Educational Technology Research and Development*, *69*(3), 1355–1386. doi:10.1007/s11423-021-09996-1

Shams, S. (n.d.). *E-Learning And The Fate Of Right To Education In India*. Lexlife India. https://lexlife.in/2021/07/02/e-learning-and-the-fate-of-right-to-education-in-india/

Shareefa, M., Zin, R. H., Abdullah, N. Z., & Hawawi, R. (2019). Differentiated Instruction: Definition and Challenging Factors Perceived by Teachers. *Advances in Social Science, Education and Humanities Research*, *388*, 322–327.

Shekhar. D. (2021, May 6). Inside the reshaping of CSR in India during Covid-19. *India Forbes*. https://www.forbesindia.com/article/take-one-big-story-of-the-day/inside-the-reshaping-of-csr-in-india-during-covid19/67821/1

Shrier, D. L. (2021). From Shock to Awe: How the Pandemic Crisis has Opened Up the Dialogue for A True Reinvention of Education. *Horizons: Journal of International Relations and Sustainable Development, 19*, 72. https://www.jstor.org/stable/48617354

Simel, D. L., Goldman, L., & Schafer, A.I. (2020). Goldman-Cecil Medicine (26th ed.). Philadelphia PA: Elsevier.

Singer, M. (1996). A dose of drugs, a touch of violence, a case of AIDS: Conceptualizing the SAVA syndemic. *Free Inquiry in Creative Sociology*, *24*, 99–110.

Singer, M. (2009). *Introduction to Syndemics: A Systems Approach to Public and Community Health*. Jossey-Bass.

Singer, M., & Clair, S. (2003). Syndemics and public health: Reconceptualizing disease in bio-social context. *Medical Anthropology Quarterly*, *17*(4), 423–441. doi:10.1525/maq.2003.17.4.423 PMID:14716917

Singer, M., Erickson, P. I., Badiane, L., Diaz, R., Ortiz, D., Abraham, T., & Nicolaysen, A. M. (2006). Syndemics, sex, and the city: Understanding sexually transmitted diseases in social and cultural context. *Social Science & Medicine*, *63*(8), 2010–2021. doi:10.1016/j.socscimed.2006.05.012 PMID:16782250

Singh, G. M. (2022, December 22). Accessibility to personal data by employees of data fiduciary, and the Digital Personal Data Protection Bill. *The Leaflet*. https://theleaflet.in/accessibility-to-personal-data-by-employees-of-data-fiduciary-and-the-digital-personal-data-protection-bill/

Singh, B., Lopez, D., & Ramadan, R. (2023). Internet of things in healthcare: A conventional literature review. *Health and Technology*, *13*(5), 699–719. doi:10.1007/s12553-023-00771-1

Singh, J. D. (2011). Higher education in India–Issues, challenges and suggestions. In S. P. Singh & K. L. Dangwal (Eds.), *Higher education (pp* (pp. 93–103). Lambert Academic Publishing.

Sistermans, I. J. (2020). Integrating competency-based education with a case-based or problem-based learning approach in online health sciences. *Asia Pacific Education Review*, *21*(4), 683–696. doi:10.1007/s12564-020-09658-6

Smilde, D., & Ulmer, A. (2018). Repression, resistance, and democratic backsliding in Venezuela. *Annual Review of Political Science*, *21*, 201–216. doi:10.1146/annurev-polisci-050317-070836

Sofi-Karim, M., Bali, A. O., & Rached, K. (2023). Online education via media platforms and applications as an innovative teaching method. *Education and Information Technologies*, *28*(1), 507–523. doi:10.1007/s10639-022-11188-0 PMID:35791317

Solerte, S., Cravello, L., Ferrari, E., & Fioravanti, M. (2000). Overproduction of IFN-γ and TNF-α from natural killer (NK) cells is associated with abnormal NK reactivity and cognitive derangement in Alzheimer's disease. *Annals of the New York Academy of Sciences*, *917*(1), 331–340. doi:10.1111/j.1749-6632.2000.tb05399.x PMID:11268360

Song, L., Che, W., Min-Wei, W., Murakami, Y., & Matsumoto, K. (2006). Impairment of spatial learning and memory induced by learned helplessness and chronic mild stress. *Pharmacology, Biochemistry, and Behavior*, *83*(2), 186–193. doi:10.1016/j.pbb.2006.01.004 PMID:16519925

Song, Z., Wang, C., & Bergmann, L. (2020). China's prefectural digital divide: Spatial analysis and multivariate determinants of ICT diffusion. *International Journal of Information Management*, *52*, 102072. doi:10.1016/j.ijinfomgt.2020.102072

Soomro, S. A., Casakin, H., Nanjappan, V., & Georgiev, G. V. (2023). Makerspaces Fostering Creativity: A Systematic Literature Review. *Journal of Science Education and Technology*, *32*(4), 1–19. doi:10.1007/s10956-023-10041-4

Sosa-Díaz, M., Guerra-Antequera, J., & Cerezo-Pizarro, M. (2021). Flipped classroom in the context of education: Learning, satisfaction, and interaction. *Education Sciences*, *11*(8), 416–433. doi:10.3390/educsci11080416

Srinivasan, P., Ayub Khan, A., Prabu, T., Manoj, M., & Ranjan, M. (2020). Heartbeat sensor using fingertip through Arduino. *Journal of Critical Review, 7*(7).

Srivastava, A. (2022, July 1). Akhilesh Yadav distributes laptops to students on his 49th birthday. *India Today*. https://www.indiatoday.in/education-today/news/story/akhilesh-yadav-distributes-laptops-to-students-on-his-49th-birthday-1969017-2022-07-01

Srividya, B. & Satyanarayana, V. (2018). Personal lung function monitoring system for asthma using Internet of things. *International Journal of Research in Electronics and Computer Engineering, 6.*

Statista Research Department. (2022, July 6). *Size of the global e-learning market in 2019 and 2026, by segment*. Statista. https://www.statista.com/statistics/1130331/e-learning-market-size-segment-worldwide/

Stevanović, A., Božić, R., & Radović, S. (2021). Higher education students' experiences and opinion about distance learning during the Covid-19 pandemic. *Journal of Computer Assisted Learning*, *37*(6), 1682–1693. doi:10.1111/jcal.12613 PMID:34903902

Suh, S. A. (2017). Structural Violence and the Possibility of Transformative Education. *Journal of Transformative Education*, *15*(2), 106–120.

SUNY COIL Center. (2020). *What is COIL?* Suny. https://online.suny.edu/introtocoil/suny-coil-what-is/

Sutradhar, I., Das, G. R., Hasan, M., Wazib, A., & Sarker, M. (2019). Prevalence and risk factors of chronic obstructive pulmonary disease in Bangladesh: a systematic review. *Cureus, 11.*

Tadesse, S., & Muluye, W. (2020). The impact of COVID-19 pandemic on education system in developing countries: A review. *Open Journal of Social Sciences*, *8*(10), 159–170. doi:10.4236/jss.2020.810011

Tamilselvi, V. (2020). *IoT based health monitoring system.* 6th International Conference on Advanced Computing and Communication Systems (ICACCS), Coimbatore, India.

Taussig, M. (1984). Culture of Terror-Space of Death: Roger Casement's Putumayo Report and the Explanation of Torture. *Comparative Studies in Society and History*, *26*(3), 467–497. doi:10.1017/S0010417500011105

Taussig, M. (1992). *The Nervous System*. Routledge.

Tay, A. Z., Huijser, H., Dart, S., & Cathcart, A. (2023). Learning technology as contested terrain: Insights from teaching academics and learning designers in Australian higher education. *Australasian Journal of Educational Technology*, 56–70. doi:10.14742/ajet.8179

Taylor, D., Bearman, M., Scarparo, S., & Thomas, M. K. E. (2022). The emotional transition to online teaching: Grief, loss, and implications for academic development. *The International Journal for Academic Development*, *27*(2), 176–190. doi:10.1080/1360144X.2022.2083141

Taylor, E. W., & Cranton, P. (2012). Learning to think like an adult: Core concepts of transformation theory. In E. W. Taylor & P. Cranton (Eds.), *The handbook of transformative learning: Theory, research and practice*. Jossey-Bass.

Tess, P. A. (2013). The role of social media in higher education classes (real and virtual)–A literature review. *Computers in Human Behavior*, *29*(5), A60–A68. doi:10.1016/j.chb.2012.12.032

Thailand Medical News. (n.d.). *News.* Thai Medical News. https://www.thailandmedical.news

Tinubu Ali, T., & Herrera, M. (2020). *Distance learning during COVID-19: 7 equity considerations for schools and districts*. Southern Education. https://www.southerneducation.org/covid-19-digital-equity/

Trust, T., & Whalen, J. (2020). Should teachers be trained in emergency remote teaching? Lessons learned from the COVID-19 pandemic. *Journal of Technology and Teacher Education*, *28*(2), 189–199. https://www.learntechlib.org/primary/p/215995/

Trust, T., & Whalen, J. (2021). Emergency remote teaching with technology during the COVID-19 pandemic: Using the whole teacher lens to examine educator's experiences and insights. *Educational Media International*, *58*(2), 145–160. doi:10.1080/09523987.2021.1930479

Turan, Z., & Akdag-Cimen, B. (2019). Flipped classroom in English language teaching: A systematic review. *Computer Assisted Language Learning*, *33*(5), 590–606. doi:10.1080/09588221.2019.1584117

UNESCO. (2019). *Education in Emergencies and Crises: a State-of-the-Art Review of Management, Programming, and Evidence*. UNESCO. https://unesdoc.unesco.org/images/0026/002614/261424e.pdf

UNESCO. (2020). *Global Education Monitoring Report 2020: Inclusion and education: All means all.* Paris: UNESCO. https://en.unesco.org/gem-report/sites/gem-report/files/2020-06/GEM-Report-2020.pdf

UNESCO. (2020). *School closures caused by Coronavirus (COVID-19)*. UNESCO. https://en.unesco.org/COVID19/educationresponse

UNESCO. (2020, November 26). *What you need to know about the right to education*. UNESCO. https://www.unesco.org/en/articles/what-you-need-know-about-right-education

UNICEF. (2019). *Out of School Children in Venezuela: A Call for Action*. UNICEF. https://www.unicef.org/venezuela/en/media_71964.html

UNICEF. (2019). *Venezuela's Children and Adolescents in Crisis*. UNICEF. https://www.unicef.org/venezuela/venezuela-crisis-children-and-adolescents

United Nations Educational, Scientific, and Cultural Organization (UNESCO). (2020). COVID-19 educational disruption and response. https://en.unesco.org/COVID19/educationresponse

United Nations. (1948). *Universal Declaration of Human Rights*. UN. https://www.un.org/en/about-us/universal-declaration-of-human-rights

United Nations. (2015). *Transforming Our World: The 2030 Agenda for Sustainable Development*. New York: UN Publishing. https://sdgs.un.org/goals

Valencia, L. I., & Orellana, D. (2019). Barreras en la implementación de la gamificación en educación superior: Revisión de literatura. *InCrescendo*, *10*(3), 635–650. doi:10.21895/incres.2019.v10n4.06

Valenza, M. V., Gasparini, I., & da S. Hounsell, M. (2019). Serious game design for children. *Journal of Educational Technology & Society, 22*(3), 19-31. https://www.jstor.org/stable/26896707

Varona, F. (2022). Perspectivas en la utilización de las tecnologías de información y comunicación de la educación superior. *Revista Visión Antataura*, *6*(2), 170–184.

Vázquez-Montilla, E., Martín-Blas, T., & Sánchez-Elvira Paniagua, A. (2020). Attention and working memory in young people with Internet Gaming Disorder: A systematic review. *Adicciones*, *32*(2), 126–139. doi:10.20882/adicciones.1271

Vera Ramírez, L. S., Villao Tomalá, D. C., & Granados Romero, J. F. (2020). Competencias digitales en el uso de herramientas digitales para el aprendizaje de inglés. *Ingenio*, *3*(1), 1–14. doi:10.18779/ingenio.v3i1.21

Villamizar, G. (2019). *Personal communication*, November 15, 2019.

Wade, C. (2019). *The state of Venezuelan democracy: The role of international actors*. Routledge.

Watts-Taffe, S., Laster, B., Broach, L., Marinak, B., Conner, C., & Walker-Dalhouse, D. (2022). Differentiated Instruction: Making Informed Teacher Decisions. *The Reading Teacher*, *66*(4), 303–314. doi:10.1002/TRTR.01126

Web Desk, I. T. (2020, August 22). Will NEP give a much-needed boost to online education in India? *India Today*. https://www.indiatoday.in/education-today/featurephilia/story/will-nep-give-a-much-needed-boost-to-online-education-in-india-1713926-2020-08-22

Web Desk, I. T. (2021, June 19). 38 universities can offer online degree courses now, says UGC: Check full list with programmes here. *India Today*. https://www.indiatoday.in/education-today/news/story/38-universities-can-offer-online-degree-courses-now-says-ugc-1816919-2021-06-19

Wekesser, L. J., & Caballero, J. (2020). The state of academic freedom in Venezuela: An analysis. Exchange. *The Journal of Public Diplomacy*, *1*(1), 17–24.

Wilson, L. O. (2016). *Anderson and Krathwohl: Bloom's Taxonomy Revised*. Quincy College.

Wing, J. M. (2006). Computational thinking. *Communications of the ACM*, *49*(3), 33–35. doi:10.1145/1118178.1118215

Wing, J. M. (2011). Research Notebook: Computational Thinking—What and Why? *The Link Magazine*, *26*(2), 27–36.

Winter, E., Costello, A., O'Brien, M., & Hickey, G. (2021). Teachers' use of technology and the impact of COVID-19. *Irish Educational Studies*, *40*(2), 235–246. doi:10.1080/03323315.2021.1916559

World Health Organization (WHO). (2020). *Violence Prevention Alliance (VPA) - Learning to Live Together - Promote Resilience in Children and Youth.* WHO. https://www.who.int/violenceprevention/alliance/advocacy/Learning.pdf

Wrist worn pulse oximeter. (n.d.). Concord Health Supply. https:// www.concordhealthsupply.com/Wrist-Oximeter-p/75006.html

Xiao, J., Sun-Lin, H. Z., & Cheng, H. C. (2019). A framework of online-merge-offline (OMO) classroom for open education: A preliminary study. *Asian Association of Open Universities Journal*, *14*(2), 134–146. doi:10.1108/AAOUJ-08-2019-0033

Yan, L., Whitelock-Wainwright, A., Guan, Q., Wen, G., Gašević, D., & Chen, G. (2021). Students' experience of online learning during the COVID-19 pandemic: A province-wide survey study. *British Journal of Educational Technology*, *52*(5), 2038–2057. doi:10.1111/bjet.13102 PMID:34219755

Yaribeygi, H., Panahi, Y., Sahraei, H., Johnston, T. P., & Sahebkar, A. (2017, July 21). The impact of stress on body function: A review. *EXCLI Journal*, *16*, 1057–1072. doi:10.17179/excli2017-480 PMID:28900385

Yatsenkov, V. (2018). *Pulse oximeterMAX30100/MAX30102-how to fix wrong board.* Reed Paper. https://reedpaper.wordpress.com/2018/08/22/pulse-oximeter-max30100-max30102-how-to-fix-wrong-board/

Yu, A. Y., Tian, S. W., Vogel, D., & Kwok, R. C. W. (2010). Can learning be virtually boosted? An investigation of online social networking impacts. *Computers & Education*, *55*(4), 1494–1503. doi:10.1016/j.compedu.2010.06.015

Zaglia, M. E. (2013). Brand communities embedded in social networks. *Journal of Business Research*, *66*(2), 216–223. doi:10.1016/j.jbusres.2012.07.015 PMID:23564989

Zarrinabadi, N., & Ebrahimi, A. (2019). Increasing peer collaborative dialogue using a flipped classroom strategy. *Innovation in Language Learning and Teaching*, *13*(3), 267–276. doi:10.1080/17501229.2018.1455688

Zhang, N., & Ouyang, F. (2023). An integrated approach for knowledge extraction and analysis in collaborative knowledge construction. *International Journal of Educational Technology in Higher Education*, *20*(1), 45. doi:10.1186/s41239-023-00414-5

Zhong, B., Zheng, J., & Zhan, Z. (2023). An exploration of combining virtual and physical robots in robotics education. *Interactive Learning Environments*, *31*(1), 370–382. doi:10.1080/10494820.2020.1786409

Related References

To continue our tradition of advancing information science and technology research, we have compiled a list of recommended IGI Global readings. These references will provide additional information and guidance to further enrich your knowledge and assist you with your own research and future publications.

Aasi, P., Rusu, L., & Vieru, D. (2017). The Role of Culture in IT Governance Five Focus Areas: A Literature Review. *International Journal of IT/Business Alignment and Governance, 8*(2), 42-61. https://doi.org/ doi:10.4018/IJITBAG.2017070103

Abdrabo, A. A. (2018). Egypt's Knowledge-Based Development: Opportunities, Challenges, and Future Possibilities. In A. Alraouf (Ed.), *Knowledge-Based Urban Development in the Middle East* (pp. 80–101). Hershey, PA: IGI Global. doi:10.4018/978-1-5225-3734-2.ch005

Abu Doush, I., & Alhami, I. (2018). Evaluating the Accessibility of Computer Laboratories, Libraries, and Websites in Jordanian Universities and Colleges. *International Journal of Information Systems and Social Change*, *9*(2), 44–60. doi:10.4018/IJISSC.2018040104

Adegbore, A. M., Quadri, M. O., & Oyewo, O. R. (2018). A Theoretical Approach to the Adoption of Electronic Resource Management Systems (ERMS) in Nigerian University Libraries. In A. Tella & T. Kwanya (Eds.), *Handbook of Research on Managing Intellectual Property in Digital Libraries* (pp. 292–311). Hershey, PA: IGI Global. doi:10.4018/978-1-5225-3093-0.ch015

Afolabi, O. A. (2018). Myths and Challenges of Building an Effective Digital Library in Developing Nations: An African Perspective. In A. Tella & T. Kwanya (Eds.), *Handbook of Research on Managing Intellectual Property in Digital Libraries* (pp. 51–79). Hershey, PA: IGI Global. doi:10.4018/978-1-5225-3093-0.ch004

Agarwal, P., Kurian, R., & Gupta, R. K. (2022). Additive Manufacturing Feature Taxonomy and Placement of Parts in AM Enclosure. In S. Salunkhe, H. Hussein, & J. Davim (Eds.), *Applications of Artificial Intelligence in Additive Manufacturing* (pp. 138–176). IGI Global. https://doi.org/10.4018/978-1-7998-8516-0.ch007

Al-Alawi, A. I., Al-Hammam, A. H., Al-Alawi, S. S., & AlAlawi, E. I. (2021). The Adoption of E-Wallets: Current Trends and Future Outlook. In Y. Albastaki, A. Razzaque, & A. Sarea (Eds.), *Innovative Strategies for Implementing FinTech in Banking* (pp. 242–262). IGI Global. https://doi.org/10.4018/978-1-7998-3257-7.ch015

Alsharo, M. (2017). Attitudes Towards Cloud Computing Adoption in Emerging Economies. *International Journal of Cloud Applications and Computing*, *7*(3), 44–58. doi:10.4018/IJCAC.2017070102

Amer, T. S., & Johnson, T. L. (2017). Information Technology Progress Indicators: Research Employing Psychological Frameworks. In A. Mesquita (Ed.), *Research Paradigms and Contemporary Perspectives on Human-Technology Interaction* (pp. 168–186). Hershey, PA: IGI Global. doi:10.4018/978-1-5225-1868-6.ch008

Andreeva, A., & Yolova, G. (2021). Liability in Labor Legislation: New Challenges Related to the Use of Artificial Intelligence. In B. Vassileva & M. Zwilling (Eds.), *Responsible AI and Ethical Issues for Businesses and Governments* (pp. 214–232). IGI Global. https://doi.org/10.4018/978-1-7998-4285-9.ch012

Anohah, E. (2017). Paradigm and Architecture of Computing Augmented Learning Management System for Computer Science Education. *International Journal of Online Pedagogy and Course Design*, *7*(2), 60–70. doi:10.4018/IJOPCD.2017040105

Anohah, E., & Suhonen, J. (2017). Trends of Mobile Learning in Computing Education from 2006 to 2014: A Systematic Review of Research Publications. *International Journal of Mobile and Blended Learning*, *9*(1), 16–33. doi:10.4018/IJMBL.2017010102

Arbaiza, C. S., Huerta, H. V., & Rodriguez, C. R. (2021). Contributions to the Technological Adoption Model for the Peruvian Agro-Export Sector. *International Journal of E-Adoption*, *13*(1), 1–17. https://doi.org/10.4018/IJEA.2021010101

Bailey, E. K. (2017). Applying Learning Theories to Computer Technology Supported Instruction. In M. Grassetti & S. Brookby (Eds.), *Advancing Next-Generation Teacher Education through Digital Tools and Applications* (pp. 61–81). Hershey, PA: IGI Global. doi:10.4018/978-1-5225-0965-3.ch004

Baker, J. D. (2021). Introduction to Machine Learning as a New Methodological Framework for Performance Assessment. In M. Bocarnea, B. Winston, & D. Dean (Eds.), *Handbook of Research on Advancements in Organizational Data Collection and Measurements: Strategies for Addressing Attitudes, Beliefs, and Behaviors* (pp. 326–342). IGI Global. https://doi.org/10.4018/978-1-7998-7665-6.ch021

Banerjee, S., Sing, T. Y., Chowdhury, A. R., & Anwar, H. (2018). Let's Go Green: Towards a Taxonomy of Green Computing Enablers for Business Sustainability. In M. Khosrow-Pour (Ed.), *Green Computing Strategies for Competitive Advantage and Business Sustainability* (pp. 89–109). Hershey, PA: IGI Global. doi:10.4018/978-1-5225-5017-4.ch005

Basham, R. (2018). Information Science and Technology in Crisis Response and Management. In M. Khosrow-Pour, D.B.A. (Ed.), Encyclopedia of Information Science and Technology, Fourth Edition (pp. 1407-1418). Hershey, PA: IGI Global. doi:10.4018/978-1-5225-2255-3.ch121

Batyashe, T., & Iyamu, T. (2018). Architectural Framework for the Implementation of Information Technology Governance in Organisations. In M. Khosrow-Pour, D.B.A. (Ed.), Encyclopedia of Information Science and Technology, Fourth Edition (pp. 810-819). Hershey, PA: IGI Global. doi:10.4018/978-1-5225-2255-3.ch070

Bekleyen, N., & Çelik, S. (2017). Attitudes of Adult EFL Learners towards Preparing for a Language Test via CALL. In D. Tafazoli & M. Romero (Eds.), *Multiculturalism and Technology-Enhanced Language Learning* (pp. 214–229). Hershey, PA: IGI Global. doi:10.4018/978-1-5225-1882-2.ch013

Bergeron, F., Croteau, A., Uwizeyemungu, S., & Raymond, L. (2017). A Framework for Research on Information Technology Governance in SMEs. In S. De Haes & W. Van Grembergen (Eds.), *Strategic IT Governance and Alignment in Business Settings* (pp. 53–81). Hershey, PA: IGI Global. doi:10.4018/978-1-5225-0861-8.ch003

Bhardwaj, M., Shukla, N., & Sharma, A. (2021). Improvement and Reduction of Clustering Overhead in Mobile Ad Hoc Network With Optimum Stable Bunching Algorithm. In S. Kumar, M. Trivedi, P. Ranjan, & A. Punhani (Eds.), *Evolution of Software-Defined Networking Foundations for IoT and 5G Mobile Networks* (pp. 139–158). IGI Global. https://doi.org/10.4018/978-1-7998-4685-7.ch008

Bhatt, G. D., Wang, Z., & Rodger, J. A. (2017). Information Systems Capabilities and Their Effects on Competitive Advantages: A Study of Chinese Companies. *Information Resources Management Journal*, *30*(3), 41–57. doi:10.4018/IRMJ.2017070103

Bhattacharya, A. (2021). Blockchain, Cybersecurity, and Industry 4.0. In A. Tyagi, G. Rekha, & N. Sreenath (Eds.), *Opportunities and Challenges for Blockchain Technology in Autonomous Vehicles* (pp. 210–244). IGI Global. https://doi.org/10.4018/978-1-7998-3295-9.ch013

Bhyan, P., Shrivastava, B., & Kumar, N. (2022). Requisite Sustainable Development Contemplating Buildings: Economic and Environmental Sustainability. In A. Hussain, K. Tiwari, & A. Gupta (Eds.), *Addressing Environmental Challenges Through Spatial Planning* (pp. 269–288). IGI Global. https://doi.org/10.4018/978-1-7998-8331-9.ch014

Boido, C., Davico, P., & Spallone, R. (2021). Digital Tools Aimed to Represent Urban Survey. In M. Khosrow-Pour D.B.A. (Ed.), *Encyclopedia of Information Science and Technology, Fifth Edition* (pp. 1181-1195). IGI Global. https://doi.org/10.4018/978-1-7998-3479-3.ch082

Borkar, P. S., Chanana, P. U., Atwal, S. K., Londe, T. G., & Dalal, Y. D. (2021). The Replacement of HMI (Human-Machine Interface) in Industry Using Single Interface Through IoT. In R. Raut & A. Mihovska (Eds.), *Examining the Impact of Deep Learning and IoT on Multi-Industry Applications* (pp. 195–208). IGI Global. https://doi.org/10.4018/978-1-7998-7511-6.ch011

Brahmane, A. V., & Krishna, C. B. (2021). Rider Chaotic Biography Optimization-driven Deep Stacked Auto-encoder for Big Data Classification Using Spark Architecture: Rider Chaotic Biography Optimization. *International Journal of Web Services Research*, *18*(3), 42–62. https://doi.org/10.4018/ijwsr.2021070103

Burcoff, A., & Shamir, L. (2017). Computer Analysis of Pablo Picasso's Artistic Style. *International Journal of Art, Culture and Design Technologies*, *6*(1), 1–18. doi:10.4018/IJACDT.2017010101

Byker, E. J. (2017). I Play I Learn: Introducing Technological Play Theory. In C. Martin & D. Polly (Eds.), *Handbook of Research on Teacher Education and Professional Development* (pp. 297–306). Hershey, PA: IGI Global. doi:10.4018/978-1-5225-1067-3.ch016

Calongne, C. M., Stricker, A. G., Truman, B., & Arenas, F. J. (2017). Cognitive Apprenticeship and Computer Science Education in Cyberspace: Reimagining the Past. In A. Stricker, C. Calongne, B. Truman, & F. Arenas (Eds.), *Integrating an Awareness of Selfhood and Society into Virtual Learning* (pp. 180–197). Hershey, PA: IGI Global. doi:10.4018/978-1-5225-2182-2.ch013

Carneiro, A. D. (2017). Defending Information Networks in Cyberspace: Some Notes on Security Needs. In M. Dawson, D. Kisku, P. Gupta, J. Sing, & W. Li (Eds.), Developing Next-Generation Countermeasures for Homeland Security Threat Prevention (pp. 354-375). Hershey, PA: IGI Global. https://doi.org/ doi:10.4018/978-1-5225-0703-1.ch016

Carvalho, W. F., & Zarate, L. (2021). Causal Feature Selection. In A. Azevedo & M. Santos (Eds.), *Integration Challenges for Analytics, Business Intelligence, and Data Mining* (pp. 145-160). IGI Global. https://doi.org/10.4018/978-1-7998-5781-5.ch007

Chase, J. P., & Yan, Z. (2017). Affect in Statistics Cognition. In *Assessing and Measuring Statistics Cognition in Higher Education Online Environments: Emerging Research and Opportunities* (pp. 144–187). Hershey, PA: IGI Global. doi:10.4018/978-1-5225-2420-5.ch005

Chatterjee, A., Roy, S., & Shrivastava, R. (2021). A Machine Learning Approach to Prevent Cancer. In G. Rani & P. Tiwari (Eds.), *Handbook of Research on Disease Prediction Through Data Analytics and Machine Learning* (pp. 112–141). IGI Global. https://doi.org/10.4018/978-1-7998-2742-9.ch007

Cifci, M. A. (2021). Optimizing WSNs for CPS Using Machine Learning Techniques. In A. Luhach & A. Elçi (Eds.), *Artificial Intelligence Paradigms for Smart Cyber-Physical Systems* (pp. 204–228). IGI Global. https://doi.org/10.4018/978-1-7998-5101-1.ch010

Cimermanova, I. (2017). Computer-Assisted Learning in Slovakia. In D. Tafazoli & M. Romero (Eds.), *Multiculturalism and Technology-Enhanced Language Learning* (pp. 252–270). Hershey, PA: IGI Global. doi:10.4018/978-1-5225-1882-2.ch015

Cipolla-Ficarra, F. V., & Cipolla-Ficarra, M. (2018). Computer Animation for Ingenious Revival. In F. Cipolla-Ficarra, M. Ficarra, M. Cipolla-Ficarra, A. Quiroga, J. Alma, & J. Carré (Eds.), *Technology-Enhanced Human Interaction in Modern Society* (pp. 159–181). Hershey, PA: IGI Global. doi:10.4018/978-1-5225-3437-2.ch008

Cockrell, S., Damron, T. S., Melton, A. M., & Smith, A. D. (2018). Offshoring IT. In M. Khosrow-Pour, D.B.A. (Ed.), Encyclopedia of Information Science and Technology, Fourth Edition (pp. 5476-5489). Hershey, PA: IGI Global. https://doi.org/ doi:10.4018/978-1-5225-2255-3.ch476

Coffey, J. W. (2018). Logic and Proof in Computer Science: Categories and Limits of Proof Techniques. In J. Horne (Ed.), *Philosophical Perceptions on Logic and Order* (pp. 218–240). Hershey, PA: IGI Global. doi:10.4018/978-1-5225-2443-4.ch007

Dale, M. (2017). Re-Thinking the Challenges of Enterprise Architecture Implementation. In M. Tavana (Ed.), *Enterprise Information Systems and the Digitalization of Business Functions* (pp. 205–221). Hershey, PA: IGI Global. doi:10.4018/978-1-5225-2382-6.ch009

Das, A., & Mohanty, M. N. (2021). An Useful Review on Optical Character Recognition for Smart Era Generation. In A. Tyagi (Ed.), *Multimedia and Sensory Input for Augmented, Mixed, and Virtual Reality* (pp. 1–41). IGI Global. https://doi.org/10.4018/978-1-7998-4703-8.ch001

Dash, A. K., & Mohapatra, P. (2021). A Survey on Prematurity Detection of Diabetic Retinopathy Based on Fundus Images Using Deep Learning Techniques. In S. Saxena & S. Paul (Eds.), *Deep Learning Applications in Medical Imaging* (pp. 140–155). IGI Global. https://doi.org/10.4018/978-1-7998-5071-7.ch006

De Maere, K., De Haes, S., & von Kutzschenbach, M. (2017). CIO Perspectives on Organizational Learning within the Context of IT Governance. *International Journal of IT/Business Alignment and Governance, 8*(1), 32-47. https://doi.org/doi:10.4018/IJITBAG.2017010103

Demir, K., Çaka, C., Yaman, N. D., İslamoğlu, H., & Kuzu, A. (2018). Examining the Current Definitions of Computational Thinking. In H. Ozcinar, G. Wong, & H. Ozturk (Eds.), *Teaching Computational Thinking in Primary Education* (pp. 36–64). Hershey, PA: IGI Global. doi:10.4018/978-1-5225-3200-2.ch003

Deng, X., Hung, Y., & Lin, C. D. (2017). Design and Analysis of Computer Experiments. In S. Saha, A. Mandal, A. Narasimhamurthy, S. V, & S. Sangam (Eds.), Handbook of Research on Applied Cybernetics and Systems Science (pp. 264-279). Hershey, PA: IGI Global. doi:10.4018/978-1-5225-2498-4.ch013

Denner, J., Martinez, J., & Thiry, H. (2017). Strategies for Engaging Hispanic/Latino Youth in the US in Computer Science. In Y. Rankin & J. Thomas (Eds.), *Moving Students of Color from Consumers to Producers of Technology* (pp. 24–48). Hershey, PA: IGI Global. doi:10.4018/978-1-5225-2005-4.ch002

Devi, A. (2017). Cyber Crime and Cyber Security: A Quick Glance. In R. Kumar, P. Pattnaik, & P. Pandey (Eds.), *Detecting and Mitigating Robotic Cyber Security Risks* (pp. 160–171). Hershey, PA: IGI Global. doi:10.4018/978-1-5225-2154-9.ch011

Dhaya, R., & Kanthavel, R. (2022). Futuristic Research Perspectives of IoT Platforms. In D. Jeya Mala (Ed.), *Integrating AI in IoT Analytics on the Cloud for Healthcare Applications* (pp. 258–275). IGI Global. doi:10.4018/978-1-7998-9132-1.ch015

Doyle, D. J., & Fahy, P. J. (2018). Interactivity in Distance Education and Computer-Aided Learning, With Medical Education Examples. In M. Khosrow-Pour, D.B.A. (Ed.), Encyclopedia of Information Science and Technology, Fourth Edition (pp. 5829-5840). Hershey, PA: IGI Global. https://doi.org/ doi:10.4018/978-1-5225-2255-3.ch507

Eklund, P. (2021). Reinforcement Learning in Social Media Marketing. In B. Christiansen & T. Škrinjarić (Eds.), *Handbook of Research on Applied AI for International Business and Marketing Applications* (pp. 30–48). IGI Global. https://doi.org/10.4018/978-1-7998-5077-9.ch003

El Ghandour, N., Benaissa, M., & Lebbah, Y. (2021). An Integer Linear Programming-Based Method for the Extraction of Ontology Alignment. *International Journal of Information Technology and Web Engineering*, *16*(2), 25–44. https://doi.org/10.4018/IJITWE.2021040102

Elias, N. I., & Walker, T. W. (2017). Factors that Contribute to Continued Use of E-Training among Healthcare Professionals. In F. Topor (Ed.), *Handbook of Research on Individualism and Identity in the Globalized Digital Age* (pp. 403–429). Hershey, PA: IGI Global. doi:10.4018/978-1-5225-0522-8.ch018

Fisher, R. L. (2018). Computer-Assisted Indian Matrimonial Services. In M. Khosrow-Pour, D.B.A. (Ed.), Encyclopedia of Information Science and Technology, Fourth Edition (pp. 4136-4145). Hershey, PA: IGI Global. doi:10.4018/978-1-5225-2255-3.ch358

Galiautdinov, R. (2021). Nonlinear Filtering in Artificial Neural Network Applications in Business and Engineering. In Q. Do (Ed.), *Artificial Neural Network Applications in Business and Engineering* (pp. 1–23). IGI Global. https://doi.org/10.4018/978-1-7998-3238-6.ch001

Gardner-McCune, C., & Jimenez, Y. (2017). Historical App Developers: Integrating CS into K-12 through Cross-Disciplinary Projects. In Y. Rankin & J. Thomas (Eds.), *Moving Students of Color from Consumers to Producers of Technology* (pp. 85–112). Hershey, PA: IGI Global. doi:10.4018/978-1-5225-2005-4.ch005

Garg, P. K. (2021). The Internet of Things-Based Technologies. In S. Kumar, M. Trivedi, P. Ranjan, & A. Punhani (Eds.), *Evolution of Software-Defined Networking Foundations for IoT and 5G Mobile Networks* (pp. 37–65). IGI Global. https://doi.org/10.4018/978-1-7998-4685-7.ch003

Garg, T., & Bharti, M. (2021). Congestion Control Protocols for UWSNs. In N. Goyal, L. Sapra, & J. Sandhu (Eds.), *Energy-Efficient Underwater Wireless Communications and Networking* (pp. 85–100). IGI Global. https://doi.org/10.4018/978-1-7998-3640-7.ch006

Gauttier, S. (2021). A Primer on Q-Method and the Study of Technology. In M. Khosrow-Pour D.B.A. (Eds.), *Encyclopedia of Information Science and Technology, Fifth Edition* (pp. 1746-1756). IGI Global. https://doi.org/10.4018/978-1-7998-3479-3.ch120

Ghafele, R., & Gibert, B. (2018). Open Growth: The Economic Impact of Open Source Software in the USA. In M. Khosrow-Pour (Ed.), *Optimizing Contemporary Application and Processes in Open Source Software* (pp. 164–197). Hershey, PA: IGI Global. doi:10.4018/978-1-5225-5314-4.ch007

Ghobakhloo, M., & Azar, A. (2018). Information Technology Resources, the Organizational Capability of Lean-Agile Manufacturing, and Business Performance. *Information Resources Management Journal, 31*(2), 47–74. doi:10.4018/IRMJ.2018040103

Gikandi, J. W. (2017). Computer-Supported Collaborative Learning and Assessment: A Strategy for Developing Online Learning Communities in Continuing Education. In J. Keengwe & G. Onchwari (Eds.), *Handbook of Research on Learner-Centered Pedagogy in Teacher Education and Professional Development* (pp. 309–333). Hershey, PA: IGI Global. doi:10.4018/978-1-5225-0892-2.ch017

Gokhale, A. A., & Machina, K. F. (2017). Development of a Scale to Measure Attitudes toward Information Technology. In L. Tomei (Ed.), *Exploring the New Era of Technology-Infused Education* (pp. 49–64). Hershey, PA: IGI Global. doi:10.4018/978-1-5225-1709-2.ch004

Goswami, J. K., Jalal, S., Negi, C. S., & Jalal, A. S. (2022). A Texture Features-Based Robust Facial Expression Recognition. *International Journal of Computer Vision and Image Processing, 12*(1), 1–15. https://doi.org/10.4018/IJCVIP.2022010103

Hafeez-Baig, A., Gururajan, R., & Wickramasinghe, N. (2017). Readiness as a Novel Construct of Readiness Acceptance Model (RAM) for the Wireless Handheld Technology. In N. Wickramasinghe (Ed.), *Handbook of Research on Healthcare Administration and Management* (pp. 578–595). Hershey, PA: IGI Global. doi:10.4018/978-1-5225-0920-2.ch035

Hanafizadeh, P., Ghandchi, S., & Asgarimehr, M. (2017). Impact of Information Technology on Lifestyle: A Literature Review and Classification. *International Journal of Virtual Communities and Social Networking*, *9*(2), 1–23. doi:10.4018/IJVCSN.2017040101

Haseski, H. İ., Ilic, U., & Tuğtekin, U. (2018). Computational Thinking in Educational Digital Games: An Assessment Tool Proposal. In H. Ozcinar, G. Wong, & H. Ozturk (Eds.), *Teaching Computational Thinking in Primary Education* (pp. 256–287). Hershey, PA: IGI Global. doi:10.4018/978-1-5225-3200-2.ch013

Hee, W. J., Jalleh, G., Lai, H., & Lin, C. (2017). E-Commerce and IT Projects: Evaluation and Management Issues in Australian and Taiwanese Hospitals. *International Journal of Public Health Management and Ethics*, *2*(1), 69–90. doi:10.4018/IJPHME.2017010104

Hernandez, A. A. (2017). Green Information Technology Usage: Awareness and Practices of Philippine IT Professionals. *International Journal of Enterprise Information Systems*, *13*(4), 90–103. doi:10.4018/IJEIS.2017100106

Hernandez, M. A., Marin, E. C., Garcia-Rodriguez, J., Azorin-Lopez, J., & Cazorla, M. (2017). Automatic Learning Improves Human-Robot Interaction in Productive Environments: A Review. *International Journal of Computer Vision and Image Processing*, *7*(3), 65–75. doi:10.4018/IJCVIP.2017070106

Hirota, A. (2021). Design of Narrative Creation in Innovation: "Signature Story" and Two Types of Pivots. In T. Ogata & J. Ono (Eds.), *Bridging the Gap Between AI, Cognitive Science, and Narratology With Narrative Generation* (pp. 363–376). IGI Global. https://doi.org/10.4018/978-1-7998-4864-6.ch012

Hond, D., Asgari, H., Jeffery, D., & Newman, M. (2021). An Integrated Process for Verifying Deep Learning Classifiers Using Dataset Dissimilarity Measures. *International Journal of Artificial Intelligence and Machine Learning*, *11*(2), 1–21. https://doi.org/10.4018/IJAIML.289536

Horne-Popp, L. M., Tessone, E. B., & Welker, J. (2018). If You Build It, They Will Come: Creating a Library Statistics Dashboard for Decision-Making. In L. Costello & M. Powers (Eds.), *Developing In-House Digital Tools in Library Spaces* (pp. 177–203). Hershey, PA: IGI Global. doi:10.4018/978-1-5225-2676-6.ch009

Hu, H., Hu, P. J., & Al-Gahtani, S. S. (2017). User Acceptance of Computer Technology at Work in Arabian Culture: A Model Comparison Approach. In M. Khosrow-Pour (Ed.), *Handbook of Research on Technology Adoption, Social Policy, and Global Integration* (pp. 205–228). Hershey, PA: IGI Global. doi:10.4018/978-1-5225-2668-1.ch011

Huang, C., Sun, Y., & Fuh, C. (2022). Vehicle License Plate Recognition With Deep Learning. In C. Chen, W. Yang, & L. Chen (Eds.), *Technologies to Advance Automation in Forensic Science and Criminal Investigation* (pp. 161-219). IGI Global. https://doi.org/10.4018/978-1-7998-8386-9.ch009

Ifinedo, P. (2017). Using an Extended Theory of Planned Behavior to Study Nurses' Adoption of Healthcare Information Systems in Nova Scotia. *International Journal of Technology Diffusion*, *8*(1), 1–17. doi:10.4018/IJTD.2017010101

Ilie, V., & Sneha, S. (2018). A Three Country Study for Understanding Physicians' Engagement With Electronic Information Resources Pre and Post System Implementation. *Journal of Global Information Management*, *26*(2), 48–73. doi:10.4018/JGIM.2018040103

Ilo, P. I., Nkiko, C., Ugwu, C. I., Ekere, J. N., Izuagbe, R., & Fagbohun, M. O. (2021). Prospects and Challenges of Web 3.0 Technologies Application in the Provision of Library Services. In M. Khosrow-Pour D.B.A. (Ed.), *Encyclopedia of Information Science and Technology, Fifth Edition* (pp. 1767-1781). IGI Global. https://doi.org/10.4018/978-1-7998-3479-3.ch122

Inoue-Smith, Y. (2017). Perceived Ease in Using Technology Predicts Teacher Candidates' Preferences for Online Resources. *International Journal of Online Pedagogy and Course Design*, *7*(3), 17–28. doi:10.4018/IJOPCD.2017070102

Islam, A. Y. (2017). Technology Satisfaction in an Academic Context: Moderating Effect of Gender. In A. Mesquita (Ed.), *Research Paradigms and Contemporary Perspectives on Human-Technology Interaction* (pp. 187–211). Hershey, PA: IGI Global. doi:10.4018/978-1-5225-1868-6.ch009

Jagdale, S. C., Hable, A. A., & Chabukswar, A. R. (2021). Protocol Development in Clinical Trials for Healthcare Management. In M. Khosrow-Pour D.B.A. (Ed.), *Encyclopedia of Information Science and Technology, Fifth Edition* (pp. 1797-1814). IGI Global. https://doi.org/10.4018/978-1-7998-3479-3.ch124

Jamil, G. L., & Jamil, C. C. (2017). Information and Knowledge Management Perspective Contributions for Fashion Studies: Observing Logistics and Supply Chain Management Processes. In G. Jamil, A. Soares, & C. Pessoa (Eds.), *Handbook of Research on Information Management for Effective Logistics and Supply Chains* (pp. 199–221). Hershey, PA: IGI Global. doi:10.4018/978-1-5225-0973-8.ch011

Jamil, M. I., & Almunawar, M. N. (2021). Importance of Digital Literacy and Hindrance Brought About by Digital Divide. In M. Khosrow-Pour D.B.A. (Ed.), *Encyclopedia of Information Science and Technology, Fifth Edition* (pp. 1683-1698). IGI Global. https://doi.org/10.4018/978-1-7998-3479-3.ch116

Janakova, M. (2018). Big Data and Simulations for the Solution of Controversies in Small Businesses. In M. Khosrow-Pour, D.B.A. (Ed.), Encyclopedia of Information Science and Technology, Fourth Edition (pp. 6907-6915). Hershey, PA: IGI Global. doi:10.4018/978-1-5225-2255-3.ch598

Jhawar, A., & Garg, S. K. (2018). Logistics Improvement by Investment in Information Technology Using System Dynamics. In A. Azar & S. Vaidyanathan (Eds.), *Advances in System Dynamics and Control* (pp. 528–567). Hershey, PA: IGI Global. doi:10.4018/978-1-5225-4077-9.ch017

Kalelioğlu, F., Gülbahar, Y., & Doğan, D. (2018). Teaching How to Think Like a Programmer: Emerging Insights. In H. Ozcinar, G. Wong, & H. Ozturk (Eds.), *Teaching Computational Thinking in Primary Education* (pp. 18–35). Hershey, PA: IGI Global. doi:10.4018/978-1-5225-3200-2.ch002

Kamberi, S. (2017). A Girls-Only Online Virtual World Environment and its Implications for Game-Based Learning. In A. Stricker, C. Calongne, B. Truman, & F. Arenas (Eds.), *Integrating an Awareness of Selfhood and Society into Virtual Learning* (pp. 74–95). Hershey, PA: IGI Global. doi:10.4018/978-1-5225-2182-2.ch006

Kamel, S., & Rizk, N. (2017). ICT Strategy Development: From Design to Implementation – Case of Egypt. In C. Howard & K. Hargiss (Eds.), *Strategic Information Systems and Technologies in Modern Organizations* (pp. 239–257). Hershey, PA: IGI Global. doi:10.4018/978-1-5225-1680-4.ch010

Kamel, S. H. (2018). The Potential Role of the Software Industry in Supporting Economic Development. In M. Khosrow-Pour, D.B.A. (Ed.), Encyclopedia of Information Science and Technology, Fourth Edition (pp. 7259-7269). Hershey, PA: IGI Global. doi:10.4018/978-1-5225-2255-3.ch631

Kang, H., Kang, Y., & Kim, J. (2022). Improved Fall Detection Model on GRU Using PoseNet. *International Journal of Software Innovation*, *10*(2), 1–11. https://doi.org/10.4018/IJSI.289600

Kankam, P. K. (2021). Employing Case Study and Survey Designs in Information Research. *Journal of Information Technology Research*, *14*(1), 167–177. https://doi.org/10.4018/JITR.2021010110

Karas, V., & Schuller, B. W. (2021). Deep Learning for Sentiment Analysis: An Overview and Perspectives. In F. Pinarbasi & M. Taskiran (Eds.), *Natural Language Processing for Global and Local Business* (pp. 97–132). IGI Global. https://doi.org/10.4018/978-1-7998-4240-8.ch005

Kaufman, L. M. (2022). Reimagining the Magic of the Workshop Model. In T. Driscoll III, (Ed.), *Designing Effective Distance and Blended Learning Environments in K-12* (pp. 89–109). IGI Global. https://doi.org/10.4018/978-1-7998-6829-3.ch007

Kawata, S. (2018). Computer-Assisted Parallel Program Generation. In M. Khosrow-Pour, D.B.A. (Ed.), Encyclopedia of Information Science and Technology, Fourth Edition (pp. 4583-4593). Hershey, PA: IGI Global. doi:10.4018/978-1-5225-2255-3.ch398

Kharb, L., & Singh, P. (2021). Role of Machine Learning in Modern Education and Teaching. In S. Verma & P. Tomar (Ed.), *Impact of AI Technologies on Teaching, Learning, and Research in Higher Education* (pp. 99-123). IGI Global. https://doi.org/10.4018/978-1-7998-4763-2.ch006

Khari, M., Shrivastava, G., Gupta, S., & Gupta, R. (2017). Role of Cyber Security in Today's Scenario. In R. Kumar, P. Pattnaik, & P. Pandey (Eds.), *Detecting and Mitigating Robotic Cyber Security Risks* (pp. 177–191). Hershey, PA: IGI Global. doi:10.4018/978-1-5225-2154-9.ch013

Khekare, G., & Sheikh, S. (2021). Autonomous Navigation Using Deep Reinforcement Learning in ROS. *International Journal of Artificial Intelligence and Machine Learning, 11*(2), 63–70. https://doi.org/10.4018/IJAIML.20210701.oa4

Khouja, M., Rodriguez, I. B., Ben Halima, Y., & Moalla, S. (2018). IT Governance in Higher Education Institutions: A Systematic Literature Review. *International Journal of Human Capital and Information Technology Professionals, 9*(2), 52–67. doi:10.4018/IJHCITP.2018040104

Kiourt, C., Pavlidis, G., Koutsoudis, A., & Kalles, D. (2017). Realistic Simulation of Cultural Heritage. *International Journal of Computational Methods in Heritage Science, 1*(1), 10–40. doi:10.4018/IJCMHS.2017010102

Köse, U. (2017). An Augmented-Reality-Based Intelligent Mobile Application for Open Computer Education. In G. Kurubacak & H. Altinpulluk (Eds.), *Mobile Technologies and Augmented Reality in Open Education* (pp. 154–174). Hershey, PA: IGI Global. doi:10.4018/978-1-5225-2110-5.ch008

Lahmiri, S. (2018). Information Technology Outsourcing Risk Factors and Provider Selection. In M. Gupta, R. Sharman, J. Walp, & P. Mulgund (Eds.), *Information Technology Risk Management and Compliance in Modern Organizations* (pp. 214–228). Hershey, PA: IGI Global. doi:10.4018/978-1-5225-2604-9.ch008

Lakkad, A. K., Bhadaniya, R. D., Shah, V. N., & Lavanya, K. (2021). Complex Events Processing on Live News Events Using Apache Kafka and Clustering Techniques. *International Journal of Intelligent Information Technologies*, *17*(1), 39–52. https://doi.org/10.4018/IJIIT.2021010103

Landriscina, F. (2017). Computer-Supported Imagination: The Interplay Between Computer and Mental Simulation in Understanding Scientific Concepts. In I. Levin & D. Tsybulsky (Eds.), *Digital Tools and Solutions for Inquiry-Based STEM Learning* (pp. 33–60). Hershey, PA: IGI Global. doi:10.4018/978-1-5225-2525-7.ch002

Lara López, G. (2021). Virtual Reality in Object Location. In A. Negrón & M. Muñoz (Eds.), *Latin American Women and Research Contributions to the IT Field* (pp. 307–324). IGI Global. https://doi.org/10.4018/978-1-7998-7552-9.ch014

Lee, W. W. (2018). Ethical Computing Continues From Problem to Solution. In M. Khosrow-Pour, D.B.A. (Ed.), Encyclopedia of Information Science and Technology, Fourth Edition (pp. 4884-4897). Hershey, PA: IGI Global. doi:10.4018/978-1-5225-2255-3.ch423

Lin, S., Chen, S., & Chuang, S. (2017). Perceived Innovation and Quick Response Codes in an Online-to-Offline E-Commerce Service Model. *International Journal of E-Adoption*, *9*(2), 1–16. doi:10.4018/IJEA.2017070101

Liu, M., Wang, Y., Xu, W., & Liu, L. (2017). Automated Scoring of Chinese Engineering Students' English Essays. *International Journal of Distance Education Technologies*, *15*(1), 52–68. doi:10.4018/IJDET.2017010104

Ma, X., Li, X., Zhong, B., Huang, Y., Gu, Y., Wu, M., Liu, Y., & Zhang, M. (2021). A Detector and Evaluation Framework of Abnormal Bidding Behavior Based on Supplier Portrait. *International Journal of Information Technology and Web Engineering*, *16*(2), 58–74. https://doi.org/10.4018/IJITWE.2021040104

Mabe, L. K., & Oladele, O. I. (2017). Application of Information Communication Technologies for Agricultural Development through Extension Services: A Review. In T. Tossy (Ed.), *Information Technology Integration for Socio-Economic Development* (pp. 52–101). Hershey, PA: IGI Global. doi:10.4018/978-1-5225-0539-6.ch003

Mahboub, S. A., Sayed Ali Ahmed, E., & Saeed, R. A. (2021). Smart IDS and IPS for Cyber-Physical Systems. In A. Luhach & A. Elçi (Eds.), *Artificial Intelligence Paradigms for Smart Cyber-Physical Systems* (pp. 109–136). IGI Global. https://doi.org/10.4018/978-1-7998-5101-1.ch006

Manogaran, G., Thota, C., & Lopez, D. (2018). Human-Computer Interaction With Big Data Analytics. In D. Lopez & M. Durai (Eds.), *HCI Challenges and Privacy Preservation in Big Data Security* (pp. 1–22). Hershey, PA: IGI Global. doi:10.4018/978-1-5225-2863-0.ch001

Margolis, J., Goode, J., & Flapan, J. (2017). A Critical Crossroads for Computer Science for All: "Identifying Talent" or "Building Talent," and What Difference Does It Make? In Y. Rankin & J. Thomas (Eds.), *Moving Students of Color from Consumers to Producers of Technology* (pp. 1–23). Hershey, PA: IGI Global. doi:10.4018/978-1-5225-2005-4.ch001

Mazzù, M. F., Benetton, A., Baccelloni, A., & Lavini, L. (2022). A Milk Blockchain-Enabled Supply Chain: Evidence From Leading Italian Farms. In P. De Giovanni (Ed.), *Blockchain Technology Applications in Businesses and Organizations* (pp. 73–98). IGI Global. https://doi.org/10.4018/978-1-7998-8014-1.ch004

Mbale, J. (2018). Computer Centres Resource Cloud Elasticity-Scalability (CRECES): Copperbelt University Case Study. In S. Aljawarneh & M. Malhotra (Eds.), *Critical Research on Scalability and Security Issues in Virtual Cloud Environments* (pp. 48–70). Hershey, PA: IGI Global. doi:10.4018/978-1-5225-3029-9.ch003

McKee, J. (2018). The Right Information: The Key to Effective Business Planning. In *Business Architectures for Risk Assessment and Strategic Planning: Emerging Research and Opportunities* (pp. 38–52). Hershey, PA: IGI Global. doi:10.4018/978-1-5225-3392-4.ch003

Meddah, I. H., Remil, N. E., & Meddah, H. N. (2021). Novel Approach for Mining Patterns. *International Journal of Applied Evolutionary Computation*, *12*(1), 27–42. https://doi.org/10.4018/IJAEC.2021010103

Mensah, I. K., & Mi, J. (2018). Determinants of Intention to Use Local E-Government Services in Ghana: The Perspective of Local Government Workers. *International Journal of Technology Diffusion*, *9*(2), 41–60. doi:10.4018/IJTD.2018040103

Mohamed, J. H. (2018). Scientograph-Based Visualization of Computer Forensics Research Literature. In J. Jeyasekar & P. Saravanan (Eds.), *Innovations in Measuring and Evaluating Scientific Information* (pp. 148–162). Hershey, PA: IGI Global. doi:10.4018/978-1-5225-3457-0.ch010

Montañés-Del Río, M. Á., Cornejo, V. R., Rodríguez, M. R., & Ortiz, J. S. (2021). Gamification of University Subjects: A Case Study for Operations Management. *Journal of Information Technology Research*, *14*(2), 1–29. https://doi.org/10.4018/JITR.2021040101

Moore, R. L., & Johnson, N. (2017). Earning a Seat at the Table: How IT Departments Can Partner in Organizational Change and Innovation. *International Journal of Knowledge-Based Organizations*, *7*(2), 1–12. doi:10.4018/IJKBO.2017040101

Mukul, M. K., & Bhattaharyya, S. (2017). Brain-Machine Interface: Human-Computer Interaction. In E. Noughabi, B. Raahemi, A. Albadvi, & B. Far (Eds.), *Handbook of Research on Data Science for Effective Healthcare Practice and Administration* (pp. 417–443). Hershey, PA: IGI Global. doi:10.4018/978-1-5225-2515-8.ch018

Na, L. (2017). Library and Information Science Education and Graduate Programs in Academic Libraries. In L. Ruan, Q. Zhu, & Y. Ye (Eds.), *Academic Library Development and Administration in China* (pp. 218–229). Hershey, PA: IGI Global. doi:10.4018/978-1-5225-0550-1.ch013

Nagpal, G., Bishnoi, G. K., Dhami, H. S., & Vijayvargia, A. (2021). Use of Data Analytics to Increase the Efficiency of Last Mile Logistics for Ecommerce Deliveries. In B. Patil & M. Vohra (Eds.), *Handbook of Research on Engineering, Business, and Healthcare Applications of Data Science and Analytics* (pp. 167–180). IGI Global. https://doi.org/10.4018/978-1-7998-3053-5.ch009

Nair, S. M., Ramesh, V., & Tyagi, A. K. (2021). Issues and Challenges (Privacy, Security, and Trust) in Blockchain-Based Applications. In A. Tyagi, G. Rekha, & N. Sreenath (Eds.), *Opportunities and Challenges for Blockchain Technology in Autonomous Vehicles* (pp. 196–209). IGI Global. https://doi.org/10.4018/978-1-7998-3295-9.ch012

Naomi, J. F. M., K., & V., S. (2021). Machine and Deep Learning Techniques in IoT and Cloud. In S. Velayutham (Ed.), *Challenges and Opportunities for the Convergence of IoT, Big Data, and Cloud Computing* (pp. 225-247). IGI Global. https://doi.org/10.4018/978-1-7998-3111-2.ch013

Nath, R., & Murthy, V. N. (2018). What Accounts for the Differences in Internet Diffusion Rates Around the World? In M. Khosrow-Pour, D.B.A. (Ed.), Encyclopedia of Information Science and Technology, Fourth Edition (pp. 8095-8104). Hershey, PA: IGI Global. https://doi.org/ doi:10.4018/978-1-5225-2255-3.ch705

Nedelko, Z., & Potocan, V. (2018). The Role of Emerging Information Technologies for Supporting Supply Chain Management. In M. Khosrow-Pour, D.B.A. (Ed.), Encyclopedia of Information Science and Technology, Fourth Edition (pp. 5559-5569). Hershey, PA: IGI Global. doi:10.4018/978-1-5225-2255-3.ch483

Negrini, L., Giang, C., & Bonnet, E. (2022). Designing Tools and Activities for Educational Robotics in Online Learning. In N. Eteokleous & E. Nisiforou (Eds.), *Designing, Constructing, and Programming Robots for Learning* (pp. 202–222). IGI Global. https://doi.org/10.4018/978-1-7998-7443-0.ch010

Ngafeeson, M. N. (2018). User Resistance to Health Information Technology. In M. Khosrow-Pour, D.B.A. (Ed.), Encyclopedia of Information Science and Technology, Fourth Edition (pp. 3816-3825). Hershey, PA: IGI Global. doi:10.4018/978-1-5225-2255-3.ch331

Nguyen, T. T., Giang, N. L., Tran, D. T., Nguyen, T. T., Nguyen, H. Q., Pham, A. V., & Vu, T. D. (2021). A Novel Filter-Wrapper Algorithm on Intuitionistic Fuzzy Set for Attribute Reduction From Decision Tables. *International Journal of Data Warehousing and Mining*, *17*(4), 67–100. https://doi.org/10.4018/IJDWM.2021100104

Nigam, A., & Dewani, P. P. (2022). Consumer Engagement Through Conditional Promotions: An Exploratory Study. *Journal of Global Information Management*, *30*(5), 1–19. https://doi.org/10.4018/JGIM.290364

Odagiri, K. (2017). Introduction of Individual Technology to Constitute the Current Internet. In *Strategic Policy-Based Network Management in Contemporary Organizations* (pp. 20–96). Hershey, PA: IGI Global. doi:10.4018/978-1-68318-003-6.ch003

Odia, J. O., & Akpata, O. T. (2021). Role of Data Science and Data Analytics in Forensic Accounting and Fraud Detection. In B. Patil & M. Vohra (Eds.), *Handbook of Research on Engineering, Business, and Healthcare Applications of Data Science and Analytics* (pp. 203–227). IGI Global. https://doi.org/10.4018/978-1-7998-3053-5.ch011

Okike, E. U. (2018). Computer Science and Prison Education. In I. Biao (Ed.), *Strategic Learning Ideologies in Prison Education Programs* (pp. 246–264). Hershey, PA: IGI Global. doi:10.4018/978-1-5225-2909-5.ch012

Olelewe, C. J., & Nwafor, I. P. (2017). Level of Computer Appreciation Skills Acquired for Sustainable Development by Secondary School Students in Nsukka LGA of Enugu State, Nigeria. In C. Ayo & V. Mbarika (Eds.), *Sustainable ICT Adoption and Integration for Socio-Economic Development* (pp. 214–233). Hershey, PA: IGI Global. doi:10.4018/978-1-5225-2565-3.ch010

Oliveira, M., Maçada, A. C., Curado, C., & Nodari, F. (2017). Infrastructure Profiles and Knowledge Sharing. *International Journal of Technology and Human Interaction*, *13*(3), 1–12. doi:10.4018/IJTHI.2017070101

Otarkhani, A., Shokouhyar, S., & Pour, S. S. (2017). Analyzing the Impact of Governance of Enterprise IT on Hospital Performance: Tehran's (Iran) Hospitals – A Case Study. *International Journal of Healthcare Information Systems and Informatics*, *12*(3), 1–20. doi:10.4018/IJHISI.2017070101

Otunla, A. O., & Amuda, C. O. (2018). Nigerian Undergraduate Students' Computer Competencies and Use of Information Technology Tools and Resources for Study Skills and Habits' Enhancement. In M. Khosrow-Pour, D.B.A. (Ed.), Encyclopedia of Information Science and Technology, Fourth Edition (pp. 2303-2313). Hershey, PA: IGI Global. https://doi.org/ doi:10.4018/978-1-5225-2255-3.ch200

Özçınar, H. (2018). A Brief Discussion on Incentives and Barriers to Computational Thinking Education. In H. Ozcinar, G. Wong, & H. Ozturk (Eds.), *Teaching Computational Thinking in Primary Education* (pp. 1–17). Hershey, PA: IGI Global. doi:10.4018/978-1-5225-3200-2.ch001

Pandey, J. M., Garg, S., Mishra, P., & Mishra, B. P. (2017). Computer Based Psychological Interventions: Subject to the Efficacy of Psychological Services. *International Journal of Computers in Clinical Practice*, *2*(1), 25–33. doi:10.4018/IJCCP.2017010102

Pandkar, S. D., & Paatil, S. D. (2021). Big Data and Knowledge Resource Centre. In S. Dhamdhere (Ed.), *Big Data Applications for Improving Library Services* (pp. 90–106). IGI Global. https://doi.org/10.4018/978-1-7998-3049-8.ch007

Patro, C. (2017). Impulsion of Information Technology on Human Resource Practices. In P. Ordóñez de Pablos (Ed.), *Managerial Strategies and Solutions for Business Success in Asia* (pp. 231–254). Hershey, PA: IGI Global. doi:10.4018/978-1-5225-1886-0.ch013

Patro, C. S., & Raghunath, K. M. (2017). Information Technology Paraphernalia for Supply Chain Management Decisions. In M. Tavana (Ed.), *Enterprise Information Systems and the Digitalization of Business Functions* (pp. 294–320). Hershey, PA: IGI Global. doi:10.4018/978-1-5225-2382-6.ch014

Paul, P. K. (2018). The Context of IST for Solid Information Retrieval and Infrastructure Building: Study of Developing Country. *International Journal of Information Retrieval Research*, *8*(1), 86–100. doi:10.4018/IJIRR.2018010106

Paul, P. K., & Chatterjee, D. (2018). iSchools Promoting "Information Science and Technology" (IST) Domain Towards Community, Business, and Society With Contemporary Worldwide Trend and Emerging Potentialities in India. In M. Khosrow-Pour, D.B.A. (Ed.), Encyclopedia of Information Science and Technology, Fourth Edition (pp. 4723-4735). Hershey, PA: IGI Global. https://doi.org/ doi:10.4018/978-1-5225-2255-3.ch410

Pessoa, C. R., & Marques, M. E. (2017). Information Technology and Communication Management in Supply Chain Management. In G. Jamil, A. Soares, & C. Pessoa (Eds.), *Handbook of Research on Information Management for Effective Logistics and Supply Chains* (pp. 23–33). Hershey, PA: IGI Global. doi:10.4018/978-1-5225-0973-8.ch002

Pineda, R. G. (2018). Remediating Interaction: Towards a Philosophy of Human-Computer Relationship. In M. Khosrow-Pour (Ed.), *Enhancing Art, Culture, and Design With Technological Integration* (pp. 75–98). Hershey, PA: IGI Global. doi:10.4018/978-1-5225-5023-5.ch004

Prabha, V. D., & R., R. (2021). Clinical Decision Support Systems: Decision-Making System for Clinical Data. In G. Rani & P. Tiwari (Eds.), *Handbook of Research on Disease Prediction Through Data Analytics and Machine Learning* (pp. 268-280). IGI Global. https://doi.org/10.4018/978-1-7998-2742-9.ch014

Pushpa, R., & Siddappa, M. (2021). An Optimal Way of VM Placement Strategy in Cloud Computing Platform Using ABCS Algorithm. *International Journal of Ambient Computing and Intelligence, 12*(3), 16–38. https://doi.org/10.4018/IJACI.2021070102

Qian, Y. (2017). Computer Simulation in Higher Education: Affordances, Opportunities, and Outcomes. In P. Vu, S. Fredrickson, & C. Moore (Eds.), *Handbook of Research on Innovative Pedagogies and Technologies for Online Learning in Higher Education* (pp. 236–262). Hershey, PA: IGI Global. doi:10.4018/978-1-5225-1851-8.ch011

Rahman, N. (2017). Lessons from a Successful Data Warehousing Project Management. *International Journal of Information Technology Project Management, 8*(4), 30–45. doi:10.4018/IJITPM.2017100103

Rahman, N. (2018). Environmental Sustainability in the Computer Industry for Competitive Advantage. In M. Khosrow-Pour (Ed.), *Green Computing Strategies for Competitive Advantage and Business Sustainability* (pp. 110–130). Hershey, PA: IGI Global. doi:10.4018/978-1-5225-5017-4.ch006

Rajh, A., & Pavetic, T. (2017). Computer Generated Description as the Required Digital Competence in Archival Profession. *International Journal of Digital Literacy and Digital Competence*, *8*(1), 36–49. doi:10.4018/IJDLDC.2017010103

Raman, A., & Goyal, D. P. (2017). Extending IMPLEMENT Framework for Enterprise Information Systems Implementation to Information System Innovation. In M. Tavana (Ed.), *Enterprise Information Systems and the Digitalization of Business Functions* (pp. 137–177). Hershey, PA: IGI Global. doi:10.4018/978-1-5225-2382-6.ch007

Rao, A. P., & Reddy, K. S. (2021). Automated Soil Residue Levels Detecting Device With IoT Interface. In V. Sathiyamoorthi & A. Elci (Eds.), *Challenges and Applications of Data Analytics in Social Perspectives* (Vol. S, pp. 123–135). IGI Global. https://doi.org/10.4018/978-1-7998-2566-1.ch007

Rao, Y. S., Rauta, A. K., Saini, H., & Panda, T. C. (2017). Mathematical Model for Cyber Attack in Computer Network. *International Journal of Business Data Communications and Networking*, *13*(1), 58–65. doi:10.4018/IJBDCN.2017010105

Rapaport, W. J. (2018). Syntactic Semantics and the Proper Treatment of Computationalism. In M. Danesi (Ed.), *Empirical Research on Semiotics and Visual Rhetoric* (pp. 128–176). Hershey, PA: IGI Global. doi:10.4018/978-1-5225-5622-0.ch007

Raut, R., Priyadarshinee, P., & Jha, M. (2017). Understanding the Mediation Effect of Cloud Computing Adoption in Indian Organization: Integrating TAM-TOE- Risk Model. *International Journal of Service Science, Management, Engineering, and Technology*, *8*(3), 40–59. doi:10.4018/IJSSMET.2017070103

Rezaie, S., Mirabedini, S. J., & Abtahi, A. (2018). Designing a Model for Implementation of Business Intelligence in the Banking Industry. *International Journal of Enterprise Information Systems*, *14*(1), 77–103. doi:10.4018/IJEIS.2018010105

Rezende, D. A. (2018). Strategic Digital City Projects: Innovative Information and Public Services Offered by Chicago (USA) and Curitiba (Brazil). In M. Lytras, L. Daniela, & A. Visvizi (Eds.), *Enhancing Knowledge Discovery and Innovation in the Digital Era* (pp. 204–223). Hershey, PA: IGI Global. doi:10.4018/978-1-5225-4191-2.ch012

Rodriguez, A., Rico-Diaz, A. J., Rabuñal, J. R., & Gestal, M. (2017). Fish Tracking with Computer Vision Techniques: An Application to Vertical Slot Fishways. In M. S., & V. V. (Eds.), Multi-Core Computer Vision and Image Processing for Intelligent Applications (pp. 74-104). Hershey, PA: IGI Global. https://doi.org/doi:10.4018/978-1-5225-0889-2.ch003

Romero, J. A. (2018). Sustainable Advantages of Business Value of Information Technology. In M. Khosrow-Pour, D.B.A. (Ed.), Encyclopedia of Information Science and Technology, Fourth Edition (pp. 923-929). Hershey, PA: IGI Global. doi:10.4018/978-1-5225-2255-3.ch079

Romero, J. A. (2018). The Always-On Business Model and Competitive Advantage. In N. Bajgoric (Ed.), *Always-On Enterprise Information Systems for Modern Organizations* (pp. 23–40). Hershey, PA: IGI Global. doi:10.4018/978-1-5225-3704-5.ch002

Rosen, Y. (2018). Computer Agent Technologies in Collaborative Learning and Assessment. In M. Khosrow-Pour, D.B.A. (Ed.), Encyclopedia of Information Science and Technology, Fourth Edition (pp. 2402-2410). Hershey, PA: IGI Global. doi:10.4018/978-1-5225-2255-3.ch209

Roy, D. (2018). Success Factors of Adoption of Mobile Applications in Rural India: Effect of Service Characteristics on Conceptual Model. In M. Khosrow-Pour (Ed.), *Green Computing Strategies for Competitive Advantage and Business Sustainability* (pp. 211–238). Hershey, PA: IGI Global. doi:10.4018/978-1-5225-5017-4.ch010

Ruffin, T. R., & Hawkins, D. P. (2018). Trends in Health Care Information Technology and Informatics. In M. Khosrow-Pour, D.B.A. (Ed.), Encyclopedia of Information Science and Technology, Fourth Edition (pp. 3805-3815). Hershey, PA: IGI Global. doi:10.4018/978-1-5225-2255-3.ch330

Sadasivam, U. M., & Ganesan, N. (2021). Detecting Fake News Using Deep Learning and NLP. In S. Misra, C. Arumugam, S. Jaganathan, & S. S. (Eds.), *Confluence of AI, Machine, and Deep Learning in Cyber Forensics* (pp. 117-133). IGI Global. https://doi.org/10.4018/978-1-7998-4900-1.ch007

Safari, M. R., & Jiang, Q. (2018). The Theory and Practice of IT Governance Maturity and Strategies Alignment: Evidence From Banking Industry. *Journal of Global Information Management, 26*(2), 127–146. doi:10.4018/JGIM.2018040106

Sahin, H. B., & Anagun, S. S. (2018). Educational Computer Games in Math Teaching: A Learning Culture. In E. Toprak & E. Kumtepe (Eds.), *Supporting Multiculturalism in Open and Distance Learning Spaces* (pp. 249–280). Hershey, PA: IGI Global. doi:10.4018/978-1-5225-3076-3.ch013

Sakalle, A., Tomar, P., Bhardwaj, H., & Sharma, U. (2021). Impact and Latest Trends of Intelligent Learning With Artificial Intelligence. In S. Verma & P. Tomar (Eds.), *Impact of AI Technologies on Teaching, Learning, and Research in Higher Education* (pp. 172-189). IGI Global. https://doi.org/10.4018/978-1-7998-4763-2.ch011

Sala, N. (2021). Virtual Reality, Augmented Reality, and Mixed Reality in Education: A Brief Overview. In D. Choi, A. Dailey-Hebert, & J. Estes (Eds.), *Current and Prospective Applications of Virtual Reality in Higher Education* (pp. 48–73). IGI Global. https://doi.org/10.4018/978-1-7998-4960-5.ch003

Salunkhe, S., Kanagachidambaresan, G., Rajkumar, C., & Jayanthi, K. (2022). Online Detection and Prediction of Fused Deposition Modelled Parts Using Artificial Intelligence. In S. Salunkhe, H. Hussein, & J. Davim (Eds.), *Applications of Artificial Intelligence in Additive Manufacturing* (pp. 194–209). IGI Global. https://doi.org/10.4018/978-1-7998-8516-0.ch009

Samy, V. S., Pramanick, K., Thenkanidiyoor, V., & Victor, J. (2021). Data Analysis and Visualization in Python for Polar Meteorological Data. *International Journal of Data Analytics*, *2*(1), 32–60. https://doi.org/10.4018/IJDA.2021010102

Sanna, A., & Valpreda, F. (2017). An Assessment of the Impact of a Collaborative Didactic Approach and Students' Background in Teaching Computer Animation. *International Journal of Information and Communication Technology Education*, *13*(4), 1–16. doi:10.4018/IJICTE.2017100101

Sarivougioukas, J., & Vagelatos, A. (2022). Fused Contextual Data With Threading Technology to Accelerate Processing in Home UbiHealth. *International Journal of Software Science and Computational Intelligence*, *14*(1), 1–14. https://doi.org/10.4018/IJSSCI.285590

Scott, A., Martin, A., & McAlear, F. (2017). Enhancing Participation in Computer Science among Girls of Color: An Examination of a Preparatory AP Computer Science Intervention. In Y. Rankin & J. Thomas (Eds.), *Moving Students of Color from Consumers to Producers of Technology* (pp. 62–84). Hershey, PA: IGI Global. doi:10.4018/978-1-5225-2005-4.ch004

Shanmugam, M., Ibrahim, N., Gorment, N. Z., Sugu, R., Dandarawi, T. N., & Ahmad, N. A. (2022). Towards an Integrated Omni-Channel Strategy Framework for Improved Customer Interaction. In P. Lai (Ed.), *Handbook of Research on Social Impacts of E-Payment and Blockchain Technology* (pp. 409–427). IGI Global. https://doi.org/10.4018/978-1-7998-9035-5.ch022

Sharma, A., & Kumar, S. (2021). Network Slicing and the Role of 5G in IoT Applications. In S. Kumar, M. Trivedi, P. Ranjan, & A. Punhani (Eds.), *Evolution of Software-Defined Networking Foundations for IoT and 5G Mobile Networks* (pp. 172–190). IGI Global. https://doi.org/10.4018/978-1-7998-4685-7.ch010

Siddoo, V., & Wongsai, N. (2017). Factors Influencing the Adoption of ISO/IEC 29110 in Thai Government Projects: A Case Study. *International Journal of Information Technologies and Systems Approach*, *10*(1), 22–44. doi:10.4018/IJITSA.2017010102

Silveira, C., Hir, M. E., & Chaves, H. K. (2022). An Approach to Information Management as a Subsidy of Global Health Actions: A Case Study of Big Data in Health for Dengue, Zika, and Chikungunya. In J. Lima de Magalhães, Z. Hartz, G. Jamil, H. Silveira, & L. Jamil (Eds.), *Handbook of Research on Essential Information Approaches to Aiding Global Health in the One Health Context* (pp. 219–234). IGI Global. https://doi.org/10.4018/978-1-7998-8011-0.ch012

Simões, A. (2017). Using Game Frameworks to Teach Computer Programming. In R. Alexandre Peixoto de Queirós & M. Pinto (Eds.), *Gamification-Based E-Learning Strategies for Computer Programming Education* (pp. 221–236). Hershey, PA: IGI Global. doi:10.4018/978-1-5225-1034-5.ch010

Simões de Almeida, R., & da Silva, T. (2022). AI Chatbots in Mental Health: Are We There Yet? In A. Marques & R. Queirós (Eds.), *Digital Therapies in Psychosocial Rehabilitation and Mental Health* (pp. 226–243). IGI Global. https://doi.org/10.4018/978-1-7998-8634-1.ch011

Singh, L. K., Khanna, M., Thawkar, S., & Gopal, J. (2021). Robustness for Authentication of the Human Using Face, Ear, and Gait Multimodal Biometric System. *International Journal of Information System Modeling and Design*, *12*(1), 39–72. https://doi.org/10.4018/IJISMD.2021010103

Sllame, A. M. (2017). Integrating LAB Work With Classes in Computer Network Courses. In H. Alphin Jr, R. Chan, & J. Lavine (Eds.), *The Future of Accessibility in International Higher Education* (pp. 253–275). Hershey, PA: IGI Global. doi:10.4018/978-1-5225-2560-8.ch015

Smirnov, A., Ponomarev, A., Shilov, N., Kashevnik, A., & Teslya, N. (2018). Ontology-Based Human-Computer Cloud for Decision Support: Architecture and Applications in Tourism. *International Journal of Embedded and Real-Time Communication Systems*, *9*(1), 1–19. doi:10.4018/IJERTCS.2018010101

Smith-Ditizio, A. A., & Smith, A. D. (2018). Computer Fraud Challenges and Its Legal Implications. In M. Khosrow-Pour, D.B.A. (Ed.), Encyclopedia of Information Science and Technology, Fourth Edition (pp. 4837-4848). Hershey, PA: IGI Global. doi:10.4018/978-1-5225-2255-3.ch419

Sosnin, P. (2018). Figuratively Semantic Support of Human-Computer Interactions. In *Experience-Based Human-Computer Interactions: Emerging Research and Opportunities* (pp. 244–272). Hershey, PA: IGI Global. doi:10.4018/978-1-5225-2987-3.ch008

Srilakshmi, R., & Jaya Bhaskar, M. (2021). An Adaptable Secure Scheme in Mobile Ad hoc Network to Protect the Communication Channel From Malicious Behaviours. *International Journal of Information Technology and Web Engineering, 16*(3), 54–73. https://doi.org/10.4018/IJITWE.2021070104

Sukhwani, N., Kagita, V. R., Kumar, V., & Panda, S. K. (2021). Efficient Computation of Top-K Skyline Objects in Data Set With Uncertain Preferences. *International Journal of Data Warehousing and Mining, 17*(3), 68–80. https://doi.org/10.4018/IJDWM.2021070104

Susanto, H., Yie, L. F., Setiana, D., Asih, Y., Yoganingrum, A., Riyanto, S., & Saputra, F. A. (2021). Digital Ecosystem Security Issues for Organizations and Governments: Digital Ethics and Privacy. In Z. Mahmood (Ed.), *Web 2.0 and Cloud Technologies for Implementing Connected Government* (pp. 204–228). IGI Global. https://doi.org/10.4018/978-1-7998-4570-6.ch010

Syväjärvi, A., Leinonen, J., Kivivirta, V., & Kesti, M. (2017). The Latitude of Information Management in Local Government: Views of Local Government Managers. *International Journal of Electronic Government Research, 13*(1), 69–85. doi:10.4018/IJEGR.2017010105

Tanque, M., & Foxwell, H. J. (2018). Big Data and Cloud Computing: A Review of Supply Chain Capabilities and Challenges. In A. Prasad (Ed.), *Exploring the Convergence of Big Data and the Internet of Things* (pp. 1–28). Hershey, PA: IGI Global. doi:10.4018/978-1-5225-2947-7.ch001

Teixeira, A., Gomes, A., & Orvalho, J. G. (2017). Auditory Feedback in a Computer Game for Blind People. In T. Issa, P. Kommers, T. Issa, P. Isaías, & T. Issa (Eds.), *Smart Technology Applications in Business Environments* (pp. 134–158). Hershey, PA: IGI Global. doi:10.4018/978-1-5225-2492-2.ch007

Tewari, P., Tiwari, P., & Goel, R. (2022). Information Technology in Supply Chain Management. In V. Garg & R. Goel (Eds.), *Handbook of Research on Innovative Management Using AI in Industry 5.0* (pp. 165–178). IGI Global. https://doi.org/10.4018/978-1-7998-8497-2.ch011

Thompson, N., McGill, T., & Murray, D. (2018). Affect-Sensitive Computer Systems. In M. Khosrow-Pour, D.B.A. (Ed.), Encyclopedia of Information Science and Technology, Fourth Edition (pp. 4124-4135). Hershey, PA: IGI Global. doi:10.4018/978-1-5225-2255-3.ch357

Triberti, S., Brivio, E., & Galimberti, C. (2018). On Social Presence: Theories, Methodologies, and Guidelines for the Innovative Contexts of Computer-Mediated Learning. In M. Marmon (Ed.), *Enhancing Social Presence in Online Learning Environments* (pp. 20–41). Hershey, PA: IGI Global. doi:10.4018/978-1-5225-3229-3.ch002

Tripathy, B. K. T. R., S., & Mohanty, R. K. (2018). Memetic Algorithms and Their Applications in Computer Science. In S. Dash, B. Tripathy, & A. Rahman (Eds.), Handbook of Research on Modeling, Analysis, and Application of Nature-Inspired Metaheuristic Algorithms (pp. 73-93). Hershey, PA: IGI Global. https://doi.org/ doi:10.4018/978-1-5225-2857-9.ch004

Turulja, L., & Bajgoric, N. (2017). Human Resource Management IT and Global Economy Perspective: Global Human Resource Information Systems. In M. Khosrow-Pour (Ed.), *Handbook of Research on Technology Adoption, Social Policy, and Global Integration* (pp. 377–394). Hershey, PA: IGI Global. doi:10.4018/978-1-5225-2668-1.ch018

Unwin, D. W., Sanzogni, L., & Sandhu, K. (2017). Developing and Measuring the Business Case for Health Information Technology. In K. Moahi, K. Bwalya, & P. Sebina (Eds.), *Health Information Systems and the Advancement of Medical Practice in Developing Countries* (pp. 262–290). Hershey, PA: IGI Global. doi:10.4018/978-1-5225-2262-1.ch015

Usharani, B. (2022). House Plant Leaf Disease Detection and Classification Using Machine Learning. In M. Mundada, S. Seema, S. K.G., & M. Shilpa (Eds.), *Deep Learning Applications for Cyber-Physical Systems* (pp. 17-26). IGI Global. https://doi.org/10.4018/978-1-7998-8161-2.ch002

Vadhanam, B. R. S., M., Sugumaran, V., V., V., & Ramalingam, V. V. (2017). Computer Vision Based Classification on Commercial Videos. In M. S., & V. V. (Eds.), Multi-Core Computer Vision and Image Processing for Intelligent Applications (pp. 105-135). Hershey, PA: IGI Global. https://doi.org/ doi:10.4018/978-1-5225-0889-2.ch004

Vairinho, S. (2022). Innovation Dynamics Through the Encouragement of Knowledge Spin-Off From Touristic Destinations. In C. Ramos, S. Quinteiro, & A. Gonçalves (Eds.), *ICT as Innovator Between Tourism and Culture* (pp. 170–190). IGI Global. https://doi.org/10.4018/978-1-7998-8165-0.ch011

Valverde, R., Torres, B., & Motaghi, H. (2018). A Quantum NeuroIS Data Analytics Architecture for the Usability Evaluation of Learning Management Systems. In S. Bhattacharyya (Ed.), *Quantum-Inspired Intelligent Systems for Multimedia Data Analysis* (pp. 277–299). Hershey, PA: IGI Global. doi:10.4018/978-1-5225-5219-2.ch009

Vassilis, E. (2018). Learning and Teaching Methodology: "1:1 Educational Computing. In K. Koutsopoulos, K. Doukas, & Y. Kotsanis (Eds.), *Handbook of Research on Educational Design and Cloud Computing in Modern Classroom Settings* (pp. 122–155). Hershey, PA: IGI Global. doi:10.4018/978-1-5225-3053-4.ch007

Verma, S., & Jain, A. K. (2022). A Survey on Sentiment Analysis Techniques for Twitter. In B. Gupta, D. Peraković, A. Abd El-Latif, & D. Gupta (Eds.), *Data Mining Approaches for Big Data and Sentiment Analysis in Social Media* (pp. 57–90). IGI Global. https://doi.org/10.4018/978-1-7998-8413-2.ch003

Wang, H., Huang, P., & Chen, X. (2021). Research and Application of a Multidimensional Association Rules Mining Method Based on OLAP. *International Journal of Information Technology and Web Engineering, 16*(1), 75–94. https://doi.org/10.4018/IJITWE.2021010104

Wexler, B. E. (2017). Computer-Presented and Physical Brain-Training Exercises for School Children: Improving Executive Functions and Learning. In B. Dubbels (Ed.), *Transforming Gaming and Computer Simulation Technologies across Industries* (pp. 206–224). Hershey, PA: IGI Global. doi:10.4018/978-1-5225-1817-4.ch012

Wimble, M., Singh, H., & Phillips, B. (2018). Understanding Cross-Level Interactions of Firm-Level Information Technology and Industry Environment: A Multilevel Model of Business Value. *Information Resources Management Journal, 31*(1), 1–20. doi:10.4018/IRMJ.2018010101

Wimmer, H., Powell, L., Kilgus, L., & Force, C. (2017). Improving Course Assessment via Web-based Homework. *International Journal of Online Pedagogy and Course Design, 7*(2), 1–19. doi:10.4018/IJOPCD.2017040101

Wong, S. (2021). Gendering Information and Communication Technologies in Climate Change. In M. Khosrow-Pour D.B.A. (Eds.), *Encyclopedia of Information Science and Technology, Fifth Edition* (pp. 1408-1422). IGI Global. https://doi.org/10.4018/978-1-7998-3479-3.ch096

Wong, Y. L., & Siu, K. W. (2018). Assessing Computer-Aided Design Skills. In M. Khosrow-Pour, D.B.A. (Ed.), Encyclopedia of Information Science and Technology, Fourth Edition (pp. 7382-7391). Hershey, PA: IGI Global. doi:10.4018/978-1-5225-2255-3.ch642

Wongsurawat, W., & Shrestha, V. (2018). Information Technology, Globalization, and Local Conditions: Implications for Entrepreneurs in Southeast Asia. In P. Ordóñez de Pablos (Ed.), *Management Strategies and Technology Fluidity in the Asian Business Sector* (pp. 163–176). Hershey, PA: IGI Global. doi:10.4018/978-1-5225-4056-4.ch010

Yamada, H. (2021). Homogenization of Japanese Industrial Technology From the Perspective of R&D Expenses. *International Journal of Systems and Service-Oriented Engineering, 11*(2), 24–51. doi:10.4018/IJSSOE.2021070102

Yang, Y., Zhu, X., Jin, C., & Li, J. J. (2018). Reforming Classroom Education Through a QQ Group: A Pilot Experiment at a Primary School in Shanghai. In H. Spires (Ed.), *Digital Transformation and Innovation in Chinese Education* (pp. 211–231). Hershey, PA: IGI Global. doi:10.4018/978-1-5225-2924-8.ch012

Yilmaz, R., Sezgin, A., Kurnaz, S., & Arslan, Y. Z. (2018). Object-Oriented Programming in Computer Science. In M. Khosrow-Pour, D.B.A. (Ed.), Encyclopedia of Information Science and Technology, Fourth Edition (pp. 7470-7480). Hershey, PA: IGI Global. doi:10.4018/978-1-5225-2255-3.ch650

Yu, L. (2018). From Teaching Software Engineering Locally and Globally to Devising an Internationalized Computer Science Curriculum. In S. Dikli, B. Etheridge, & R. Rawls (Eds.), *Curriculum Internationalization and the Future of Education* (pp. 293–320). Hershey, PA: IGI Global. doi:10.4018/978-1-5225-2791-6.ch016

Yuhua, F. (2018). Computer Information Library Clusters. In M. Khosrow-Pour, D.B.A. (Ed.), Encyclopedia of Information Science and Technology, Fourth Edition (pp. 4399-4403). Hershey, PA: IGI Global. doi:10.4018/978-1-5225-2255-3.ch382

Zakaria, R. B., Zainuddin, M. N., & Mohamad, A. H. (2022). Distilling Blockchain: Complexity, Barriers, and Opportunities. In P. Lai (Ed.), *Handbook of Research on Social Impacts of E-Payment and Blockchain Technology* (pp. 89–114). IGI Global. https://doi.org/10.4018/978-1-7998-9035-5.ch007

Zhang, Z., Ma, J., & Cui, X. (2021). Genetic Algorithm With Three-Dimensional Population Dominance Strategy for University Course Timetabling Problem. *International Journal of Grid and High Performance Computing, 13*(2), 56–69. https://doi.org/10.4018/IJGHPC.2021040104

About the Contributors

***

Kathirvel Ayyaswamy, acquired, B.E.(CSE), M.E. (CSE) from Crescent Engineering College affiliated to University of Madras and Ph. D (CSE.) from Anna University. He is currently working as Professor, Dept of Computer Science and Engineering, Karunya Institute of Technology and Sciences, Coimbatore. He is a studious researcher by himself, completed 18 sponsored research projects worth of Rs 103 lakhs and published more than 110 articles in journals and conferences. 4 research scholars have completed Ph. D and 3 under progress under his guidance. He is working as scientific and editorial board member of many journals. He has reviewed dozens of papers in many journals. He has author of 13 books. His research interests are protocol development for wireless ad hoc networks, security in ad hoc network, data communication and networks, mobile computing, wireless networks, WSN and DTN. He is a Life member of the ISTE (India), IACSIT (Singapore), Life Member IAENG (Hong Kong), Member ICST (Europe), IAES, etc. He has given a number of guest lecturers/expert talks and seminars, workshops and symposiums.

Jonathan Castañeda Fernández is a professor at the University of Oviedo affiliated with the area of Research Methods and Diagnosis in Education (MIDE). Holds a degree in Pedagogy (receiving the National Award for University Studies Completion) and a Doctorate with international mention from the University of Oviedo, achieved through a University Teaching Training Fellowship (FPU) and a predoctoral research stay at Universidade Lusiada de Lisboa. In terms of teaching, he has delivered courses primarily related to research and educational evaluation. On the research front, he has participated in various projects (themes: evaluation of training activities, learning approaches, ecosystems to build global citizenship, etc.) and is currently a member of the "TECN@: Technology and Learning" research group at the University of Oviedo.

Esther del Moral Pérez is a professor at the University. Teaches ICT applied to Education. Faculty of Teacher Training and Education. University of Oviedo (Spain). Holds 4 six-year research periods. Coordinates the TECN@ Research Group: Technology and Learning. Principal investigator of competitive projects, author of impactful articles in prestigious journals. Research areas: media, digital literacy, TV and childhood, video games, social networks, augmented reality, digital applications, gamification, education in rural areas, etc. Conducted research stays in: Calgary (Canada), Poitiers (France), Freiburg (Germany), ITD Genoa (Italy). Taught courses at Ibero-American universities (Chile, Mexico, and Peru).

Henk Huijser is Strategic Lead, Educator Development and Recognition at Queensland University of Technology, and he has been an academic developer for almost 20 years in Australia, China and the Middle East. He is the co-author (with Megan Yih Chyn A Kek) of Problem-based Learning into the Future (2017) and the lead editor on a volume called Student Support Services (2022). His latest co-edited book is called Technology-enhanced Learning and the Virtual University (2023).

José Luis Jiménez is project coordinator VE/COIL-UCAB. Researcher in virtual exchange topics, a specialist in curriculum design, and a university professor with more than 35 years of international experience. Research areas: Online collaborative learning, journalism, democratic processes, human rights, complex systems, the environment, sustainable development, and human ecology. Ph.D. Candidate in Comparative Studies at Florida Atlantic University. In 1993 he was honored with a scholarship from the Organization of American States to do his Master of Arts at The American University, Washington D.C.

Antonio Juan Rubio has a degree in English Studies from the University of Murcia and a PhD from the National University of Distance Education (UNED) with the positive accreditation by the ANECA body, being given the Extraordinary Doctorate Award. He is currently working as a professor at the University of Granada. He has been awarded a scholarship by University College (Cork, Ireland), the Franklin Institute (University of Alcala de Henares, Spain) and the Radcliffe Institute for Advanced Study (Harvard University, USA), where he conducted a pre-doctoral research visit in the year 2012. He is currently a member of the scientific committee of several national and international journals as well as a member of the editorial board of several international journals. He also belongs to the organizing and scientific committee of several conferences organized by the Athens Institute for Education and Research (Greece). Among his main lines of research we can emphasize the following aspects: cultural studies in the United States; gender issues associated with the role of women in the Anglo-American literature; or the teaching practice and process of English.

Xiuping Li works as Lecturer in Chinese, Course Director, and Lecturer in Multicultural Education and Language Learning, supervisor of MA, PhD research students, and Chair of the Research Filter Committee at School of Education, Ulster University, UK. She has several decades' experience in teaching and supervising. Her research interests are mainly in language teaching/learning skills and strategies, intercultural communications, and adaptations.

Nerea López-Bouzas is a doctoral student in Education and Psychology with a University Teaching Training Fellowship (FPU). Early Childhood Education teacher and Master's degree in Research and Innovation in Early Childhood and Primary Education. Collaborates with the Department of Education Sciences and is a member of the TECN@ Research Group: Technology and Learning at the University of Oviedo. Research interests focus on the integration of technological resources in the teaching-learning process, inclusive education, digital applications, augmented reality, gamification, analysis of audiovisual narratives, etc. Research stay at L'Istituto Tecnologie Didattiche (CNR-ITD) (Genoa, Italy).

Ritu Punhani is Assistant Professor in Department of Information Technology in Amity University having total experience of 25 years in Education and Industry (DRDO). She handled many responsibilities at University level & Department level. Published 27 research papers in field of information technology, 10 Book Chapters and write books for MBA, M.Sc and MCA courses. She has two copyrights and four patents. She was conducted corporate training for South African High Commission to train their employees the concept of Software Project Management. Earned "YOUNG RESEARCHER" Award for research proposal "ISMS Process Maturity Standardization for Data Mining Industry", held at Central University of Rajasthan in collaboration with IIT Kharagpur, National School of Leadership (NSL) Pune and International Association of Research Scholars (IARS). Received Vidya Ratan Samman Award on Hindi Mahotsav on 18th September 2022 from Arunabha Welfare Society, Faridabad. Received Nari Ratan Samman Award on International Women's Day on 6th March 2023 from Bal Yuva Nari Jagriti Manch, New Delhi. Received Women's Elegance Award on International Women's Day Celebration for the valuable contribution in the field of Education and Social Work on 31st March 2023 from Arunabha Welfare Society, Faridabad. Received Global Peace Earth Protection Award 2023 on World Earth Day on 22nd April 2023 from Bhavana Earth and Literature Foundation, Jaipur. The main work done is educating the underprivileged students and is associated with several NGO's. I conducted group lessons with my students. My students visit numerous non - governmental organisations (NGO) to encourage education in all areas, such as hygiene, saving girl children, school education, etc.

Shalini Puri was awarded Ph.D. in Engineering from the Birla Institute of Technology, Mesra, Ranchi, Jharkhand. Presently, she works as Assistant Professor (Senior Scale) in the Information Technology Department at Manipal University Jaipur, Rajasthan, India. She has 21 years of teaching experience and has 12 years of research experience. She has published 36 research papers and attended more than national FDPs, workshops, and training programs. The indexing of most of her research works is in various ESCI, SCOPUS, Web of Science, Elsevier, and Compendex Journals. She has published other research works in IEEE, Springer, and other international and national conferences. She has got the grant of an Australian patent and published two Indian Patents. She has received many awards and recognitions at the professional level from Government, private institutes, and other agencies. She has authored three books related to Software Engineering and computer fundamentals. Her research interests include Machine Learning, Image Processing, Pattern Recognition, and Artificial Intelligence. She has a strong base in Hindi Document Image Processing.

Fatema Wali is an Assistant Professor of English at Bahrain Polytechnic, and she has been teaching English as a Second Language, developing curricula, designing e-learning courses and managing teams. Her research interests include On-line language learning, English as a Second Language, Computer Assisted Language Learning, Interdisciplinary Education, Entrepreneurship Education and Problem Based Learning.

Index

O

P

S

T

V

W

www.ingramcontent.com/pod-product-compliance
Lightning Source LLC
LaVergne TN
LVHW061545290926
849162LV00004B/912